SECURITY *and* PRIVACY

SECURITY *and* PRIVACY

Global Standards for Ethical Identity Management in Contemporary Liberal Democratic States

John Kleinig • Peter Mameli • Seumas Miller • Douglas Salane
Adina Schwartz

THE AUSTRALIAN NATIONAL UNIVERSITY

E PRESS

Centre for
Applied Philosophy
and **Public Ethics**
An Australian Research Council Funded Special Research Centre

Practical Ethics and Public Policy Monograph 2
Series Editor: Michael J. Selgelid

E PRESS

Published by ANU E Press
The Australian National University
Canberra ACT 0200, Australia
Email: anuepress@anu.edu.au
This title is also available online at http://epress.anu.edu.au

---

National Library of Australia Cataloguing-in-Publication entry

Title:	Security and privacy : global standards for ethical identity management in contemporary liberal democratic states / John Kleinig ... [et al.]
ISBN:	9781921862571 (pbk.) 9781921862588 (ebook)
Notes:	Includes bibliographical references.
Subjects:	Terrorism--Moral and ethical aspects. Transnational crime--Moral and ethical aspects. Terrorism--Political aspects. Transnational crime--Political aspects.

Other Authors/Contributors:

Kleinig, John, 1942-

Dewey Number: 363.325

Cover design and layout by ANU E Press

Contents

Preface vii

Contributors ix

Acknowledgments xi

I.   Crime Scenes and the Terroir of Terror 1

II.   Security and the Challenge to Liberal Values 7

III. The Blessing and Bane of the Liberal Democratic Tradition 11

IV.   Divergent Formalities 19

V.   When the Rubber Hits the Road 77

VI.   Securitization Technologies 89

VII. Surveillance Technologies and Economies 129

VIII. The Underlying Values and their Alignment 151

IX.   The Complexities of Oversight and Accountability 225

X.   Recommendations 241

Appendix: Security and Privacy Institutional Arrangements:
Australia and India 247

References 263

Preface

This study is principally concerned with the ethical dimensions of identity management technology – electronic surveillance, the mining of personal data, and profiling – in the context of transnational crime and global terrorism. The ethical challenge at the heart of this study is to establish an acceptable and sustainable equilibrium between two central moral values in contemporary liberal democracies, namely, security and privacy. Both values are essential to individual liberty but they come into conflict in times when civil order is threatened, as has been the case from late in the twentieth century, with the advent of global terrorism and transnational crime.

We seek to articulate legally sustainable, politically possible and technologically feasible global ethical standards[1] for identity management technology and policies in liberal democracies in the contemporary global security context. Although the standards in question are to be understood as *global ethical standards* potentially to be adopted not only by the United States (US) but also by the European Union (EU), India, Australasia and other contemporary liberal democratic states, we take as our primary focus the tensions that have arisen between the US and the EU.

This tension provides a good example of the kinds of challenges involved in developing global standards. It is exemplified by the 2006 disclosure concerning the US government's access to SWIFT transactions and the controversy that has followed it, as well as the earlier and ongoing controversy over the 2004 US–EU Passenger Names Records (PNR) agreement. It also makes itself known in the ongoing debate over national identity cards. The first two conflicts make it clear that, however difficult it may be to develop global standards for the management of personal data, such standards are needed and that every effort should be made to develop them or at least to implement procedures for addressing conflicts among them.

Naturally, authoritarian states do not share the liberal values underlying this project – values such as individual autonomy and privacy. Nevertheless, to the extent that such authoritarian states are evolving or are likely to evolve toward some form of liberal democracy, the results of this study will also be relevant to these states. Our purpose is to articulate standards and institutional initiatives that are sufficiently specific to determine – or at least substantially constrain – the requisite detailed security and privacy policies and prescriptions in national as well as international and transnational jurisdictions.

---

1   Gijs de Vries, "Terrorism, Islam and Democracy", EurActiv.com, March 4, 2005, at: http://www.euractiv.com/en/security/gijs-vries-terrorism-islam-democracy/article-136245.

The project distinguishes itself from other work in this field in two major respects. Firstly, the multi-disciplinary team of experts brought together for this project has enabled the integration of: (a) ethical principles, (b) national and international legal considerations, (c) effective law enforcement practices, (d) oversight and accountability concerns and (e) knowledge of existing and emerging technology, such as database mining and knowledge discovery technology, in the development of a framework of determinate and feasible ethical standards for identity management technology in the global security context.

Secondly, the study has drawn on an international team of experts and focuses on common international standards and solutions, as befits the trans-jurisdictional and transnational nature of the problems to be addressed. Specifically, the project involves not only US personnel and institutions but also EU, Indian, and Australasian expertise.

Contributors

John Kleinig is Professor of Philosophy in the Department of Criminal Justice at John Jay College of Criminal Justice, and teaches in the PhD Programs in Philosophy and Criminal Justice at the Graduate Center, City University of New York. He is also Professorial Fellow in Criminal Justice Ethics at the Centre for Applied Philosophy and Public Ethics, Charles Sturt University, Canberra.

Peter Mameli is Associate Professor in the Department of Public Management at John Jay College of Criminal Justice and is part of the PhD Program in Criminal Justice at the Graduate Center, CUNY.

Seumas Miller is Foundation Director for the Centre for Applied Philosophy and Public Ethics (an Australian Research Council Special Research Centre) at the Australian National University and Charles Sturt University, and a senior research fellow in the Centre for Ethics and Technology at Delft University of Technology, Netherlands.

Douglas Salane is Associate Professor in the Department of Mathematics and Computer Science and in the graduate program in Forensic Computing at John Jay College of Criminal Justice. He is also Director of the Center for Cybercrime Studies.

Adina Schwartz is Professor of Law in the Department of Law, Police Science, and Criminal Justice Administration at John Jay College of Criminal Justice and the Masters Program in Forensic Computing at John Jay College of Criminal Justice. She is also the Assistant Director of the Center for Cybercrime Studies.

Acknowledgments

The initial impetus for this study was a US National Science Foundation grant (#0619226) awarded in 2006 to several researchers at John Jay College of Criminal Justice, some of whom were also associated with the Centre for Applied Philosophy and Public Ethics, Charles Sturt University, Canberra. We are particularly appreciative of the support of John Jay College and CAPPE, and for the assistance at different stages of this project of Nick Evans, Jamie Levy, Richard Lovely, Richard Lucas, Vincent Maldonado and Vincenzo Sainato. Richard Lucas was particularly helpful in reviewing and updating the technical data. Until his untimely death, one of our original grant members, Brian O'Connell, from Central Connecticut State University, brought to the early stages of this project not only his enthusiasm but also his combined expertise in philosophy, law, and computing. Our loss, along with that of others, was great.

In preparing this material for publication, we are grateful for the extensive comments of two reviewers, including Leslie Francis of the University of Utah. James Spence provided valuable editorial assistance.

During the course of this study, several items have been prepared for other venues, including: John Kleinig "Humiliation, Degradation, and Moral Capacity: A Response to Hörnle and Kremnitzer", *Israel Law Review* 44; and John Kleinig, "Liberty and Security in an Era of Terrorism", in *Criminologists on Terrorism and Homeland Security*, ed. Brian Forst, Jack Greene & James Lynch (NY: Cambridge University Press, 2011), ch. 15.

Acknowledgment is also made of permission to use material first published in Peter Mameli, "Tracking the Beast: Techno-Ethics Boards and Government Surveillance Programs", *Critical Issues in Justice and Politics*, 1, no. 1 (2008): 31–56, available at: http://www.suu.edu/hss/polscj/CIJP.htm. Professor Mameli's research benefitted from time spent as a visiting scholar at the National Policing Improvement Agency, Bramshill, in the United Kingdom during 2006. In addition, elements of his work were originally presented at the 2006 "Soft Law, Soft Regulation?" conference of Anglia Ruskin University.

We also acknowledge permission to publish in Chapter VII (pages 131–51) material from Douglas Salane, "Are Large Scale Data Breaches Inevitable?", *Cyber Infrastructure Protection*, ed. Tarek N. Saadawi and Col. Louis H. Jordan, Jr. (Carlisle, PA: Strategic Studies Institute, United States Army War College, forthcoming), ch. 4.

I. Crime Scenes and the Terroir of Terror

The latter decades of the twentieth century and now the first decade of the twenty-first century have seen considerable changes in the ethical challenges we face. Many of those changes have been technologically driven. Technologies that enable people to be kept physiologically alive have posed new and difficult questions about the time, timing and circumstances of the end of life. Other technological developments have posed new questions at the beginning of life concerning the potential use of gene enhancement therapies, cloning and the emergence of personhood. Technological developments have also done much to overcome what the historian Geoffrey Blainey spoke of as "the tyranny of distance". Blainey wanted to argue that Australia's distance (from Europe in particular) had dramatically shaped its history, but his artfully chosen phrase also characterizes a wider phenomenon that has been largely eliminated. We can travel between countries in a matter of hours rather than days, weeks or even months. We can also communicate almost instantaneously with those in far places. The means for rapid travel and communication have, moreover, made possible the development of multinational corporations, cartels, and networks that are more powerful than the countries in which they are situated – posing distinct regulatory and ethical challenges to national and global governance structures.

With such developments have come the transnationalization and globalization of some of the less-attractive aspects of human society – crime and terrorism. The events of September 11, 2001 (9/11) did not occur in a vacuum, but they managed – for reasons that we need not pursue here – to refocus attention on the transnational and global character of much that is problematic in Western, liberal democratic societies. Although we might legitimately wonder whether there are really any "good guys" in our present global situation, the simple fact of the matter is that much of crime and terrorism is no longer local or multinational but transnational and international. Even though Westphalian borders remain in place, and indeed function as critical and oftentimes problematic elements in global politics, they no longer present impenetrable or controlled barriers to outsiders.[1] For many purposes, the passport that needs to be shown if A travels

---

1   Contemporary doctrines of national sovereignty tend to go back to the Peace of Westphalia, 1648. State sovereignty is one of the factors that makes the problem of developing global standards so difficult. See Michael Walzer, *Just and Unjust Wars* (1977). For a few recent contributions to the debate, see Omar Dahbour, "Advocating Sovereignty in an Age of Globalization", *Journal of Social Philosophy* 37, no. 1 (2006): 108–26; Joelle Tanguy, "Redefining Sovereignty and Intervention", *Ethics and International Affairs*, 17, no. 1 (2003): 141–48; Michael Dusche, "Human Rights, Autonomy and National Sovereignty", *Ethical Perspectives*, 7, no. 1 (2000): 24–36.

to X from Y to see B can be circumvented by the Skype call, email or other online transaction that A can make with B. The bomb or weapons that need to be physically transported across borders may not cause as much devastation as the computer virus or hacked website that is remotely controlled. Crime and terrorism have exploited the porosity of borders, along with the opacity that encryption and other technological advances have made available.

The advent of global terrorism has created an additional problem to that posed by porous boundaries. Global terrorism, like all terrorism, stands somewhere between crime and war. Countries that have been confronted by it have had to make difficult decisions about how to deal with it. Those involved in the first terrorist attack on the Twin Towers of the World Trade Center in 1993 were treated as though they had committed a number of serious crimes – including seditious conspiracy, explosive destruction of property and interstate transportation of explosives. Their intentions were to topple one of the towers against the other, with a view to bringing both down – arguably a more radical plan than that adopted by the terrorists on September 11, 2001, who appear to have seen the actual collapse of the towers as an unexpected bonus. However, what occurred on September 11 was treated as something much closer to an act of war, leading to the US invasion of Afghanistan. Given that there was some connection between those who plotted the first attack on the Twin Towers and those who were involved in the second, what made for the difference? Was it that the second attack included other targets besides the Twin Towers? Was it the death toll? Admittedly, the events of 1993 already raised questions about the sufficiency of law enforcement strategies for dealing with terrorism.[2] Nevertheless, terrorism seems to occupy a broad space between crime and war, intersecting with each and thus blurring once-clear conceptual boundaries. We tend to think of crimes as serving the personal interests of those who perpetrate them; war, on the other hand, is politically motivated as one state seeks to take control of the affairs of another. But Timothy McVeigh's (and Terry Nichols's) terroristic destruction of the Alfred P. Murrah Building in Oklahoma City, though politically motivated, was treated as a crime, as was the first World Trade Center bombing. Terrorism does not clearly constitute war either, even though it is usually politically motivated. If we generally think of war as armed conflict between states, terrorism does not clearly constitute an act of war. There is no standing army to fight or head of state with whom to negotiate.

---

2 See Dale Watson, "Foreign Terrorists in America: Five Years After the World Trade Center" (Senate Judiciary Committee), February 24, 1998, available at: http://fas.org/irp/congress/1998_hr/s980224w.htm. See also Seumas Miller, *Terrorism and Counter-terrorism: Ethics and Liberal Democracy* (Oxford: Blackwell, 2010), ch. 5.

This is not the place to engage in an extended discussion of what constitutes terrorism.[3] Perhaps it is enough for our purposes to say that terrorism seeks to further some political or politico-religious end, using, as the name implies, indiscriminate violence to intimidate a people. Unlike war, which may also involve terror – though not generally as a strategy – terrorism does not usually constitute armed conflict between jurisdictionally bound political communities.[4]

What we designate as crimes are generally jurisdictionally defined. That is, the designation of "doing φ" as a crime applies only in country P, though country Q may in some cases also designate "doing φ_1", an act similar to φ, as a crime. That will commonly be the case with respect to crimes that are said to be *mala in se*, but less frequently so with respect to *mala prohibita* crimes. The firearm whose possession is illegal in jurisdiction P may be permitted in Q. Technological advances, however, may enable A, who wishes to do what is criminalized in P, to accomplish it by transacting it in Q. Secret offshore bank accounts can hide the proceeds of criminal activity or avoid tax requirements (or both). Of course, a jurisdiction may choose to make illegal acts that would move doing φ offshore, but it is much more difficult if the evidence of an offense in P is hidden in Q. This is only one of many possible options and a particularly simple one. A may not be in P when the offense takes place. If A is in Q and by means of a computer transaction defrauds C in P, A may be beyond the reach of investigatory authorities unless there is some agreement between the authorities in P and Q. Such agreements are frequently absent, but even when such an agreement exists it may take time and effort to implement it if there are local sensitivities to be negotiated[5] and, if there are significant differences in the legal understandings of P and Q, it may be impossible for C to get redress. Although Westphalian boundaries are sometimes flouted or quietly subverted,[6] they continue to pose

---

3   Some of the diversity of definitions and complexities involved are discussed in Alex P. Schmid, A.J. Jongman, and Irving Horowitz, *Political Terrorism: A New Guide to Actors, Authors, Concepts, Data Bases, Theories, and Literature* (Amsterdam: Transaction Books, 1998); Bruce Hoffman, "Defining Terrorism", in *Terrorism and Counterterrorism: Understanding the New Security Environment*, ed. Russell D. Howard, Reid L. Sawyer, Natasha E. Bajema, third ed. (NY: McGraw-Hill, 2009), 4–33; Miller, *Terrorism and Counter-terrorism*, ch. 2.

4   However, we leave to one side what is often referred to as state terrorism (as was evident in Stalin's Soviet Union) as well as terrorism used in the course of war (say, British carpet bombing of German cities during World War II) and state support for terrorism (say, Syrian support for Hezbollah).

5   A recent case concerned the extradition of a permanent resident of Australia (of 37 years) to the US for cracking copy-protected software and then distributing it free of charge over the internet. Although the scale of the offense was not great, because there was an extradition treaty between the US and Australia it still raised eyebrows. Some felt that extraditing "simply" to protect US commercial interests gave the US excessive influence in Australia. See Kenneth Nguyen, "Australia Hands over Man to US Courts", *The Age* (Melbourne), May 7, 2007; P.W. Young, "Extradition to the US", *Australian Law Journal* 81 (April, 2007): 225. On June 22, 2007, he was sentenced to 51 months imprisonment in the US, though because of the time served in Australia during extradition proceedings he served less than 15 months. See http://www.sys-con.com/read/393715. htm. He returned to Australia in March, 2008.

6   There is evidence of both subversion and flouting in the so-called extraordinary renditions of suspected terrorists that were carried out by US authorities. See Association of the Bar of the City of New York & Center for Human Rights and Global Justice, *Torture by Proxy: International and Domestic Law Applicable to*

major obstacles to the effective control and prosecution of much criminality. When transactions become more complex than the simple ones noted, as indeed they often do, then the problems of investigation, prosecution and, perhaps, recovery can become even more difficult. If A, in P, steals B's identifiers from Q (either by hacking or phishing or some other ruse), opens an account under B's name in R, transfers B's assets to R and then arranges for them to be cashed out by an accomplice in R, the task of investigation and prosecution may become almost impossibly intricate. Moreover, actual criminality, especially at the high end, may be much more complex than this. The point is simply that technology has made possible forms of criminality that challenge the traditional means for their control, creating ethical quandaries as those committed to their control find that time-tested tools are no longer sufficient.

ATM card fraud is an example of the type of fraud that is becoming increasingly international in nature. ATM card numbers and even complete track 2 information[7], as well as card security codes, are available for purchase on websites that have been located in former eastern bloc countries, Russia, China, and other nations that often do not cooperate with US and European law enforcement authorities.[8] Access to this contraband is available to cyber thieves throughout the world who frequently work in highly organized groups and make use of the information to withdraw funds at ATMs located in various nations before financial institutions can detect the fraud and invalidate the cards. Access to contraband sites often requires a password or a cryptographic key available only to cyber thieves who establish a trust relationship with the criminal organization that sponsors the site.[9] Sensitive personal financial information, including social security and bank account numbers, captured in major data breaches at American retailers, banks and card processors have frequently turned up on these foreign sites.[10] Although the current discourse consistently weighs privacy against national security needs, the widespread availability of personally identifiable financial information puts individuals at risk for fraud.

"Extraordinary Renditions", New York: ABCNY & NYU School of Law, 2004; available at The Record (of the Bar Association of the City of New York) 60 (2005): 13–193; David Weissbrodt and Amy Bergquist, "Extraordinary Rendition: A Human Rights Analysis", Harvard Human Rights Journal, 19 (Spring, 2006): 123–60; idem, "Extraordinary Rendition and the Torture Convention", Virginia Journal of International Law, 46 (Summer, 2006): 585–650; idem, "Extraordinary Rendition and the Humanitarian Law of War and Occupation", Virginia Journal of International Law, 47 (Winter, 2007): 295–356; Michael V. Sage, "The Exploitation of Legal Loopholes in the Name of National Security", California W. International Law Journal 37 (Fall, 2006): 121–42.

7   Track 2 information is the information contained on the card's magnetic strip and can be used to fabricate a duplicate card.

8   K. Perreti, "Data Breaches: What the Underground World of Carding Reveals", Santa Clara Computer and High Tech Law Journal 25, no. 2 (2009): 375–413.

9   Statement of Rita Glavin, Acting Assistant Attorney General, Criminal Division, US Department of Justice, before the House of Representatives Subcommittee on Emerging Threats, Cybersecurity, and Science and Technology, March 31, 2009.

10   Douglas Salane, "Are Large Scale Data Beaches Inevitable?", Cyber Infrastructure Protection Conference '09, City College and SSI US Army War College, the City University of New York, June 2009. Available at: http://www.jjay.cuny.edu/centers/cybercrime_studies/D_SalaneLargeScaleDataBreaches.pdf.

Terrorism has also moved across territorial boundaries. Although localized terrorism still occurs (in places such as Egypt and Spain, and until recently in Northern Ireland and Sri Lanka), the attacks of 9/11 were a sharp reminder that terrorist activity does not need to be grounded in local discontent but may reflect disaffection from afar. The attacks of 9/11, moreover, were not the work of another "state" but of a much more amorphous group with no clear political identity. Whatever we may think of the responses to those events, they posed a challenge that had not been clearly thought through – attackers from afar and an operational center or centers that could not be identified with a government or country (even though an insurgent Taliban gave cover in Afghanistan). Furthermore, it was clear that the coordination required for the attack was possible only because it had become technologically feasible to move money and messages electronically. For the US authorities, it presaged things to come.

Reactive responses

Political authorities have responded to these transnational, international, and global challenges in a number of ways. One obvious response has been to try to increase border security (fences, patrols, etc.), but important as border interceptions have been, it has been argued that these have not been sufficient. Westphalian constraints have for the most part required that intergovernmental agreements are sought. Agreements between and among sovereign states have ranged from extradition treaties to exchanges of salient information. They have operated at a number of levels, sometimes through international organizations such as Interpol or through high-level memoranda of understanding.

As well as monitoring the incoming, outgoing and through-passing movement of human beings, there have also been efforts to monitor incoming, outgoing and through-passing transactions such as phone calls, internet communications and financial wire dealings. Indeed, these activities are increasingly conducted by specialized agencies set up for this very purpose. For example, AUSTRAC in Australia monitors international financial transactions of AU$5,000 or above.[11] These monitoring activities have sometimes proved problematic. In the US, for example, certain legal constraints have traditionally been applicable to many of these transactions. Most significantly for the contemporary era – at least until quite recently – the Foreign Intelligence Security Act of 1978 (FISA) was set up to ensure that any monitoring of cross-border communications satisfied a range of conditions. FISA was introduced to place stringent – though not insuperable – conditions on governmental monitoring of communications, generally communications between the US and foreign countries. It provided for

---

11   See Appendix.

a special court to handle requests for monitoring. These conditions, however, were relaxed in cascading fashion by both the USA PATRIOT Act of 2001 and the FISA Amendments Act of 2008. In addition, as we see later, widespread commercial collection and mining of digitalized data has also been accessed by government agents.

Although Westphalian constraints have for the most part required that intergovernmental agreements are sought, more has been thought necessary. Agreements that allow for exchanges of information or other actions that enable the interception and prosecution of criminal or terroristic enterprises have not always been thought adequate. If the security of borders cannot be achieved at the borders they can perhaps be achieved by unilateral actions taken beyond the borders. Sovereign states have instituted their own means of monitoring communications and transactions in their efforts to curb transnational, international and global criminal and terrorist activity.

To counter both crime and terrorism, technology is being turned to. In itself, this is not intrinsically inappropriate. But warring on crime and counter-terrorism strategies may overreach and the values of those in whose defense they are employed may be in danger of being undermined. No less problematic is that we may find that the coordination of effort that is required is jeopardized by jurisdictional differences.

The purpose of this study is to address such counter-crime and counter-terrorism concerns and offer some best practice recommendations.

II. Security and the Challenge to Liberal Values

Security is valuable to any society. For each society, security offers a form of stability in the face of vulnerability, but within liberal democratic polities, security also provides – at least in theory – a social environment within which individual citizens and other dwellers can flourish. That is, security offers to citizens and others a stable framework for the pursuit of the various goods that they seek to realize for themselves. Henry Shue speaks of individual security as a basic right – indeed, as a right that underwrites all other rights, including, in his view, other basic rights such as subsistence and liberty.[1]

How security is to be understood and how it is most appropriately achieved are questions that we will address in the course of this study (especially in Chapter VIII). What is to be noted here, however, is the impact that the events of 9/11 had on conceptions of security and the ways of achieving it, as well as on the relations between security and other important liberal values such as liberty, autonomy, privacy, dignity and the maintenance of one's identity.

It is indisputable that the events of 9/11 constituted a massive failure of security – not only of security procedures at various US airports but also of larger federal security processes directed against terrorism and threats to national security. Such failures naturally raised questions concerning the adequacy of security at both local and federal levels.

More than one response to such circumstances might be proffered:

1. It might be argued that the security measures in place were as good as they could have been expected to be and that the breaches that occurred represented a cost that needed to be borne. That is, it might be argued that even with our best efforts it could not be expected that we would be impervious to all breaches. Relatively few have been willing to argue that (and even fewer since the Christmas 2009 bombing attempt). The benefits of hindsight have made it clear that even though we might expect there to be unanticipated and unpreventable breaches of security, the particular failures that occurred were realistically preventable and should not have happened. We need not have accepted what occurred as the cost of remaining a decent society.

---

1   Henry Shue, *Basic Rights:* Subsistence, *Affluence, and U.S. Foreign Policy*, second ed. (Princeton, NJ: Princeton University Press, 1996), ch. 1.

2. It might be argued that although the security measures already in place could have been utilized to prevent the particular attacks from occurring they occurred as a result of technical or human failings. No more was needed except for what already existed to have worked better than it did.[2] Although this position was taken by some, and might indeed have much to be said for it, it was not a politically popular one.[3] In part, dissatisfaction with such a position was associated with the view that the magnitude of the threat had been underestimated and that for such threats heightened measures need to be in place.

3. Although many accepted that some failures of otherwise adequate security procedures had occurred, they argued that what was really called for was not simply that the existing system be made to work but also that security measures needed to be dramatically increased. We needed much tighter security to ensure such events would not happen again.

One significant cost of giving most weight to the third of these responses was that ramping up security placed pressure on other values also held dear within liberal democratic polities. In particular, it was argued that an "imbalance" had occurred between liberty and security and that this needed rectification.[4] We would need to give up some liberty in order to bring our security to an acceptable level, but liberty – in the sense of social freedom – was not the only value placed under pressure. Privacy was also compromised and along with it autonomy, or the inner freedom that is so greatly prized within liberal democratic theory. Furthermore, insofar as certain people were more heavily targeted than others as a result of enhanced security measures, issues of identity, dignity and equality, or non-discrimination, were brought to the fore.

We will later have occasion to question the metaphor of "balance" to characterize the relations between security and other values, such as liberty. For one thing, increased security does not necessarily imply a trade-off in terms of a significant reduction in freedom or privacy; it might simply involve greater expenditure of resources on security without any lessening of legal and ethical constraints on the powers of security agencies. For another thing, where trade-offs do actually occur the metaphor can mask them by misleadingly implying that the rectification of an imbalance was a costless process, as though the resulting liberty were not significantly impaired. But it is more relevant at this juncture

---

2   There are numerous white papers, news articles, podcasts and webinars that suggest ways of doing this. See, for example, the webinar of Patrick Howard, Chief Information Security Officer, Nuclear Regulatory Commission, "Creating a Culture of Security – Top 10 Elements of an Information Security Program", available at: www.govinfosecurity.com/webinarsDetails.php.

3   The point was made just as plausibly – though hardly more popularly – with respect to the Christmas Day 2009 bombing. See: http://i.cdn.turner.com/cnn/2010/images/01/07/summary.of.wh.review.pdf.

4   Here the term "imbalance" was often implicitly understood in terms of a trade-off.

to note some of the ways in which the ramping up of security has impinged on these other values. We confine ourselves here to cases involving the use of digital technologies.

There has, first of all, been a growth in the use of surveillance technologies. This is no doubt partly a function of the increased availability and greatly enhanced power of these technologies. After all, they are being used in a wide variety of settings for reasons other than security, such as in the workplace.[5] However, security concerns have been a key driver. The uses of these technologies have included the proliferation of closed-circuit television (CCTV) and other visual surveillance devices, along with their greater centralization. Increased use has been made of wiretapping and other measures designed to access communications between people. The use of X-ray-type devices to scan persons and their possessions has also greatly expanded.

Secondly, increasing use has been made of data gathering and data mining activities. Vast numbers of public – and not so public – documents that once needed to be sought on an as-needed basis, often with some effort, have now been digitalized and their data centralized in huge databases where they are available for access or purchase (by commercial, private and government organizations). Such data have enabled the construction of identity narratives for the purpose of investigation or profiling.

Thirdly, data mining has enabled the development of profiles for various purposes, including the investigation (and even perpetration) of crime and terrorism. Although profiling (especially where race was implicated) came under heavy criticism during the latter years of the twentieth century it made a powerful comeback after the events of 9/11. Aspects of this issue pose serious challenges for liberal democratic values.

In this study we seek to outline the development of these technologies in order to identify the ethical, social and legal risks associated with them, to examine possible responses to those risks and to make some recommendations concerning best practice.

---

5   See Seumas Miller and John Weckert, "Privacy, the Workplace and the Internet", *Journal of Business Ethics* 28, no. 3 (2000): 255–65, and John Weckert (ed.), *Electronic Monitoring in the Workplace: Controversies and Solutions* (Hershey, PA: Idea Group Publishing, 2005).

III. The Blessing and Bane of the Liberal Democratic Tradition

One of the important virtues of liberalism – and, by extension, a liberal democratic polity – is that, in theory at least, it acknowledges the diversity of human goods and ends. A liberal democratic polity seeks to accommodate within its social order a recognition of this diversity and to enable the realization of differing ends. A liberal democratic polity will therefore include among its important goals the fostering of – or at least a decision not to inhibit – the diversity of ways in which humans can flourish. No doubt there will be limits or at least challenges to such support – when, for example, the form that human flourishing appears to take requires the suppression of others' flourishing (what is sometimes referred to as the paradox of liberalism). Even so, there will be the recognition and promotion of a broad range of human possibilities along with the conditions for their social and associational realization.

The acute challenge that liberalism poses is of incompatible diversity or at least of diversity in tension. Although we commonly see such tensions at the individual level – say, between the libertarian and social democrat – these tensions may also be manifest at a macro-level. One country's liberal democratic tradition may develop in one direction whereas another liberal democratic polity may develop in a different direction. Consider, for example, the contrast between the US and the Netherlands, or the even greater contrast between both of these countries and India. These differences may manifest themselves not only with respect to, say, forms of governance and social institutions but also in the traditions of understanding that underpin shared values, such as those of liberty, autonomy, privacy and dignity.

There is no guarantee, even, and perhaps especially within liberalism, that central concepts will be understood in exactly the same way. Liberals are themselves divided on this. There are those who are committed to the univocity of liberalism's central concepts but who recognize diversity in the ways in which they may be realized. However, there are others who see the diversity reaching to its core concepts, liberalism itself being seen as at best an overlapping consensus of traditions.[1]

It is this latter challenge that we must confront in this study, for although the polities with which we will be concerned – primarily those of the US and the EU but also those of Australia and India, albeit to a much lesser extent – can

---

1   See P.F. Strawson, "Social Morality and Individual Ideal", *Philosophy* 36 (January, 1961): 1–17.

reasonably be characterized as liberal democratic, their traditions have diverged in important ways that have come to a head in the response to international crime and global terrorism.

The possibility of intractable diversity within liberalism has long exercised its theorists. In 1956, W. B. Gallie published his influential essay on the essential contestability of many – perhaps most – social concepts, and then in 1987 John Rawls, in response to objections made to his classic political treatise, *A Theory of Justice* (1971), published his paper on the idea of an overlapping consensus. Here we summarize a few of the main contentions of these two papers to illustrate some of the challenges created by the liberal commitment to diversity.

First, Gallie.[2] In his original paper, Gallie argued that many and perhaps most concepts employed in social life are not merely contested, but "essentially contested". He gives as examples art, democracy, social justice, religion and championship, but other writers have added to the list with medicine, education, music, liberty, power, rule of law, rhetoric, security, the Christian tradition, justice, academic freedom, privacy and so on. It would not be too much of an exaggeration to claim that almost any social concept that is likely to be of importance to us will be contested, though whether it is contested in Gallie's sense remains to be seen. Gallie articulates and develops several conditions that will qualify a concept as "essentially contested". They include the following:

1. They are *appraisive*. That is, although they characterize an activity, they are also normative characterizations. "Art" is not simply a human activity but one that we value. "Disease", on the other hand, is something we disvalue. What constitutes art or a disease will depend on the kinds of normative considerations that we allow to inform our understanding of each. Similar claims might be made about privacy or security. To characterize a matter as private is not simply to identify it but also to indicate certain claims that are made on us – that we respect and not intrude on what is deemed private. Security no less implies the appropriate provision or protection of that which is valued.

---

2   W.B. Gallie, "Essentially Contested Concepts", *Proceedings of the Aristotelian Society* 56 (1955–56), 167–98 (also in *Essentially Contested Concepts and the Historical Understanding*, London: Chatto and Windus, 1964, ch. 8). The idea has also been taken up and discussed by others – e.g. A.C. MacIntyre, "The Essential Contestability of Some Social Concepts", *Ethics* 84 (October, 1973), 1–9; Norman S. Care, "On Fixing Social Concepts", *Ethics* 84 (October, 1973), 10–21; Steven Lukes, "Relativism: Cognitive and Moral", *Proceedings of the Aristotelian Society*, Supp. Vol. 48 (1974), 165–89; A.P. Montefiore (ed.), *Neutrality and Impartiality: The University and Political Commitment* (Cambridge, UK: Cambridge University Press, 1975), Part I; John N. Gray, "The Contestability of Concepts", *Political Theory* 5 (1977), 330–48; John N. Gray, "On Liberty, Liberalism, and Essential Contestability", *British Journal of Political Science* 8 (1978), 385–402; Christine Swanton, "On the 'Essential Contestedness' of Political Concepts", *Ethics* 95 (July, 1985), 811–27; Andrew Mason, "On Explaining Political Disagreement: The Notion of an Essentially Contested Concept", *Inquiry* 33 (1990), 81–98; William E. Connolly, *The Terms of Political Discourse* (Princeton, NJ: Princeton University Press, 1993).

2. They denote an *essentially complex* activity. What makes something a piece of music or a religion is not a single feature but a complex of features of varying importance, and it may be that not all are necessarily present if other features are present. One might be inclined to think that worship of a god is essential to a religion but in the case of certain other belief traditions this might be less important as long as other features are present. We do not usually deny that Buddhism is a religion, even though some of its main strands are nontheistic. Should Marxism also be seen as a religion? In the case of security we meet some of these complexities in the debate about whether (national) security is to be thought of in terms of territorial integrity or the integrity of a way of life, whether any threat to national security interests is, *ipso facto*, a threat to national security or whether an attack on a national symbol can be seen as an attack on the nation, and so on. No less complex is the idea of privacy, a chameleon-like concept that yields the possibility that what takes place in private is not therefore private.[3]

3. They are initially *variously describable*, and differences are likely among their users about the relative importance of different elements in the complex activity. This is clearly the case in matters of religion and art but applies equally when a broad enough group of people start talking about what philosophy or democracy is. Sometimes the gulf between Western and Eastern philosophy can seem pretty broad, almost unbridgeable. Those of us who still remember the DDR, the German Democratic Republic, know that what counts as democratic is a matter of contestation. Notions of privacy and security are not immune to such variations and, certainly in the case of privacy, such variability has been of critical importance.

4. They are *open ended* and subject to considerable modification in the light of changing times, and such modification cannot be predicted or prescribed in advance. What Gallie has in mind here are the historical changes to which such concepts are susceptible. What forty years ago was encompassed by the term "medicine" has changed, not merely because we have learned more about what does and what does not fulfill our criteria for medicine, but also because our criteria for what constitutes something as medicine have changed (consider acupuncture, homeopathy etc.). We see this in the discussion of (national) security in the shift from border security to a variety of challenges to a state's equanimity, such as pandemics, economic crises and threats of war. Our conception of privacy has also evolved as our capacity to integrate information, previously considered as public, has grown.

5. Each party to a dispute *recognizes that its own use of the concept is contested* by those of other parties. To use an essentially contested concept means to

---

3   See S.I. Benn and G.F. Gaus, "Public and Private – Concepts in Action", in *Public and Private in Social Life*, ed. S.I. Benn and G.F. Gaus (NY: St. Martin's Press, 1983), 3–27.

use it against other users. To use such a concept means to use it aggressively and defensively. This was very clear in debates during the seventies over the (often feminist) slogan, "the personal is the political", but it is also true in the case of terms such as "terrorism", which can be used not only as a term of criticism but also to distinguish one's own activity from that of terrorists. The ongoing conflict between Israelis and Palestinians is in part a contest of characterizations. What Israelis have often viewed as acts of terrorism Palestinians have characterized as acts of retaliation, and vice versa. Privacy is viewed rather differently by the United States and Europe. Members of the EU consider all personal data as private, accessible by others only under fairly stringent conditions. In the US, however, privacy is construed primarily as a shield against governmental intrusion, not against the data gathering and mining activities of commercial enterprises. In contrast with both the US and the EU, individual privacy in a developing country such as India is not a very high priority, whether *vis-à-vis* government or private sector intrusion. Even within a culture there may be variable recognitions. Arguably, the upper and middle classes in India are more likely to be concerned about individual privacy than the members of lower socio-economic groups. Although we have appealed unabashedly to "liberal values", that which is deemed liberal is often spoken of disparagingly in the US political context, to the point where their advocates now often speak of themselves as "progressive."

6. Such concepts must be derived from an *original exemplar* (or exemplars) whose authority is acknowledged by all the contestant users of the concept. This condition is required to ensure that we are dealing with a single concept and not two or more distinct or confused concepts. Nobody disputes that a Rembrandt painting is art or that Christianity is a religion. Few would dispute that what happened on 9/11 was a terrorist act or that the proliferation of nuclear weapons by other countries is likely to constitute a challenge to national security. The problems arise as we move out from acknowledged cases to more problematic ones – say, to Ron Hubbard's scientology in the case of religion, or to the British area bombing of Dresden during World War II or the atom bombing of the cities of Hiroshima and Nagasaki in the case of terrorism.

7. Use of these concepts requires the probability or plausibility of the claim that the continuous competition for acknowledgment among contesting users enables the original exemplar's achievement to be sustained and/or developed in optimum fashion. The contestation does not split the original exemplars of the concept from ongoing inclusion or from conceptual evolution. What is contested is how that evolution is to be appropriately constructed. So it is with security and many other social concepts – an overlapping of underlying considerations that has evolved in somewhat divergent ways.

Gallie's position has not gone unchallenged. Nor, according to some writers, is it altogether clear what Gallie's exact thesis is or is intended to reflect. Is he saying that concepts such as security are characterized by multiple and evaluatively-charged criteria and that there is no settled priority among them? Is he saying that terms such as security arise within and express particular and competing moral positions or outlooks? Is he arguing that there is no way of extracting oneself from some particular normative position so that one can, *sub species aeternitatis*, determine one account to be better than others? It would take us too far afield to explore and seek to resolve these possibilities at any length. (Swanton offers a useful overview.) Our point here is simply that Gallie's thesis helps to provide some understanding of the problems that we encounter as we seek to articulate an account of security and other concepts that will be central to our discussion: privacy, autonomy and identity. Definitions do not simply precede justificatory discussions – to some extent they already embody and reflect them.

Now, Rawls.[4] In *A Theory of Justice* Rawls argued for the priority of justice as a principle of social organization, a principle that he subsequently articulated in terms of a number of other principles arrived at through the artifice of what was called "the original position", a strategy designed to devise social principles untainted by the particularities of their collective architects. Rawls later came to accept that the strategy he devised and the principles at which he arrived were not as immune from partisan values as he had hoped. Contributing to this was the liberal recognition of diversity of ends and of the justificatory structures grounding them. The diversity is too deep for Rawls's original strategy to work as it was intended.

And so, in a later development of his position, Rawls argues that stability within a liberal society may be achieved not because of shared principles derived from reflections on an original position, nor from some general and comprehensive moral doctrine, but from an overlapping consensus in which a sufficient core of political principles is shared, albeit grounded in diverse frameworks or comprehensive doctrines. Rawls argues that the political conception of justice that constitutes this overlapping consensus will have three features. It will first of all be a moral or normative conception tailored explicitly to the basic political, social and economic institutions of society (whether or not it can later be extended more broadly to international relations[5]). Second, the principles constitutive of this overlapping consensus will not be derivable from or be articulations of a general and comprehensive moral or political doctrine such

---

4   John Rawls, "The Idea of an Overlapping Consensus", *Oxford Journal of Legal Studies*, 7, no. 1 (1987): 1–25. The material was later incorporated into his *Political Liberalism* (1993).

5   Clearly, however, the possibility of extending a political conception of justice to relations between states is of importance to the present study. For discussion at the level of interstate relations see Thomas Pogge, *Realizing Rawls* (Ithaca, NY: Cornell University Press, 1989), Part III.

as utilitarianism, for it is precisely about such general and comprehensive doctrines that liberal democratic societies are pluralistic. Such pluralism is endemic to liberal democracies. Third, the political conception of justice will be formulated "in terms of certain fundamental intuitive ideas viewed as latent in the public culture of a democratic society."[6] By means of this strategy, Rawls hopes (though without guarantee) that the resulting conception of justice will garner the support of an overlapping social consensus. It is not Rawls's purpose here to argue for the relevant substantive principles, though he offers his own conception of "justice as fairness" as one such candidate along with Ronald Dworkin's liberal conception of equality.

Rawls seeks to distinguish his idea of an overlapping consensus based on a political conception of justice from that of a *modus vivendi* based on self interest, and to argue for the superiority of the former. A *modus vivendi* (of the kind advocated by Hobbes) lacks any principled basis and as such is inherently unstable: it will be abandoned in the event that one of the parties to it thinks it advantageous to do so. The principles that comprise the consensus, however, are moral principles, ultimately grounded in internally affirmed moral doctrines, and adherence to them is likely to persist in the face of shifting advantage.

Both Gallie and Rawls confront the difficulties that must be acknowledged in any attempt to develop global standards across a number of issues (e.g. ethical identity management), and though they are optimistic that it is not a lost cause they do not underestimate the problems that may be involved. The difficulties they confront are not precisely the same difficulties; they occur at different levels of the socio-political process. Rawls confronts basic structural difficulties that may need to be addressed whereas Gallie is concerned for the most part with divergences that occur among seemingly shared social concepts that are likely – much more than Rawls's – to be reflective of general and comprehensive doctrines. In both cases, however – and this is perhaps characteristic of a liberal approach – there is a willingness to engage in ongoing reflection and deliberation concerning the issues at stake. It may not be quite true that liberal societies do not war against each other, but there are deep social, political and intellectual resources within those societies for addressing such differences.

An illustration

An apposite instance of this contestability is privacy, for which we will draw upon James Q. Whitman's provocative paper, "The Two Western Cultures of

---

6 "The Idea of an Overlapping Consensus", 6.

Privacy: Dignity versus Liberty."[7] The history of the development of privacy in Europe and in the US nicely illustrates the divergence from a common history (prior to US Independence) as well as the possibilities for rapprochement.

It is Whitman's contention that European (by which he tends to mean German and French) conceptions of privacy view it as an aspect of dignity whereas the US conception of privacy tends to see it as an aspect of liberty. Whitman argues that the European tradition informing privacy has its origins in late eighteenth century notions of honor and dignity (in France) and Kantian notions of personality (in Germany) and places great store on control over one's public image. Much of European privacy consists in "our right to a public image of our own making, as the right to control of our public face." Whitman draws attention to what he sees as European wariness about allowing the free market to be the umpire on privacy matters. To illustrate this he looks at credit reporting and consumer data protection. Europeans, he writes, believe that "one's financial information is information 'of a personal character,' over which one must have control just as one must have control over one's image."

It is Whitman's contention that the seminal article by Samuel Warren and Louis Brandeis on "The Right to Privacy"[8] attempted to import a European conception of privacy into the US. However, influential though their article has been it was an unsuccessful transplant. Although privacy eventually made its way into American constitutional values through *Griswold v. Connecticut*[9], it did so in a different form and with a different rationale. Whitman does not want to argue that "Americans don't understand the moral imperative of privacy in the creation of 'personhood'", an idea that is central to European conceptions. Rather, what is central to the US conception of privacy is liberty: "Suspicion of the state has always stood at the foundation of American privacy thinking, and American scholarly writing and court doctrine continue to take it for granted that the state is the prime enemy of our privacy." And so privacy is seen as something that protects individuals from state intrusion – hence the sanctity of the home in American privacy law.

We have, then, two different frameworks for thinking about privacy which clearly overlap but do not coincide. Though they are hard to reconcile at a political level – reflecting "local social anxieties and local ideals" – at a conceptual and normative level they can be brought into much closer alignment. As Whitman puts it: "There is no logical inconsistency in pursuing both forms of privacy protection: it is perfectly possible to advocate both privacy against the state

---

7   James Q. Whitman, "The Two Western Cultures of Privacy: Dignity versus Liberty", *Yale Law Journal*, 113 (2004): 1151–1221.
8   Samuel D. Warren and Louis D. Brandeis, "The Right to Privacy", *Harvard Law Review* 4, no. 5 (1890): 193–20.
9   *Griswold v. Connecticut*, 381 US 479 (1965).

and privacy against non-state information gatherers to argue that protecting privacy means both safeguarding the presentation of self, and inhibiting the investigative and regulatory excesses of the state."

No doubt Whitman's account can be questioned in a number of respects.[10] To talk, as he does, as though there are only two cultures, is somewhat tendentious, especially as his accounts of German and French conceptions of privacy point to rather different roots. Nevertheless, Europeans appear to have developed a unified public policy on privacy that now stands in serious tension with American public policy. We might take some comfort from this, however, for despite the differences between Germany and France they were able to develop a unified public policy. Perhaps the same can be achieved in relation to the US and even globally within liberal democratic communities.

---

10 See, for example, Francesca Bignami, "European versus American Liberty: A Comparative Privacy Analysis of Anti-Terrorism Data-Mining", *Boston College Law Review*, 48 (May 2007): 609.

IV. Divergent Formalities

There is wide divergence in the ways that liberal democracies view and protect individual privacy and identity. A recent multinational report sponsored by the European Commission compares legal and regulatory measures to enhance privacy and trust in the European Union, the United States, Japan, South Korea and Malaysia.[1] For each jurisdiction, the report examines self-regulatory and co-regulatory arrangements, enforcement mechanisms and the effectiveness of privacy and trust practices. Jurisdictions in which privacy is considered an inherent human right and is constitutionally protected tend to have a uniform regulatory framework that limits the way in which a data controller can collect and process information. These jurisdictions typically have statutory regulations that apply to all economic sectors and types of activities.[2] Jurisdictions in which personal information is not recognized in constitutional guarantees, even though privacy rights may be inferred from court decisions, tend to lack a uniform regulatory framework for privacy and identity protections. Typically, legal protections arise to address some demonstrated harm and protections tend to apply only to a given economic sector. Thus a complex tapestry of laws and regulation arises in these jurisdictions and, as the report notes, it often includes significant gaps in protection. Enforcement is scattered across a range of agencies, often with no strong original mandate to enforce privacy legislation. The report also found that even in jurisdictions in which constitutional privacy provisions exist, a prominent security threat such as that posed by South Korea's northern neighbor has a profound influence on the regulatory framework.

Nations such as Australia and India (see Appendix), which have no constitutional privacy provisions, have developed a diverse array of laws, regulations and other institutional mechanisms to accommodate privacy concerns. In part this is because they have close commercial ties to nations that do have these provisions. India in particular has developed a very large IT, software and associated international outsourcing industry that has led it to address privacy concerns above and beyond those emanating exclusively from domestic sources.

---

1   "Comparison of Privacy and Trust Policies in the Area of Electronic Communications", July 20, 2007. Available at: http://ec.europa.eu/information_society/policy/ecomm/doc/library/ext_studies/privacy_trust_policies/final_report_20_07_07_pdf.pdf.

2   As will be seen in Section (B) below, however, limits on the European unification project mean that, despite the explicit recognition of a right to privacy in EU law, the EU statutory framework has thus far provided individuals with very little protection against intrusions on their privacy by governmental, as opposed to private, entities.

In India, the right to privacy derives from the Constitution as well as the common law of torts. The Constitution does not explicitly recognize the right to privacy but Article 21 provides for personal liberty,[3] and in various cases this has been taken by the Supreme Court to include the right to privacy against the state.

Although data protection is not explicitly provided for in India's Constitution, under its constitutional right to legislate in relation to matters not enumerated in the relevant lists, the central government has taken it to be an appropriate matter for its involvement. In 2009, the Information Technology (Amendment) Act 2008 was enacted in part to address domestic and regional security issues, including cybercrimes and cyberterrorism, but also, and importantly, the security concerns of foreign companies with respect to India's huge outsourcing industry. The Act provides penalties for various new cybercrimes (for example, cyberterrorism and identity theft), the recognition of new electronic documents (for example, electronic documents with e-signatures) and enhanced data security (for example, for intermediaries (any person who receives, stores, or transmits data for another person such as internet service providers)).

The establishment by the National Association of Software and Services Companies (NASSCOM) of the Data Security Council of India (DSCI) is part of the broader institutional response – in this instance, a self-regulatory part for the DSCI represents software companies and the business process outsourcing (BPO) and related IT industries. The function of DSCI is to establish, disseminate, monitor and enforce privacy and data protection standards for India's IT and outsourcing industry. Obviously, enforcement is the key challenge for DSCI – it is difficult to see how what is essentially a voluntary organization can effectively enforce the standards it establishes other than by the threat of expulsion.

The Information Technology Act 2000 and the Information Technology (Amendment) Act 2008 do not set out a comprehensive set of specific privacy and data protection principles in the manner of, say, the EU Directive or the OECD Guidelines. Rather, they require the use of "reasonable security practices and procedures", defined in terms of practices and procedures designed to protect sensitive personal information from unauthorized access, damage, use, modification, disclosure etc. The DSCI has recommended that companies implement one of the available industry-recognized standards such as the OECD Privacy Principles for Information Management Systems. Nevertheless, there is no requirement that companies undergo an audit to verify the existence and efficacy of the controls they have in place to meet any such industry standards.

---

3   This also enables India to partially fulfil its international obligations under the International Covenant on Civil and Political Rights, in which a basic right to privacy is recognized.

In India there is thus a heavy reliance on self-regulation and contractual provisions to protect individual privacy and identities, particularly for foreign citizens whose data are processed in that country.

Although Australia, like India, has no constitutional protection of privacy, it provides for a greater degree of privacy protection than does India. The key piece of Australian legislation pertaining to privacy is the Privacy Act 1988. The Office of the Privacy Commissioner is the federal agency responsible for overseeing the operation of the Privacy Act. Most law enforcement agencies in Australia are covered by the Privacy Act. The intelligence and defense intelligence agencies are, however, partially or completely exempt from it.

The Privacy Act gives effect to Article 17 of the International Covenant on Civil and Political Rights and the OECD's Guidelines on the Protection of Privacy and Trans-border Flows of Personal Data. The Privacy Act regulates the collection, use, storage, disclosure and correction of personal information. The requirements of the Act include the National Privacy Principles (NPP) (applying to private sector organizations) and the Information Privacy Principles (IPP) (applying to Australian government agencies).

The Office of the Privacy Commissioner's (OPC) responsibilities include overseeing and monitoring compliance with the Privacy Act, investigating breaches of the Data-matching Program (Assistance and Tax) Act 1990 and monitoring compliance with record-keeping requirements of the Telecommunications Act 1997. As a consequence, the OPC conducts audits and examines records, receives and investigates privacy complaints and enforces the Act through determinations and court proceedings.[4]

Although the Privacy Act applies to private sector organizations as well as Australian government agencies, the OPC does not have the power to conduct audits of organizations in the private sector. Moreover, there are various public sector agencies that are exempt from the Privacy Act and, therefore, from oversight and monitoring by the OPC. Further, the Privacy Act does not cover businesses with less than AU$3 million annual turnover (that is, the majority of businesses in Australia).

The federal Privacy Act does not cover state public sector agencies and the OPC does not have jurisdiction with respect to state public sector agencies. These come under the jurisdiction of the various state privacy commissioners – for example, the Office of the Victorian Privacy Commissioner – and are covered by state legislation. Not all the states have privacy legislation or privacy commissioners.

---

4   See *The Operation of the Privacy Act: Annual Report 2008-2009* (Canberra: Office of the Privacy Commissioner, 2009).

In Australia, other than the Victorian Commissioner for Law Enforcement Data Security, there is no statutory body concerned exclusively with data security. At the federal level and in other states data security – specifically, law enforcement data security – is simply one of the functions of oversight agencies with a wider remit. Thus the Crime and Conduct Commission in Queensland oversees the Queensland Police (and other Queensland public sector agencies) and has a concern with data security.

Accordingly, although it does not have a constitutional protection of individual privacy and there are various gaps in its privacy legislation and enforcement mechanisms, Australia does have statutory protection of privacy from both government and non-government intrusion and it does have a range of enforcement mechanisms. Moreover, as will become evident, Australia affords a greater degree of privacy for individuals, notably from intrusion by corporations, other organizations and individuals in the private sector, than a country such as the US which has constitutional guarantees that do not apply to non-government intrusion.[5]

For our present purposes we will provide a detailed treatment of the particularities of liberal disagreement as they manifest themselves in differences between the US and the EU. In this chapter we endeavor to provide:

(A) An overview of US constitutional and statutory protections of the privacy of personal data and telephone and internet communications. We will also include some discussion of how US post-9/11 law "on the books" (primarily FISA and the Patriot Act) dealt with the tensions between national boundaries, cyberspace and globalization; how these statutes were contravened by the executive branch's post-9/11 surveillance of phone and cybercommunications; the lawsuits brought to remedy these violations and the barriers raised in response (e.g. telecommunications immunity and assertions of state secrets privilege); and, finally, brief general reflections on the (in)efficacy of the separation of powers in reining in surreptitious government abuses of power;

(B) An overview and comparison of EU data protection law with US law.

In Chapter V we provide an explanation of how the differences between EU and US law underlie the PNR and SWIFT disputes, and a discussion of the national identity card issue within the framework of EU law's weaker concern with data protection from government rather than from private parties (the reverse of the priorities of US law).

---

5   As will be explained in Section (A) below, however, some protections against intrusions on individual privacy are contained in the statutory law of the United States.

(A) United States of America

The basic structure of United States law

Three basic principles underlie the legal system of the United States: (i) the existence of constitutional, statutory and common law, (ii) federalism and (iii) the separation of powers. Under federalism, each of the fifty states has its own legal system which is separate and distinct from the federal legal system. The autonomy of state law is limited, however, by the Supremacy Clause of the US Constitution, which provides that the federal constitution is "the supreme law of the land".[6] The Due Process Clause of the Fourteenth Amendment places a further major limit on the autonomy of state law by providing that no state "shall deprive any person of life, liberty or property, without due process of law."

The basic American principle of judicial review, as first enunciated by the United States Supreme Court in *Marbury v. Madison*,[7] provides that as part of its power to "say what the law is" the judicial branch of the US government, as opposed to the executive or legislative branch, has the final say in interpreting the Constitution. This in turn means that the federal courts have the power to decide whether federal or state legislation or actions by federal or state officials conform to the Constitution's commands. Under the common law tradition of the United States, the meaning and application of various constitutional provisions is determined by precedent; that is, previous case law. As the highest federal court, the United States Supreme Court is the ultimate authority on the meaning and application of the Constitution; its interpretations are binding on the lower federal courts and the state courts. The Supreme Court and the lower federal courts also have the power to interpret and apply federal statutes and regulations. However, absent a determination of unconstitutionality, the legislature or executive has the power to rewrite statutes or regulations to counter judicial interpretations with which it disagrees.

In contrast with federal legislation and regulations, state law is not within the power of the federal courts to interpret or apply. The highest court of each state is the ultimate authority on the meaning and application of the state's constitution, legislation, regulations, and common law. Although a state's constitution and enacted laws cannot deprive its citizens of the rights guaranteed by the Due Process Clause of the Fourteenth Amendment, or other provisions of the Constitution, a state court can interpret its state constitution to provide its citizens with greater rights than the federal Constitution, as interpreted by the

---

6   United States Constitution, Article VI, 2.
7   5 U.S. (1 Cranch) 137 (1803).

Supreme Court, provides.[8] A state's legislature and executive can also issue laws and regulations that expand individual rights beyond the floor provided by the Supreme Court's interpretation of federal constitutional rights.

The protection of privacy under the United States Constitution

Although the word "privacy" is absent from the United States Constitution, rights to privacy are implicit in the Fourth Amendment's prohibition of unreasonable searches and seizures and the First Amendment's protection of freedom of speech and association.[9] These rights, like all those in the Bills of Rights, protect individuals only against the federal government. The United States Supreme Court has held, however, that the Due Process Clause of the Fourteenth Amendment incorporates both First and Fourth Amendment rights; in other words, it makes these rights effective against the governments of the states.[10] Individual rights under the United States Constitution are exclusively rights against government action; the federal Constitution does nothing to protect individuals against intrusions on their privacy by corporations, associations or private individuals.[11]

The protection of privacy under the Constitution has been importantly shaped by the Fourth Amendment exclusionary rule and the Sixth Amendment's right to counsel. The exclusionary rule, which the Supreme Court made effective against the federal government in *Weeks v. United States* (1914) and effective against the states in *Mapp v. Ohio* in 1961, makes evidence obtained through violations of the Fourth Amendment inadmissible in criminal prosecutions.[12]

---

8   Justice William Brennan was a vigorous advocate of interpreting state constitutions to expand individual rights. See, e.g., Justice William F. Brennan, Jr., "The Bill of Rights and the States", *New York University Law Review* 61 (1986): 535. For another view of the relations between judicial interpretations of the federal and state constitutions of the United States, see Paul W. Kahn, "Interpretation and Authority in State Constitutionalism", *Harvard Law Review*, 106 (1993): 1147.

9   The Ninth Amendment, which provides that the "enumeration in the Constitution, of certain rights, shall not be construed to deny or disparage other rights retained by the people", has also been interpreted to protect individual privacy. See e.g. *Griswold v. Connecticut*, 381 U.S. 479, 486 (1965) (Goldberg, J., concurring); Charles Black, *Decision According to Law* (New York: Norton, 1981).

10   See e.g. *Gitlow v. New York*, 268 U.S. 652 (1925) (Fourteenth Amendment Due Process Clause incorporates First Amendment right to free speech); *National Association for the Advancement of Colored People v. Alabama*, 357 U.S. 449 (1958) (freedom of expressive association applied against the states); *Mapp v. Ohio*, 367 U.S. 643 (1961) (incorporating Fourth Amendment protections into the Due Process Clause of the Fourteenth Amendment).

11   See *Katz v. United States*, 389 U.S. 347, 351 (1967) (stating that "the protection of a person's general right to privacy – his right to be let alone by other people – is, like the protection of his property and of his very life, left largely to the law of the individual States" (footnotes omitted)).

12   *Weeks v. United States*, 232 U.S. 383 (1914); *Mapp v. Ohio*, 367 U.S. 643 (1961). Although the subject is beyond the scope of this study, it should be noted that the US Supreme Court has carved out increasingly severe exceptions to the exclusionary rule. See e.g. *United States v. Leon*, 468 U.S. 897 (1984); *Hudson v. Michigan*, 547 U.S. 586 (2006); *Herring v. United States*, 129 S.Ct. 695 (2009).

As a practical matter, criminal defendants are unlikely to obtain the suppression remedy unless they are represented by attorneys. In *Johnson v. Zerbst* (1938) the Supreme Court established that the Sixth Amendment entitles all indigent criminal defendants in federal court to government-provided attorneys.[13] In *Gideon v. Wainwright* (1963) the Supreme Court extended the Sixth Amendment right to government-provided counsel to indigent defendants in state courts.[14] Since the overwhelming majority of criminal defendants in the US are indigents,[15] the joint effect of these Fourth and Sixth Amendment cases was to increase the number of motions by criminal defendants to suppress evidence on Fourth Amendment grounds. This, together with the paucity of civil law suits brought to vindicate Fourth Amendment rights,[16] means that Fourth Amendment claims are typically brought by factually guilty people. Unless a criminal defendant was caught red handed there is no incriminating evidence to suppress. The case law interpreting the protection of privacy under the Constitution has been importantly shaped by the typical Fourth Amendment litigant's dual status as both (i) an apprehended criminal who seeks to suppress incriminating evidence and (ii) an assertor of the people's rights against government.[17]

The *Katz* expectation of privacy test and Fourth Amendment protections of telephone communications

Since the Fourth Amendment protects people from "unreasonable searches or seizures" a government intrusion must count as a search or seizure for Fourth Amendment requirements to apply. In *Katz v. United States* (1967) the United States Supreme Court was faced with the question of whether Charles Katz had been subject to a search or seizure when by means of a device attached to the outside of a public telephone booth law enforcement agents listened in to his side of telephone conversations transmitting illegal gambling information. In a departure from existing precedent, the Supreme Court reasoned that whether there had been a Fourth Amendment search or seizure did not depend on whether a public telephone booth was "a constitutionally protected area",

---

13   304 U.S. 458.

14   372 U.S. 335.

15   See e.g. Bureau of Justice Statistics, *State and Local Public Defender Offices*, at: http://bjs.ojp.usdoj.gov/index.cfm?ty=tp&tid=215 ("Publicly financed counsel represented about 66% of federal felony defendants in 1998 as well as 82% of felony defendants in the 75 most populous counties in 1996.").

16   Civil actions seeking damages for Fourth Amendment violations by federal and state agents are respectively available under *Bivens v. Six Unknown Named Agents of Federal Bureau of Narcotics*, 403 U.S. 388 (1971) and 42 U.S.C. § 1983. See Anthony G. Amsterdam, "Perspectives on the Fourth Amendment", *Minnesota Law Review*, 58 (1974): 349, 428–34, and Yale Kamisar, "Remembering the Old World of Criminal Procedure: A Reply to Professor Grano", *University of Michigan Journal of Law Reform*, 23 (1990): 537, 562–65, for discussions of why such suits are difficult to win and seldom brought.

17   For an extended discussion of how these two views of the criminal defendant have shaped Fourth Amendment case law, see Adina Schwartz, "Homes as Folding Umbrellas: Two Recent Supreme Court Decisions on 'Knock and Announce'", *American Journal of Criminal Law*, 25 (1998): 545–94.

as "the Fourth Amendment protects people, not places."[18] Further departing from precedent, the Supreme Court reasoned that the fact that the wiretap was effected without physical penetration of the telephone booth did not mean that there was no Fourth Amendment search or seizure. "[T]he reach of [the Fourth] Amendment cannot turn upon the presence or absence of a physical intrusion into any given enclosure."[19] The Supreme Court replaced those tests with the test that Fourth Amendment protections apply only when government action intrudes on (i) a person's "actual (subjective) expectation of privacy" and (ii) the subjective expectation is "one that society is prepared to recognize as 'reasonable.'"[20] Under this test, Katz was subject to a Fourth Amendment search or seizure when the agents listened in to his side of the conversations because he had sought to keep his conversations private by closing the door of the phone booth. Moreover, Katz's subjective expectation that his conversations would be kept private was objectively reasonable because of "the vital role that the public telephone has come to play in private communication."[21]

The consensual wiretap exception

Four years later in *United States v. White*, the United States Supreme Court carved out the so-called "consensual wiretapping" exception to Fourth Amendment protections of the privacy of telephone conversations. *White* dealt with the technique of third party bugging, wherein informants engage in conversations with suspects and simultaneously transmit those conversations to law enforcement agents who record them. The justices in *White* acknowledged that third-party bugging was possible only because suspects subjectively expected that their conversations would be kept private. "Our problem is not what the privacy expectations of particular defendants in particular situations may be or the extent to which they may in fact have relied on the discretion of their companions. Very probably, individual defendants neither know nor suspect that their colleagues have gone or will go to the police or are carrying recorders or transmitters. Otherwise, conversation would cease . . ."[22] The Supreme Court reasoned, however, that third-party bugging does not count as a Fourth Amendment search or seizure because it is not reasonable for criminals to expect that their conversations with their cohorts will remain private. "Inescapably, one contemplating illegal activities must realize and risk that his companions

---

18   *Katz v. U.S.*, 389 U.S. 347, 351 (1967).
19   *Ibid.*, 353.
20   This classic formulation of the *Katz* test is in Justice Harlan's concurrence. Interestingly, Harlan departed from the majority in reasoning that a person's location will usually determine whether he or she has a subjective expectation of privacy that counts as reasonable and is, accordingly, subject to Fourth Amendment protections. *Ibid.*,361 (Harlan, J., concurring).
21   *Ibid.*, 352.
22   *United States v. White*, 401 U.S. 745, 751–52 (1971).

may be reporting to the police. If he sufficiently doubts their trustworthiness, the association will very probably end or never materialize. But if he has no doubts, or allays them, or risks what doubt he has, the risk is his."[23]

In this assumption of risk analysis, the Supreme Court assumed that the only people who may be subject to third-party bugging are those who are, in fact, engaged in crime. The language about the risks that "one contemplating illegal activities" assumes contrasts interestingly with the language that the Supreme Court used in the *Katz* case in holding that Katz was entitled to Fourth Amendment protections. "No less than an individual in a business office, in a friend's apartment, or in a taxicab, a person in a telephone booth may rely upon the protection of the Fourth Amendment. One who occupies it, shuts the door behind him, and pays the toll that permits him to place a call is surely entitled to assume that the words he utters into the mouthpiece will not be broadcast to the world."[24] No mention is made of the fact that Katz (like White) was seeking to suppress conversations that revealed he was engaged in crime.

The pen register exception

In *Smith v. Maryland* in 1979, the United States Supreme Court carved out a further exception to the Fourth Amendment protections of telephone communications. There, at the behest of the police, a telephone company had used a pen register to record the numbers dialed from the defendant's home telephone. In reasoning that the use of the pen register did not constitute a search under the Fourth Amendment, the Supreme Court expanded on the idea, implicit in *White*, that one has no reasonable expectation that information one reveals to a third party will not, in turn, be revealed to the government. Since, under this analysis, one is entitled either to expect privacy against everyone or to expect it against no one, and telephone company employees have access to the numbers one dials from one's phone, the government's use of a pen register cannot infringe on any privacy one can reasonably expect.[25] However, the application of the *Katz* test to deny Fourth Amendment protections to information revealed to third parties would seem to be inconsistent with the holding that Katz was entitled to Fourth Amendment protections. Telephone company employees cannot only access numbers dialed; they can listen in on conversations as well. The *Smith* Court distinguished *Katz* away on the ground that "a pen register differs significantly from the listening device employed in *Katz*, for pen registers do not acquire the *contents* of communications."[26]

---

23   *Ibid.*, 752.
24   *Katz*, 389 U.S. at 352.
25   The *Smith* Court also reasoned that "people in general [do not] entertain any actual expectation of privacy in the numbers they dial." 442 U.S. 735, 742 (1979).
26   *Ibid.*, 741.

Fourth Amendment protections of email and internet communications

Thus far, the United States Supreme Court has avoided the question of whether individuals enjoy reasonable expectations of privacy and, hence, Fourth Amendment protections in regard to internet and other electronic communications. *City of Ontario v. Quon* (2010) is the Supreme Court's only Fourth Amendment decision on electronic communications.[27] The issue there was whether a police officer's Fourth Amendment rights were violated when police department officials requested from the service provider and read transcripts of text messages that the police officer had sent with a two-way pager provided by the department over the wireless service to which the department subscribed. In his opinion for the majority, Justice Kennedy avoided the question of whether the officer had reasonable expectations of privacy and hence Fourth Amendment rights in regard to his text messages, holding that even if this were the case, the department officials' acts of requesting and reading the transcripts of his text message were reasonable, and thus did not violate any Fourth Amendment protection that the officer might have enjoyed. Despite holding that the issue of the reasonableness of the officer's expectations of privacy need not be reached, Justice Kennedy dwelt at length on the difficulty that emerging changes in communications technology create for determining the reasonable expectations of privacy that individuals have today.

> The Court must proceed with care when considering the whole concept of privacy expectations in communications made on electronic equipment owned by a government employer. The judiciary risks error by elaborating too fully on the Fourth Amendment implications of emerging technology before its role in society has become clear. In *Katz*, the Court relied on its own knowledge and experience to conclude that there is a reasonable expectation of privacy in a telephone booth. It is not so clear that courts at present are on so sure a ground. . .
>
> Rapid changes in the dynamics of communication and information transmission are evident not just in the technology itself but in what society accepts as proper behavior. As one *amici* brief notes, many employers expect or at least tolerate personal use of such equipment by employees because it often increases worker efficiency. Another *amicus* points out that the law is beginning to respond to these developments, as some States have recently passed statutes requiring employers to notify employees when monitoring their electronic communications. At present, it is uncertain how workplace norms, and the law's treatment of them, will evolve.

---

27   30 S.Ct. 2619.

. . . [T]he Court would have difficulty predicting how employees' privacy expectations will be shaped by those changes or the degree to which society will be prepared to recognize those expectations as reasonable. Cell phone and text message communications are so pervasive that some persons may consider them to be essential means or necessary instruments for self-expression, even self-identification. That might strengthen the case for an expectation of privacy. On the other hand, the ubiquity of those devices has made them generally affordable, so one could counter that employees who need cell phones or similar devices for personal matters can purchase and pay for their own.

A broad holding concerning employees' privacy expectations vis-à-vis employer-provided technological equipment might have implications for future cases that cannot be predicted. It is preferable to dispose of this case on narrower grounds.[28]

The Supreme Court's decision in *City of Ontario v. Quon* reversed the decision of the United States Court of Appeals for the Ninth Circuit's in *Quon v. Arch Wireless*.[29] There, the Ninth Circuit had faced the question that the Supreme Court subsequently avoided, holding both that the officer enjoyed reasonable expectations of privacy, and hence Fourth Amendment rights in regard to his text messages, and that the officer's Fourth Amendment rights were violated because department officials acted unreasonably in accessing and reading the transcripts of his text messages. In deciding in *Quon* in 2008 that reasonable expectations of privacy apply to text messages, the Ninth Circuit built on its decision in regard to email communications in *United States v. Forrester* (2007), reasoning that there is "no meaningful difference between the emails at issue in *Forrester* and the text messages at issue here."[30] The *Forrester* Court had applied the *Katz* test, as further developed in *Smith v. Maryland*, to hold that neither email addressing information nor the IP addresses of websites accessed from a particular email account were subject to Fourth Amendment protection.[31] Building on the principle articulated in *Katz*, *Smith v. Maryland*, and *Forrester* that Fourth Amendment protections apply to the contents of communications but not to addressing information on communications, *Quon* reasoned that users have reasonable expectations of privacy and hence Fourth Amendment protections in regard to the content of text or email messages. *Quon* further

---

28 130 S.Ct. at 2629-30 (citations omitted). Cf.City of Ontario v. Quan, 130 S.Ct. 2633, 2634–35 (Scalia, J., concurring in part and concurring in the judgment) (severely criticizing J. Kennedy's discussion of reasonable expectations of privacy).

29 529 F.3d 892 (9th Cir. 2008).

30 *United States v. Forrester,* 512 F.3d 500; *Quon v. Arch Wireless,* 529 F.3d 892, 905.

31 In a footnote (512 F.3d 500, 510 n.6), the *Forrester* Court indicated that since URLs provide more information than IP addresses about the information a person accesses on the web, Fourth Amendment protections might apply to surveillance techniques that enabled the government to determine the URLs of the web pages a person visited.

reasoned that the police department's formal policy of auditing officers' use of communications facilities provided by the department did not abrogate the officers' reasonable expectations of privacy because the department's informal policy was not to audit text messages so long as officers paid for any messages they sent beyond the quota allocated to their accounts.

The *Katz* test and the protection of personal records

In *United States v. Miller* (1976) the United States Supreme Court extended the notion that privacy is possessed by everyone or no one to imply that a person has no Fourth Amendment rights with regard to documents or records that he or she stores with a third party. The specific issue was whether Mitch Miller was subject to a search or seizure when, in response to a subpoena, his bank delivered his bank records to agents from the Alcohol, Tobacco and Firearms Bureau. In holding that Miller had no reasonable expectation of privacy and thus no Fourth Amendment rights in regard to his bank records, the Supreme Court cited *White* for the proposition that whenever one reveals information to a third party one assumes the risk that the information will in turn be conveyed to the government. "The depositor takes the risk, in revealing his affairs to another, that the information will be conveyed by that person to the Government. *United States v. White*, 401 U.S. 745, 751-752 (1971). This Court has held repeatedly that the Fourth Amendment does not prohibit the obtaining of information revealed to a third party and conveyed by him to Government authorities, even if the information is revealed on the assumption that it will be used only for a limited purpose and the confidence placed in the third party will not be betrayed."[32] In other words, if Miller did not want the government to learn of his financial affairs he should have kept his money under his mattress.

Although the Supreme Court has not considered the issue, lower courts have applied the *Katz* test to hold that a subscriber's Fourth Amendment rights are not implicated when an ISP responds to a government request by providing the subscriber information corresponding to a particular email address, including the subscriber's name, address, telephone number, billing and account information and any other email addresses that he or she has with the ISP. In *Freedman v. America Online, Inc.* the United States District Court for the District of Connecticut applied *Smith v. Maryland's* distinction between contents of communications and non-content information to conclude that a person has no reasonable expectation of privacy with regard to his or her subscriber information. In so reasoning, the District Court did not so much as advert to the possibility of disagreement with its classification of an individual's credit card number and other financial information as "non-content information".[33]

---

32 *United States v. Miller*, 425 U.S. 435, 443 (1976) (footnotes and some citations omitted).
33 *Freedman v. America Online, Inc.*, 412 F.Supp.2d 174, 181 (D.Conn. 2005).

In addition, the *Freedman* Court relied on the notion that one has no reasonable expectation of privacy in regard to information revealed to a third party: "He [the subscriber] provided his name, address, credit card number, and telephone number to AOL when he registered to obtain internet access from AOL. That information was exposed to AOL employees in the normal course of business . . ."[34] In other words, anyone who subscribes to an ISP enjoys no Fourth Amendment protection in regard to the information he or she must provide in order to obtain an account.

The Fourth Amendment rights of record keepers

By contrast to the total absence of Fourth Amendment protection that an individual enjoys with regard to personal records in the possession of corporations or other entities, record-keeping entities have limited Fourth Amendment rights. Although the Fourth Amendment protects an entity that is subpoenaed for records, the United States Supreme Court has reasoned that because a subpoena is only a "figurative search" neither a warrant nor probable cause is required for its issuance. Rather, the Fourth Amendment requires that *after* a subpoena is issued, the party to whom it is addressed is able to obtain judicial review of the reasonableness of the subpoena's demands.[35] The reasonableness requirement for a subpoena is much less stringent than the probable cause requirement for a full-blown search. The requirement is met so long as an administrative subpoena is (1) "within the authority of the [issuing] agency"; (2) its demands are "not too indefinite"; and (3) the information sought is "reasonably relevant" to a proper inquiry.[36]

The Fourth Amendment and domestic and foreign threats to national security

In *Katz*, Justice White concurred separately for the purpose of insisting that, despite the decision's extension of the Fourth Amendment warrant requirement to wiretapping, the President or the Attorney General was still empowered to authorize warrantless wiretaps for national security purposes.[37] Justice Douglas, joined by Justice Brennan, wrote a separate concurrence in response to Justice White, asserting that a national security exception to the warrant requirement would violate the Fourth Amendment.[38] The *Katz* majority disposed of the issue

---

34 *Ibid.*, 183.

35 *See v. Seattle*, 387 U.S. 541, 541–45 (1967); *Oklahoma Press Pub. Co. v. Walling*, 327 U.S. 186, 217 (1946).

36 *United States v. Morton Salt Co.*, 338 U.S. 632, 652 (1950); *Oklahoma Press*, 327 U.S., 208.

37 *Katz v. United States*, 389 U.S. 347, 363 (White, J., concurring). In his concurrence, Justice White also insisted that the *Katz* test did not impinge on the government's right to use informants to obtain information, including through third-party bugging.

38 *Ibid.*, 359-60 (Douglas, J., concurring).

in a footnote that stated that the facts of the case did not present the question of whether the Fourth Amendment would allow warrantless wiretaps for national security purposes.

In *United States v. United States District Court* (1972), commonly known as the *Keith* case, the United States Supreme Court held that the Fourth Amendment does not allow the President to authorize warrantless wiretaps of domestic organizations for national security purposes. The Court emphasized, however, that the case did not require a "judgment on the scope of the President's surveillance power with respect to the activities of foreign powers, within or without this country."[39] While acknowledging that the distinction between domestic and foreign threats to national security might sometimes be difficult to draw, the Court stated that it was not faced with the issue. "No doubt there are cases where it will be difficult to distinguish between 'domestic' and 'foreign' unlawful activities directed against the Government of the United States where there is collaboration in varying degrees between domestic groups or organizations and agents or agencies of foreign powers. But this is not such a case."[40]

The Supreme Court has yet to decide whether there is a foreign intelligence exception to the warrant requirement. However, on January 12, 2009 the Foreign Intelligence Surveillance Court of Review (the FISA Court of Review) released a redacted version of a decision made on August 22, 2008, which held that under the Fourth Amendment there is an exception to the warrant requirement for surveillance directed at a foreign power or agent of a foreign power, where such person(s) are reasonably believed to be outside the United States and where foreign intelligence (as opposed to criminal investigation) is a significant purpose of the surveillance.[41]

Federal statutory protections of privacy

Federal statutes and state constitutions, statutes and case law expand on the protection of privacy that individuals are afforded under the Fourth Amendment. Neither state law nor such important federal statutes as the Right to Financial Privacy Act (RFPA), the Health Insurance Portability and Accountability Act of 1996 (HIPPA), the Cable Communications Policy Act of 1984 (Cable Act), the Video Privacy Protection Act of 1988 (VPPA), the Fair Credit Reporting Act (FCRA) or the Privacy Act of 1974 will be discussed here. The statutes to be discussed will be the Electronic Communications Privacy Act (ECPA),

---

39   407 U.S. 297, 308 (1972).
40   *Ibid.*
41   In re Directives [Redacted] Pursuant to 105B of Foreign Intelligence Surveillance Act, 551 F.3d 1004 (Foreign Int. Surv. Ct. Rev. 2008). This is one of only two published decisions by the FISA Court of Review.

which applies to surveillance of phone and internet communications by both government and private entities, and the Foreign Intelligence Surveillance Act (FISA), which regulates foreign intelligence surveillance. Also to be discussed are some of the post-9/11 amendments to ECPA and FISA and the US Federal Government's systemic evasion of the statutory limits on wiretapping.

The Electronic Communications Privacy Act (ECPA)

Enacted in 1986, ECPA is the successor to Title III of the Omnibus Crime Control and Safe Streets Act of 1968. Whereas Title III dealt with private as well as government wiretapping of oral (face-to-face) and wire (telephone) communications, in response to changing technology Congress made the purview of ECPA extend to electronic (roughly, internet) as well as oral and wire communications. The protections of communications privacy in ECPA include not only those in its Wiretap Act but also those in its Stored Communications and Pen/Trap Acts. The Wiretap Act applies to the contemporaneous acquisition of the contents of communications and updates the protections provided in Title III of the Omnibus Crime Control and Safe Streets Act of 1968. The Stored Communications Act deals with subscriber records and subscriber communications stored by communication service providers (telephone companies and ISPs), while the Pen/Trap Act deals with "to" and "from" (addressing information) on telephone and electronic communications (roughly, phone numbers, email addressing information, URL's and IP addresses of websites and ISP subscriber accesses). As noted above, FISA, not ECPA, governs foreign intelligence wire taps and pen/traps.

The Wiretap Act of ECPA

The Wiretap Act prohibits wiretapping by the government or any individual or private entity, subject to three major exceptions. Firstly, a communications services provider may intercept communications where this is necessary for providing its services or for protecting its rights or property. A communications service provider may also record the fact that a communication was initiated or completed in order to protect itself, another provider providing services toward the completion of the communication, or someone using its services from fraudulent, unlawful or abusive use of the communication service.

Secondly, there is an exception for consensual wiretapping where the requisite consent is that of only one party to a communication. Thus, the ECPA, like the Fourth Amendment, does not protect individuals against the government's use of informants, including third-party bugging. Moreover, under the ECPA a person may be deemed to have implicitly consented to the interception of communications. For example, the consent exception may apply if an employer "banners" employees' computers so that when they log on a screen informs them that their use of the computer is exclusively for business purposes and that internet communications will be periodically screened. Consent to interceptions may also be inferred if telephone callers are informed that their calls may be monitored and recorded.

Thirdly, state and Federal Government officials may intercept communications either by obtaining a warrant from a judge or magistrate or without a warrant in exigent circumstances. To obtain a warrant, the government must provide probable cause to believe that (i) a particular person(s) has committed or is about to commit one of certain enumerated crimes,[42] (ii) communications pertaining to the offense will be obtained through the interception and (iii) the facilities from which or the location at which the oral, wire or electronic communications are to be intercepted are being used or are about to be used to commit the particular offense, or are leased or commonly used by the suspect(s). A showing must also be made that other techniques besides wiretapping for investigating the crime have failed or would be too dangerous or unlikely to succeed. Judicial orders authorizing interceptions must specify that the interception is to last no longer than necessary to achieve the objectives of the interception and, in any event, no longer than thirty days, subject to an extension by the court for another such period. In addition, interceptions are to be conducted so as to minimize the acquisition of communications other than those specified in the warrant. A judicial order may direct a communications services provider or landlord to provide information, facilities or technical services to assist government officials in the authorized interception, subject to compensation for reasonable expenses.

The Stored Communications Act of ECPA

As a result of its definitions of "electronic storage", "electronic communication service" and "remote computing service"[43] the Stored Communications Act (SCA) protects only voicemail or email stored on a public ISP once it is opened; it does not protect opened emails stored on a university or other non-public ISP. The SCA does, however, protect unopened voicemail or email regardless of whether it is stored on a public or private system.[44] In addition, the SCA accords some protection to records or other information that telecommunications services and communications storage facilities hold about subscribers.

The SCA criminalizes unauthorized access to a telecommunications service for purposes of obtaining, altering or preventing access to unopened email or voicemail, with exceptions for the provider of the service or a user of the service

---

42   The PATRIOT Act expanded the list of enumerated crimes.
43   The terms are defined, respectively, in 18 U.S.C. Sec. 2510 (17), 118 U.S.C. Sec. 2510 (15) and 18 U.S.C. Sec. 2711 (2).
44   The PATRIOT Act amended ECPA so that the acquisition of voicemail was no longer governed by the stricter requirements of the Wiretap Act.

with regard to his or her own communications. Telecommunication services and communications storage facilities are prohibited from disclosing the contents of their subscribers' wire or electronic communications, whether opened or unopened, to private individuals or entities, with exceptions for (i) addressees or intended recipients of the communications and their agents, (ii) employees or persons whose facilities are used to forward communications, (iii) disclosures that are necessary for rendition of the service or for protecting the rights and property of the service provider and (iv) disclosures with the consent of one of the parties to a communication. By contrast, telecommunication services and facilities are free to disclose records or information about their subscribers or customers to "anyone other than a governmental entity", so long as the records or information do not include the contents of communications.[45]

Under the SCA, the government must meet escalating requirements in order to be entitled to have telecommunications services and computer storage facilities disclose (i) subscriber records, (ii) opened email stored with a provider of computer services or facilities to the public or email or voicemail that the addressee or intended recipient has not opened for more than 180 days or (iii) email or voicemail that the addressee or intended recipient has not opened for 180 days or less.

To obtain records, including the subscriber's name, address, local and long distance telephone connection records or records of session times and durations, length of service (including start date) and types of service utilized, telephone or instrument number or other subscriber number or identity, including any temporarily assigned network address, and means and source of payment for such service (including any credit card or bank account number), the government need present the telecommunications company or communications storage facility with only a federal or state administrative, grand jury or trial subpoena.[46] Notice need not be provided to the subscriber.

To obtain opened email or voicemail from a communications storage facility or unopened email or voicemail that has been stored with a telecommunications provider for more than 180 days, the government may use either a federal or state administrative, grand jury, or trial subpoena or obtain a court order for such disclosure by presenting "specific and articulable facts" that provide "reasonable grounds to believe that the contents of a wire or electronic communication . . . are relevant and material to an ongoing criminal investigation."[47] In either case, prior notice to the subscriber is necessary. However, if it uses a subpoena, the government may delay giving notice for up to ninety days, subject to a further period of ninety days, if the prosecutor or other officials in charge of an

---

45   18 U.S.C. Sec. 2702 (c)(6).
46   The PATRIOT Act added "records of session times and durations" and "any temporarily assigned network address" to the information that the government can obtain with a subpoena under 18 U.S.C. Sec. 2703 (c) (2).
47   18 U.S.C. 2703(b), (d).

investigation certifies that the delay is necessary to avoid endangering a person's life or safety, jeopardizing the investigation or unduly delaying a trial. If the government obtains a court order for the emails, similar delays in notification may be obtained if the court finds them necessary to avoid endangering a person's life or safety, jeopardizing the investigation or unduly delaying a trial.[48] The requirement of notice does not apply, however, if the government obtains a warrant using the procedures described in the Federal Rules of Criminal Procedure.

By contrast to the more lax requirements that apply to records and voicemail and email that is either opened or unopened for more than 180 days, the government may require a telecommunications provider to disclose unopened email that has been stored with it for 180 days or less only if it obtains a warrant using the procedures described in the Federal Rules of Criminal Procedure.[49]

Does the SCA violate the Fourth Amendment by allowing the government to access opened emails or emails stored for more than 180 days without a warrant?

In *United States v. Warshak* (2011), the United States Court of Appeals for the Sixth Circuit confronted the question that the Supreme Court had declined to resolve in *City of Ontario v. Quon,* holding that "a subscriber enjoys a reasonable expectation of privacy in the contents of emails 'that are stored with, or sent or received through, a commercial ISP.'"[50] On this basis, the *Warshak* Court further held that the Fourth Amendment requires the government to obtain a warrant backed by probable cause before it can compel a commercial ISP to turn over the contents of a subscriber's emails. As the *Warshak* decision recognized, this reasoning implies that it is unconstitutional for the SCA to provide that the government need only obtain a warrant in order to obtain emails that have been stored for 180 days or less: "[T]o the extent that the SCA purports to permit the government to obtain . . . emails warrantlessly, the SCA is unconstitutional."[51]

An unresolved controversy: Is email in transit covered by the wiretap or the stored communications provisions of ECPA?

Unless the *Warshak* decision results in a change in the Stored Communications Act, the Wiretap Act requires that the government meet more stringent conditions to obtain a warrant than the government is required to meet in order to obtain emails under the Stored Communications Act. The unresolved controversy over

---

48   18 U.S.C. Sec. 2705.
49   18 U.S.C. Sec. 2703(a).
50   631 F.3d 266, 288 (citation omitted).
51   *Ibid.*

whether the interception of an email before it reaches its intended recipient's mailbox counts as a wiretap or as access to a stored communication therefore has major implications regarding the protection of email from government intrusion.

This controversy arises because the Wiretap Act applies to "intercepts" or disclosures of intercepts of "electronic communications." An electronic communication is defined as "any transfer of signs, signals, writing, images, sounds, data, or intelligence of any nature transmitted in whole or in part by a wire, radio, electromagnetic, photoelectronic or photo-optical system that affects interstate or foreign commerce."[52] Although this definition does not mention "electronic storage" of communications, in the course of traveling between their senders and recipients emails are broken into packets and then passed from one computer to another on the internet. "[E]ach computer along the route stores the packets in memory, retrieves the address of their destination, and then determines where to send it next based on the packet's destination."[53] This implies that, as they travel between sender and recipient, emails are in "electronic storage", which ECPA defines in part as "any temporary, intermediate storage of a wire or electronic communication incidental to the electronic transmission thereof."[54] The question is whether the absence of the term "electronic storage" in the definition of "electronic communication" means that an interception of an email as it travels between sender and receiver cannot count as an "interception of an electronic communication" and thus cannot be subject to the provisions of the Wiretap Act. In other words, does the fact that emails are temporarily stored in the course of their transition over the internet mean that they are stored communications subject to the lesser protections of ECPA's Stored Communications Act?

In *United States v. Councilman* (2005), the United States Court of Appeals for the First Circuit held in an *en banc* decision that the Wiretap Act applies to email messages that are temporarily stored in the course of transit.[55] In *United States v. Szymuszkiewicz* (2010) the United States Court of Appeals for the Seventh Circuit adopted *Councilman's* position.[56]

The Pen/Trap Act of ECPA

The Pen/Trap Act includes a general prohibition of the installation and use of "pen registers" and "trap and trace devices". These are defined respectively as devices that record or decode the "to" and "from" addressing information, but not the contents, of wire and electronic communications (e.g. telephone numbers,

---

52 18 U.S.C. 2510 (15).
53 *United States v. Councilman*, 373 F.3d 197, 205 (1st Cir. 2004) (Lipez, J., dissenting), *rev'd on rehearing en banc*, 418 F.3d 67 (1st Cir. 2005).
54 18 U.S.C. 2510 (17) (A).
55 418 F.3d 67, 79.
56 622 F.3d 701, 706.

email addresses, IP addresses of websites).[57] An exception to this prohibition exists for telecommunications providers with the consent of a subscriber, or in connection with providing, operating or testing their services, protecting their rights or property or protecting their users from unlawful or abusive use of their services. In addition, telecommunications providers may record the initiation and completion of communications in order to protect themselves, their users or other providers involved in the completion of a communication from fraudulent, illegal or abusive use of the service.

Federal and state courts may issue orders authorizing federal or state government officials to install and use pen/trap devices either on their own or with the assistance of telecommunication service providers. To obtain an order, an attorney for the Federal Government or a state law enforcement or investigative officer must certify "to the court that the information likely to be obtained by such installation and use is relevant to an ongoing criminal investigation."[58] Although courts are to take such certifications at face value and not independently assess their veracity, the Pen/Trap Act does not allow the government to engage in dragnet surveillance. An order authorizing the installation and use of a pen/trap must specify (i) the offense to which the information likely to be obtained from the pen/trap relates, (ii) the identity, if known, of the person who is the subject of the investigation, (iii) the number or other identifier and, if known, the telephone line or other facility to which the pen/trap is to be attached and (iv) the identity, if known, of the person who leases or in whose name is listed the telephone line or other facility to which the telephone line is to be attached. A court is not to order the installation and use of a pen/trap for more than sixty days, though an order may be extended, upon application, but for no more than sixty days. In addition, the government is to use reasonably available technology to ensure that its recording or decoding of addressing information does not capture the contents of communications.

An exception to the requirement of a court order exists where the principal prosecuting attorney of a state, or various high level officials in the United States Attorney General's Office, "reasonably determines" that an emergency involving an immediate danger of death or serious bodily injury, conspiracy characteristic of organized crime, an immediate threat to national security or an ongoing attack on a "protected computer" (roughly, a computer connected to the internet) requires a pen/ trap to be installed and used before a court order

---

57   The PATRIOT Act expanded the definitions in ECPA so that pen registers and trap and trace devices include devices recording internet addressing information as well as telephone numbers. Pub. L. 107–56, Sec. 216 (c)(2) and (3) (2001).
58   18 U.S.C. Sec. 3123 (a) (1) and (2).

can be obtained. The use of the pen/trap must immediately terminate if a court order approving the installation or use is not obtained within forty-eight hours from the beginning of the installation.

Penalties for violations of ECPA

There are civil and criminal penalties for violations of the Wiretap, Stored Communications, and Pen/Trap acts of ECPA. Government wiretaps of oral and wire (telephone) communications are subject to a strong suppression remedy which prohibits the use of any illegally intercepted communication or part thereof "in any trial, hearing, or other proceeding in or before any court, grand jury, department, officer, agency, regulatory body, legislative committee, or other authority of the United States, a State, or a political subdivision thereof."[59] The suppression remedy does not extend to illegal wiretaps of electronic communications or to violations of the Stored Communications or Pen/Trap acts.

FISA

The Foreign Intelligence Surveillance Act of 1978 (FISA) established a secret court to hear applications for warrants to conduct foreign intelligence surveillance. The FISA Court's hearings are closed to the public, and records of proceedings have been made available to the public only with classified information redacted.

The target of a FISA warrant must be a "foreign power" or an "agent of a foreign power", where a foreign power is defined as a foreign government or component, faction or entity directed by such or a group engaged in international terrorism or preparations for such. To obtain a warrant to wiretap telephone or internet communications, a national security or defense executive designated by the President must certify that the information sought is "foreign intelligence information". This is defined as information that is *relevant* to protection against foreign attacks, sabotage or international terrorism, or to the conduct of the national defense or foreign affairs. Information concerning a United States citizen or legal resident counts as "foreign intelligence information" only if it is *necessary* for the protection of the US against foreign attacks, sabotage or international terrorism, or for the conduct of national defense or foreign affairs. To issue a FISA warrant, a judge need find only probable cause to believe that the target of the surveillance is a foreign power or an agent of a foreign power and that the facilities or places at which the surveillance is directed are being used or about to be used by a foreign power or an agent of a foreign power. Activities protected by the First Amendment to the US Constitution cannot be the sole basis for a judicial finding of probable cause to believe that a citizen or permanent resident of the US is an agent of a foreign power.

---

59   18 U.S.C. Sec. 2515.

Instead of using FISA warrants for the purpose of obtaining foreign intelligence information, government officials might be tempted to use them to circumvent the stricter requirements that ECPA places on the use of wiretaps for criminal investigations. In 2001 the Patriot Act increased this danger by amending FISA so that the government no longer needs to certify in a warrant application that obtaining foreign intelligence information is "the primary purpose" of the surveillance. The designated government official need only certify that "a significant purpose" of the surveillance is obtaining foreign intelligence information. In 2002, in a decision considering the first appeal ever from a FISA court's decision on a warrant application, the FISA Court of Review held that the court had wrongly imposed the condition that the "primary purpose" of the surveillance could not be criminal prosecution of foreign agents for their foreign intelligence activities.[60] According to the court, the "primary purpose" test and its mandated wall between foreign intelligence and criminal investigations misinterprets FISA, especially as amended by the "significant purpose" language of the Patriot Act. The FISA Court of Review further held that the amendment did not violate the Fourth Amendment.

The Terrorist Screening Program

Debates about the legitimacy of the Patriot Act's extension of surveillance powers may be tantamount to debates about a distracting side show. On December 16, 2005, the *New York Times* reported for the first time that since 2001 the Bush Administration had engaged in massive, warrantless surveillance of telephone and email communications. In response to the article, Attorney General Gonzales confirmed the existence of a Terrorist Screening Program (TSP), conducted by the National Security Agency, and claimed that the FISA warrant requirements had been superseded by the Authorization for Use of Military Force Against Terrorists Act that Congress had passed on September 18, 2001. The Attorney General further claimed that the warrantless intercepts had been conducted only where the government had a reasonable basis to conclude that at least one party to the communication was outside the United States and that at least one party was affiliated with al-Qaeda or a related organization, or working in support of al-Qaeda. This claim was belied, however, when whistle blower Mark Klein informed the Electronic Frontier Foundation (EFF) that in its Folsom Street facility in San Francisco AT&T had given the NSA access to the contents of all of its subscribers' communications with subscribers of other ISPs.

---

60   *In re Sealed Case,* 310 F.3d 717 (FISC Rev. 2002).

Separation of powers and the difficulty of preventing surreptitious violations of the law by the executive power

This information about the massive evasion of the requirements of ECPA and FISA by the government and AT&T was brought to the attention of the Federal Court system in *Hepting v. AT&T*, a law suit in which the EFF sought damages against AT&T. This and other law suits were mooted, however, when Congress provided retroactive immunity to telecommunications providers who had participated in the Terrorist Screening Program. The FISA Amendments Act of 2008 required the dismissal of lawsuits against telecommunications providers if the government secretly certified to the court that the surveillance did not occur, was legal or was authorized by the President. In response to Congress' passage of the telecommunications immunity provision, EFF sued the government and named government officials directly in *Jewel v. NSA*, filed in September 2008. *Jewel* sought to stop the warrantless wiretapping and to hold the government officials behind the TSP accountable. On January 21, 2010, a federal district judge dismissed the *Jewel* case on the ground that the plaintiffs lacked standing to bring the lawsuit because they had not alleged an injury sufficiently peculiar to themselves or the class they represented: "[T]he harm alleged is a generalized grievance shared in substantially equal measure by all or a large class of citizens."[61] In other words, the judge held that legal redress was precluded by the enormous extent of the Executive's violation of the limits on surveillance that the Fourth Amendment, ECPA and FISA mandated. Although EFF plans to appeal the decision, the judge's interpretation of federal standing law may be correct.[62]

(B) European Union

The desire to remove barriers to commerce has been the primary impetus towards European unification since World War II. At the same time, state sovereignty has continued to be valued, particularly in the areas of national security and protection against crime. Reflecting these two aspects of the European unification project, EU law comprehensively and strictly regulates the collection, transmission and use of data about individuals by private entities, but its regulation of such activity by states is much less strict and much less comprehensive. In addition, private parties' obligations to protect data may be weakened for state purposes.

---

61 *Jewel v. NSA*, No. C 08-cv-4373, 2–3 (N.D.Cal. Jan.21, 2010).
62 *EFF Plans Appeals of Jewel v. NSA Warrantless Wiretapping Case,* January 21, 2010, at: http://www.eff. org/press/archives/2010/01/21.

Constitutional protections

The privacy of EU citizens is constitutionally protected by both the Convention for the Protection of Human Rights and Fundamental Freedoms (the European Convention on Human Rights (ECHR)) and the Charter of Fundamental Rights of the European Union. The constitutions of some of the individual states of the EU also give individuals rights to privacy, but the constitutional law of multiple member states cannot be given detailed treatment here. Instead we will provide only passing discussion of member states. However, at the end of this section on the EU we provide a somewhat more extensive discussion of the protection of individual privacy rights in one of the EU's member states, namely, the Netherlands. Accordingly, the Netherlands serves as an exemplification of the institutional embodiment of the EU's privacy rights.

The European Convention on Human Rights (ECHR)

The ECHR, which opened for signature in 1950 and went into effect in 1953, established rights that are incorporated in both EU law and the laws of each of the individual states of the EU. The ECHR also established the European Court of Human Rights, before which cases may be brought by any person who claims that a state party to the ECHR (including the EU states, other European states that belong to the Council of Europe and EU bodies such as the European Commission, the Council or the European Parliament) has violated his or her rights under the ECHR. State parties to the ECHR may also bring cases against other parties before the European Court of Human Rights, but this power is rarely used.

By contrast to the United States Constitution, the ECHR provides an explicit right to privacy. Article 8 states that:

> **Right to respect for private and family life**
>
> 1. Everyone has the right to respect for his private and family life, his home and his correspondence.
>
> 2. There shall be no interference by a public authority with the exercise of this right except such as is in accordance with the law and is necessary in a democratic society in the interests of national security, public safety or the economic well-being of the country, for the prevention of disorder or crime, for the protection of health or morals, or for the protection of the rights and freedoms of others.

Unlike the right to privacy that courts have inferred from the First, Fourth, Ninth and Fourteenth Amendments to the United States Constitution, the right to privacy that Article 8 of the ECHR confers is not merely a negative right against state interference but also a positive right to the enjoyment of privacy. The ECHR right to privacy does, however, resemble the right to privacy that courts have inferred from the US Constitution in not being an absolute right, but one that may be restricted for legitimate state purposes. National security, public safety and the prevention of disorder or crime are among the listed purposes for which Article 8, Section 2 of the ECHR allows states to interfere with privacy, subject to the requirements that such interference be in "accordance with law and . . . necessary in a democratic society" for furthering a listed purpose(s).

As discussed above, in *City of Ontario v. Quon* the United States Supreme Court explicitly declined to decide whether reasonable expectations of privacy and hence Fourth Amendment rights extend to electronic communications.[63] By contrast, the European Court of Human Rights has held that the protections of "private life" and "correspondence" in ECHR Article 8, Section 1 extend to emails and other internet communications as well as telephone calls, regardless of whether such communications take place in the workplace or at home.[64]

In a further contrast with US law, the European Court of Human Rights has reasoned that "information relating to the date and length of telephone conversations and in particular the numbers dialled . . . constitutes an 'integral element of the communications made by telephone'" that Article 8, Section 1 of the ECHR protects, and has extended that principle to email and other internet communications.[65] This contrasts with the US Supreme Court's position in *Smith v. Maryland* that reasonable expectations of privacy and Fourth Amendment protections extend to the contents of telephone communications but not to the numbers dialed, and with lower courts extensions of the distinction between protected contents and unprotected addressing information to email and other internet communications.[66]

The Charter of Fundamental Rights of the European Union

The Charter of Fundamental Rights of the European Union (the "EU Charter"), which was adopted in 2000 and went into effect with the Lisbon Treaty on December 1, 2009, applies to EU institutions. Individual countries of the EU are also subject to the Charter, but only insofar as they are implementing EU law, as opposed to matters on which the EU either has failed or lacks the competence to legislate.

---

63 130 S.Ct. 2619 (2010).
64 *Copland v. United Kingdom*, 45 Eur. Ct. H.R. 253, Section 41 (citing *Halford v. the United Kingdom*, *Reports of Judgments and Decisions* 1997–III, Section 44, and *Amann v. Switzerland*, 2000–II Eur. Ct. H.R. 247, Sec. 43).
65 *Ibid.*, Sec 43 (quoting *Malone v. the United Kingdom*, 82 Eur. Ct. H.R. (ser. A) Sec. 84).
66 See e.g. *Smith v. Maryland*, 442 U.S. 735 (1979); *United States v. Forrester*, 512 F.3d 500 (9th Cir. 2007); *Quon v. Arch Wireless*, 529 F.3d 892 (9th Cir. 2008).

The Charter's protections of privacy include Article 7 of the Charter, which is identical to the Article 8, Section 1 of the ECHR, and a special provision for protection of personal data in Article 8 of the Charter. The Charter provisions are:

Article 7

Respect for private and family life

Everyone has the right to respect for his or her private and family life, home and communications.

Article 8

Protection of personal data

1. Everyone has the right to the protection of personal data concerning him or her.

2. Such data must be processed fairly for specified purposes and on the basis of the consent of the person concerned or some other legitimate basis laid down by law. Everyone has the right of access to data which has been collected concerning him or her, and the right to have it rectified.

3. Compliance with these rules shall be subject to control by an independent authority.

The interpretation of articles 7 and 8 of the Charter is guided by the European Court of Human Rights' interpretation of the right to privacy in the ECHR. The preamble to the Charter reaffirms the rights granted by the ECHR and by the case law of the European Court of Human Rights. Article 52(3) of the Charter indicates that the ECHR provides a floor, but not a ceiling, for interpreting the rights that the Charter provides.

The Lisbon Treaty entitles individuals to bring claims about an EU country's violation of their Charter rights in the courts of that country. The European Court of Justice can also rule on individual countries' obligations under the Charter, but only if a case is referred to it by the European Commission or a national court. Individuals may bring claims as to the violation of their Charter rights by an EU institution or body before the General Court (court of first instance) of the European Court of Justice, but only if a measure adopted by the EU institution or body has directly and individually affected them.

EU legislation

EU legislation on the collection, use and transmission of personal data is principally composed of three directives and one framework decision. These set forth goals that are binding on all EU states and that require each state to legislate forms and methods for achieving the goals. The directives and framework decision are:

- Directive 95/46/EC on the protection of individuals with regard to the processing of personal data and the free movement of such data (the "Data Protection Directive");[67]

- Directive 2002/58/EC concerning the processing of personal data and the protection of privacy in the electronic communications sector (Directive on privacy and electronic communications) (the "e-Privacy Directive"),[68] as updated by Directive 2009/136/EC of the European Parliament and of the Council;[69]

- Directive 2006/24/EC on the retention of data generated or processed in connection with the provision of publicly available electronic communications services or of public communications networks and amending Directive 2002/58/EC (the "Data Retention Direction");[70] and

- Council Framework Decision 2008/977/JHA on the protection of personal data processed in the framework of police and judicial cooperation in criminal matters.[71]

Before turning to the specifics of the Directives and Framework Decision, it is crucial to note that although it is often claimed that EU law provides comprehensive standards for data protection, this is true only in regard to the collection, use and transmission of personal data by private parties for private purposes.[72] Until the Lisbon Treaty went into effect on December 1, 2009, policing and criminal justice in individual EU countries were outside the purview of EU law.[73] In a policy review of EU data protection law issued

---

67   Available at: http://ec.europa.eu/justice_home/fsj/privacy/docs/95-46-ce/dir1995-46_part1_en.pdf and http://ec.europa.eu/justice/policies/privacy/docs/95-46-ce/dir1995-46_part2_en.pdf.

68   Available at: http://eur-lex.europa.eu/LexUriServ/LexUriServ.do?uri=CELEX:32002L0058:EN:HTML.

69   Available at: http://eur-lex.europa.eu/LexUriServ/LexUriServ.do?uri=OJ:L:2009:337:0011:0036:En:PDF.

In addition to updating the e-Privacy Directive, the 2009 Directive updated Directive 2002/22/E on universal service and users' rights relating to electronic communications networks and services and Regulation (EC) N. 2006/2004 on cooperation between national authorities responsible for the enforcement of consumer protection laws.

70   Available at: http://eur-lex.europa.eu/LexUriServ/LexUriServ.do?uri=CELEX:32006L0024:EN:HTML.

71   Available at: http://eur-lex.europa.eu/LexUriServ/LexUriServ.do?uri=OJ:L:2008:350:0060:01:EN:HTML.

72   For the notion that EU data protection law is comprehensive see e.g. Monique Altheim, "The Review of the EU Data Protection Framework v. The State of Online Consumer Privacy in the US", EDiscoveryMap, March 17, 2011, available at: http://ediscoverymap.com/2011/03/the-review-of-the-eu-data-protection-framework-v-the-state-of-online-consumer-privacy-in-the-us; "Data Protection in the European Union", available at: http://ec.europa.eu/justice/policies/privacy/docs/guide/guide-ukingdom_en.pdf

73   This limitation of the scope of EU law resulted from the three-pillar structure which the Lisbon Treaty abolished. For a brief overview of the relations between the three pillars, the Lisbon Treaty and data

in November 2010 the European Commission stated that the Lisbon Treaty provided an opportunity "to lay down comprehensive and coherent rules on data protection for all sectors, including police and criminal justice. Under the review, data retained for law enforcement purposes should also be covered by the new legislative framework."[74] In particular, the Commission's policy review recognized, as will be discussed below, that in order to protect individuals' privacy, amendments are needed to Council Framework Decision 2008/977/JHA on Personal Data and Police and Judicial Cooperation.[75]

The Data Protection Directive

Scope

As discussed above, United States constitutional law limits only government activity, and the only further limits that federal law places on the collection, use and transfer of personal data consist of legislation and regulations that apply only to certain types of data collected by certain types of private or governmental entities (e.g. the Right to Financial Privacy Act (RFPA), the Health Insurance Portability and Accountability Act of 1996 (HIPPA), the Cable Communications Policy Act of 1984 (Cable Act), the Video Privacy Protection Act of 1988 (VPPA), the Fair Credit Reporting Act (FCRA) and the Privacy Act of 1974 (applying only to federal agencies)).[76] By contrast, the EU Data Protection Directive regulates

---

protection in the EU, see Daniel Cooper, Henriette Tielemans, and David Fink, "The Lisbon Treaty and Data Protection: What's Next for Europe's Privacy Rules?" *The Privacy Advisor*, at http://www.cov.com/files/Publication/44dd09f7-3015-4b37-b02e-7fe07d1403f4/Presentation/PublicationAttachment/8a89a612-f202-410b-b0c8-8c9b34980318/The%20Lisbon%20Treaty%20and%20Data%20Protection%20What%E2%80%99s%20Next%20for%20Europe%E2%80%99s%20Privacy%20Rules.pdf

74 EUROPA Press Releases Rapid, "European Commission Sets Out Strategy to Strengthen EU Data Protection Rules", IP/10/1462, Brussels, November 4, 2010, available at http://europa.eu/rapid/pressReleasesAction.do?reference=IP/10/1462. The full text of the Commission's policy review, Communication from the Commission to the European Parliament, the Council, the Economic and Social Committee and the Committee of the Regions, "A Comprehensive Approach on Personal Data Protection in the European Union", IP/10/1462, Brussels, November 4, 2010 ("Commission, 'A Comprehensive Approach on Personal Data Protection") is available at http://ec.europa.eu/justice/news/consulting_public/0006/com_2010_609_en.pdf. On the basis of the policy review and public consultation, the Commission intends to propose legislation in 2011 revising EU data protection law.

The European Commission, comprising Commissioners from each EU country, has the function of representing and upholding the interests of the EU as a whole by proposing new laws to Parliament and the Council, managing the EU's budget and allocating funding, enforcing EU law (together with the Court of Justice) and representing the EU internationally, for example, by negotiating agreements between the EU and other countries. See Europa, "European Commission", at http://europa.eu/about-eu/institutions-bodies/european-commission/index_en.htm.

75 Such amendment of the Council Framework Decision might assuage one scholar's concern that "[i]n the field of data-related police cooperation the importance of the EU is increasing. . . These developments on [sic] intelligence-led policing create enormous problems of legal protection, privacy and control as the legal framework of the EU does not focus on the rule of law questions in regard to police cooperation." Konrad Lachmayer, "European Police Cooperation and its Limits: From Intelligence-led to Coercive Measures", in *The Outer Limits of European Union Law*, ed. Catherine Barnard and Okeoghene Odudu (Oxford: Hart Publishing 2009), 106–07.

76 For an interesting discussion of how the development of the regulatory state under the New Deal may have led to diminished Fourth Amendment protections for records kept by third parties, see William J. Stuntz, "Privacy's Problem and the Law of Criminal Procedure", *Michigan Law Review* 93 (1995): 1016.

the collection, use and distribution of all records about individuals by private parties, except when this is done "by a natural person in the course of a purely personal or household activity."[77]

The broad scope of the Data Protection Directive comes from its application to all automatic processing of personal data and to all non-automatic processing of personal data that are contained or intended to be contained in filing systems that are structured so as to make personal data readily accessible. Processing is defined as any automatic or non-automatic operations on data, "such as collection, recording, organization, storage, adaptation or alteration, retrieval, consultation, use, disclosure by transmission, dissemination or otherwise making available, alignment or combination, blocking, erasure or destruction."[78] Under the Directive, personal data include any information pertaining to an identified person or to a person who can be directly or indirectly identified, "in particular by reference to an identification number or to one or more factors specific to his physical, physiological, mental, economic, cultural or social identity." [79]

Although the data controllers on whom the Directive imposes obligations include public authorities and agencies as well as natural persons and private legal entities, the Directive does not apply to data processing in connection with government activity that the EU was not empowered to regulate before the Lisbon Treaty. Accordingly, the Directive does not regulate "processing operations concerning public security, defence, State security (including the economic well-being of the State when the processing operation relates to State security matters) and the activities of the State in areas of criminal law."[80] Nor does the Directive apply to the "processing of sound and image data, such as . . . video surveillance" where this is done "for the purposes of public security, defence, national security, or in the course of State activities relating to the area of criminal law."[81] Even where the Directive applies, governments may enact legislation limiting the rights to access data and gain information that the Directive grants to individuals and restricting the obligations in regard to the quality of data that the Directive imposes on data controllers when such legislation is necessary to safeguard a broad variety of state functions. Article 12 of the Directive lists the state functions that may justify restrictions on the Directive's protections as national security, defense, public security, the prevention, investigation and prosecution of crime or professional breaches of ethics, important economic or financial interests of a State or the EU (including

---

77   Data Protection Directive, Article 3, Section 2. See also *ibid.*, Recital 12.

78   *Ibid.*, Art. 2(b).

79   *Ibid.*, Art. 2(a).

80   *Ibid.*, Art. 3, Sec. 2.

81   *Ibid.*, Recital 16. The video-surveillance that the Directive fails to regulate includes the use of CCTV in the United Kingdom which, with three million cameras in use, was the most extensive in the world as of 2009. See Alan Travis, "Lords: CCTV is Threat to Freedom", *The Guardian*, Feb. 9, 2009, available at: http://www. guardian.co.uk/uk/2009/feb/06/surveillance-freedom-peers.

monetary, budgetary and taxation matters) and monitoring, inspection, or regulatory functions that are connected, even occasionally, to the state's exercise of its powers in regard to public security and the preventing, investigating or prosecuting of crime or professional breaches of ethics or the state's or EU's important economic or financial interests. States may also limit data subjects' rights to information and access, and data controllers' obligations in regard to the quality of data in order to protect data subjects or the rights and freedoms of others.

Where it applies, the Directive requires EU countries to enact legislation that grants data subjects the following principal protections.

When can personal data be processed?

Sensitive data

The Directive imposes especially stringent conditions on the processing of sensitive data "revealing racial or ethnic origin, political opinions, religious or philosophical beliefs, trade-union membership, [or] concerning health or sex life."[82] States are to prohibit the processing of sensitive data without the explicit consent of the data subject except where such processing is necessary for the fulfillment of the data controller's rights and obligations under employment law, for the vital interests of the data subject or another where the data subject is physically or legally incapable of consenting to the data processing, or for health-related reasons where the processing is done by persons who are legally obligated to confidentiality. Trades unions, political and religious groups and other non-profit entities with religious, political or philosophical aims may also process sensitive data about their members without the members' consent if this is done in the course of their legitimate activities with appropriate guidelines and if the data are not disclosed to third parties without the data subject's consent.

States are empowered to enact additional exceptions to the requirement that sensitive data not be processed without the subject's consent for "reasons of substantial public interest", subject "to the provision of suitable safeguards",[83] and they are also free to determine when "a national identification number or any other identification of general application may be processed."[84] States may also enact exceptions, subject to specific legally established safeguards, to the rule that the processing of data relating to criminal offenses, convictions or security measures is to be controlled by official authorities.[85]

---

82   *Ibid.*, Art. 8.
83   *Ibid.*, Art.8, sec.4.
84   *Ibid.*, Art.8, sec.7.
85   *Ibid.*, Art.8, sec.5.

Other personal data

For other personal data, there are much broader exceptions to the requirement that data processing occur only with the subject's unambiguous consent.[86] Data may be processed in order to enable a data subject to enter into a contract, if necessary for the execution of a contract to which he or she is a party or if necessary to fulfill the data controller's legal obligations or to protect the data subject's vital interests. In addition, processing may occur where this is necessary for the public interest or for the exercise of official authority by the data controller or a third party to whom the data is disclosed. The legitimate interests of either the data controller or third party may also allow data to be processed without the subject's consent so long as these interests are not overridden by the data subject's rights to privacy or other fundamental rights.

However, the processing of non-sensitive personal data is limited by the data subject's right to object. Article 14 of the Directive provides that at least with regard to data whose processing is justified by the public interest or the legitimate interests or official functions of data controllers or third parties, a data subject has the right to object "on compelling legitimate grounds relating to his particular situation" at any time, and the processing must stop if the objection is justified.[87] Although the right to object does not apply where states have "otherwise provided by national legislation", the Directive prohibits states from limiting data subjects' right to object to the processing of personal data for direct marketing purposes on request and free of charge whenever data controllers anticipate such use of their data.[88] Data subjects must also be informed before their data are disclosed for the first time to third parties or used on these parties' behalf for direct marketing purposes, and explicitly offered the right to object free of charge to such disclosures or uses.[89]

The quality of data

The obligations of data controllers under Article 6 to ensure the quality of data include ensuring that processing is lawful and fair, that data are accurate and up-to-date and that reasonable steps are taken to rectify or erase inaccurate or incomplete data. In addition, data are to be collected only for specified, explicit and legitimate purposes and are not to be further processed for purposes that are incompatible with the original purpose of collection. The data controller's

---

86 *Ibid.*, Art. 7. Under the Directive, a data subject is deemed to consent only if there is a "freely given specific indication of his wishes by which the data subject signifies his agreement to personal data relating to him being processed." *Ibid.*, Art. 2 (h). This requirement of explicit consent contrasts with the notion of implicit consent that underlies much of United States law, including, among other instances, the lack of legal protection for information revealed to third parties, the notion of consensual wiretapping and the notion that people consent to certain uses of their data unless they opt out.

87 *Ibid.*, Art. 14 (a).

88 *Ibid.*, Art. 14 (a) and (b).

89 *Ibid.*, Art. 14(b).

obligations with regard to the quality of data also include ensuring that data be relevant and adequate to the stated purpose for collection and/or further processing, and that no more data than are needed for the stated purpose are collected or processed. Moreover, data are to be kept in a form that permits the identification of data subjects for no more time than is necessary to fulfill the stated purposes for collection and/or processing.

Data subjects' rights to information and access

Articles 10 and 11 of the Directive provide that, in regard to personal data obtained from either data subjects themselves or other sources, data subjects have the right to be informed of the purposes of the intended processing of the data and the identity of the data controller and any of his or her representatives. Where fairness to the data subject requires, he or she is also entitled to be informed of the recipients of the data and of his or her rights to access and to rectify data. Where the data subject is the source of personal data, he or she may also be entitled to learn whether replying to questions is mandatory, as well as the possible consequences of not replying. Where data is collected from sources other than the data subject, the subject may be entitled to learn the categories of data that the controller possesses or intends to disclose to a third party if this is required for the data processing to be fair.

Under Article 12, data subjects also have the right to obtain confirmation, at reasonable intervals and without undue expense or delay, of whether a data controller is processing data about them and, if so, to learn what data are being processed for what purposes and for what recipients. They are also entitled to any available information about the source of the data being processed and to be apprised of the logic underlying any automatic data processing operations that result in decisions that subject them to legal or other significant effects, such as determinations of creditworthiness or evaluations of their work. This right of access to one's personal data is linked to a right to correct the data held on one. Data subjects are entitled to have incomplete or inaccurate data, or data whose processing does not otherwise conform to the Directive's requirements, rectified, erased or blocked as appropriate and to have third parties notified of such changes.

Security and confidentiality of processing

Article 16 of the Directive provides that data processors and anyone acting under their authority or the authority of the data controller are not to process personal data except on the authority of the data controller.

Under Article 17, states are to mandate that data controllers "implement appropriate technical and organizational measures" to protect personal data from being accidentally or unlawfully destroyed, lost, altered, disclosed or accessed without authorization or otherwise unlawfully processed.[90] Data controllers' obligations to ensure the security of data apply "in particular where processing involves the transmission of data over a network."[91] The security provided must be "appropriate to the risks represented by the processing and the nature of the data to be protected", taking account of "the state of the art and the cost of their implementation."[92] Even if they choose to have external providers perform the processing, data controllers remain obligated to ensure the security of data.

Transfer of data to non-EU countries

The Directive provides, in Article 25, that personal data may be transferred from an EU country to a third country only if the third country "ensures an adequate level of protection" for personal data. Adequacy is to be assessed by both the European Commission and individual EU countries, and beyond stating that adequacy should be assessed "in the light of all the circumstances surrounding a data transfer operation", the Directive provides no standards for assessing whether a third country's level of data protection is adequate.[93]

Article 26 provides a broad list of conditions under which states may allow data to be transferred to a third country even if the adequacy requirement is not met, including with the consent of the data subject, for contractual reasons, if "the transfer is necessary or legally required on important public interest grounds" and if the transfer is made from a register that is legally intended to provide information to the public and the legal conditions for consulting the register are met. In addition, individual states may authorize transfers of personal data on the basis of contractual obligations that data controllers impose on the entities to whom the data are transferred, and the Commission is empowered to decide that certain standard contractual clauses provide sufficient safeguards for transfers to countries whose overall level of data protection is inadequate.[94]

The Commission's criticisms of the Data Protection Directive's provisions for transfers to third countries

In its policy review of EU data protection law in November 2010, the European Commission opined that the ever-increasing globalization of data processing created a "general need to improve the current mechanisms allowing for international transfers of personal data, while at the same time ensuring that personal data are adequately protected when transferred and processed outside the EU and the EEA."[95] According to the Commission, "the Internet makes it

---

90 *Ibid.*, Art.17, sec. 1.
91 *Ibid.*
92 *Ibid.*
93 *Ibid.*, Art. 25, secs. 1 and 2.
94 *Ibid.*, Art. 26 (2) and (4).
95 Commission, 'A Comprehensive Approach on Personal Data Protection," *supra*, at 2.4.1, available at: http://ec.europa.eu/justice/news/consulting_public/0006/com_2010_609_en.pdf.

much easier for data controllers established outside the European Economic Area (EEA) to provide services from a distance and to process personal data in the online environment; and it is often difficult to determine the location of personal data and of equipment used at any given time (e.g., in 'cloud computing' applications and services)."[96]

Among other things, the Commission criticized the lack of standards in the Directive for assessing the adequacy of a third country's level of data protection, stating that "the exact requirements for recognition of adequacy by the Commission are currently not specified in satisfactory detail in the Data Protection Directive."[97] In addition, the Commission criticized the lack of procedural guidelines for individual states' determinations of adequacy: "This situation may lead to different approaches to assessing the level of adequacy of third countries, or international organisations, and involves the risk that the level of protection of data subjects provided for in a third country is judged differently from one Member State to another."[98] In accord with its view that the Lisbon Treaty provides an opportunity for the extension of data protection principles to government operations, the Commission criticized "the current Commission standard clauses for the transfer of personal data to controllers and to processors [in third countries whose level of data protection is inadequate on the ground] that they are not designed for non-contractual situations and, for example, cannot be used for transfers between public administrations."[99]

Enforcement mechanisms in the Data Protection Directive

Under Article 28, each EU state is required to appoint an independent supervisory authority (or authorities) with the power to monitor compliance with the Directive within its territory, including investigative powers and effective powers of intervening to prevent the illegal processing of data or to order the blocking, erasure or destruction of illegally processed data. States' data supervisors are also to be empowered to bring legal proceedings when their state's laws implementing the Directive are violated and to hear claims concerning the protection of people's rights and freedoms with regard to

---

All European Economic Area (EEA) countries, including both the EU countries and the non-EU countries of Norway, Liechtenstein and Iceland, adhere to the Data Protection Directive. Strictly speaking, the Directive's provisions for data transfers to third countries are therefore provisions for transfers to non-EEA, as opposed to non-EU, countries. See School of African and Oriental Studies, University of London, "Transfer Outside the EU", available at: http://www.soas.ac.uk/infocomp/dpa/policy/outside.

96 Commission, 2.2.3. For an illustration of the tensions between the globalized nature of data processing and the EU's attempt to protect the privacy of its citizens, see Zach Whittaker, "Microsoft Admits Patriot Act Can Access EU-Based Cloud Data", ZDNet, June 28, 2011, available at: http://www.zdnet.com/blog/igeneration/microsoft-admits-patriot-act-can-access-eu-based-cloud-data/11225.

97 *Ibid.*, 2.4.1.

98 *Ibid.*

99 *Ibid.*

the processing of personal data, including claims about the lawfulness of the abridgement of rights under the Directive for reasons of national security or other state purposes.

Although a state's supervisory authority may provide individuals with administrative remedies, each EU state is also required, under Articles 22–24, to provide individuals with judicial remedies for violations of their rights under the state's laws implementing the Directive, including the right to have data controllers compensate them for damages.

The Article 29 Working Party

Article 29 creates a Working Party comprising one representative each of the data supervisory authority (or authorities) of each EU state, the data supervisory authority (or authorities) established for EU institutions and bodies and the European Commission, for the purpose of contributing to the uniform implementation of the Data Protection Directive in the EU. Under Article 30, the Working Party is empowered to provide the Commission with opinions on the levels of protection of personal data in the EU and in third countries, to advise the Commission on amendments to the Data Protection Directive or other measures to safeguard individuals' rights and freedoms regarding personal data and to make recommendations on its own initiative on all matters relating to the protection of personal data. The Working Party is to present publicly available annual reports to the Commission, the European Parliament and the Council on the processing of personal data in the EU and third countries.

The e-Privacy Directive

Scope and relation to the Data Protection Directive

The principal United States legislation on telecommunications privacy, the Electronic Communications Privacy Act (ECPA) of 1986, is widely criticized for being based on outmoded assumptions about the technology it regulates.[100] By contrast, in enacting the e-Privacy Directive in 2002, the European Parliament and the Council recognized that the "development of the information society is characterised by the introduction of new electronic communications services."[101] It went on to say, "New advanced

---

100   See e.g. Mike Masnick, "Privacy: Senator Leahy Wants to Update Digital Privacy Law: Some Good, Some Bad", *TechDirt*, May 17, 2011, available at: http://www.techdirt.com/blog/?tag=ecpa; IAPP (International Assoc. of Privacy Professionals), "House Subcommittee Hears Call for ECPA Updates", June 25, 2010, available at: https://www.privacyassociation.org/.../2010_06_25_house_subcommittee_hears_call_for_ecpa_updates.
101   Directive 2002/58/EC concerning the processing of personal data and the protection of privacy in the electronic communications sector (Directive on privacy and electronic communications) (the "e-Privacy Directive"), Recital 5, available at: http://eur-lex.europa.eu/LexUriServ/LexUriServ.do?uri=CELEX:32002L0058:EN:HTML.

digital technologies are currently being introduced in public communications networks in the Community, which give rise to specific requirements concerning the protection of personal data and privacy of the user."[102]

The provisions of the e-Privacy Directive apply to personal data processed in connection with the provision of publicly available electronic communications services and networks. Thus its protections of privacy extend to telephone calls and any voice, text, sound or image messages sent over public communications networks and capable of being stored in the network or on recipients' terminals, and also apply to users' terminal equipment and information stored therein.[103] However, when communications are made over non-public electronic communications services and networks (e.g. university or corporate networks) the Data Protection Directive applies. In addition, the Data Protection Directive applies to any matters pertaining to the processing of personal data in connection with publicly available services or networks that the e-Privacy Directive does not specifically address.[104]

Like the Data Protection Directive, the e-Privacy Directive does not protect individuals' privacy against any government action that the EU was not empowered to regulate before the Lisbon Treaty. Therefore, the e-Privacy Directive does not limit individual states' power to intercept or otherwise limit the privacy of electronic communications when this is "necessary for the protection of public security, defence, State security (including the economic well-being of the State when the activities relate to State security matters) and the enforcement of criminal law."[105] However, as indicated above, and as the Directive recognizes, the ECHR as interpreted by the European Court of Human Rights limits government power to restrict the privacy of electronic communications. The Directive states that any government restrictions "must be appropriate, strictly proportionate to the intended purpose, and necessary within a democratic society."[106]

The most important provisions of the e-Privacy Directive can be summarized as follows.

Confidentiality of communications

As discussed above, the Wiretap Provision of the ECPA accords individuals more protection against real-time interception of communications than the Stored

---

102   *Ibid.* In recognition of the continuing need for the law to keep abreast of technological changes, the e-Privacy Directive was amended by Directive 2009/136/EC of the European Parliament and of the Council, available at: http://eur-lex.europa.eu/LexUriServ/LexUriServ.do?uri=OJ:L:2009:337:0011:0036:En:PDF.
103   *Ibid.*, E-Privacy Directive, Articles 2(e) and (h) and 3(1), and Recital 14.
104   *Ibid.*, Recital 10.
105   *Ibid.*, Recital 11.
106   *Ibid.* See also *ibid.*, Art. 15(1).

Communications Provision provides against access to communications stored on terminals or other telecommunications equipment. By contrast, Article 5 requires EU states to enact laws prohibiting "listening, tapping, storage, or other kinds of interception or surveillance of communications and related traffic data" by anyone other than the parties to communications, unless they receive the consent of all the parties. This prohibition of all kinds of "interception or surveillance of communications" seems broad enough to cover both real-time interceptions and access to stored communications.

Article 5's prohibition of interception or surveillance of communications extends to "traffic data", defined in Article 2 as "any data processed for the purpose of the conveyance of a communication on an electronic communications network or for the billing thereof". Thus, the term "traffic data" in the e-Privacy Directive includes, but is not limited to, what US law counts as addressing information: the telephone numbers between which calls are made, the IP addresses of accessed websites and the "to" and "from" information on email headers. This implies that, in contrast to the US Constitution and the ECPA and in accordance with the European Court of Human Rights' interpretation of the ECHR, the e-Privacy Directive accords equal protection to the contents of communications and associated addressing information.

Exceptions to the e-Privacy Directive's limits on interception or surveillance

As implied above, the e-Privacy Directive's broad prohibition of interception or surveillance does not limit a state's power to authorize interception or surveillance of communications and traffic data for national security, criminal defense and related state purposes.[107]

The only other exceptions to Article 5's prohibition of interception or surveillance are for technical storage or access to information stored in a user or subscriber's terminal by a telecommunication provider for the sole purpose of transmitting communications.[108] In addition, people may be legally authorized to record communications and related traffic data in the course of lawful business practices for the purposes of providing evidence of business transactions and communications.[109]

Retention of traffic data

Article 6 of the e-Privacy Directive limits telecommunication service or network providers' use of the information that Article 5 allows them to store and access by requiring providers to erase or make anonymous traffic data when they are

---

107   *Ibid.*, Art. 5(1) and 15(1).
108   *Ibid.*, Art. 5(1) and (3).
109   *Ibid.*, Art.5(2).

longer needed for the transmission of a communication, for billing purposes or for marketing purposes to which the user or subscriber has consented. Article 15(1) carves out a major exception, however, to the Article 6 limits on the retention of data, providing that member states may "adopt legislative measures providing for the retention of data for a limited period justified on the grounds laid down in this paragraph", namely, "to safeguard national security (i.e. State security), defence, public security, and the prevention, investigation, detection and prosecution of criminal offences or of unauthorised use of the electronic communication system."

Although the e-Privacy Directive thus *permits* individual states to enact data retention legislation, the Data Retention Directive *requires* all EU states to mandate the retention of traffic data by telecommunications providers. The Data Retention Directive's provisions for the retention of traffic data are highly controversial.

Location data

The e-Privacy Directive defines location data as "any data processed in an electronic communications network, indicating the geographic position of the terminal equipment of a user of a publicly available communications service.[110] While some location data are part of the traffic data needed for transmitting or billing electronic communications (e.g. the location of a mobile phone *vis-à-vis* cell phone towers), Article 9 applies to processing of location data that are not part of traffic data. Subject to a state's decision to legislate an exception for law enforcement or other purposes under Article 15(1), location data other than traffic data can be processed only if made anonymous, or if the subscriber or user of the electronic communications service or network consents to the processing after being informed of the purposes of the processing, the types of data that will be processed and any third party to whom data will be transmitted. The user or subscriber must also be able to withdraw consent at any time.

Security of processing and data breach notification

Like Article 17 of the Data Protection Directive, Article 4 of the e-Privacy Directive contains provisions for the security of personal data. However, unlike the Data Protection Directive provision, the e-Privacy Directive provides for notifying individuals in the case of breaches of personal data. The 2009 Amendment to the e-Privacy Directive considerably strengthened its data breach notification requirements by providing that not only affected individuals and subscribers but also a competent national authority must be notified without

---

110   *Ibid.*, Art. 2 (c).

delay. The national authority may adopt guidelines for notification and for security practices and will audit the adequacy of providers' measures to notify individuals and mitigate the effects of the breach.[111]

The need for more comprehensive data breach notification

In its policy review of EU data protection law in November 2010, the European Commission recognized the importance of data breach notification and suggested that the 2009 Amendment's provisions for notifications of data breaches in telecommunications services and networks need to be extended to other fields.

> It is . . . important for individuals to be informed when their data are accidentally or unlawfully destroyed, lost, altered, accessed by or disclosed to unauthorised persons. The recent revision of the e-Privacy Directive introduced a mandatory personal data breach notification covering, however, only the telecommunications sector. Given that risks of data breaches also exist in other sectors (e.g. the financial sector), the Commission will examine the modalities for extending the obligation to notify personal data breaches to other sectors.[112]

The need for comprehensive and uniform standards for data breach notification may be even greater in the US than in the EU. An article on the Citigroup data breach in June 2011 reported that, "Security is . . . hampered by a patchwork of data protection laws and regulatory agencies, each with limited mandates. 'We need a uniform national standard for data security and data breach notification,' said Representative Mary Bono Mack, a California Republican who is pushing for legislation on better consumer safeguards."[113]

The Data Retention Directive

The Data Retention Directive was issued in 2006 in response to the 2004 Madrid terrorist bombings and the 2005 London terrorist bombings.[114]

---

111   See Directive 2009/136/EC of the European Parliament and of the Council, Article 2(4).

112   Commission, "A Comprehensive Approach on Personal Data Protection", 2.1.2.

113   Eric Dash, "City Data Theft Points Up a Nagging Problem", NY Times, June 10, 2011, B1 and 7. See also Editorial, "The Cloud Darkens: As Online Security Threats Grow, Companies and Government Are Scarily Unprepared", NY Times, June 30, 2011, A26.

114   Data Retention Directive, Recitals 8, 10, available at: http://eur-lex.europa.eu/LexUriServ/LexUriServ. do?uri=CELEX:32006L0024:EN:HTML. See also European Data Protection Supervisor (EDPS), "Opinion of the European Data Protection Supervisor on the Evaluation Report from the Commission to the Council and the European Parliament on the Data Retention Directive (Directive 2006/24/EC)", May 31, 2011, I.2, para. 4, available at: http://www.edps.europa.eu/EDPSWEB/webdav/site/mySite/shared/Documents/Consultation/Opinions/2011/11-05-30_Evaluation_Report_DRD_EN.pdf

Scope

The Directive requires EU states to enact laws requiring providers of publicly available telecommunications services and networks to retain traffic and location data that they generate or process in the course of providing their communications services, as well as related data needed to identify the subscriber or user of the service. Article 5 of the Directive lists the data to be retained as: data identifying the source and destinations of communications, including telephone numbers, user IDs and IP addresses and names and addresses of associated subscribers or registered users; data identifying the date, time, and duration of communications; data necessary to identify the type of communication (i.e. the ISP or telephone service used); data necessary to identify the users' equipment (e.g. the International Mobile Subscriber Identity (IMSI) and International Mobile Equipment Identity (IMEI) for both parties to a mobile phone conversation); and data necessary to identify the location of mobile communications equipment. By contrast, data revealing the contents of communications are not to be stored.

Article 6 of the Directive requires individual states to enact legislation requiring the listed data to be retained for a period, to be selected by each state, of between six months and two years from the time of a communication.

Access to the data

States have broad discretion as to the conditions for government officials' access to the retained data. Although the Directive specifies that the retained data be available only "for the purpose of the investigation, detection and prosecution of serious crime", each state may provide its own legal definition of a serious crime.[115] In addition, if a state's law so provides, data may be retained for any or all of the further purposes beyond the investigation, detection and prosecution of serious crimes for which Article 15(1) of the e-Privacy Directive allows states to order the retention of data.[116]

Article 4 further provides that only "competent national authorities in specific cases and in accordance with national law" are to access retained data and that the procedures and conditions for access are to accord with necessity and proportionality requirements. However, each state is left to define the requirements of necessity and proportionality in its own laws "subject to the relevant provisions of European Union law or public international law, and in particular the ECHR as interpreted by the European Court of Human Rights."

115　*Ibid.*, Recital 21 and Art. 1. See also EDPS, II, para. 24.
116　Data Protection Directive, Recital 12 ("Article 15(1) of Directive EC 2002/58/ED continues to apply to data . . . the retention of which is not specifically required under this Directive and which therefore falls outside the scope thereof, and to retention for purposes, including judicial purposes, other than those covered by this Directive"). See also EDPS, IV.3, paras. 71 and 72.

States' resistance to implementing the Directive

Although EU states were required to enact laws implementing the Directive by September 15, 2007, as of April 2011 Austria and Sweden had not enacted such laws. After the European Court of Justice ruled against Austria on July 29, 2010, for failing to implement the Directive, Austrian authorities transmitted drafts of implementing legislation to the Commission. By contrast, although the European Court of Justice issued a similar ruling against Sweden on February 4, 2010, the Swedish Parliament voted on March 16, 2011, to defer a vote on proposed implementing legislation for twelve months. The Commission then brought proceedings against Sweden in the European Court of Justice for a second time.[117]

In addition, the laws that Germany, Romania and the Czech Republic issued to implement the Directive were struck down by each of their constitutional courts as unconstitutional.[118] Although none of the courts found that the Data Retention Directive was unconstitutional *per se*, the German Constitutional Court found that the German law was unconstitutional because it did not contain sufficient protections for the security of the retained data or sufficient limitations on law enforcement access to the data. The German Court further reasoned that since data retention created a perception of surveillance that could interfere with people's exercise of fundamental rights, six months was the maximum period for which data could be retained.

Relying on decisions of the European Court of Human Rights, the Romanian Constitutional Court found that the Romanian law's imposition of an obligation to retain all traffic data for a continuous period of six months was too ambiguous in its scope and purpose and had too few safeguards to be compatible with Article 8 of the ECHR.

The Czech Constitutional Court found that the Czech law's definitions of the officials who were competent to access data and its procedures for access and use of data were not sufficiently clear to protect people's fundamental rights against abuse of power by government officials.

---

117 EUROPA – Press Releases – Frequently Asked Questions: Evaluation Report of the Data Retention Directive, April 18, 2011, available at: http://europa.eu/rapid/pressReleasesAction.do?reference=MEMO/11/251&format=HTML&aged=0&language=EN&guiLanguage=en.

118 *Ibid*. See also European Commission, Evaluation Report on the Data Retention Directive (Directive 2006/24/EC), April 18, 2011 ("Commission Evaluation of Data Retention"), Sec. 4.9, available at: http://ec.europa.eu/commission_2010-2014/malmstrom/archive/20110418_data_retention_evaluation_en.pdf.

The decisions of the Romanian, German and Czech Constitutional Courts are Decision No. 1258 from 8 October 2009 of the Romanian Constitutional Court, Romanian Official Monitor No 789, 23 November 2009; judgement of the Bundesverfassungsgericht 1 BvR 256/08, of 2 March 2010; Official Gazette of 1 April 2011, Judgment of the Constitutional Court of 22 March on the provisions of section 97 paragraph 3 and 4 of Act No. 127/2005 Coll. on electronic communications and amending certain related acts as amended, and Decree No 485/2005 Coll. on the data retention and transmission to competent authorities.

On May 5, 2010, the Irish High Court granted a civil rights group the right to refer the question of the legality of the Data Retention Directive's requirement of blanket and indiscriminate retention of individuals' traffic, location and subscriber data to the European Court of Justice.[119]

The European Commission's evaluation report

In accord with Article 14 of the Data Retention Directive, the Commission issued an evaluation report on the Directive to the Council and European Parliament on April 18, 2011. Despite acknowledging that the "evidence, in the form of statistics and examples, provided by Member States is limited in some respects", the Commission concluded that the EU should continue to require the retention of traffic, location and subscriber data. According to the Commission, the evidence established "the very important role of retained data for criminal investigation. These data provide valuable leads and evidence in the prevention and prosecution of crime and ensuring criminal justice."[120]

The Commission voiced its intent to propose revisions in the data retention framework on the basis of a thorough assessment of "the implications for the effectiveness and efficiency of the criminal justice system and of law enforcement, for privacy and for costs to public administration and operators, of more stringent regulation of storage, access to and use of traffic data."[121] The possible changes whose impact the Commission deemed particularly worthy of assessment were:

- consistency in limitation of the purpose of data retention and types of crime for which retained data may be accessed and used;
- more harmonisation of, and possibly shortening, the periods of mandatory data retention;
- ensuring independent supervision of requests for access and of the overall data retention access regime applied in all Member States;
- limiting the authorities authorised to access the data;
- reducing the data categories to be retained;
- guidance on technical and organisational security measures for access to data including handover procedures;
- guidance on use of data including the prevention of data mining; and
- developing feasible metrics and reporting procedures to facilitate comparisons of application and evaluation of a future instrument.[122]

---

119   Commission Evaluation of Data Retention, 7.2.
120   *Ibid.*, 8.1.
121   *Ibid.*, 8.5 and 8.6.
122   *Ibid.*, 8.5.

The Commission also proposed to consider how data retention might be complemented by data preservation or, in other words, court orders that obligate operators to retain data prospectively on specific individuals who are suspected of being engaged in crime.

The opinion of the European Data Protection Supervisor

The European Data Protection Supervisor (EDPS) issued an opinion on May 31, 2011, that was highly critical of both the Data Retention Directive and the Commission's Evaluation Report. Contrary to the Commission's exclusion of the possibility of repealing the Data Retention Directive, the EDPS claimed that the quantitative and qualitative data the Commission had obtained from EU states were not sufficient to show that data retention was necessary for law enforcement purposes. In particular, the EDPS criticized the Commission for only assessing data from states that had implemented the Directive and not comparing the criminal justice outcomes there with outcomes in states in which the Directive either had not been implemented or had been annulled.[123]

Furthermore, according to the EDPS, the Commission had not adequately considered whether data retention could be replaced by data preservation or some other less intrusive method of providing law enforcement with data.

> [I]t is unfortunate that in the conclusions of the report the Commission commits itself to examining whether – and if so how – an EU approach on data preservation might complement (i.e. not replace) data retention. . . the EDPS recommends the Commission during the impact assessment also to consider whether a system of data preservation, or other alternative means, could fully or partly substitute the current data retention scheme.[124]

The EDPS also faulted the Commission for failing to recognize that even if a data retention regime is necessary the Directive's restrictions on privacy were not proportionate to the purposes served. In particular, the EDPS claimed that the Directive left individual states too much discretion over the purposes for which retained data can be used and as to the authorities with access to the

---

123 EDPS, IV.1, para. 50. In accord with the EDPS's recognition of the need to compare crime control outcomes in EU countries that had and had not implemented the Directive, a recent study by the Scientific Services of the German Parliament of the effects of data retention on crime clearance rates in EU Member States concluded that, "In most States crime clearance rates have not changed significantly between 2005 and 2010. Only in Latvia did the crime clearance rate rise significantly in 2007. However, this is related to a new Criminal Procedure Law and is not reported to be connected to the transposition of the EU Data Retention Directive." See A.K. Vorrat, "Police Statistics Prove Data Retention Superfluous", *EDRI-gram*, Number 9.12, June 15, 2011, http://www.edri.org/edrigram/number9.12. Statistics published by Germany's Federal Crime Agency show that after the Constitutional Court's annulment of the German law implementing the Data Retention Directive on March 3, 2010, "registered crime continued to decline and the crime clearance rate was the highest ever recorded (56.0%)." Vorrat, *supra*.
124 EDPS, IV.1, para.57.

data.[125] Pointing to statistics in the Commission's evaluation report showing that 86% of requests were for access to data that had been retained for no more than six months, 12% were for access to data retained between six and twelve months and two per cent were for access to data retained for more than one year, the EDPS further concluded that the Directive allowed states to retain data for longer periods than necessary.[126] The requirement of proportionality was also violated, according to the EDPS, because the absence of adequate measures for the security of data in the Directive caused the privacy of personal data to be unnecessarily threatened.[127]

Further, the EDPS opined that the Directive failed to conform to the requirement, established by the European Court of Human Rights, that intrusions on privacy be foreseeable or, in other words, that they "have a legal basis in law and . . . be compatible with the rule of law."[128] The absence of predictability was created by the Directive's leaving states free to determine which officials are entitled to access retained data, and by the Directive's leaving individual states to define what counts as a serious crime and whether data can be accessed, under Article 15(1) of the e-Privacy Directive, for purposes other than combating serious crime.

Council Framework Decision 2008/977/JHA on Personal Data and Police and Judicial Cooperation[129]

Scope

Council Framework Decision 2008/977/JHA is the first EU legislation that establishes common standards for all EU states with regard to personal data processed as part of policing and criminal justice operations. The Decision governs the processing, "for the purpose of the prevention, investigation, detection, or prosecution of criminal offences or the execution of criminal penalties", of personal data exchanged between EU states.[130] The Decision also

---

125   *Ibid.*, IV.2, para. 59.
126   *Ibid.*, IV.2, para. 60 and n.51.
127   Cf. Lukas Feiler, "The Legality of the Data Retention Directive in Light of the Fundamental Right to Privacy and Data Protection", *European Journal of Law & Technology* 1, no. 3 (2010), available at: http://ejlt. org//article/view/29/75 (arguing that the Directive's restrictions on privacy conform to the requirement of necessity, but are not proportional to the stated purpose of combating serious crime, therefore violating the rights to privacy and data protection in articles 7 and 8 of the EU Charter); Lachmayer, "European Police Cooperation and its Limits", 108–09 ("The scope of the directive is very broad as the categories of data to be retained are manifold and the retention period is 'not less than six months and not more than two years from the date of the communication.' Its effects on the general human rights situation are dramatic."). But see Francesca Bignami, "Privacy and Law Enforcement in the European Union: The Data Retention Directive", *Chicago Journal of International Law* 8 (2007): 233 (finding that "privacy – as guaranteed under Article 8 of the European Convention on Human Rights and the Council of Europe's Convention on Data Protection – is adequately protected in the Directive").
128   EDPS, IV.3.
129   Available at http://eur-lex.europa.eu/LexUriServ/LexUriServ.do?uri=OJ:L:2008:350:0060:01:EN:HTML.
130   Council Framework Decision 2008/977/JHA, Article 1(2)(a).

applies to individual EU states' transmission of personal data received from other EU states to private parties for criminal justice purposes and the prevention of serious threats to public safety or serious harm to human rights.[131]

The scope of the Framework Decision is limited by the fact that it does not replace "various sector-specific legislative instruments for police and judicial co-operation in criminal matters adopted at the EU level, in particular those governing the functioning of Europol, Eurojust, the Schengen Information System (SIS) and the Customs Information System (CIS)."[132]

In addition, the Framework Decision only partially governs EU states' transfers to non-EU states or international bodies of data received from other EU states. Article 13 requires EU states to provide that such transfers will occur only for criminal justice purposes and that data will be given only to non-EU authorities responsible for those purposes. In addition, personal data are to be transferred only to non-EU states or international bodies that ensure adequate levels of data protection and only with the consent of the EU state that originally provided the data. However, Article 13 of the Framework Decision leaves individual states to decide on the conditions under which they will consent to such transfers of data. In addition, the adequacy of the level of data protection in a non-EU country or international body is left up to the laws of the state that provided the data, and the conditions for waiving the requirement of an adequate level of data protection are left up to the laws of the state that transferred the data.

EU regulation of the use of personal data for policing and criminal justice is further limited as the Framework Decision does not apply to the collection, use or transmission of personal data within the confines of individual EU states, or to an EU state's transmission of data received from another EU state to private parties, such as defense lawyers and victims, in the context of criminal proceedings.[133] Nor does the Framework Decision apply to data received by an EU state from a non-EU country or to the processing of data for "essential national security interests and specific intelligence activities in the field of national security."[134]

Requirements for the processing of data

The Framework Decision's principal requirements for the processing of data exchanged between EU states for criminal justice purposes can be compared

---

131 *Ibid.*, Article 14.
132 Commission, 'A Comprehensive Approach on Personal Data Protection", 2.3; Council Framework Decision 2008/977/JHA, Art. 1(2)(b) and (c), Recitals 39-41.
133 *Ibid.*, Recitals 9 and 18.
134 *Ibid.*, Article 1 (4); Information Policy Division, UK Ministry of Justice, Circular 2011/01, "Council Framework Decision on the protection of personal data processed in the framework of police and judicial cooperation in criminal matters 2008/977/JHA', Jan. 25, 2011, 2, available at: http://www.justice.gov.uk/publications/docs/data-protection-framework-decision-circular.pdf.

with those that the Data Protection Directive imposes for the processing of personal data for other purposes. While the Framework Decision agrees with the Directive in imposing especially stringent conditions for the processing of sensitive data "revealing racial or ethnic origin, political opinions, religious or philosophical beliefs, trade-union membership, [or] concerning health or sex life", it does not follow the Directive in making the data subject's consent the principal requirement for such processing.[135] Instead, Article 6 of the Framework Decision allows sensitive data to be processed "only when this is strictly necessary and when the national law provides adequate safeguards."

With regard to other personal data, Article 3 of the Framework Decision provides, similarly to Article 6 of the Data Protection Directive, that data are to be collected only for specified, explicit and legitimate purposes, are not to be further processed for purposes that are incompatible with the original purpose for collection and are to be relevant and adequate to the stated purpose for collection and/or further processing. In addition, no more data than are needed for the stated purposes are to be collected or processed. Under Article 11 of the Framework Decision, the permissible purposes for which data can be further processed beyond those for which they were originally transmitted are broad, extending to additional criminal justice purposes and related judicial and administrative proceedings, the prevention of serious and immediate threats to public security and any other purpose to which the EU state that transmitted the data consents in advance or to which the data subject consents in accord with national law.

Although the Framework Decision also resembles the Data Protection Directive in requiring that personal data be kept accurate and up-to-date and providing data subjects with rights to information and access, these protections are weaker than those in the Directive. Under Article 8 of the Framework Decision, competent authorities are to verify the accuracy of personal data "as far as practicable" and to take "all reasonable steps" to ensure that inaccurate, incomplete or outdated personal data are not transmitted. Article 4 requires rectifying inaccurate data or updating or completing them where "possible and necessary", and erasing, making anonymous or blocking data that are no longer needed for the original purposes or further purposes for which they were lawfully processed. Although Article 16 of the Framework Decision provides data subjects with the right to be informed of the collection or processing of their personal data, this right may be limited by the laws of both their own state and any other EU state with which their data are exchanged. Similarly, although Article 17 grants data subjects rights to receive confirmation that their personal data have or have not been transmitted, as well as information as to the recipients of the data and the data being processed, the right to access may be limited by individual EU states

---

135   Data Protection Directive, Art. 8; Council Framework Decision, Art. 6.

where this is necessary and proportional to avoid obstructing judicial or police procedures, to protect public or national security or to protect data subjects or the rights and freedoms of others.

Perhaps reflecting increasing awareness of the risk of data breaches, the Framework Decision's provisions in Article 22 for the security of data are more elaborate than those in the Data Protection Directive.

Enforcement

The Framework Decision requires each EU state to appoint an independent supervisory authority (or authorities) which may or may not be same as the Data Protection Supervisor appointed in accord with the Data Protection Directive.[136] Under Article 25 of the Framework Decision, each state's supervisory authority (or authorities) is to have the power to advise and monitor the application of the Framework Decision within its territory, including investigative powers and effective powers of intervening to deliver opinions before the processing of data or to order the blocking, erasure or destruction of processed data. States are also to empower data supervisors to bring legal proceedings when the state's laws implementing the Framework Decision are violated, and to hear individuals' claims concerning the protection of their rights and freedoms regarding the processing of personal data.

Although Article 20 of the Framework Decision grants data subjects rights to judicial remedies for breaches of the rights provided to them by their state's law implementing the Framework Decision, these rights may be limited by administrative remedies.

Criticisms of the Council Framework Decision by the EDPS and the European Commission

The European Data Protection Supervisor and the European Commission separately opined that the Council Framework Decision is an important – though only a first – step toward the goal of adequately protecting personal data in the context of policing and criminal justice.[137] In regard to cross-border exchanges of personal data within the EU, the EDPS and the Commission agreed that more limits are needed on the purposes for which the Framework Decision allows data to be further processed. In addition, both agreed on "the need to

---

136   Council Framework Decision, Recitals 33 and 34, Art. 25.
137   European Data Protection Supervisor Press Release, "EDPS Sees Adoption of Data Protection Framework for Police and Judicial Cooperation Only as a First Step", Nov. 28, 2008, available at http://www.edps.europa. eu/EDPSWEB/webdav/shared/Documents/EDPS/PressNews/Press/2008/EDPS-2008-11_DPFD_EN.pdf; Commission, 2.3.

distinguish between different categories of data subjects, such as suspects, criminals, witnesses and victims, to ensure that their data are processed with more appropriate safeguards."[138]

More fundamentally, the Commission and EDPS both criticized the limitations on the scope of the Framework Decision, stressing the need for common EU law to govern exchanges of data with non-EU countries and for EU legislation to extend to domestic policing and criminal justice operations. Notably, the Commission recognized that the distinction between cross-border data exchanges and domestic processing of data "is difficult to make in practice and can complicate the actual implementation and application of the Framework Decision."[139]

Institutional arrangements in an EU Member State: The Netherlands

It is now time to exemplify the institutional embodiment of the EU's privacy rights in a member state. We have selected the Netherlands for this purpose.

The Kingdom of the Netherlands is a constitutional monarchy and a representative parliamentary democracy. It has territory in the Caribbean (the former colonies of Aruba and Netherlands Antilles) as well as in Europe (the Netherlands). The Charter for the Kingdom of the Netherlands provides for the autonomy of the Caribbean territories. The Constitution of the Kingdom of the Netherlands provides for the regulation of the government of the Netherlands (but not of the government of the territories). It grants citizens an explicit right to privacy.

The monarch and the Council of Ministers of the Netherlands are the government of the Kingdom. The Dutch Prime Minister chairs the Council of Ministers of the Kingdom. Under Article 14 of the Charter, the Netherlands can conduct kingdom affairs if this does not affect Aruba or Netherlands Antilles; neither of the latter has this right. The Parliament is known as the States-General of the Netherlands and has two houses, the House of Representatives (which can propose legislation, as can the monarch) and the Senate (the upper house). The Netherlands is divided into twelve provinces. The Supreme Court of the Netherlands is the highest court. However, it cannot rule on the constitutionality of laws passed by the States-General or on treaties. In contrast to some countries in the EU, the Netherlands has no constitutional court. (There is a council of state that advises the government on serious judicial matters, including issues relating to international law.) However, the Dutch Constitution obliges the courts to review all domestic legislation, including acts of parliament, in

---

138   EDPS, see also Commission.
139   *Ibid.* (footnote omitted).

respect of their compatibility with relevant parts of the international treaties to which the Netherlands is a party (for example, the European Convention for the Protection of Human Rights and Fundamental Freedoms 1950). Where there is incompatibility, the domestic legislation must give way. In particular, it must give way to conventions and directives that bind all member states of the EU, such as the 1995 directive 95/46/EC of the European Parliament and of the Council of Europe on the protection of personal data.

The Dutch Criminal Code defines many but not all criminal offenses. Various other statutes complement criminal law legislation – for example, the Economic Offenses Act 1950, the Narcotic Drug Offenses Act 1928 and the Military Criminal Code 1991. The Computer Crime Act 1993 allowed for the interception of all forms of telecommunications, including by means of long-distance target microphones.

Criminal procedure in the Netherlands has two phases: investigation by the police (under the direction of a public prosecutor – see below) and judicial investigation by an examining judge. The purpose of the police investigation is simply to gather evidence. Although the police have a right to ask questions of suspects, no one is required to answer questions put by the police. Under Dutch law there needs to be reasonable suspicion before a criminal investigation may be started. Police are able to use covert policing methods, such as surveillance, undercover operatives and the use of informants, under the Special Powers of Investigation Act 2000.

The Dutch police system is based on the Police Act of 1993. Law enforcement in the Netherlands is provided by twenty-five regional police forces and the Dutch National Police Agency (KLPD). The latter is responsible for the transport systems of the Netherlands (e.g. motorways and waterways). The National Criminal Investigation Department (responsible for serious and organized crime and cross-regional crimes) comes under the KLPD. The KLPD also has its own intelligence service, the National Criminal Intelligence Service (NRI). Each regional police force has a Criminal Intelligence Service (CIS). However, the establishment of communication systems and the processing and availability of information obtained from investigations is done at a national level. Currently, the records services are converting to a fully computerized system that will comprise criminal records, photographs of crime scenes and offenders, fingerprints etc.

The States-General generates the regulations governing the police while the Minister of the Interior is responsible for their central administration and the mayor of the largest municipality in the region for their regional administration (except in the case of the directly centrally administered KLPD). The regional police chiefs are responsible for day-to-day management. However, the relevant public prosecutor (belonging to the Public Prosecution Service (OM) which is managed by the Board of Procurators General within the Ministry of Justice) is responsible for the police with respect to crime investigation. Although the police actually conduct most investigations, sometimes the public prosecutors take direct control of investigations into serious crimes. The OM is responsible for investigating and prosecuting criminal offenders and is the only body in the Netherlands that may prosecute criminal suspects. Accordingly, no single body in the Netherlands has sole authority over the police.

The prosecution office attached to the Supreme Court is not part of the OM. It is an independent statutory body concerned with the prosecution of the members of Parliament and the ministers in relation to criminal matters.

The duties and powers of the intelligence and security services in the Netherlands are set forth in the Intelligence and Security Services Act 2002. The General Intelligence and Security Service (AIVD) focuses on domestic intelligence and non-military threats including, in recent times, Islamic fundamentalism. It collects and assesses information and monitors suspected terrorists and the like. The Ministry of the Interior is responsible for the AIVD (see below). The Military Intelligence and Security Service (MIVD) focuses on foreign intelligence and international threats, specifically military- and government-sponsored threats such as espionage. It collects and assesses information. The MIVD works closely with NATO. The Minister of Defense is responsible for the MIVD. The MIVD is overseen by a committee appointed by the Committee for the Intelligence and Security Services and comprising the leaders of the four main political parties represented in the House of Representatives of the States-General.

The National Coordinator for Counter-terrorism (NCTb) exists to ensure coordination between these and other relevant agencies.

The Information and Communications Technology Agency is an agency of the Ministry of the Interior and is responsible for the provision of reliable and secure ICT services and for information management in the security and criminal justice sectors.

Under the Treaty of Lisbon (2009), the Treaty of Amsterdam (1999) and other treaties, the Netherlands is required to cooperate with other EU countries in criminal matters, including corruption, organized crime, terrorism, arms trafficking, trafficking in drugs and trafficking in human beings. Europol (based in The Hague) is the central police office for sharing and analyzing information on criminal matters among EU members. The Schengen Information System has been established to facilitate EU information sharing. Under the Europol Convention (1999), EU countries have agreed to share information and to institute measures for data protection. As of 2010, Europol functions on the basis of a Council Decision that gives it Community status and subjects its budget to control by the European Parliament.

Post-9/11 cooperation on security among EU states and between the EU, including the Netherlands, and the US has increased. Within the EU, extradition processes have been simplified and expedited, agreement has been reached on the definition of the constituent elements of terrorism and the minimum sentences to be applied, and Europol's Terrorism Task Force has been established and thereby enables the exchange of information between the various counter-terrorism authorities. A cooperation agreement exists between Europol and the US.

These attempts at cooperation notwithstanding, the EU and the US standpoints on privacy and data protection are somewhat different. Thus in the US the approach to regulation in the private sector is essentially self-regulation whereas in the EU there is comprehensive privacy and data protection legislation as well as oversight bodies. In the case of the Netherlands, the Data Protection Authority has oversight and investigative powers, including with respect to the private sector (see below).

Privacy rights and data protection

As noted above, Dutch citizens have an explicit right to privacy under the Constitution of the Netherlands. Article 10 of the Constitution states:

1. Everyone shall have the right to respect for his privacy, without prejudice to restrictions laid down by, or pursuant to, Act of Parliament.

2. Rules to protect privacy shall be laid down by Act of Parliament in connection with the recording and dissemination of personal data.

3. Rules concerning the rights of persons to be informed of data recorded concerning them, of the use that is made thereof, and to have such data corrected shall be laid down by Act of Parliament.

Article 12 states:

1. Entry into a home against the will of the occupant shall be permitted only in the cases laid down by, or pursuant to, Act of Parliament, by those designated for this purpose by, or pursuant to, Act of Parliament.

2. Prior identification and notice of purpose shall be required in order to enter a home under the preceding paragraph, subject to the exceptions by Act of Parliament. A written report of the entry shall be issued to the occupant.

Article 13 states:

1. The privacy of correspondence shall not be violated, except in the cases laid down by Act of Parliament or by order of the courts.

2. The privacy of the telephone and telegraph shall not be violated, except in the cases laid down by Act of Parliament, by or with the authorization of those designated for this purpose by Act of Parliament.

The Dutch Data Registration Act 1988, which preceded the EU Data Protection Directive, protects personal data files and, speaking generally, requires consent, accuracy of data, use of data only for the purpose for which they were originally collected, security of data, disclosure only by consent or by statute and so on.

The Data Registration Act established the Dutch Data Protection Authority, which advises the government, deals with complaints and undertakes investigations.

The Decree on Sensitive Data under the Data Registration Act sets out the limited circumstances under which data on an individual's political and sexual persuasion, religious beliefs, race and medical and criminal history may be included on a personal data file. The Decree on Regulated Exemption under the Data Registration Act exempts certain organizations from the requirements of the Data Registration Act.

The Dutch Personal Data Protection Act of 2000 supersedes earlier legislation, including the Data Registration Bill 1998 and the Data Registration Act 1988. It brings Dutch law in line with the European Data Protection Directive; *inter alia* it regulates the disclosure of personal data to countries outside of Europe.

As noted above, interception of communications is regulated by the Criminal Code and requires a court order. The intelligence services (e.g. the AIVD and the MIVD) do not need a court order for interception of communications; their authorization comes from the Minister of the Interior.

The Telecommunications Act 1998 requires all internet service providers to have the capacity to intercept all traffic in the event of a court order.

The Intelligence and Security Services Act authorizes the interception, search and keyword scanning of satellite communications. Intelligence services can store intercepted communications for up to one year.

As noted above, the Netherlands has ratified the European Convention for the Protection of Human Rights and Fundamental Freedoms 1950, which recognizes a right to privacy. Article 8 states: "Everyone has the right to respect for his private and family life, his home and his correspondence." As a member of the Council of Europe in 1993 the Netherlands ratified the Convention for the

Protection of Individuals with Regard to Automatic Processing of Personal Data. Moreover, the Netherlands is a member of the Organization for Economic Cooperation and Development and has adopted the OECD Guidelines for the Protection of Privacy and Trans-border Flows of Personal Data.

The 2006 directive (Directive 2006/24/EC) on retention of data generated or processed in connection with the provision of publicly available electronic communication services or of public communication networks is highly controversial in the Netherlands. The directive allows the retention for lengthy periods – twelve months in the Netherlands, longer than the Directive's minimum requirement of six months – of so-called traffic data, including not simply who has been communicated with and when but also a person's movements (based on, for example, location of a mobile phone caller) and patterns of internet use. The claim of the authorities who have passed this legislation is that the data in question are not communicative of content and, therefore, that the legislation respects privacy. Moreover, the data are held to be useful in counter-terrorism initiatives and in combating organized crime. However, the counter-claim is that the traffic data are sufficiently rich and comprehensive to enable the creation of a map of the human associations and activities of any individual with respect to whom it has been retained – a profile of sorts – and their retention is, therefore, an infringement of the privacy of ordinary citizens.

The Netherlands has recently passed legislation that introduces biometric passports with an RFID-microchip containing digital information about the passport holder. The passport holder's fingerprints and a digital facial image are stored on the microchip for identification. Although this increases security by, for example, reducing the possibility of fraudulent use, the data on all biometric passports is stored in a central database accessible by law enforcement agencies in relation to criminal investigations and counter-terrorist activities. Because this central database contains information about all citizens who are passport holders it contains data about virtually every Dutch citizen irrespective of their criminality or suspected criminality. Accordingly, this new law would appear to breach the right to privacy and, arguably, Dutch privacy legislation.

Another controversy that has recently arisen is the decision by the Dutch government to direct Amsterdam's Schiphol airport to install full-body scanners and to use them to scan passengers traveling to the US. The decision comes in the wake of a Nigerian man carrying a non-metallic explosive device undetected through airport security at Amsterdam on Christmas Day 2009 before boarding a US plane and traveling to Detroit. His attempt to trigger the device was unsuccessful. There are privacy concerns – including from a legal perspective – about the intrusive nature of the images and the possibility of these images being stored, transferred or accessed without authorization.

Agencies

Dutch Data Protection Authority

The Data Protection Authority (DPA) is an independent statutory authority that supervises compliance with the legislation that regulates the use of personal data. The legislation in question includes the Personal Data Protection Act, the Police Data Act and the Municipal Database (Personal Records) Act.

The DPA makes recommendations regarding legislation, receives complaints, conducts audits and official investigations and initiates prosecutions. Appeals can be made against the DPA's decisions to the administrative law court and complaints can be made to the National Ombudsman.

In the past, the DPA has: conducted random investigations of the practices of Criminal Intelligence Service Units to determine the extent to which the regulations governing data processing were actually being observed; conducted an investigation in 2004 into the privacy aspects of data processing in police wiretapping rooms; conducted random checks on municipalities to see whether they had complied with their notification obligations in respect of the collection of personal data; approved in 2004 the Code of Conduct for processing personal data of the Netherlands Association of Business Information Agencies; and conducted in 2003 an investigation into a business information agency, finding that it had processed personal data illegitimately and informing the Public Prosecutor, with the result that a criminal investigation was conducted leading to prosecution of members of the agency.

General Intelligence and Security Service

The General Intelligence and Security Service (AIVD) is responsible for non-military intelligence gathering and assessment, conducting threat analyses, issuing warnings of risks to national security and monitoring individuals suspected of involvement in organized crime, cybercrime, terrorist activities (including radicalization) and the like. It passes information that is relevant to the investigation or prosecution of offenses in the form of official reports to the police and/or the relevant judicial authorities within the Public Prosecutions Service. The regional intelligence services conduct activities on behalf of the AIVD and for which the AIVD has ultimate responsibility. It also has an investigative capacity, for example, of terrorist incidents and it conducts background checks on individuals in sensitive positions, including public offices and important positions in industry.

The AIVD makes use of covert methods, including undercover operatives, use of informants and interception of electronic communications. As noted above, the AIVD intercepts telephone and internet communications and does so under the authorization of the Minister of the Interior (rather than judicial warrant). It has unrestricted access to police intelligence and works closely with Dutch police intelligence agencies, other EU intelligence agencies and foreign intelligent agencies such as the CIA.

The Minister of the Interior is responsible for the AIVD. However, the Council for National Security, which is a Cabinet sub-committee comprising the Prime Minister, two Deputy Prime Ministers and the ministers of the Interior, Justice, Defense and Foreign Affairs, gives general direction to the AIVD and delegates much of the tasking of the AIVD to other bodies, such as the Joint Intelligence Services Committee (CVIN) (chaired by the Intelligence and Security Services Coordinator and various public servants) and the Joint Counter-terrorism Committee (GCT).

The AIVD is overseen by the Intelligence and Security Supervisory Committee (CTIVD), which is appointed by the Committee for the Intelligence and Security Services (CIVD). The CIVD comprises the leaders of all the political parties represented in the House of Representatives of the States-General (with the exception of the Socialist Party, which opted not to join). The Minister of the Interior is accountable to Parliament via the CIVD. When AIVD matters cannot be publicly disclosed, the CIVD meets in closed sessions.

The AIVD publishes an annual report including its budget. Sensitive information is omitted.

Under the freedom of information rules, the AIVD can be required by the courts to provide any records held on a private citizen to that citizen unless it is relevant to a current case. Moreover, even outdated material cannot be provided if it would compromise the AIVD's sources or methods.

Conclusions

Returning to the framework for data protection that is provided by EU law and is binding on all EU member states, and to a comparison of EU and US law, the criticisms of the Council Framework Decision by the EDPS and the European Commission highlight two crucial unresolved issues about the protection of privacy in the twenty-first century. First, how can state sovereignty be reconciled with the globalized nature of personal data and the concomitant globalized nature of threats to both individual privacy and national security? Second, what, if any, differences in restrictions on the collection, use and transfer of personal data are justified by differences between state and private entities and state and private purposes?

With regard to the second question, the preceding discussion has shown that the United States lags behind the EU in recognizing the need for comprehensive restrictions on the collection, use and transfer of personal data by private entities. There is a clear need for additional legislation in the US to protect the individual's privacy rights from intrusion by private entities. However, the EU has yet to face the major challenge of extending its legislative framework for data protection to policing and criminal justice within the individual EU states. The difficulty of doing this is evident in the Commission's statement that "the notion of a comprehensive data protection scheme does not exclude specific rules for data protection for the police and the judicial sector within the general framework, taking due account of the specific nature of these fields."[140] In the opinion of the authors, neither the US nor the EU has arrived at an adequate understanding of what it means for data protection safeguards to take "due account of the specific nature" of policing and criminal justice.

Nonetheless, our discussion suggests that the EU may be aided in answering this question by the expertise on technological and legal issues about data protection that its law has created through the institutions of the Article 29 Working Party, the European Data Protection Supervisor and the Data Protection Supervisors of the individual states. By contrast, although some governmental bodies in the US, such as the Federal Trade Commission, have become interested in questions of data protection, these bodies are interested in data protection only as it impacts on some other governmental function, for example, protecting consumers or advancing commerce.[141] Unlike the European Data Protection Supervisor, no American governmental body has the power or institutional competence to advocate and argue for a data protection framework that extends to both public and private entities and functions and that accounts for the globalized nature of personal data in the twenty-first century.

Given increasing inroads on personal privacy in the US, it seems unreasonable to advocate not only additional privacy legislation (both federal and state) in relation to intrusions by private sector entities but also, and related, the creation of a National Office of Data Protection that would seek to provide a set of national guidelines for the protection of personal data. This has occurred in a number of other countries and even if, as was the case with the American Law Institute's (ALI) projects,[142] such guidelines could not be enforced in the absence of relevant legislation, they would at least constitute a respected benchmark for

---

140   *Ibid.*
141   See e.g. The Department of Commerce Internet Policy Task Force, "Commercial Data Privacy and Innovation in the Internet Economy: A Dynamic Policy Framework", 2010, available at: http://www.commerce.gov/sites/default/files/documents/2010/december/iptf-privacy-green-paper.pdf; Federal Trade Commission, "Protecting Consumer Privacy in an Era of Rapid Change", December 2010, available at: http://www.ftc.gov/os/2010/12/101201privacyreport.pdf.
142   See The American Law Institute web site at: http://www.ali.org/.

the review and revision of existing privacy protections as well as the initiation of others. Although we envisage a federally funded agency, the analogy with the ALI indicates that we also believe that it should be heavily populated by those who have an expertise in privacy issues: conceptual, moral, legal and political. Such a body would not only be charged with the development of privacy guidelines for consideration by both commercial and governmental bodies, and of recommendations for legislation, but it would also have a public responsibility to communicate its findings to a wide audience.[143] We further suggest that there is a need for a statutory body (whether the National Office of Data Protection and/or some other body or bodies) with the responsibility to oversee and monitor compliance with privacy legislation. Such a body should conduct audits and examine records as well as receive privacy complaints. It should also have the power to conduct investigations of breaches of the legislation.

We advocate that the process of developing a National Office of Data Protection for the US begin with a national public discussion concerning the legitimate extent and limits of privacy and of ways of protecting it. Such a debate would need to take into account not only the governmental collection, retention and use of personal data but also its collection, retention and use by commercial organizations. We believe that once it is widely recognized that the division between governmental and commercial collection, retention and use of personal data has been all but eroded under the current regulatory arrangements, such a national office will be seen as both reasonable and feasible.

It is our hope that in advocating a National Office of Data Protection we will see the development of a graduated series of guidelines and associated legislation for the oversight of personal data collection, use and retention by private and public agencies, including but not limited to soft law self-regulatory measures, privacy enhancement of software and administrative measures designed to protect privacy, along with recommendations concerning situations in which criminal penalties ought to be levied. The National Office of Data Protection should also have a communicative responsibility to ensure that the American public is aware of current concerns about the privacy of personal data as well as its recommendations concerning protection enhancements. Moreover, there is a need for an oversight body (perhaps the National Office of Data Protection) with statutory powers to monitor, receive complaints, conduct audits and investigate infringements of privacy rights.

---

143   We imagine some sort of parallel – inexact, to be sure – with the Law Reform Commission of Australia. The latter has produced impressive reviews of existing privacy regulations as well as conceptually rich accounts of privacy. See http://www.alrc.gov.au/media/2008/mr11108.html. A better understanding of how this adjustment to the US system may be achieved is provided in Chapter IX.

We further believe that it would be essential for a National Office of Data Protection to confer regularly with the EDPS of other similar institutions in other countries in order to develop a set of standards that can be generally implemented within such societies. As the EDPS and European Commission have recognized, the globalized nature of data in the twenty-first century means that no country can effectively protect its citizens' privacy on its own. A globalized problem demands globalized solutions.

V. When the Rubber Hits the Road

What Gallie had in mind when articulating the idea of essential contestability were comprehensive normative traditions and ideologies that range across the whole spectrum of social and political belief. His observations about social conceptualization might be applied equally to variations within the liberal tradition and, even more relevantly to our purposes in this inquiry, to differences in liberal cultural traditions. Indeed, what Rawls aspires to as an overlapping consensus is grounded in *liberal* diversity rather than the whole range of normative difference.

Although this study could have attempted to explore the wide range of differences among liberal polities – and it will indeed advert to a reasonably broad group of such polities, including those in Australia and India – it will most conveniently and manageably serve our purposes if it focuses primarily on differences that have come to notice in relations between the countries that form the EU and the US. Of course, even that is a simplification, because both the EU and the US embody a variety of traditions and understandings, and what we refer to as the views of each are but prominent and shifting expressions within each rather than an exhaustive characterization.

This has already been presaged in our brief comparative discussion of the roots of privacy in Europe and the US (Chapter III) and in our account of the regulatory traditions found in each (Chapter IV). The different constructions of privacy have played a large part in the ongoing debates between the EU and the US regarding digital technologies and the access to and use of digital data. In addition there are larger socio-political concerns that have informed their divergences.

Three cases will serve to illustrate the problems addressed by this study. They are: (A) the Passenger Name Record (PNR) controversy that has for several years dogged EU–US relations; (B) the US subpoenaing of SWIFT data; and (C) the National Identity (ID) card debate.

(A) The PNR Controversy

The PNR (Passenger Name Record) controversy began after 9/11 when the US began demanding certain personal information of passengers traveling to or from the United States, information that the EU considered to be private and therefore not appropriately demanded except under much narrower conditions than the US observed. Here we trace its main outlines.

Whenever a person books a flight from country A to country B,[1] a Passenger Name Record (PNR) is created. That record contains various *data*; it has a *location*; and it acquires a *history*.[2]

Data. The PNR will contain a lot of personal data that the traveler is asked to provide—formal data such as name, address, date of birth, credit card information, frequent flyer numbers and billing and approval codes (if relevant), as well as informal data concerning preferences such as meals or religious preferences, sleeping preferences if the traveler is also booking a hotel or even notes from the agent if they are thought pertinent.[3] There will also be various ancillary data about the agent who is making the booking or about some other person if that person is making the booking for the person who is traveling. All told, over thirty different fields are usually represented.

Location. This information is then stored — not usually on the airline or travel agent's computer system but in the centralized database of a Computerized Reservation System (CRS) or Global Distribution System (GDS) such as Sabre, Galileo/Apollo, Amadeus or Worldspan. These CRSs are owned by private- or publicly-traded companies. Amadeus, a Spanish corporation with its primary operations in Germany, is largely owned by the airlines that use it. The others are based in the US and are used but not owned by US-based airlines.

History. As travelers make changes or buy additional tickets, and even if they cancel, the information is updated and to some extent consolidated. An audit trail is created, and though data can be changed they are not expunged. An approximation of such a procedure is as follows:

> When a travel agent makes a reservation, they enter data on a CRS/GDS terminal, and create a PNR in that CRS/GDS. If the airline is hosted in a different CRS/GDS, information about the flight(s) on that airline is sent to the airline's host system, and a PNR is created in the airline's partition in that system as well. What information is sent between airlines, and how, is specified in the Airline Interline Message Procedures (AIRIMP) manual, although many airlines and CRS's/GDS's have their own direct connections and exceptions to the AIRIMP standards.

> If, for example, you make a reservation on United Airlines (which outsources the hosting of its reservations database to the Galileo CRS/GDS) through the Internet travel agency Travelocity.com (which is a division of Sabre, and uses the Sabre CRS/GDS), Travelocity.com creates

---

1 It need not be an international flight, but we are restricting the example to those.
2 See Edward Hasbrouck, "What's in a Passenger Name Record (PNR)?" at: http://hasbrouck.org/articles/PNR.html.
3 Most airline bookings are made through travel agents and so PNRs will often contain other details concerning car hires, hotel rooms, companions, special requests etc.

a PNR in Sabre. Sabre sends a message derived from portions of the Sabre PNR data to Galileo, using the AIRIMP (or another bilaterally-agreed format). Galileo in turn uses the data in the AIRIMP message to create a PNR in United's Galileo "partition."

If a set of reservations includes flights on multiple airlines, each airline is sent the information pertaining to its flights. If information is added later by one of those airlines, it may or may not be transmitted back to the CRS/GDS in which the original reservation was made, and almost never will be sent to other airlines participating in the itinerary that are hosted in different CRS's/GDS's. So there can be many different PNR's, in different CRS's/GDS's, for the same set of reservations, none of them containing all the data included in all of the others.[4]

The relevance of this is that there is little control over the uses to which these private companies can put their data. They may make commitments about how they will use it and share it, but there is little effective oversight.[5]

In addition, as the US government's Secure Flight Program[6] (formerly CAPPS II) becomes operational, these PNRs will be accessed and fed into the Passenger and Aviation Security Screening Records (PASSR) database of the Transportation Security Agency (TSA), which is a division of the Department of Homeland Security (DHS). The information will be used by the US government (along with other information) to fill out passenger profiles, including "selectee" and "no-fly" watch lists, as well as to match passenger data with existing lists.[7] Although Secure Flight was expected to be operational in 2005, its full implementation was significantly delayed – partly for privacy-related reasons – until 2009, when

---

4   Hasbrouck, "What's in a Passenger Name Record (PNR)?", 3.

5   Recognizing these weaknesses, we have undertaken to provide a means by which the companies themselves, along with external oversight bodies, can query the state of accountability in a given organization and identify where shortcomings exist. The Surveillance Technology Accountability Assessment Tool (STAAT) in Chapter IX of this study allows those interested in exercising greater control over questions of data construction, data mining and data sharing a means for grounding their efforts to improve these and other areas of digital technology use. The application of this tool is available to any entity engaged in digital technology surveillance.

6   See http://www.tsa.gov/what_we_do/layers/secureflight/editorial_1716.shtm. CAPPS II (Computer Assisted Passenger Prescreening System) was to be the successor of CAPPS I, developed in 1997. Opposition to the proposed CAPPS II led to its "demise" and reconstitution as Secure Flight.

7   Security lists were first developed in 1990 (and were originally administered by the FBI) to keep an eye on people "determined to pose a direct threat to U.S. civil aviation", but they moved to center stage only after 9/11. Being on a "selectee" list will heighten the security that a person will be required to undergo; being on a "no fly" list will lead to a person's being prevented from flying. "No-fly" lists are also distributed to other agencies concerned with visas, border crossings and law enforcement. It is thought that well over 300,000 names are on the lists, though information is not readily available on either numbers or the criteria used to make determinations.

it began to be implemented in stages.[8] Until now, the airlines themselves have been charged with matching names to the existing lists (which have been drawn up using other data).[9]

There appears to be no legal barrier to the US government using PNR data for security purposes.[10] However, in the case of German citizens based in Europe who wish to fly to the US, the US does *not* have jurisdiction over them at that point and there may even be laws against some of that data being transmitted without authorization. Indeed, as we have already noted, the European Parliament has a directive that severely limits the circumstances under which such data may be shared and used.[11] After 9/11 an interim agreement between Europe and the US was reached regarding access to PNR data for security purposes. That agreement was subsequently determined to be incompatible with European law and work then proceeded on a new agreement that was supposed to be concluded by July 2007, when the sun set on an interim arrangement. Controversy continues, though temporary understandings have been in place, allowing EU–US traffic to continue.

The proposed agreement reduced the number of pieces of PNR data to which US authorities could get access to nineteen, though some of the reduction involved combining data that had otherwise been kept discrete. Data concerning ethnicity, however, could not be accessed. It was further proposed that the US could store the data "actively" for a period of seven years, with the possibility of "dormant storage" for a further eight years. Although this involved a significant extension of the storage period (from three years), it was argued that better safeguards had been put in place. Significantly, the July 2007 bombings in Glasgow and London prompted PNR data-gathering initiatives in Europe similar to those in the US.

However, the proposed agreement ran into trouble with the European Parliament, with an overwhelming majority of its members determining that it was "substantively flawed". The main objections were that: (a) the agreement on

---

8 "Secure Flight was implemented in two phases. The program initially assumed the watch list matching responsibility for passengers on domestic flights from aircraft operators beginning early 2009. In a second stage of implementation, begun in late 2009, the Secure Flight program assumed, from Customs and Border Protection and the international air carriers, the watch list matching function for passengers on international flights." See "TSA to Assume Watch List Vetting with Secure Flight Program" http://www.tsa.gov/press/releases/2008/1022.shtm. The program has now been fully implemented.

9 If a "no fly" match occurs, the airline agent is required to call a law enforcement officer to detain and question the passenger. In the case of a "selectee", the boarding pass will be marked and the person given additional screening by security.

10 49 U.S.C. § 44909 (c) (3). However, there may be more than "actual passenger" data in a PNR, and the statute does not require the data in advance.

11 Directive 95/46/EC of the European Parliament and of the Council of 24 October 1995 on the protection of individuals with regard to the processing of personal data and on the free movement of such data: ec.europa.eu/justice_home/fsj/privacy/docs/95-46-ce/dir1995-46_part1_en.pdf. This led, in 2000, to an EU/US agreement on "safe harbor" privacy principles: http://www.epic.org/privacy/intl/EP_SH_resolution_0700.html.

the collection, use and storage of PNR data was constituted simply by the non-binding assurances contained in a letter (that could be unilaterally changed); (b) there were no assurances that the data would be used only for counter-terrorism (though allowance was made for its use by the US Government for "unspecified additional purposes"); (c) in exceptional cases, information on travelers' ethnicity, political opinions or sexual orientation could be accessed; (d) that the reduction of fields was "largely cosmetic due to the merging of data fields instead of actual deletion"; and (e) retention of data under the proposed agreement was inordinate and raised the possibility of massive profiling. At the same time, the Parliament raised concerns about the proposed European data-gathering initiative.[12]

Even so, an agreement was reached with the European Union on July 23, 2007,[13] followed by a Letter (July 26) explaining how the US Department of Homeland Security (DHS) intended to collect, use and store the data it gained.[14] A DHS Report released in December 2008 came to an irenic conclusion about DHS compliance with the Agreement. However, it was an internal report including no EU representatives and, according to some reviewers, had failed to be adequately responsive to requests by travelers to see data (or all the data) held concerning them.[15]

The PNR controversy raises a number of important ethical questions, some specific and some general. The most general question relevant to the focus of this study is whether it is possible to develop standards for personal data collection, use and management that can be accepted by all the parties. Although we are concerned fairly specifically here with the EU and the US, the question can be cast to range over liberal democratic polities generally. More specifically, there are issues raised by the PNR controversy narrowly but which are also transferable to other contexts in which data are gathered. Here is a sample:

- Ever since "selectee" and "no-fly" watch lists have been compiled, errors have occurred and innocent passengers have been inconvenienced, sometimes quite seriously. It has not proven easy to rectify such errors.

---

12   However, the European Commission introduced such a plan – very similar to that which was so roundly criticized in the European Parliament – on November 6, 2007.

13   See: *Agreement Between the United States of America and the European Union on the Processing and Transfer of Passenger Name Record (PNR) Data by Air Carriers to the United States Department of Homeland Security (DHS) (2007 PNR Agreement)*, http://www.dhs.gov/xlibrary/assets/pnr-2007agreement-usversion.pdf.

14   Appended to *A Report Concerning Passenger Name Record Information Derived from Flights between the U.S. and the European Union*, http://www.dhs.gov/xlibrary/assets/privacy/privacy_pnr_report_20081218.pdf.

15   See *EDRI-gram* January 14, 2009, http://www.edri.org/edri-gram/number7.1. By June, 2010, provisional agreement appeared to have been reached, pending further negotiations. However, as of June 30, 2011, a further draft agreement was criticized for many of the same reasons as previously – not being limited to terrorism and serious crime, unnecessarily long data retention, lack of judicial redress for data subjects and an absence of any guarantees of independent oversight. See "EU-US PNR Agreement Found Incompatible with Human Rights", *EDRI-gram*, 9, no. 3 (June 29, 2011), available at: http://www.edri.org/edrigram/number9.13.

- Especially from the side of the EU, there has been a concern about personal data being collected for one reason – to combat terrorism – and then being used or being available to be used for other reasons (say, tax evasion or money laundering). Apart from such data being used for purposes to which consent has not been given, there are serious issues of disproportionality in collecting personal data for less serious social concerns.

- There is very little transparency with national security data collection. For example, it is not known or disclosed how many people are on watch lists. There is secrecy about the numbers of people on watch lists, or whether the personal data of some citizens is as likely to be surveilled as that of others.

- The lack of transparency extends to information about who is responsible for the compilation, protection and correction of watch lists.

- The lack of transparency further extends to the criteria used to compile watch lists and to disclosures concerning their effectiveness. For example, is Secure Flight really needed or will it simply add to the amount of information that government may amass about individuals? Transparency is an important liberal democratic value, and though it is recognized that security interests may sometimes require secrecy of data and strategies, the limits to such secrecy ought to be determined in the light of public debate.[16]

- Although transparency is typically a necessary condition for accountability it is not sufficient. So what oversight and accountability mechanisms are in place to ensure regulatory and ethical compliance?

Behind these more specific questions about the collection of PNR data there stand some more general ethical questions. For example:

- What privacy, if any, do we have a right to, and why? What are the limits to such a right?

- What security do we have a right to, and how should it best (ethically and practically) be enabled/protected?

- What is the appropriate role of government in ensuring security and what constraints should be placed on its security activities?

- To what extent may one government legitimately make demands of another government or on those under the jurisdiction of another?

---

16 These issues of practical policy implementation have led us to consider recommending that an internal body be developed within law enforcement and intelligence organizations that would be responsible for aiding surveillance practitioners in sorting out such problems. The creation of Techno-ethics Boards, discussed in Chapter IX, offers one means to build capacity within government agencies engaged in surveillance operations of this and other types (see Peter Mameli, "Tracking the Beast: Techno-Ethics Boards and Government Surveillance Programs", *Critical Issues in Justice and Politics* 1, no. 1 (2008): 31–56).

These are large questions – perhaps too large to be adequately resolved within the framework of the present study. Yet they cannot be wholly sidestepped. We will take some steps toward addressing them in later chapters.

(B) The Terrorist Finance Tracking Program and SWIFT Controversy

The events related to this second controversy came to light with a *New York Times* article on June 23, 2006, in which it was revealed that not long after 9/11 the CIA, through the US Treasury Department, secretly put (via administrative subpoena[17]) pressure on a Belgian cooperative – SWIFT – that routes over 11 million international financial transactions per day (amounting to US$6 trillion) to give it access to its records.[18] The US Government claimed that the emergency powers granted by Congress soon after 9/11 allowed it to do so and that it was not prevented from doing so by "American laws restricting government access to private financial records because the cooperative was considered a messaging service, not a bank or financial institution."[19]

Exactly what was looked at is not known, though US authorities have naturally argued that the data reviewed were limited and that they focused on terrorism, not tax fraud or drug trafficking. It appears that the primary tool used on the subpoenaed data was "link analysis", whereby those who had suspected ties then had all wired financial transfers tracked in which they were involved. It was claimed that the analyses had yielded positive results (though this has been disputed).[20]

When the US actions were made public (initially by a whistle blower), the Belgian Government immediately protested and a European Parliament resolution (July 7, 2006) alleged that "the SWIFT transfers were undertaken without regard to legal process . . . and . . . without any legal basis or authority." Although the

---

17   Unlike other subpoenas, administrative subpoenas do not have to be reviewed by judges or juries. They are issued under the International Emergency Economic Powers Act 1977. For discussion, see Charles Doyle, *Administrative Subpoenas and National Security Letters in Criminal and Foreign Intelligence Investigations* (Congressional Research Service, 2005), http://www.fas.org/sgp/crs/natsec/RL32880.pdf.

18   Eric Lichtblau and James Risen, "Bank Data is Sifted by U.S. in Secret to Block Terror," *The New York Times*, June 23, 2006, A1. Other articles appeared in the *Wall Street Journal* and *Los Angeles Times* on the same day. SWIFT is an acronym for the Society for Worldwide Interbank Financial Telecommunication: "SWIFT is the industry-owned co-operative supplying secure, standardised messaging services and interface software to nearly 8,100 financial institutions in 207 countries and territories." It was founded in 1973. http://www.swift.com/index.cfm?item_id=43232.

19   Stuart Levey, Under Secretary, Terrorism and Financial Intelligence, US Treasury. This was backed up by reference to *US v. Miller*, 425 US 435 (1976).

20   The claim is that it was helpful in the tracking of Hambali, the Indonesian leader of the al-Qaeda-related terrorist organization, Jemaah Islamiyah. Other suggestions about its usefulness were reported in the original *New York Times* and *Wall Street Journal* articles.

Belgian Privacy Protection Commission sympathized with the US's concern about terrorism and security, it argued that the requests were not focused on individuals suspected of terrorist activities and involved the transfer of massive amounts of data. Moreover, SWIFT was not a mere "messenger" but a "controller" in the processing of personal data. It concluded that European law concerning personal data was more stringent than US law with respect to "the principle of proportionality, the limited retention period, the principle of transparency, the requirement for independent control and an adequate protection level."[21] SWIFT had, furthermore, failed to get assurances that were required under European law concerning data of the kind involved.[22] Talks subsequently commenced to try to work out a common framework for the sharing of data.

US authorities argued that disclosure of the SWIFT actions had been very damaging to the fight against terrorism. In addition there was a back story about pressure that was placed on the *New York Times* to refrain from publishing the results of its journalistic investigation.

Here, too, a whole series of questions emerged, some specific and others more general. The specific questions focused on:

- the degree of specificity that desired disclosures of private financial information ought to have;
- whether those whose financial transactions were disclosed to US authorities ought to have been informed;
- whether SWIFT ought to have informed European authorities about its actions;
- whether the differences between European law and US law were significant and, if so, why;
- whether the privacy invasions had, in fact, yielded any information of significance, assuming that it would have been of justificatory value;
- whether a measure that might have been justified in emergency terms could still be justified five years later (since the gathering of such data had been ongoing);
- what controls US authorities placed on the program and the data it received, and whether those controls were enforced;

---

21 "Summary of the Opinion on the Transfer of Personal Data by SCRL SWIFT Following the UST (OFAC) Subpoenas", http://www.privacycommission.be/communiqu%E9s/summary_opinion_Swift_%2028_09_2006.pdf. A non-official translation of the whole opinion can be found at: http://www.privacycommission.be/communiqu%C3%A9s/opinion_37_2006.pdf. See also Dan Bilefsky, "Data Transfer Broke Rules, Report Says", *The New York Times*, September 28, 2006.

22 Embarrassed, SWIFT tried to wriggle out of the rebuke by claiming that because it had offices in the US it was required to obey the subpoenas.

- whether the newspapers that published the articles revealing the program were justified in doing so (in the face of US Administration opposition); and

- whether the whistleblower who disclosed what was going on was justified in doing so.[23]

No doubt there are other questions. As with the PNR data controversy, the SWIFT one generated similar broad questions concerning the scope of privacy, what constitutes private data, what kinds of actions compromise privacy, the ethical demands that appeals to security can make, issues of efficacy and probability and the trade-off between security and privacy.

In the follow up to the SWIFT controversy there were, as in the case of PNR data, further negotiations between the EU and the US regarding European financial transactions operated through SWIFT, with an agreement reached on June 28–29, 2007.[24] The US committed itself to using SWIFT data exclusively for counterterrorism purposes and to retaining the data for no longer than five years. For its part, SWIFT was to observe privacy requirements according to EU principles promulgated in 2000. Banks using SWIFT were to inform their customers about any transfers of data to US authorities. Moreover, the EU gained a right to inspect US investigators' use of European data, given that US laws regarding the use of data are not as stringent as those of the EU.

But even these concessions have not stilled the controversy and there has been continuing debate within the EU over their adequacy. An agreement signed on November 30, 2009, was possible only because of a politically necessary German abstention.[25]

(C) The Controversy over National Identity (ID) Cards[26]

One might infer, from an examination of the PNR and SWIFT debates, that the European Union has a much stronger and better developed concern for privacy than the US. That inference would seem to be justified. However,

---

23   As with the PNR, we believe that by forcing deeper consideration of the accountability questions at hand prior to action being taken the utilization of both STAAT and Techno-ethics Boards could aid in mitigating abuses in the areas that we noted when discussing the SWIFT case.

24   Reported in *EDRI-gram* (biweekly newsletter about digital civil rights in Europe), Number 5.13, 4 July 2007. See also: http://www.statewatch.org/news/2007/jul/eu-usa-pnr-agreement-2007.pdf.

25   See text of the Agreement between the European Union and the United States of America on the Processing and Transfer of Financial Messaging Data from the European Union to the United States for the Purposes of the Terrorist Finance Tracking Program (30.10.2009), at: http://eur-lex.europa/LexUriServ/LexUriServ.do?uri=OJ:L:2010:008:00 10:0016:EN:PDF. For further follow-up see *EDRI-gram* Newsletter 8, 3 (Feb 10), 2010, available at: http://www.edri. org/edrigram/number8.3. Since then, the European Parliament has (2/11/2010) rejected the latest agreement (http:// www.privacyinternational.org/article.shtml?cmd[347]=x-347-565959) and the discussions continue.

26   For some of the early research on this section, we are grateful to Vincenzo Sainato.

the situation becomes rather more complicated when we shift our focus to a different controversy – that concerning the issuing of National Identity (ID) cards. Such is the strength of feeling against them in the US that there is at best a perfunctory discussion about the use of ID cards – it is, by and large, a political non-starter.[27] Australians are also largely opposed to ID cards. The Labor government of Bob Hawke attempted to introduce the Australia Card in the late 1980s but abandoned the attempt in 1987 (largely as a result of concerns about the accuracy and security of data). However, most countries within the EU have mandated ID cards for years and make considerable use of them for access to a variety of government services as well as for security measures. India is set to introduce an ID card for similar reasons. Needless to say, aside from privacy concerns, there are prodigious logistical and other problems in a large developing country such as India.

In this context, it is worth tracing some of the recent contours of the ID card controversy in the United Kingdom (UK) – a controversy that puts it at some odds with its fellow European Unionists. Some ten European countries have compulsory ID cards, another ten have voluntary ones while four, including the UK, as yet have none.

Though mooted in 2002, the UK Identity Cards Bill was first presented to Parliament in 2004. It contained a number of components, one of which was the development of a National Identity Card. The card was supported as a "public interest" measure, where the public interest was understood to encompass "national security", "the prevention and detection of crime", "the enforcement of immigration controls", "the enforcement of prohibitions on unauthorized working or employment" and the securing of "efficient and effective provision of public services". In later discussions, considerable weight was given to its supposed benefits in countering identity theft. The card was not required to be carried at all times.

Following a general election in early May 2005, a revised Bill was presented on May 25, 2005, to a Labour government with a reduced majority.[28] It gained narrow approval in the House of Commons in October but criticism in the House of Lords led to significant amendments in 2006. The amendments were

---

27 Although some have argued – at least in the context of health care, that some system of patient ID numbers would be more protective of privacy (as well as more efficient and less mistake-prone) than the present system for matching health data, there is strong opposition even to this. For the argument in favor of such see the RAND study, Richard Hillestad, James H. Bigelow, Basit Chaudhry, Paul Dreyer, Michael D. Greenberg, Robin C. Meili, M. Susan Ridgely, Jeff Rothenberg, Roger Taylor, *Identity Crisis: An Examination of the Costs and Benefits of a Unique Patient Identifier for the U.S. Health Care System* (Santa Monica, CA: Rand, 2008), available at: http://www.rand.org/content/dam/rand/pubs/monographs/2008/RAND_MG753.pdf. In the UK, NHS members already have an identifying number which entitles them to a European Health Insurance Card.

28 The Bill is available at: http://www.publications.parliament.uk/pa/cm200506/cmbills/009/2006009.htm.

not passed and the Bill shuttled back and forth between the House of Lords and House of Commons. After five renditions the Bill was finally passed by both houses in March 2006. The agreement reached made the card voluntary (provided a passport was held) and delayed its implementation, though 51 types of individual data including fingerprints, iris scans and face scans would still be entered into a National Identity Register (NIR), one of the Bill's other components. The major parties declared that it would be an election issue in 2010, with the Labour Party indicating that, if it won, it would make the card mandatory. The new Conservative leader, David Cameron, indicated his opposition to the card on principle. The Conservatives now govern in a coalition with the Liberal Party and, for a time, the ID card issue is dead.

In consequence, the cards have not been introduced (though some were slated to be issued in 2009), and if they had been it would have taken several years for most people to have them (or an upgraded passport). As it is, practical difficulties plagued both the development of the NIR and the introduction of the cards, and if in the future there is any end product it may not exactly match the legislation. The debate about the cards was particularly vigorous, some opposing the cards altogether and others focusing on particulars associated with the UK card. Major concerns included the following:

- that the cards would be no more (or not significantly more) effective than measures already in place to achieve what they were intended to achieve;
- the huge cost involved in introducing them – a cost for the government as well as for individuals;
- that the card would provide a pretext for discrimination against minorities, a problem that had arisen in other European countries that have identity cards;
- that, as with all governmental data gathering initiatives, government misuse of data would increase its control of individuals – such initiatives were viewed as further encroachments of the so-called surveillance society[29]; and
- the possible vulnerability of data either gathered for the NIR or inscribed on cards. Several notorious cases in which data have been lost or stolen have shaken confidence that personal data will be secure. Although it was argued that a National ID Card would help to counteract rising identity theft, it was also argued that a national register or card would, in fact, make it easier by providing a "one stop" opportunity for the theft of salient data.

---

29 Once again, the inescapable need for useful accountability mechanisms comes to the fore of the discussion. Although the existence of the "Surveillance Society" means different things to different people, what seems to be generally accepted is that the means for retaining control of its growth is accomplished through increasing transparency and monitoring of actions in a better lit environment. We believe that the utilization of tools such as STAAT and internal oversight bodies such as Techno-ethics Boards could satisfy part of this requirement.

What the three foregoing cases illustrate is the great complexity involved in developing appropriate standards for security and privacy both between and within liberal democratic societies. They constitute the practical challenge of the present study.

VI. Securitization Technologies

We noted in Chapter III that the ratcheting up of security has created a number of problems for important liberal democratic values – in relation to security itself as well as with respect to liberty, autonomy, privacy, identity and dignity.

Here our focus will be on various securitization technologies concerned with surveillance, data mining and matching/integration, and profiling. We provide descriptions of some of the main technologies in use, indicating briefly how they impact on and challenge the values identified in Chapter III (and articulated at greater length in Chapter VIII). Our concern will not be to determine the actual and potential contribution of these technologies to security. Accordingly, this chapter should not be understood as even implicitly offering an all-things-considered evaluation of the securitization technologies described.

(A) Electronic Surveillance[1]

Surveillance technology takes many forms. Whereas some are familiar, others pass unnoticed. Examples of both include: closed circuit television (CCTV), X-ray and similar devices at airports, thermal sensors, temperature screening (for SARS), keyloggers, wiretaps, bugs, parabolic microphones, Radio Frequency Identification Devices (RFID) and Global Positioning Systems (GPS).[2,3] Why should we worry about them and in what ways do they compromise, or threaten to compromise, privacy, liberty and the like?

In the US, the use of electronic surveillance to enhance security has a long history that began soon after the invention of the telegraph in 1844. As newer technology was invented it was co-opted in the name of security. These technologies have included the telephone and computers as well as the many and multiplying electronic encroachments on public space.

---

1   For background on surveillance and its theory, See David Lyon, *Surveillance Studies: An Overview* (Cambridge, UK: Polity Press, 2007).

2   It is not possible to cover all these technologies and their ethical implications in a single chapter. For more information see, for example, M.G. Michael, Sarah Jean Fusco, and Katina Michael, "A Research Note on Ethics in the Emerging Age of Überveillance", *Computer Communications* 31 (2008): 1192–99. Also, see Roger Clarke, "Person-Location and Person-Tracking: Technologies, Risks and Policy Implications", *Information Technology & People* 14, no. 2 (Summer 2001): 206–31; Christopher S. Milligan, "Facial Recognition Technology, Video Surveillance, and Privacy", *Southern California Interdisciplinary Law Journal* 9 (2000): 295–334.

3   There is always new technology being developed that can be pressed into action. For example, see H. Schneider, H. C. Liu, S. Winnerl, O. Drachenko, M. Helm, and J. Faist, "Room-temperature Midinfrared Two-photon Photodetector", *Applied Physics Letters* 93, no. 101114 (2008): 1–3.

As far as government surveillance is concerned, the checks provided by the Fourth Amendment have been of critical historical importance, though the Fourth Amendment's value has become marginalized in the face of increasing non-governmental surveillance and, even in those cases, because of problematic re-drawings of the public–private distinction and persisting (legal) doubts about the applicability of the Fourth Amendment to public space.

Recent years have seen the development of a range of strategies encompassed (more or less) by the general term "electronic surveillance". Included among these have been, most ubiquitously, closed circuit television (CCTV) cameras, more potent and prevalent in the UK than in the US, though increasingly used in the US in a more coordinated fashion.[4] Such electronic surveillance may take many other forms. We have already noted the use of X-ray-type devices at airports that penetrate clothing to the skin, and thermal sensors that can be used to detect activity in buildings (such as movement and marijuana growth). To these we might add wiretaps,[5] bugs[6] and parabolic microphones.[7] Moreover, so far as networked computers are concerned, electronic surveillance has taken a number of increasingly intrusive and sophisticated forms. There are, for example, programs developed by the FBI for scanning email traffic through particular servers. One such program, originally named Carnivore, with a later version renamed as DCS 1000, had both trap and trace[8] and full access capabilities.[9] The latest version of this is the Communications Assistance for Law Enforcement Act (CALEA), which the FBI is using "as a virtual blank check to force the communications industry to build surveillance capabilities . . . into every modern means of communication. This includes cellular and digital communications technology never even contemplated when CALEA was drafted in the early 1990s."[10] The latter are much more intrusive than the former. There are also keylogging devices that can record every keystroke made by an individual. However, data on FBI and DHS email surveillance are not easy to come by.

---

4   It has been estimated that there are several thousand CCTV cameras in Manhattan public spaces. For articles, see Anon., "A History of Surveillance in New York City", available at: http://www.notbored.org/nyc-history.html; Kareem Faheem, "Surveillance Will Expand To Midtown, Mayor Says", *The New York Times*, October 4, 2009, available at: http://www.nytimes.com/2009/10/05/nyregion/05security.html; and Al Baker, "Police Seek a Second Zone of High Security in the City", *The New York Times*, March 31, 2009, available at: http://www.nytimes.com/2009/04/01/nyregion/01kelly.html.
5   For information, see the Electronic Information Privacy Center (EPIC) links: http://www.epic.org/privacy/wiretap/.
6   For general information, see http://en.wikipedia.org/wiki/Covert_listening_device.
7   See e.g. http://www.espionageinfo.com/Nt-Pa/Parabolic-Microphones.html.
8   See http://www.cdt.org/security/000404amending.shtml.
9   See the EPIC links at http://www.epic.org/privacy/carnivore/foia_documents.html. Note that use of Carnivore was abandoned in 2003.
10   Wayne Madsen, "FBI's Communications Surveillance Capabilities Widen", *Computer Fraud & Security*, no. 10 (October 2000): 16–17.

We will briefly outline several of these electronic surveillance strategies along with the ethical problems they raise. As noted previously, US policy is officially governed primarily by two documents: the Foreign Intelligence Surveillance Act of 1978 (FISA)[11] and the Electronic Communications Privacy Act of 1986 (ECPA).[12] They have been supplemented and modified by a number of other acts, most notably the Uniting and Strengthening America by Providing Appropriate Tools Required to Intercept and Obstruct Terrorism Act of 2001 (USA PATRIOT Act, as revised),[13] the Protect America Act of 2007 and the FISA Amendment Act of 2008.

Video surveillance[14]

CCTV camera surveillance predated the events of 9/11 by well over twenty years; their use is well-established. However, the growing and accelerating ubiquity of surveillance cameras, particularly in large urban areas, has created the theoretical possibility that almost all our daily movements in public space can now be reconstructed into a continuous visual narrative.[15] There are, of course, various practical and other impediments to this theoretical possibility. For one thing, it would be hugely expensive to have continuous human monitoring of all such cameras. What is feasible is that the footage of all cameras be available after some particular event. For another thing, there are practical limits on the extent of coverage, for example, in rural or semi-rural areas, and the availability of unsurveilled areas gives rise to the possibility of displacement. On the other hand, many current practical problems in densely populated urban areas (e.g. Manhattan), such as lack of coordination, integration and (often) preservation, look to be relatively easy to overcome. The UK is much closer to constructing a coordinated CCTV network, as evidenced by follow-up to the 7/7 and later bombings. IRA terrorism preceded the jihadist variety.

The everyday security concerns that initially provided public support for the use of surveillance cameras have been taken by authorities, both private and public, as justification for something of a *carte blanche* (given the lesser protections that exist for privacy in public) for their installation in many public places. Aided

---

11　See http://www.fas.org/irp/agency/doj/fisa/. FISA's main purpose is to regulate the surveillance of those who are believed to be foreign agents.

12　See §§ 2510, 2511 http://www.law.cornell.edu/uscode/html/uscode18/usc_sup_01_18.html. ECPA's main purpose is to regulate domestic surveillance.

13　See http://thomas.loc.gov/cgi-bin/bdquery/z?d107:h.r.03162. Also see http://thomas.loc.gov/cgi-bin/cpquery/R?cp109:FLD010:@1(hr333) and http://thomas.loc.gov/cgi-bin/bdquery/z?d110:s.01927:.

14　For a survey of the latest in video surveillance see Niels Haering, Péter L. Venetianer, and Alan Lipton, "The Evolution Of Video Surveillance: An Overview", *Machine Vision and Applications* 19 (2008):279–90.

15　A city council is likely to be seen as "out of step" if it does not follow the trend. We can also add to CCTV various other "tracking" possibilities, from things such as EZ-Pass to cell phones (that now function as global positioning systems).

by the myth that what happens in public is public, the proliferation of such cameras now raises possibilities similar to those created by data mining on the internet: the development of narratives rather than simple profiles.

We can accept that what we do in public may not have as great a claim to privacy as what we do in private, but even in public we ought to have some control over personal data. For example, we should not have to conduct every conversation in public *sotto voce* – or wait until we have found some private space. The self-censoring effect of denying privacy in public would be considerable. Our freedom is not constituted simply by the absence of constraints but also by a sense of security in what we do. Should we then limit the installation of cameras and/or otherwise constrain their use?

To the extent that a CCTV unit often constitutes an unobserved observer, there is additional reason to be cautious about it, for in those cases we are not given a fair opportunity to structure our behavior/self-presentation in the knowledge that the unit is present. It does not function like the uniformed police officer. Should its use, therefore, always be accompanied by a sign to the effect that it is present?[16] In other words, should the primary use of CCTV be deterrent even as it also protects privacy? Should there also be some indication as to whether a CCTV camera is controlled by an operator who can swivel, zoom in, and focus? Should there be some contact information in the event that a person wishes to inquire about the gathered data's use, retention, security etc.? Should there be rules about data use, retention and security independent of those who might wish to inquire about such matters? The questions go on.

One problem with CCTV cameras concerns simple observability and the threat to privacy that may be involved either with live operators or later reviews of the tapes. Even our awareness of a camera's presence can be unsettling if we reflect that it may be recording and making a permanent record of what we think of as fleeting. In such cases, we cannot presume on our normal ability to blend anonymously into the situational landscape. Cameras challenge our presumption of anonymity. As Alan Westin puts it:

> [A]nonymity [as a form of privacy] occurs when the individual is in public spaces or performing public acts but still seeks, and finds, freedom from identification and surveillance. He may be riding a subway, attending a ball game, or walking the streets; he is among people and knows that he is being observed; but unless he is a well-known celebrity, he does not expect to be personally identified and held to the rules of behavior and role that would operate if he were known to those observing him. In

---

16   This is suggested by Andrew von Hirsch, "The Ethics of Public Television Surveillance", in Andrew von Hirsch, David Garland, and Alison Wakefield (eds.), *Ethical and Social Perspectives on Situational Crime Prevention* (Oxford: Hart Publishing, 2000), 68.

this state the individual is able to merge into the "situational landscape." Knowledge or fears that one is under systematic observation in public places destroys the sense of relaxation and freedom that men [and women] seek in open spaces and public arenas.[17]

The point reaches a bit deeper. Unlike targeted searches that focus on specific items, CCTV surveillance functions more like a dragnet. It makes no distinction between those items that might be of interest, say, to law enforcement, and other items that are and ought to be regarded as private. It records them all. Daniel Solove links this electronic promiscuity with old discussions concerning general warrants and writs of assistance – practices to which the framers of the US Constitution were deeply opposed because they were undiscriminating. He quotes from Patrick Henry's opposition to writs of assistance: "They may, unless the general government be restrained by a bill of rights, or some similar restrictions, go into your cellars and rooms, and search, and ransack, and measure, everything you eat, drink, and wear. They ought to be restrained within proper bounds."[18] The point is simply that because CCTV cameras record everything that occurs within their range, and therefore fail to "filter out" matters that ought to be considered private, their use imposes a significant moral burden on those who install them and, potentially, a different burden on those who have to live under their eye.

However, it is not simply a matter of our observability and subsequent capture by camera that is worrisome. Also of concern is the use to which the data are put. If, for example, what is captured is preserved in some large database (along with information gleaned from other public sources), or if the captured images are used as part of some film compilation (say, a kind of "Candid Camera"), we would also have reason to be deeply disturbed. What has been set up for one purpose may, absent controls, be used for other purposes. The principle of contextual integrity (to which we will return) will have been violated. No doubt some of those other purposes may be relatively innocent, but unless we can exercise some control over them, they may not be. In other words, we have not only an issue of privacy but also of confidentiality.

And so the main concern of CCTV's critics has been to develop adequate controls over what is gathered about us in public space. One important aspect of this control might include identification of the controller of the CCTV camera:

> Being able to identify who is watching us is crucial if we are to be able to make decisions about how to adjust our behavior (or not) in the light of such observation . . . Knowing that we are being watched by

---

17   Alan F. Westin, *Privacy and Freedom* (New York: Atheneum, 1967), 31.
18   Quoted in Daniel J. Solove, "Restructuring Electronic Surveillance Law", *George Washington Law Review* 72 (2004): 1706.

a camera is not the same as knowing the identity of who is watching us. All that we know is that we are being watched, but it is impossible for us to know why or by whom. This is the reason that we draw a distinction between being watched by a visible police officer and a CCTV camera mounted on the side of the building. Seeing, identifying, and attempting to understand the motives of whoever is watching us is an essential precursor to deciding how we feel about being observed, and to deciding on how to respond to such observation.[19]

But identification of the observer is only one step in the process of retaining some control over one's public self. More is needed if we are to ensure adequate recognition of privacy. We need to know in detail the purposes that the cameras are intended to serve and we also need to assess the weight of these purposes. That will involve some assessment of the stakes, the risks (including probabilities) and the likely effectiveness of CCTV measures. We need, in other words, to know whether the loss of privacy effected by CCTV cameras (and other surveillance technologies) is morally outweighed by gains in security (and/or other socially valued outcomes for which they are intended). The latter question can be complicated by the potential that there is for public misperception – on the one hand, an underestimation of the intrusiveness of CCTV cameras and, on the other hand, an overestimation of the risks of, say, terrorism. For many of us, the ubiquity of CCTV cameras has dulled us to what they may be recording. At the same time, our fears of terrorism have been exploited by those for whom the presence of additional CCTV cameras (*inter alia*) is desired. We also need to take account of the fact that whereas the threat of terrorism is said to be "to America" or "to Australia", the burden of CCTV tends to fall on people unequally.

Assuming that we have successfully defended particular uses of CCTV, we then need to address several other questions at whose existence we have already hinted. Some concern the storage and dissemination of information: How timely? How safely? For how long? Who has access? Another set of questions relates to the issues of implementation and oversight: Who ensures that answers to the previous questions are implemented and adhered to?

Useful, though obviously not decisive, is the American Bar Association's *Standards for Criminal Justice: Electronic Surveillance, B: Technologically-Assisted Physical Surveillance.*[20] What is required is some assurance that these standards will be observed, that they are worth more than the paper on which they are written. Some, such as Benjamin Goold, doubt whether an oversight agency could provide the requisite assurance, given the huge proliferation of

---

19   Benjamin Goold, "Privacy Rights and Public Spaces: CCTV and the Problem of the 'Unobservable Observer'", *Criminal Justice Ethics* 21, no. 1 (2002): 24.
20   Third ed. (Washington, D.C.: ABA 1999). See http://www.abanet.org/crimjust/standards/electronicb.pdf.

CCTV cameras. He thinks that the kind of spot checks that an oversight agency is likely to provide (given the funding that could be expected) would not be sufficient to assure us that significant abuses were not occurring.[21] Goold's own solution takes the form of an appeal to Bentham's Panopticon[22]:

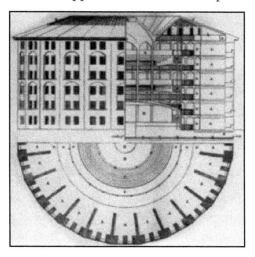

As Bentham himself puts it:

> The final application of the inspection principle was of the whole of the prison by the whole of the outside world. The central tower would enable judges and magistrates to inspect the prison quickly and safely . . . The design of the building would also enable any member of the public safely to enter the prison and to view every prisoner in it: "I take it for granted, as a matter of course, that . . . the doors of these establishments will be, as, without very special reasons to the contrary, the doors of all public establishments ought to be, thrown wide open to the body of the curious at large – the great open committee of the tribunal of the world.[23]

Taking his cue from Bentham, Goold wants to argue that all CCTV scans should be publicly available – available to all, so that those who are responsible for them can be scrutinized at any time.

---

21 Benjamin Goold, "Open to All? Regulating Open Street CCTV", *Criminal Justice Ethics* 25, no. 1 (2006): 11–12.
22 Bentham spelled out his views in an eponymous series of letters written in 1787, though he also referred to it elsewhere in his writings (see http://www.cartome.org/panopticon2.htm). See Jeremy Bentham, *The Panopticon Writings*, ed. Miran Bozovic (London: Verso, 1995). Most of the contemporary discussion takes as its point of departure Michel Foucault's discussion of Bentham in *Discipline & Punish: The Birth of the Prison*, trans. Alan Sheridan (NY: Vintage Books 1977), 195–228.
23 Jeremy Bentham, *The Works of Jeremy Bentham*, ed. John Bowring (London: W. Tait, 1838–43), vol. 4, 46.

We are not so sanguine about Goold's solution, even though we are also troubled by the frequent inadequacies of oversight agencies. There is just too much out there, and the likelihood that improper use of CCTV data will go undetected or unpenalized is substantial. Moreover, as we have learned with the doctrine of *caveat emptor*, we cannot presume that people in general will have the energy, inclination or ability to police such matters. The mere capacity to review material, though important, is not enough. Nor can we presume that complaints will be appropriately addressed any more than we can presume that oversight mechanisms will work effectively. Moreover, there is a danger that the availability of such materials could provide yet another resource for those whose perverted tastes would review, rework and distribute materials in such a way as to constitute an unacceptable invasion of privacy. True, some technological safeguards might be provided (for example, barriers on cut, paste and print options), but even these would not be foolproof. At best − and maybe it is the best − we can hope that the possibility of misuse being uncovered because of a policy of transparency might operate to deter those who would otherwise be inclined to misuse such data. As in other cases, however, the effectiveness of a policy of deterrence will depend significantly on perceptions of the likelihood of being caught and, if so, the actual penalties for misuse.[24]

To some extent, Goold's solution seems to move in exactly the wrong direction. We do wish to maintain some measure of privacy in public and surveillance technology threatens that. Making such information available to all exacerbates the problem by enabling whatever private acts took place in public to be communicated even more widely than might have been presumed when they took place. The values that informed confidentiality as well as privacy − the values of contextual integrity as well as agency − would be compromised.

The next issue we need consider is the quality of the technology itself and our reliance on its apparent infallibility.[25] In an attempt to examine the claims of facial recognition software using CCTV footage, James Meek, a journalist from the *Guardian*,[26] had his mugshot taken and then challenged the CCTV system on the streets of the east London borough of Newham to identify him. However, the software used, FaceIt, failed to recognize him. Although official results are secret, the system has, according to the Newham police, never recognized a person from its database of faces. The value of the system is apparently in

---

24 To this end, we think it is important that those engaged in surveillance operations know that they are, in fact, subject to reviews of ongoing accountability. The implementation of performance management systems, audits, program evaluations, inspections and the use of Techno-ethics Boards to address emerging concerns will put practitioners on notice that transparency is valued and, more importantly, actively pursued.

25 See Peter Kovesi, "Video Surveillance is Useless", Presentation at the 18th International Symposium of the Australia and New Zealand Forensic Society, April 2–7, 2006, Fremantle Western Australia. Also Peter Kovesi, "Video Surveillance: Legally Blind", presentation at DICTA 2009, Digital Image Computing: Techniques and Applications, December 1–3, 2009, Melbourne, Australia, http://dicta2009.vu.edu.au/, viewed December 31, 2009.

26 James Meek, "Robo Cop", *The Guardian*, 13/06/2002.

its deterrence effect, though even this is disputed. Indeed, according to the article that Meek wrote in Tampa, Florida, fourteen false positives and no true positives were recorded on one day. If this result is typical, perhaps we need not worry about any imminent actual infringement upon our privacy. Maybe we should be more concerned about government agencies spending enormous sums of money on systems that do not work! We will return to the issue of the quality of technological systems later in this study.

Even if the quality of the technology of video surveillance improves, there are some practical difficulties with serious consequences. The practical difficulties are volume and human error. The sheer volume of stored video information is overwhelming. Human evaluation capability is simply not up to the task of viewing all that information. The other problem, human error, applies to both stored and real-time video monitoring. According to the US National Institute of Justice, "Monitoring video screens is both boring and mesmerizing."[27] Smart Surveillance is being proposed as a solution to these problems.[28] Smart surveillance, of which IBM's S3[29] is but an example, offers the technological capability of providing real-time alerts (such as user-defined, generic, class specific, behavioral and high-value video capture), automatic forensic video retrieval and situation awareness. Although the current state of this technology faces challenges (both technical and evaluative), should these difficulties be resolved significant implications present themselves. The first is that these systems need to be able to prove their reliability by having few or no false positives. Another is the unprecedented challenge to privacy posed by the use of this technology to enhance privacy! The point is not that the challenge could not be met, but that it would be met only if its use could be adequately overseen, something that already constitutes a major issue.

Scanning devices[30]

Along with watch lists, there has been increased scrutiny not only of luggage but also of persons. Following the Richard Reid incident, shoes must now be

---

27   Mary W. Green, *The Appropriate and Effective Use of Security Technologies in U.S. Schools, A Guide for Schools and Law Enforcement Agencies*, Sandia National Laboratories, September 1999, NCJ 178265.

28   Arun Hampapur, Lisa Brown, Jonathan Connell, Sharat Pankanti, Andrew Senior, and Yingli Tian, "Smart Surveillance: Applications, Technologies and Implications", available at: http://domino.research.ibm.com/comm./research_projects.nsf/pages/s3.pubs.html/$FILE$/PCM03.pdf.

29   See Ying-li Tian, Lisa Brown, Arun Hampapur, Max Lu, Andrew Senior, and Chiao-fe Shu, "IBM Smart Surveillance System (S3): Event Based Video Surveillance System with an Open and Extensible Framework", *Machine Vision and Applications* 19 (2008):315–27, DOI 10.1007/s00138-008-0153-z. The article claims that such systems provide "not only the capability to automatically monitor a scene but also the capability to manage the surveillance data, perform event based retrieval, receive real time event alerts thru standard web infrastructure and extract long term statistical patterns of activity" (315).

30   For further discussion of the law and ethics relating to the use of this technology, see Julie Solomon, "Does the TSA Have Stage Fright? Then Why are they Picturing you Naked?", *Journal of Air Law and Commerce* 73, no 3 (2008): 643–71; Tobias W. Mock, "Comment: The TSA's New X-Ray Vision: The Fourth Amendment

routinely removed for X-ray inspection and, following another incident, carry-on liquids have been banned or restricted. Computers are sometimes checked for traces of explosives. To try to ensure that weapons etc. do not escape the metal detectors through which passengers must pass, some passengers are subjected to a further level of scrutiny using a wand or pat-down search.[31] However, the latter has led to complaints of sexual touching or acute anxiety, and so efforts have been made to develop technologies that will achieve the same effect without touching.

A few years ago, an X-ray backscatter imaging system was developed to detect weapons or explosives concealed on the body. The system penetrates clothing and reveals anything on the body surface (though it cannot pick up items that may be hidden in body folds).[32] It was trialed in a number of airports in the US (e.g. Orlando) and elsewhere. The technology has now developed further and the current system of choice is called an Active Millimeter Wave body scanner.[33] It uses high-frequency millimeter waves and not radiation.

Devices such as these are already in use in the UK, Netherlands, Japan and Thailand. They were tested at Phoenix Sky Harbor Airport and trialed in LA and New York[34] before becoming standard equipment in many airports around the world.

Implications of 'Body-Scan' Searches at Domestic Airport Security Checkpoints", *Santa Clara Law Review* 49 (2009): 213–51; TSA website http://www.tsa.dhs.gov/approach/tech/castscope.shtm. In addition, the technology is being considered for use in other contexts via mobile units; see Glen W. Fewkes, "New Public Surveillance Technologies May Alter Fourth Amendment Standards", *Government Security News*, March 6, 2009, available at: http://www.gsnmagazine.com.

31   However, as the recent case of Umar Farouk Abdulmutallab has shown, the problems may not be with technologies but with the humans who administer them. See Eric Lipton and Scott Shane, "Questions on Why Terror Suspect Wasn't Stopped", *The New York Times*, December 2, 2009: http://www.nytimes.com/2009/12/28/us/28terror.html?_r=1&scp=2&sq=Umar%20Farouk%20Abdulmutallab%20&st=cse.

32   See Austin Considine, "Will New Airport X-Rays Invade Privacy?", *The New York Times*, October 9, 2005, TR3; also the Rapiscan website: http://www.rapiscansystems.com/sec1000.html and, more graphically, http://www.electromax.com/rapiscan%20secure%201000.html.

33   Although a number of companies are using this technology, most of the ones being trialed at present are manufactured by L3 Communications for the Transportation Security Agency (Department of Homeland Security), http://www.l-3com.com/products-services/productservice.aspx?id=533&type=b. For technical data and assessments, see Committee on Assessment of Security Technologies for Transportation, National Research Council, *Assessment of Millimeter-Wave and Terahertz Technology for Detection and Identification of Concealed Explosives and Weapons* (Washington, DC: National Academies Press, 2007). http://books.nap.edu/openbook.php?record_id=11826&page=R1. For the latest in such technology, see S. Oka, H. Togo, N. Kukutsu, and T. Nagatsuma, "Latest Trends in Millimeter-Wave Imaging Technology", *Progress In Electromagnetics Research Letters* 1 (2008): 197–204. For discussion of ethical issues see http://www.mindfully.org/Technology/2007/Active-Millimeter-Wave1oct07.htm.

34   See Calvin Biesecker, "TSA to Test Additional Personal Imaging Systems at Airports", *Defense Daily*, 8/21/2007. For further updates, following the Christmas Day 2009 terror attempt, see "UK Introduces Full-body Screening in Heathrow Airport", available at: http://www.edri.org/edrigram/number8.3/uk-introduces-naked-body-scanners; "EU Considers Full Body Screening in Airports", available at: http://www.edri.org/edrigram/number8.1/airport-body-scanners-europe.

Critics of devices such as Rapiscan also raise the specter of X-Ray contamination, though the amounts to which people are exposed fall well below allowable levels and, as we have noted, do not constitute a problem in the case of more recent technologies.

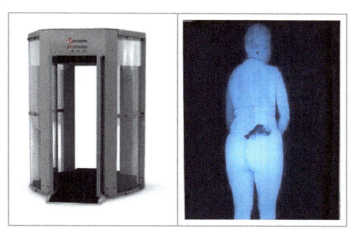

Source: http://www.thetechherald.com/media/images/200826/Provision_1.jpg; http://www.mytvmoments. com/view.php?v=14579

Nevertheless, the problem with such devices is that even though they seem[35] to avoid the privacy concerns associated with pat downs they create privacy issues of their own: screen images showing genital areas can be viewed as well as medical information that people may wish to keep private (such as colostomy bags or physiological oddities). In theory, the images may be saved and downloaded, though it appears that the machines do not need to have a save/download function.[36] New machines can also obscure the head, so that the passenger is not identifiable (though this is a feature that can be easily changed and may be not much of a hindrance to identification). A further privacy-enhancing feature is the stationing of monitors some distance from the device itself. A partial technological solution to the privacy problem is available: instead of the screen image being "what the machine sees", the raw data can be projected onto a generic outline so that all that appears are any metallic, plastic or otherwise dense objects. Although this important further step appears not to have been taken with many of the machines currently in use and under review, it has been taken in many settings, including a number of international airports. However, it should be noted that this is not sufficient for some civil liberties groups, who

---

35   It has been claimed that, because the machines cannot always disambiguate images, subsequent pat-downs are still sometimes required. Nevertheless, surveys suggest that people are more willing to have a "virtual strip search" than a pat-down.

36   There have, however, been cases in which images have been improperly saved and distributed. See Jeanne Merserve and Mike M. Ahlers, "Body Scanners Can Store, Send Images, Group Says", CNN News, January 11, 2010, available at: http://edition.cnn.com/2010/TRAVEL/01/11/body.scanners/index.html.

take the view that unless there is some other, compelling reason to think that a particular person could have terrorist connections (say, the appearance of his/her name on a watch list), no person should be subjected to such searches. This replication of pat-downs is also not without its problems. Recently the latest in body-scanning technology has raised a new problem; the seeming creation of child pornography.[37] The graphic nature of the latest technology scanning children means that the resulting images may breach child protection laws of the UK. The result is that, at the moment, individuals under the age of eighteen are exempt from scanning.[38] The problem with this is obvious: children could easily be carriers of the very objects that the scanning was devised to detect.

A further complaint concerning scanning devices has to do with their cost-effectiveness. The machines currently cost about US$200,000, have high support requirements and are time-consuming to operate and maintain. Do the gains in security match the expenditure involved? Might the money and human resources be better invested elsewhere? James Carafano of the Heritage Foundation takes the view that "where you want to spend your money is [where you have a prospect of] getting the terrorists long before they get to the TSA checkpoint."[39]

Wiretaps, bugs, and parabolic microphones

In the US, the tapping of telegraph lines goes back to the Civil War, with telephone tapping beginning in the 1890s, soon after the development of the telephone recorder. Tapping is covered primarily by FISA, ECPA and the Communications Assistance for Law Enforcement Act of 1994 (CALEA),[40] and is supplemented by the other acts that we have already referred to. CALEA requires telecommunications providers to ensure that upgrades to their technologies do not exclude the possibility of governmental tracking and interception.

Whereas wiretaps generally involve some external interception of telecommunications, bugging devices are usually located within the premises that are being monitored. They mostly take the form of microphones, often disguised as objects whose real function is unlikely to be detected: fountain pens, desk calculators, clock radios etc. Sometimes they are video-capable as well. The planting of bugs will frequently require unauthorized entry into private premises. ECPA has important provisions regarding the sale and use of bugging devices.

---

37 See Alan Travis, "New Scanners Break Child Porn Laws", *The Guardian*, Monday, January 4, 2010 22.14 GMT.

38 *Ibid.* See also Leonora LaPeter Anton, "Airport Body Scanners Reveal All, but What About When It's Your Kid?", *St Petersburg Times*, July, 17, 2010.

39 See http://www.cnsnews.com/ViewNation.asp?Page=/Nation/archive/200710/NAT20071015a.htm.

40 Available at http://www.epic.org/privacy/wiretap/calea/calea_law.html.

Parabolic microphones use satellite dish technology to focus sounds from up to about 1,000 feet (305 meters) away. There are stereo versions that give even better quality sound. Along with bugging and wiretap devices, they are easily available for purchase online. Indeed it is relatively simple to obtain product reviews of monitoring software (with a view to purchasing the most effective for one's own special purposes).[41]

Because of its invasiveness, wiretapping has always been contentious. As Justice Brandeis famously remarked:

> The evil incident to invasion of the privacy of the telephone is far greater than that involved in tampering with the mails. Whenever a telephone line is tapped, the privacy of the persons at both ends of the line is invaded, and all conversations between them upon any subject, and although proper, confidential, and privileged, may be overheard. Moreover, the tapping of one man's telephone line involves the tapping of the telephone of every other person whom he may call, or who may call him. As a means of espionage, writs of assistance and general warrants are but puny instruments of tyranny and oppression when compared with wire tapping.[42]

As we have already noted, FISA has undergone various modifications since 9/11 and there is some evidence that its provisions have been circumvented.[43] The strength of that controversy is largely expressive of Brandeis's concerns, though in the US it also taps into the ongoing controversy about the reach of the president's authority under the Constitution.[44]

In light of the potential threats to privacy posed by electronic and other interception and scanning devices, in most liberal democracies their use is legally permissible by law enforcement agencies only in the case of serious crimes. Moreover, such use is typically subject to oversight and accountability, including the requirement for independently adjudicated warrants. Nevertheless, here, as elsewhere, as a consequence of rapid technological development, there remain gaps in relevant legislation and accountability.

---

41   See, for example, the "Internet Activity Monitoring Software Consumer Guide", with recommendations on the top products reviewed, at: www.monitoringsoftwarereviews.org.consumerguide.html. This guide covers such topics as remote data access, accessibility of information, stealth, key logging (hardware and software versions), blocking, data filtering and screen shots.

42   *Olmstead v. United States*, 277 U.S. 438 (1928).

43   See "NSA Warrantless Surveillance Controversy", http://en.wikipedia.org/wiki/NSA_warrantless_surveillance_controversy.

44   This also connects with the subsequent controversy (November, 2007) about holding responsible those companies that acquiesced in executive requests while knowing FISA requirements.

Online surveillance

Even before 9/11, the US Government was developing technologies capable of scrutinizing ("sniffing") internet traffic (IP packets) and recording those that met certain security-related criteria. The main instrument for this was a software-based tool known initially as Carnivore, later to become the less predatorily-named Digital Collection System 1000 (DCS 1000). The story of Carnivore's development was broken by the *Wall Street Journal* in 2000.[45] In response to concerns *inter alia* about communicative privacy, Carnivore was tendered for an "independent" review, which was completed in September 2000.[46] This did not allay the worries of critics, though the renamed version was for a time placed on some servers. It appears that DCS 1000 was able to function in either pen-register/trap and trace (compare to the recording of outgoing phone numbers and incoming phone numbers) or full intercept (compare to wiretapping) mode. How it operates in either mode depends on what it is asked to do by way of recognizing keywords or strings. DCS 1000 is no longer used, having been abandoned in favor of commercially available technology.[47]

A key issue for the kind of technology involved in DCS 1000 (and its surrogates) has been one of accountability. Accountability can be incorporated by building into the search software constraints that will make violations of privacy or other abuses less likely and/or by ensuring (using various forms of oversight[48]) that data collected will be used only for limited, approved purposes.

Unlike telephone communications, in which the content of the call and the identifying number calling/called are quite separate, or mail, in which the envelope and its contents are clearly differentiated,[49] the IP packets that are sniffed by programs such as DCS 1000 are more closely integrated. Transactional

---

45   Neil King, Jr., "FBI's Wiretaps to Scan E-Mail Spark Concern", *Wall Street Journal*, 7/11/2000, A3. At the time, the primary purpose of Carnivore was not terrorism but crime, particularly financial crimes and child pornography.

46   The review was carried out by a Research Institute at the Illinois Institute of Technology (IIT). The terms of the review were constrained in a number of ways (critics spoke of it as a whitewash), and several prestigious institutions reputedly refused approaches to conduct it. The review, largely technical, can be found at http://www.dojgov.net/carnivore-iitri.pdf. An official public (censored) version is also available on the web at: http://www.usdoj.gov/jmd/publications/carnivore_draft_1.pdf. Nevertheless, the IIT review found that "it is not possible to determine who, among a group of agents with the password, may have set or changed filter settings. In fact, any action taken by the Carnivore system could have been directed by anyone knowing the Administrator password. It is impossible to trace the actions to specific individuals."

47   FoxNews, "FBI Ditches Carnivore Surveillance System", available at: http://www.foxnews.com/story/0,2933,144809,00.html. One of the supposed strengths of Carnivore was its capacity to track only what was authorized by court order.

48   Some of these will necessarily be internal FBI procedures along with legislative provisions and/or judicial powers. Others no doubt will take the form of external monitors such as EPIC, the Electronic Privacy Information Center (http://www.epic.org). The latter form of monitoring is made somewhat difficult because the software, its capabilities and some of its uses are classified.

49   This is not to say that envelope details are unimportant. How often *A* communicates with *B*, and how large the packets, may reveal quite a bit. One can presume some degree of anonymity in this context as well.

and substantive data are not easily separable, and that raises a problem. Whereas access to the former does not require a search warrant, access to the latter does. In addition, because of the "packet switching" that occurs (in which packets of information take the most efficient route to their destinations, where they are reassembled) a search program is likely to sniff a lot of innocent and private communications. And so, "a simple search to see if two people are emailing each other – which can be approved without a search warrant – requires that Carnivore digest the private correspondence of millions of people."[50] It is not like putting an intercept device on a particular phone number to see who is being called.

The disanalogy with telephone records has been magnified by the USA PATRIOT Act,[51] which has extended permissible searches to include IP (Internet Protocol) addresses and URLs (Uniform Resource Locators) visited. Once someone has access to an IP address (i.e. an address that refers uniquely to an internet-accessed computer) it is possible to track where that user has been. Similarly, URLs can show what content the person accessed on the internet (e.g. whether pornographic or jihadist sites were visited and, if so, how often).

Of course, the interception of communications is just one dimension of online vulnerability. There is also the issue of stored communications – say, emails on a server waiting to be read, or the inbox storage of emails. What protections should these have against the intrusions of others? Are they adequate? Do they have teeth?

Another piece of controversial software – a keystroke logging program known as Magic Lantern – embeds itself (usually via a technique known as a Trojan horse)

---

50   Joseph Goodman, Angela Murphy, Morgan Streetman, and Mark Sweet, "Carnivore: Will it Devour Your Privacy?", *Duke Law & Technology Review* (2001): 0028 http://www.law.duke.edu/journals/dltr/articles/2001dltr0028.

51   These are contained in sections 201–225 of the USA PATRIOT Act. The Act included a number of provisions relating to surveillance, including the interception of wire, oral or electronic communications. Many of its surveillance-related provisions predated the Act, but were extended to cover various terrorism-oriented investigations. Some provisions relate to the sharing of information gathered under the aegis of the Act (always a problem area, not only because of cracks in the security of data but also because such data are sometimes of questionable accuracy, de-contextualized and may be put to expanded uses). The expansion of provisions previously available under FISA to engage in extended "roving wiretaps" has also generated some controversy: normally (limited) wiretap requests require explicit detailed specifications before they are granted. Under the USA PATRIOT Act these requirements, as well as geographical requirements for warrant service, have been loosened. The use of pen registers/trap and trace devices is also made easier under the Act, it being no longer required that the person whose communications are targeted is "an agent of a foreign power". It is enough that the gathering of intelligence be a significant purpose of interception and surveillance. The focus may be domestic as well as international terrorism. Most controversial of all has been sect. 215, which allows the FBI (under FISA or through the issue of a "national security letter") to compel the handing over of any item or record that it requests and to forbid the party from whom it seeks the item from disclosing such requests to others. Libraries have been particularly reluctant to disclose loan records. The major problem with a number of these provisions is that the government is not first required to establish why some particular person is a legitimate object of its surveillance powers.

on a target's hard drive and then records all that computer's keystrokes. One of the main purposes has been to access various passwords.[52] Magic Lantern (and its predecessor, Key Logging System) also circumvents the problems/safeguards created by encryption (whereby communications are coded in such a way that only recipients with a "key" are likely to be able to read them). Again, there are significant issues of accountability, encompassing targeting, data review, data retention, data security and so on.[53]

WWWveillance

Beyond the scope of this study is the importance[54] for surveillance of the emerging trend of more and more information about individuals being available on the internet, including their social activities and private musings. This opens a new field of surveillance activities that are even harder for the individual to detect. Entire categories of new surveillance tools, such as web crawlers, cookies, bugs and webcams, have emerged. These provide surveillance agents with a plethora of new information with which to carry out new patterns of surveillance. Colin Bennett identifies glitch, default, design, possession and subject as examples of such patterns of surveillance.[55] Note that this sort of surveillance is subtly different from the online surveillance described previously.

Digitizing surveillance

Already hinted at in the previous section is the change from simple video and audio taping, which then has to be watched by humans, to the so-called digitizing of analogue recordings.[56] Indeed, with the latest technology the analogue step is bypassed completely in favor of direct digital recording. This is relatively common: these days how many do not have a digital camera with a hard drive or flash card? These "digitized" recordings can then be examined by software.[57] According to Stephen Graham and David Wood, this is important for several reasons, including widening geography and real-time monitoring. This is compounded by the increasing use of automated systems that require little or

---

52   See *US v. Scarfo*, 180 F. Supp. 2d 572 (DNJ 2001).
53   Chapter IX of this study offers accountability options to be considered when addressing these concerns.
54   For an example of the importance of this, see Tamara Dinev, Paul Hart, and Michael R. Mullen, "Internet Privacy Concerns and Beliefs about Government Surveillance – An Empirical Investigation", *Journal of Strategic Information Systems* 17 (2008): 214–33. See also Ian Brown, "Terrorism and the Proportionality of Internet Surveillance", *European Journal of Criminology* 6, no. 2 (2009): 119–134.
55   Colin J. Bennett, "Cookies, Web Bugs, Webcams and Cue Cats: Patterns of Surveillance on the World Wide Web", *Ethics and Information Technology* 3 (2001): 197–210.
56   See the James Meek article on facial recognition software applied to CCTV footage introduced earlier.
57   Stephen Graham and David Wood, "Digitizing Surveillance: Categorization, Space, Inequality", *Critical Social Policy* 23, no. 2 (2003): 227–48.

no human intervention: what Jones calls the "digital rule".[58] On the one hand, this automated processing can be used to overcome biases of human decision makers; on the other hand, the systems can be designed and built to exclude whole classes of persons with there being no overt acknowledgement that such exclusion is occurring.

Of course, these digitized recordings are stored in databases (which can be combined with other related databases and so on) which can then be further combed through in a secondary process called "dataveillance".

Dataveillance

Although not discussed in detail in this study the notion of monitoring not individuals but rather data about individuals is important.[59] Here, dataveillance is understood as the monitoring of data systems rather than of persons directly. While the ultimate end of this monitoring is to keep track of individuals it does so indirectly, making it less intrusive, more covert and less likely to be known by the individual(s) being monitored. It is important also because of the increasing acceptance of the notion that the identity of a person being watched is nothing but what is *recorded* about that person.

An important new development is the use of syndromic surveillance. This is the use of dataveillance techniques to track patterns in (nondiagnostic health information[60]) symptoms. Although originally intended to aid early intervention in the outbreak of potentially catastrophic pandemics (a worthwhile enterprise), its techniques can also be used to track patterns of any kind in any population, all without the permission or knowledge of the members of that population.[61]

RFIDs

A little-recognized form of surveillance, Radio Frequency Identification Devices (RFIDs), is beginning to be understood as a serious threat to privacy. Originally developed to manage warehouse inventories, the use of these short range devices

---

58   R. Jones, "Digital Rule: Punishment, Control and Technology", *Punishment and Society* 2, no. 1 (2001): 5–22.

59   For a history of the transition from conventional electronic surveillance to dataveillance see Mun-Cho Kim, "Surveillance Technology, Privacy and Social Control: With Reference to the Case of the Electronic National Identification Card in South Korea", *International Sociology* 19, no. 2 (2004): 193–213. For more recent attempts see Yuval Elovici, Bracha Shapira, Mark Last, Omer Azzfrany, Menahem Friedman, Moti Schneider, and Abraham Kandel, "Content Based Detection of Terrorists Browsing the Web Using an Advanced Terror Detection System", in *Terrorism Informatics: Knowledge Management and Data Mining for Homeland Security*, ed. Hsinchun Chen, Edna Reid, Joshua Sinai, Andrew Silke, and Boaz Ganor (Springer, 2008), 365–384.

60   See Lyle Fearnley, "Signals Come and Go: Syndromic Surveillance and Styles of Biosecurity", *Environment and Planning A*, 40 (2008): 1615–1632.

61   Leslie P. Francis, Margaret P. Battin, Jay Jacobson, and Charles Smith, "Syndromic Surveillance and Patients as Victims and Vectors", *Bioethical Inquiry* 6 (2009): 187–195.

has expanded to include tracking of employees while at work.[62] RFIDs can be read without the wearer's knowledge or permission. Indeed, some RFIDs can be placed on employee work badges, clothing or other work-specific apparel. According to Jeremy Gruber, once confined simply to location information they have in recent times been expanded to include information such as "fingerprints, social security number, driver's license number". Also, according to Gruber (and others), there are no legal constraints on the use of RFIDs in the workplace.

Participatory surveillance

Most of the discussion of surveillance so far has concerned covert practices or compulsory surveillance. Here we discuss a new and often overlooked form of surveillance: consensual or buying-in technology. This is technology that users must have in order to carry out their work/social activities but implicit in the technology is the ability to use it as a surveillance tool.

In the workplace, the use of "consent to be surveilled" as a means of claiming that the employee is "OK" with surveillance is used by employers to meet their moral obligations of "informed consent" and similar concepts. However, this consent frequently amounts to nothing more than coercion: no agreement to surveillance, no job. This is morally problematic, as the consent involved is at best superficial.[63]

In the context of ordinary society, twittering, tweeting and blogging are part of a new phenomenon, known as social networking or social media,[64] that has enormous potential for surveillance. In these technologies, people voluntarily post (hence the term participatory) information (often intensely personal) on websites that they believe (indeed hope) are accessible to millions. Although it is a social phenomenon of interest in its own right, we are interested here mainly in the ethical implications of such activity.

Many of the subscribers are teens and young adults with little experience in the adult world. One of the problems they face is that employers can, and do, check a prospective employee's activity on these social sites. Exuberant and youthful outbursts appropriate for the time may be seen in a less-than-favorable light.

62   For an example of this, see Jeremy Gruber, "RFID and Workplace Privacy", on the National Workrights Institute website, http://www.workrights.org/issue_electronic/RFIDWorkplacePrivacy.html, December 23, 2009, and Paul Roth, "Workplace Privacy Issues Raised by RFID Technology", Privacy Issues Forum, March 30, 2006, University of Otago, New Zealand.
63   For a more detailed treatment see, Jo Ann Oravec, "Secret Sharers: Consensual and Participatory Surveillance Concerns in the Context of Network-Based Computer Systems", *ACM SIGOIS Bulletin* 14, no. 1 (July 1993): 32–40.
64   For an excellent examination of the issues see Anders Albrechtslund, "Online Social Networking as Participatory Surveillance", *First Monday* 13, no. 3 (March 2008). Note that this omits sites such as Facebook from consideration.

Thoughts once divulged to close friends in a cloak of intimacy and presumed secrecy are now broadcast to millions of subscribers. Such disclosures can be damaging to the individual and their friendships.[65] Friendships that are physically and emotionally close can be harder to develop as a result of a loss of a sense of whether the blogger/tweeter can be trusted with confidential information.

However, as Anders Albrechtslund says, it can be empowering: "participatory surveillance is a way of maintaining friendships by checking up on information that other people share. Such a friendship might seem shallow, but it is a convenient way of keeping in touch with a large circle of friends, which can be more difficult to handle offline without updates of personal information – untold and unasked."[66]

So what is the problem for surveillance/security? As Albrechtslund puts it, although the original intention of such sites was "mutuality, empowerment and sharing", this unprecedented level of disclosure makes possible fraud, social sorting and identity theft.[67] Surveillance by anyone with an account (which can be gained with little verification of the subscriber's identity) is automatic and easy.

Some social commentators have said that, taken to its extreme, where others post information about us on their sites, this saturation of information about the everyday and mundane is not big brother but rather little sister.[68]

---

65   For a recent review, see Jeffrey Rosen, "The End of Forgetting", *The New York Times Magazine*, July 25, 2010, 30 et seq. One of the difficulties here is that privacy settings can be difficult to understand and control and, on some social networking sites, privacy policies change with some regularity and it can be difficult to keep up with the changes. Although it is arguable that young people have very different privacy expectations from those of an earlier generation, this might be questioned, see Chris Jay Hoofnagle, Jennifer King, Su Li, and Joseph Turow, "How Different Are Young Adults from Older Adults When it Comes to Information Privacy Attitudes and Policies?", available at: http://papers.ssrn.com/sol3/papers.cfm?abstract_id=1589864. See also, "In the Matter of Google, Inc." (March 30, 2011), available at: http://www.ftc.gov/os/caselist/1023136/index.shtm.

66   See also Dean Cocking and Steve Matthews, "Unreal Friends", *Ethics and Information Technology* 2, no. 4 (2001): 223–31.

67   For another excellent list of worries see Christian Fuchs, *Social Networking Sites and the Surveillance Society* (Salzburg: Förderung der Integration der Informationswissenschaften, 2009).

68   It is difficult to be certain of the origin of the phrase "little sister". Here is one claim: "The Reverend and Doctor Omed, We Are Little Sister and We Are Watching Us", http://www.dailykos.com/story/2009/4/16/720852/-We-Are-Little-Sister-and-We-Are-Watching-Us, viewed 20 January 2010:

> I would like to suggest a new meme as an overlay and even a successor to Big Brother: Little Sister. Little Sister is everyone who carries a cellphone with a digital camera that can upload pics and viddy to the intertubes. Little Sister is whoever cops a feed off Fox News, and everyone who posts it online. Little Sister is the "Macaca" who provided now former Senator George Allen an opportunity to destroy his political career. Little Sister is the 3 or more BART riders who viddied BART policeman Johannes Mehserle shooting Oscar Grant as Grant lay prone on the floor of the car. Little Sister is an emergent property of people interacting via the ever-faster global communications grid and all the technologies, software, and infrastructure that make, extend, and connect it.

Resisting surveillance[69]

Also called privacy-enhancing techniques, resisting surveillance has a history as long as surveillance itself. There are many ways in which individuals and privacy-seeking groups have sought to respond to the aforementioned surveillance techniques. Gary Marx identified some eleven ways of resisting by neutralizing the effect of surveillance.[70] In discussing ways of resisting online profiling, Ira Rubinenstein et al. mention multiple identities, cookie-blocking settings and commercially available tools such as the Anonymizer,[71] as well as techniques including onion-routing, unlinkable pseudonyms and anonymous credentials.[72] Some additional examples of resisting-surveillance technologies are: encryption (the most well-known being public key cryptography) and steganography (the art/science of secret writing. In the modern context this most commonly amounts to embedding information within images). Indeed, for almost every piece of surveillance technology there is a counter technology.

Onion-routing is the routing of a message through a series of proxies, each of which has an unpredictable path with limited information about where the message has come from or is going to.[73] *Unlinkable pseudonymy* is the creation of multiple pseudonyms for a single identity, each of which cannot be linked to any of the other pseudonyms. This allows a person to sign up anonymously to several websites without revealing that he or she is the same person. Credentials are needed to satisfy sign-on requirements for loyalty programs, website registration and the like. These are requested to ensure that the person signing on is genuine and not, for example, a web-crawler. *Anonymous credentials* have the feature of providing verification information without revealing the identity of the real or genuine person.

---

69 For a general theory of resisting surveillance, see Aaron K. Martin, Rosamunde van Brakel, and Daniel Bernhard, "Understanding Resistance to Digital Surveillance: Towards a Multi-Disciplinary, Multi-Actor Framework", *Surveillance & Society* 6 no. 3 (2009): 213–32.

70 Gary T. Marx, "A Tack in the Shoe: Neutralizing and Resisting the New Surveillance", *Journal of Social Issues* 59, no. 2 (2003): 369–90. The eleven ways are: discovery, avoidance, piggybacking, switching, distorting, blocking, masking, breaking, refusal and cooperative and counter-surveillance.

71 See http://www.freeproxy.ru/en/free_proxy/cgi-proxy.htm (viewed 20 January 2010) for an extensive list of anonymizing tools. To quote from the web page (http://www.online-proxy.net/), "Online-Proxy.net is a free web based anonymous proxy service, which allows anyone to surf the web privately and securely."

72 Ira S. Rubinstein, Ronald D. Lee, and Paul M. Schwartz, "Data Mining and Internet Profiling: Emerging Regulatory and Technological Approaches", *University of Chicago Law Review* 75, no. 1 (2008): 261–85, esp. 274–80.

73 This belongs to a class of technology called anonymous remailers. See, for example, Wayne Madsen, "FBI's Communications Surveillance Capabilities Widen", *Computer Fraud & Security*, 2000, no. 10, (October 2000): 16–17; George F. du Pont, "The Time Has Come For Limited Liability For Operators of True Anonymity Remailers in Cyberspace: An Examination of the Possibilities and Perils", *Journal of Technology Law & Policy* 6, no. 2 (2001): 175–218, available at: http://grove.ufl.edu/~techlaw/vol6/issue2/duPont.pdf.

Not only do these technologies protect the privacy of individuals but they are also indiscriminate in that they serve to block (or at least make more difficult) both commercial surveillance as well as police efforts to track or uncover criminals, terrorists and the like.

Although the above discussion has focused on ways of avoiding surveillance, there are also methods used by surveillance technology to limit its own reach. Yu et al. describe a method whereby visual surveillance technology can limit its access into personally identifying information.[74] Through the use of abstraction operators, the system known as PriSurv can limit the degree and kind of information the system can display, though the authors note that "excess visual abstraction makes video surveillance meaningless."[75] There are other techniques, such as pixelization, blurring and blacking out that also achieve the aim of making sensitive information unavailable. Of course, the use of all of these techniques is at the discretion of the operator/programmer.

Steganography[76] usually refers to the use of covert or hidden writing but can be expanded to include any form of communication. As Gary Kessler points out, this is different from *cryptography*, which makes the communication unreadable but does not seek to hide the communication itself. Combining the two technologies can make for a very powerful way of resisting digital surveillance. Steganography can take many forms – from the microdots of B-grade spy movies to more ancient techniques such as invisible ink (so-called technical steganography). This method of avoiding communications being surveilled has received renewed interest recently with the increased sophistication of digital technologies. With these new technologies communications can be hidden in image or audio files. Data can be hidden in unused file space or file headers. All digital communications are packaged into some form through protocols. The most commonly known and used protocols are Internet Protocol (IP) and Transmission Control Protocols (TCP). Information can be hidden inside segments of these carriers. Finally, hard disks can be divided into secret partitions which are undetected by normal surveillance or scanning technologies. Of course steganography is available to terrorists as well as others.[77]

---

74 Xiaoyi Yu, K. Chinomi, T. Koshimizu, N. Nitta, Y. Ito, N. Babaguchi, "Image Processing, 2008", ICIP 2008, 15th IEEE International Conference, October 12–15, 2008, 1672–75.

75 *Ibid.*, 1673.

76 See Gary C. Kessler, "An Overview of Steganography for the Computer Forensics Examiner" (an edited version), *Forensic Science Communications (Technical Report)* 6, no. 3 (July 2004), available at: http://www.fbi.gov/hq/lab/fsc/backissu/july2004/research/2004_03_research01.htm; http://www.garykessler.net/library/fsc_stego.html.

77 See Rebecca Givner-Forbes, *Steganography: Information Technology in the Service of Jihad* (Singapore: The International Centre for Political Violence and Terrorism Research, a Centre of the S. Rajaratnam School of International Studies, Nanyang Technical University, 2007).

(B) Second Data Mining[78,79] and Integration/Matching[80]

By way of introduction . . .

If you order many of your books from Amazon.com and use the Amazon web site as a convenient way to check on book data (authors' initials, exact titles, publishers, dates of publication, editions etc.), you will also be aware that you subsequently receive emailings from Amazon indicating that people who have shown interest in your book have also shown interest in other books that Amazon is now happy to let you know about. Amazon has applied an algorithm to the large amount of data that it amasses/warehouses as a result of site visits, which is used to gauge your purchasing proclivities. It then dangles before you the possibility of additional purchases in line with "interests" you have shown. The overall process of determining what data is to be retained, amassing it, patterning it and acting on it is often referred to in literature as knowledge discovery; within that knowledge discovery process data mining is the application of algorithms to enable predictions or judgments to be made.[81]

---

78   The term "data mining" is somewhat of a misnomer. It conventionally means sifting through large amounts of information, usually held in one database, in search of specific pieces of information or data. Traditional mining is always held to have a reason for believing that mining a specific location will likely result in the discovery of a particular mineral. Gold mining is looking for gold using a body of knowledge that says that certain geographical formations are likely to contain deposits of gold. Data mining does not work like this. Usually there is scant or little information that even so much as implies that specific information looked for is contained in the database being searched. In the case of Amazon, described below, the intent of the data mining is not so much to find information but to create information using the available database. Using the gold mining example at its best, the Amazon activity is like using the surrounding minerals in a deposit to create gold and then calling this activity/process gold mining. At its worst, what Amazon is doing is more like taking whatever materials can be found in a given location, combining them using the laws of chemistry and calling whatever is produced an intended result. This is hardly mining in the traditional sense.

79   Of course, data mining for national security or policing is not the only use. Perhaps of even more importance and worry for privacy is data mining by corporations in which, according to John Soma et al., there is an equating of information with financial value. See John T. Soma, et al., "Corporate Privacy Trend: The 'Value' of Personally Identifiable Information ('PII') Equals the 'Value' of Financial Assets", *Richmond Journal of Law & Technology* 15, no. 4 (2009), available at: http://law.richmond.edu/jolt /v15i4/article11.pdf.

80   A note on terminology: in some countries the common term for the aligning of information across a number of disparate sources is termed "data integration" and in others it is termed "data matching." Matching is the more correct term when discussing the use of collected information to be used as a predictive tool. Integration implies the simple putting together of information whereas matching implies the more important (in this context) putting together of information that, when put together, adds value or is said to "match".

81   Kim Taipale offers the following useful differentiation and breakdown: "The steps that compose the knowledge discovery process are (1) pre-processing (including goal identification; data collection, selection, and warehousing; and data cleansing or transformation), (2) 'data mining' itself, and (3) post-processing (including interpretation, evaluation and decision-making or action)" (see "Data Mining and Domestic Security: Connecting the Dots to Make Sense of Data", *Columbia Science and Technology Law Review* 5 (2003): 24–25). In 2005, the Department of Homeland Security Privacy Office used the following definition: "Data mining involves the use of sophisticated data analysis tools to discover previously unknown, valid patterns and relationships in large data sets. Data mining consists of more than collecting and managing data; it also includes analysis and prediction." In 2006, as the result of a House demand, the definition was changed to: "a query or search or other analysis of 1 or more electronic databases, whereas – (A) at least 1 of the databases was obtained from or remains under the control of a non-Federal entity, or the information was acquired

Although such predictions can show an uncanny ability to track books that might be of interest to you, they can also be a bit irritating if some of the books you purchased were purchased for other people or if the tracked volume was simply a footnote reference for which you needed a publisher. The algorithm should be sophisticated enough to screen out "casual" visits that do not say anything – or anything accurate – about your reading interests.

Such is one use of data mining. There are many others. Data mining can be used to provide an understanding of human behavior,[82] forecast trends and demands, track performance or transform seemingly unrelated data into meaningful information.[83]

The importance of data mining and integration was highlighted by the events of 9/11, when it subsequently turned out that a number of those involved in the attacks were already on the radar screens of security officials and that there were even data to suggest that a terrorist attack was imminent. One of the things the attack revealed was that government agencies charged with responsibility for preventing such occurrences were not adequately equipped to analyze, evaluate and integrate the data available to them. Nor, as it subsequently turned out, were they equipped to tackle the information in a manner consistent with the values of a liberal society – that is, with due regard for privacy and other civil liberties. Outcries stemming from this lack of attention to liberties resulted in the proposed Total/Terrorist Information Awareness (TIA)[84] program being abandoned and the updated Computer Assisted Passenger Prescreening (CAPPS II) program (now Secure Flight) being delayed by a number of years.

Ethical questions arise at every step of the data mining process. In what is referred to as the "pre-processing" stage, for example, decisions must be

---

initially by another department or agency of the Federal Government for purposes other than intelligence or law enforcement; (B) a department or agency of the Federal Government or a non-Federal entity acting on behalf of the Federal Government is conducting the query or search or other analysis to find a predictive pattern indicating terrorist or criminal activity; and (C) the search does not use a specific individual's personal identifiers to acquire information concerning that individual." The change had consequences: some "data mining" activities discussed in the 2005 report were not reviewed in the 2006 report, and some reviewed in the 2006 report had not been considered in the 2005 report.

82   In an unusual take on the problem, Andrew McClurg, "A Thousand Words Are Worth a Picture: A Privacy Tort Response to Consumer Data Profiling", *Northwestern University Law Review* 98, no. 1 (2006): 63–143, claims that a serious concern is that data mining by businesses could result in complete dossiers of individuals that would give businesses a better understanding of an individual's purchasing patterns than the individual themselves is consciously aware of. According to McClurg, this better profile could then be appropriated without permission and used to target similar in-profile persons.

83   The algorithms used for data mining vary considerably in kind and sophistication. There are many commercial packages available, often directed at or customized for niche concerns (marketing, law enforcement etc.), and purpose-oriented institutions (e.g. Google) often develop their own. Organizations concerned with tracking terrorist activity (e.g. the FBI, the CIA) may draw on commercial as well as internal databases in seeking to identify links and patterns that warrant further investigation. See Chapter VII.

84   For an overview of TIA see Leslie Regan Shade, "The Culture of Surveillance: G-Men Redux and Total Information Awareness", *Topia* 9 (2003): 35–45.

made about the goals to be served by the data mining. Is it simply to identify (potential) terrorists or are other goals also contemplated (e.g. organized crime, money laundering, tax fraud)? The moral worthiness of the goals will obviously have some bearing on the privacy risks that might be justified. "Potential" also operates as something of a weasel word: what level of probability will satisfy that?[85] Goals will also need to be tempered by ethical considerations (for example, those mandated by liberal democratic values).[86] When it comes to data collection, decisions will need to be made about where the data are to come from and whether their sources avoid illegitimate breaches of privacy. Data given to institutions for certain limited purposes should not normally be used for other purposes.

The Department of Homeland Security's (DHS) Office of Inspector General (OIG) helpfully classifies data mining activities into two groups; commercial and government. In this security context we are interested primarily in those of the government.[87] These include: monitoring employee expenditures; speeding up employees' security clearance investigation process; identifying improper payments under federal benefit and loan programs and helping to detect instances of fraud, waste, and abuse; ranking government programs quickly; and assisting law enforcement in combating terrorism.

Government data mining is more or less coincident with the development of data mining technologies. Prior to 9/11 it was employed to combat various kinds of criminal activities, (such as money laundering, drug trafficking and tax fraud) but since 9/11 significant data mining efforts have also been directed at the prevention of terroristic acts and the apprehension of aspiring terrorists. An array of software has been developed and/or used to discover patterns and relationships and to make predictions or define rules that can be used in the so-called war on terror.

In August 2006 the OIG released its *Survey of DHS Data Mining Activities*, in which it described 12 data mining activities carried out under the aegis of the DHS. The list was not meant to be exhaustive, nor was it confined to operational data mining activities – it included several that were "under development",

---

85   Cf. the old feminist slogan: "All men are potential rapists."

86   As with any means-end reasoning, the use of data mining techniques must satisfactorily respond to the relevant questions that such reasoning generates.

87   The commercial uses are given as: to analyze and segment customer buying patterns and identify potential goods and services that are in demand; to identify and prevent fraudulent and abusive billing practices; to analyze sales trends and predict the effectiveness of promotions; to predict the effectiveness of surgical procedures, medical tests and medications; to search information from a number of documents and written sources on a particular topic (text mining); and to identify trends and present statistics in ways that are easily understood and useful. From the Office of Inspector General, Department of Homeland Security, *Survey of DHS Data Mining Activities*, OIG-06-56 (Washington, DC: Office of Information Technology, August 2006), 6, http://www.dhs.gov/xoig/assets/mgmtrpts/OIG_06-56_Aug06.pdf. Although the survey distinguishes commercial and government uses, it does not as clearly say that government purposes are outsourced to commercial data miners. See Chapter VII.

and there may well have been others that were "classified". Nevertheless, it is interesting to review some of the kinds of data mining activities because of the different ethical challenges that they provide.

The OIG survey distinguished several types of analytical processes that arguably come under the umbrella of data mining:

- *Expert systems*: programs designed to analyze information about a specific class of problems, analyze the problems themselves and, usually, to recommend courses of action (e.g. the Automated Commercial Environment Screening and Targeting Release S1 (ACE S1) that, from a centralized data base, identifies high risk cargo shipments for further detailed examination).

- *Association processes*:[88] processes which link two or more variables (e.g. persons and place), for example, the Immigration and Customs Enforcement Pattern Analysis and Information Collection System (ICEPIC) that works with various DHS databases to detect patterns and relationships and enable investigators to conduct targeted checks of non-resident aliens.

- *Threat and risk assessment tools*: tools that identify, prioritize and help to reduce risks. These include the Risk Management Reporting System (RMRS) that collects information and scores it based on the level of risk posed to national assets (such as maritime facilities, airports and mass transit).

- *Collaboration and visualization processes*: processes that collect, tag, classify, organize and apply appropriate material and expertise and then represent it in an illuminating visual form (e.g. Numerical Integrated Processing System (NIPS), a web-based tool that assists agents in identifying anomalies indicative of criminal activity – immigration violations, customs fraud, drug smuggling and terrorism).

- *Advanced analytics*: analytics that ingest information and facts from diverse types of data, both structured and unstructured, and then provide simulation and modeling tools for analysts (e.g. Analysis, Dissemination, Visualization, Insight and Semantic Enhancement (ADVISE), a meta-tool that had not been implemented at the time of the report but which was intended to incorporate and integrate comprehensive chemical, biological, radiological, nuclear and explosive threat and effects data).

Means and ends

What privacy and other ethical issues are raised by such data mining activities? Because data mining is a purposive activity – a means employed to achieve

---

88   This is also known as relational surveillance. See, for example, Katherine J. Strandburg, "Freedom of Association in a Networked World: First Amendment Regulation of Relational Surveillance", *Boston College Law Review* 49, no. 1 (2008): 1–81.

certain ends – it is important to keep in mind the following questions: Are the ends good or good enough? Are the ends proportionate to the means? Can the ends be secured in a less-invasive manner? Will the means secure the ends? Is there something intrinsically problematic about the means? Will the means have deleterious consequences making their use inappropriate?

These questions, which are overlapping rather than completely discrete, can more or less arise at every step of the data mining process: definition of the problem to be solved, data identification and collection, data quality assessment and data cleansing and, finally, data modeling (building, validation and deployment). Such a process is iterative, because information learned in later steps may lead to a clarification of and adjustments to earlier steps.[89]

Good (enough) ends

It needs to be determined that the purposes for which data are being gathered and manipulated are legitimate, both ethically and legally. So data that are oriented more to the detection of political dissent than to the prevention of clearly defined national disasters are likely to be problematic just because the legitimacy of the ends to be served is questionable. Legitimate ends, moreover, will need to be sufficiently important to warrant the devotion of the government resources that will be required. There may also need to be a determination of whether the interest of a particular agency is legitimate – that is, whether it falls within its authority to gather and analyze such data. That may be problematic for cases in which (for reasons of efficiency) different agencies jointly gather data. Connected with this requirement (and touching on others as well) will be questions about confining the use of data to the purposes for which they were originally gathered; there are often memoranda of understanding between agencies that allow information that is gathered for one purpose (say, terrorism) to be shared with other agencies concerned with another (say, financial crime). Are such extensions justified? "Mission creep" is a common problem; although it seems cost-efficient, it may violate important privacy protections. Apart from any impropriety that may be involved, it is also possible that data collected for one purpose are not in a form that is well-suited (or of adequate quality) for another purpose. Moreover, as data are shared, control over the uses to which they are put and security controls on the data themselves are often lost.

---

89   Useful documents are Maureen Cooney, *Report to Congress on the Impact of Data Mining Technologies on Privacy and Civil Liberties* (Washington, DC: DHS, July 6, 2006), available at: http://www.dhs.gov/xlibrary/ assets/privacy/privacy_data_%20mining_%20report.pdf; and Hugo Teufel III, *2007 Report to Congress on the Impact of Data Mining Technologies on Privacy and Civil Liberties* (Washington, DC: DHS, July 6, 2007), available at: http://www.dhs.gov/xlibrary/assets/privacy/privacy_rpt_datamining_2007.pdf.

Proportionate means/ends

Ends may be legitimate without being important enough to justify the kinds of means that are contemplated or employed to achieve them. Data mining, given the risks to civil liberties associated with it, is likely to be justifiable only if important ends are at stake. Some – but not all – crime is likely to qualify, and a judgment needs to be made about the legitimacy of using scarce government resources to mine data for particular purposes, given the seriousness of the issues and the available alternatives.

Restrictive means/ends

As well as some proportionality of means and ends, the means should be as little restrictive/invasive as possible. Could anonymized data be used rather than identifiable data? – a critical question when data might be shared among agencies. *Ceteris paribus*, other ways of achieving the ends, if less invasive, should be chosen. Such a requirement impacts on the issue of data retention: are the data to be kept permanently or should they be discarded after a determinate period of time? Agencies are strongly tempted to hold onto data "just in case" they turn out to be useful at some future date. However, the longer data are kept the more likely it is that they will become outdated. The principle of the least restrictive alternative may also have an important bearing on the target data: whether the software should operate dragnet style or be more tightly circumscribed.

Calibrated means/ends

The means have to be appropriately calibrated to the ends so that they are likely to be effective in achieving the ends for which they are employed. It needs to be established that accessing a particular raw data set is appropriate to the investigation at issue – that is, that it is likely to contain relevant information – and that the software used is likely to capture it and process it in a way that will enable the ends to be realized.

The ethics of scientific/experimental design

This is also important with regard to the "cleansing" of raw data – that is, the removing of inaccuracies and coping with incompleteness in such a way that patterns, relationships and rules will be accurately depicted. The issue of reliability is important not only when developing the modeling software but also at the point of its application to actual data, lest false positives lead to unwarranted invasions of rights. (False negatives can be a problem too.) Furthermore, the kinds of patterns that software tracks do not *ipso facto* constitute meaningful or causal relationships, and so caution needs to be exercised with respect to the kinds of conclusions that are drawn from them. They should be seen as investigative tools rather than probative techniques.

Appropriate means/ends

Although some data sets are likely to be public and involve no breaches of privacy that is not always the case. The privacy-invasive character of the means will have to be taken into account along with more instrumental questions about the suitability of the means to achieving the ends. These are not simple "balancing" issues – they require attention to the trade-offs involved. Where collected data are privacy-invasive there should be sufficient transparency and oversight for there to be effective means of redress in the event that privacy is improperly invaded or inappropriate conclusions are drawn.

Unintended consequences

Finally, unintended side effects will need to be addressed, for example, the augmentation of governmental power and the increased vulnerability of a (particular) population should governmental policies shift in a demagogical direction. Other side effects might include the vulnerability of a population to other threats as a result of inadequately secured data. Hackers, spies and others may have reasons for wanting to access data that has now been conveniently gathered for them.[90]

As we have already noted by implication, conceptions of privacy and formulations of privacy law have not developed *in vacuo* but have been significantly influenced by historical circumstances. Consider a few salient ones. Americans, because of their founding history, have always had an issue with the power of central government and hence with activities – such as surveillance – that would appear to enhance governmental power. At the same time, American dedication to the market as a distributor of social goods has often left it less concerned with the private mining and assembling of data. Offsetting this has been the concern that Warren and Brandeis expressed about the growth of the media and telecommunications, and the potential that they had for both governmental and private intrusions into space/activities that should be left alone. European countries have similarly been affected by historical events. In 1944, during the Nazi occupation of Norway, the Nazis decided that the German army needed a further infusion of soldiers. It was decided to conscript Norwegian men based on factors such as their age, using government files. Unable to destroy the files and thus to thwart this initiative, the Norwegian resistance succeeded in

---

90 In each of the scenarios of means/ends relationships and unintended consequences the value of Techno-ethics Boards is clear. As bodies charged with unpacking these problems, the insight and guidance that emerge would, it is hoped, clear away many thickets early rather than forcing retroactive action.

destroying the two machines used to sort the files, so the conscription plan had to be dropped. The lesson about the vulnerability of innocently centralized data was, however, imported into European privacy law.[91] Combine this with the accusation that IBM was instrumental in assisting the genocide program of the Nazis through allowing them access to their sorting machines, and it can be seen why there is a special nervousness about privately gathered data in the EU.[92]

Overall, Americans seem more complacent than Europeans[93] about the centralized gathering of certain kinds of data about its citizens. Although it caused an uproar when discovered in May 2006, the revelation that the National Security Agency (NSA) database contained at least five years' worth of the call records of tens of millions of US citizens — calls that had been routed through AT&T and Verizon/MCI — indicated the ease with which governmental authorities were able to get access.[94] The NSA may have acted illegally, though the activity was probably not as dicey as the earlier-discovered warrantless wiretapping that the US government subsequently made efforts to kosher.[95] In the European context, the mining of such data would have required a public law reviewed by an independent privacy agency and, even if access could have been gained by an intelligence agency, the data would not have been able to be retained for as long as the NSA had retained its data.

The NSA data gathering occurred shortly after 9/11, when it approached the major telecommunications carriers for customer call records (from one number to another, giving time and duration of call) and for regular updates of such. Some

---

91 It would have been interesting to see whether the recent loss of data in the UK would have derailed plans for a national ID card. See Eric Pfanner, "Data Leak in Britain Affects 25 Million", *The New York Times*, November 22, 2007. However, the change of government has rendered this moot.

92 Edwin Black, *IBM and the Holocaust* (New York: Time Warner Paperbacks, 2001).

93 "Europe" is somewhat ambiguous. It may refer — more narrowly — to those countries that constitute the European Union (currently comprising twenty-seven states: http://en.wikipedia.org/wiki/European_Union_member_state) or — more broadly — to those forty-seven countries that comprise the Council of Europe (http://en.wikipedia.org/wiki/Council_of_Europe). The discussion here will (primarily) concern the second, though it generally encompasses the first.

94 See Leslie Cauley, "NSA Has Massive Database of Americans' Phone Calls", *USA Today*, May 11, 2006, A1; Susan Page, "Lawmakers: NSA Database Incomplete", *USA Today*, June 30, 2006, A1.

95 See "Legal Authorities Supporting the Activities of the National Security Agency Described by the President", *Indiana Law Journal* 81 (2006): 1374. With regard to the call records, most of the current debate concerns whether the telecommunications companies involved should be granted immunity if it turns out that they acted contrary to legal requirements. ECPA (1986), which bears on the NSA initiative, requires — in its Stored Communications Act (U.S.C. §§2701 – 2711) – that companies can disclose their records to the government only under certain conditions, for example, if the government obtains a warrant, court order or administrative subpoena such as a national security letter (18 U.S.C. §2702 (c)). In the present instance, the information was handed over without any warrant. However, if it can be established that the President's inherent constitutional power takes precedence, that may relieve the telecommunications companies from liability. With regard to the warrantless wiretapping, however, FISA almost certainly required a warrant – hence the koshering activity of the Protect America Act of 2007. Given FISA's explicitness, the appeal to Article II of the Constitution was not very convincing (see *Youngstown Tube & Sheet, Co. v. Sawyer*, 343 U.S. 579, 635–38 (1952, J. Jackson, concurring), for the president's powers are at their "lowest ebb" when exercised contrary to "the expressed or implied will of Congress".

companies complied; others (Qwest, BellSouth) did not. This information was subsequently mined, though exactly how is not clear. Were they, for example, used to generate certain hypotheses about who might be engaged in terrorist activities, or were they used to target those who had previously been suspected of terrorist sympathies?

However the data were (or are) being used, the situation in the US is markedly different from what is possible in Europe for a number of reasons. Firstly, in the US a distinction is drawn between content and incidents, that is, between the *substance* of a communication between A and B and *date-time stamps* of communication between A and B (i.e. between the "letter" and the "envelope"). The former is generally well-protected in the US, but in Europe both kinds of data are protected (though even there it is recognized that content deserves greater protection than incidents). Secondly, there is a distinction that functions more stringently in Europe than in the US between personal and other kinds of communication data. European countries are far more protective (with respect to both government and private actors) of a broad category that encompasses "all types of personal data", whereas US law focuses on specific kinds of personal data, such as health and financial information, video-store records etc. Thirdly, a further distinction concerns the purposes for which data are collected, whether for law enforcement or national security. In both Europe and the US, constraints on law enforcement data gathering are more stringent than those on national security data gathering. In part this is because law enforcement has more dramatic consequences for individuals than national security intelligence gathering. Finally, as far as national security interests are concerned, European agencies pay attention to domestic as well as foreign threats to national security, whereas the US has until recently viewed national security in terms of foreign threats (covered by the CIA and NSA) regulated by FISA. The FBI, which covers both federal criminal investigations and domestic intelligence, is covered by regulations mostly attuned to law enforcement matters. It was the lack of an assigned domestic national security agency that led to the NSA taking it on.

Fourth Amendment jurisprudence allows the mining of call records. It is argued that because the records are available to the phone companies themselves they are not private in the way that the content of a phone conversation is.[96] Rather than doing the mining itself the NSA simply requested the information from telecommunications providers. The failure of such jurisprudence to provide for the comprehensive protection of personal data constitutes a major difference between US and European law on data protection/privacy.

---

96   Compare *Smith v. Maryland*, 442 U.S. 735 (1979) with *Katz v. United States*, 389 U.S. 347 (1967). Cf. also *United States v. Miller*, 425 U.S. 435 (1976), where it is argued that users of certain services "assume the risk" that their information will be made known to others.

Nor does the Privacy Act of 1974 provide much solace. True, it imposes several duties on government agencies: to alert the public to the existence of a records system; to reveal its purposes; to collect data that are relevant to those purposes only; to ensure the accuracy and timeliness of the mined data; to not transfer information to other agencies without the consent of those whose data are being mined; to guarantee the security and confidentiality of the acquired data; and to give those concerned a right to check and have corrected the data concerning them. This sounds pretty good, but closer inspection suggests otherwise. The Act has few teeth and it provides for many exceptions that cover most of the current contested uses, provided that notice is given to that effect (for example, unless secrecy is in the interest of national defense).

In Europe, the situation is significantly different. Data mining of the kind indicated by call records requires a law to permit it that explicitly specifies the purposes for which the data are being gathered and the limits that will be observed in their gathering, use and retention. Because data mining requires a specific law allowing it, there is likely to be public debate over its purposes and the kinds of data that will be aggregated and mined. It is most likely that only anti-terrorist purposes would be legitimated and then only in the event of a "concrete danger." Even an intelligence agency would have to conform to the latter expectation, in which there is some individualized suspicion,[97] and would not be permitted to retain the data for as long as the NSA has had it: three years is about the European limit (though between six months and two years is more common). In European law, individuals also have a right to check on the accuracy of information gathered about them, something that is denied to Americans.

Data mining has the potential to provide many legitimate benefits, especially to law enforcement agencies. However, data mining, in many of its forms and with the right sort of technology,[98] can also represent a serious threat to democratic values such as privacy and autonomy. Accordingly, there is a need to determine the ethical constraints that should apply to data mining and to devise and implement appropriate accountability mechanisms.

Of course, data mining can be an important tool in profiling.[99]

---

97 German law, however, does permit strategic surveillance of international phone calls as part of an anti-terrorism initiative.

98 Such technologies are being developed all the time. For a recent example of such technology see N. Memon, H.L. Larsen, "Investigative Data Mining Toolkit: A Software Prototype for Visualizing, Analyzing and Destabilizing Terrorist Networks", in *Visualising Network Information* (2006), 14-1–14-24. See also the so-called Investigative Data Mining techniques, Nasrullah Memon, "Detecting Terrorist Activity Patterns Using Investigative Data Mining Tool", IFSR 2005: Proceedings of the First World Congress of the International Federation for Systems Research: The New Roles of Systems Sciences For a Knowledge-based Society, Nov. 14–17, 2123, Kobe, Japan.

99 As an example of this crossover, see Ira Rubinstein, Ronald D. Lee, and Ira Schwartz, "Data Mining and Internet Profiling: Emerging Regulatory and Technological Approaches". Other technologies can also be

(C) Profiling[100, 101]

The process of reaching out to foreign nationals and their communities
fostered new trust between law enforcement and these communities.[102]

In the introduction to *Profiles, Probabilities and Stereotypes*, Frederick Schauer
states that his purpose is to challenge "the primacy of the particular" – that
is, the view that our decisions have to be guided exclusively or primarily by
the particulars of a case rather than by generalities that we can bring to it. As
he puts it, he seeks to "defend the morality of decisions by categories and by
generalizations, even with its consequent disregard for the fact that decision-
making by generalization often seems to produce an unjust result in particular
cases."[103] He makes it very clear, however, that what follows from this is not that
all generalizations (in the form of stereotypes or profiles) will pass ethical muster
– even when they have a sound statistical basis – only that some may.

The notorious profiled New Jersey Turnpike stops were almost certainly based
on spotty evidence. Schauer compares the profiling involved there with that
developed by Bob Vogel, the Florida Highway Patrol officer who became famous
for his drug interdiction work. Vogel's profile was based on his thirty biggest
drug arrests; it was not meshed with the experience of others or moderated by
the experience of stops that yielded nothing. New Jersey's profiling was hardly
better grounded and, Schauer writes, "the original New Jersey procedure ought
not to be glorified by referring to it as a 'profile,' for it would be more accurate
to call it a 'guess'."[104]

---

difficult to classify according to the standard grouping such as surveillance and profiling. See, for example,
Sudhir Saxena, K. Santhanam, and Aparna Basu, "Application of Social Network Analysis (SNA) to Terrorist
Networks", *Strategic Analysis* 28, no.1 (January–March 2004): 84–101.

100   Although this study focuses on profiling in military and criminal contexts, its uses in the commercial
sector can be just as worrying, morally speaking. See, for example, Axiom software's DISC system, in which
they offer commercial, personal, reselling, and hosting and profiling services at http://www.axiomsoftware.
com, viewed December 10, 2009.

101   An emerging technology for profiling (and other security issues) is translation technology. Roughly, this
is the use of computers to translate documents, audio and sundry foreign (i.e. not English) language sources
used in profiling. It is justified as a way of speeding up the processing of such sources. For Érika Nogueira de
Andrade Stupiello, there is the fundamental problem of "the illusion that the machine is able to translate", in
"Ethical Implications of Translation Technologies", *Translation Journal*, 2007, at http://translationjournal.net/
journal/43ethics.htm, viewed January 3, 2010.

102   Attorney General John Ashcroft, commenting (March 20, 2002) on the "voluntary" interview program
initiated by the US government on November 9, 2001 http://www.yale.edu/lawweb/avalon/sept_11/
ashcroft_018.htm. Some 5,000+ young men who had recently entered the United States on visas from
"countries with suspected terrorist links" were individually "invited" to talk with government agents about
their reasons for visiting, past movements, knowledge concerning 9/11 and feelings about the same. Few felt
able to refuse. A follow-up group of a further 3,000+ was indicated in the March 20 announcement.

103   Frederick Schauer, *Profiles, Probabilities and Stereotypes* (Cambridge, MA: Harvard University Press,
2003), ix.

104   Schauer, 192. This irks David Harris, who sees the kind of profiling that the New Jersey state police
engaged in as exactly what the public thinks of as profiling. It might have been smarter for Schauer to have

A far more sophisticated example, one that Schauer holds up as something of a model, is the FBI's serial killer profile. The people who constructed this profile studied everything they could on serial killings, interviewed serial killers where they were able and gathered whatever other information they could that would be relevant, before painstakingly analyzing it in the process of developing a profile of "serial killer indicators". These, however, were to be used only after a field of suspects had been narrowed in order to determine who might be the most likely one. As we saw several years ago, however, in the case of the Washington snipers, too great a dependence on a profile, even a well-developed one, can lead one astray. On more than one occasion, John Muhammad and Lee Malvo were "passed over" by searching police because the profile had pointed them in the direction of a lone white male.[105] Indeed, Simon Cole and Michael Lynch suggest that "the construction of DNA databases in Britain, the United States, and elsewhere shifts criminal investigation toward suspect populations and statistical suspects."[106]

CAPPS

Since 9/11 there has been an upsurge in the profiling of airline passengers.[107] Early profiling was done by way of CAPPS (Computer-Assisted Passenger Prescreening System), developed initially in 1997 by a White House Committee chaired by Al Gore.

The first CAPPS profile made no reference to race or ethnicity except to exclude it (without providing reasons). It focused on factors such as gender, age, form of purchasing the ticket (cash or credit card, last minute or well in advance, direct or through a travel agent), membership of a frequent flyer program, time of check-in, type of luggage, presence or absence of a hotel or rental car reservation at destination, demeanor etc.[108] Even so, it was shown that CAPPS could be easily circumvented through such algorithms as Carnival Booth.[109]

---

seen it as a profile informed more by prejudice or guesswork than by careful development, rather than not seeing it as a profile at all. See Harris's review of Schauer in "Profiling: Theory and Practice", *Criminal Justice Ethics* 23, no. 2 (2004): 51–57.

105   Jennifer Daw Holloway, "The Perils of Profiling for the Media: Forensic Psychologists Speak Out on the Lessons Learned from the Washington-Area Sniper Case", APA Online http://www.apa.org/monitor/jan03/perils.html.

106   Simon A. Cole and Michael Lynch, "The Social and Legal Construction of Suspects", *Annual Review of Law and Social Science* 2 (December 2006): 39–60 (doi: 10.1146/annurev.lawsocsci.2.081805.110001).

107   A practice that was upheld by the Supreme Court in *US v. Sokolow*, 490 US 1 (1989).

108   Schauer, 184.

109   Samidh Chakrabarti and Aaron Strauss, "Carnival Booth: An Algorithm for Defeating the Computer-Assisted Passenger Screening System", *Electrical-Engineering-and-Computer-Science* (2002), available at: http://www.mit.strathmore.edu/NR/rdonlyres/Electrical-Engineering-and-Computer-Science/6-805Fall-2005/4E484655-6947-4D60-B789-32F2FFE6199A/0/caps.pdf, viewed December 18, 2009.

The events of 9/11 prompted calls for the revision of CAPPS, one that would provide a "risk score" for air travelers. As we have already had occasion to observe, the proposed revision – CAPPS II – came to grief in 2004 over civil rights and privacy issues, and the new system, Secure Flight, was frequently delayed by privacy concerns.[110]

Geographic profiling

Geographic profiling is the use of "knowledge about the relative locations of an offender's crime sites to predict the highest probable location of his or her residence (or some other anchor point, such as a work place)."[111] Although this technology has its origin in domestic serial crimes, recent work has attempted to use it to find the home base of other kinds of offenders, particularly terrorists.[112] Such profiling uses several assumptions about the criminal/terrorist/insurgent (here we shall refer to them as offenders). These assumptions are: multiple offenses by a single offender; the relative closeness of the offenses to the home base of the offender; the distribution of the offenses; and a stationary home base. The profile identifies an area within which the probability of an offender's home base is measured. This then allows those using the profile to target locations with the highest probability. Further it is used to prioritize probable offenders based on how closely their home base is to the site of the offense.

This form of profiling is highly dependent upon the accuracy of the underlying assumptions. If any of the assumptions is inaccurate then the profile is useless. However, as has been observed:

> An analysis of such factors was not possible within this chapter because of a lack of detailed data, but such an analysis must be carried out before any firm conclusions can be reached about whether geographic profiling techniques have the potential to be effective [for profiling terrorists].[113]

---

110   For official materials, see http://www.tsa.gov/public/display?theme=5&content=09000519800cf3a7.

111   Craig Bennell and Shevaun Corey, "Geographic Profiling of Terrorist Attacks", in *Criminal Profiling: International Theory, Research, and Practice*, ed. R. N. Kocsis (Totowa, NJ: Humana Press, 2007), 190.

112   National Technology Alliance, *Geographic Profiling and the Hunt for Insurgents* (2007), available at: http://www.nta.org/docs/Geoprofiling.pdf, accessed on February 15, 2007.

113   Bennell and Corey, "Geographic Profiling of Terrorist Attacks," in *Criminal Profiling: International Theory, Research, and Practice*, 201.

(D) Limitations of Technology[114]

All this discussion of the use of technology in trying to secure our society may incline us to the conclusion that all technology does is cloud the security issue with both certainty (though this, as it turns out, is false) for those ignorant of the actual capabilities and limitations of technology, and pessimism in those who are not.[115] John Gentry succinctly summarizes the systemic problems stemming from the US military's approach to technology.[116] According to him, these problems are: narrow applicability; vulnerable infrastructure; easy counter-measures; and institutional impediments.

The efficacy of technology can be assessed on (at least) two fronts: the quality of the technology and the information needed to make it useful; and the way the technology is used.

Quality of information and quality of technology

There is a common phrase in the information technology field – "garbage in, garbage out"[117] – which is both a swipe at the unwarranted trust that people put in the output of computers and a succinct way of saying that the quality of the output is absolutely dependent upon the quality of the source of the information used. Although the military does not reveal the nature or extent of the quality of its information or information technology, we can, given its record in the rest of technology development and use, deduce that its record is similar to commercial systems and that there are significant problems with its

---

114   The point of this is not to deny that technology, especially information technology, can be used effectively in the military or security fields. See Nicholas S. Argyres, "The Impact of Information Technology on Coordination: Evidence from the B-2 'Stealth' Bomber", *Organization Science* 10, no. 2 (1999): 162–80 for an example of where it has assisted the development of a significant piece of military (and surveillance) technology. Our point here is that this is not always the case. Indeed, as the following examples show, the success of IT is more the exception than the rule. The GOA regularly issues reports on the failure of US government agencies and departments to adhere to proper IT project management techniques. This failure costs billions of dollars, according to the GOA. See, for example, David A. Powner, Director, United States Government Accountability Office, Information Technology Management Issues, *Management and Oversight of Projects Totaling Billions of Dollars Need Attention*, Testimony before the Subcommittee on Federal Financial Management, Government Information, Federal Services, and International Security, Committee on Homeland Security and Governmental Affairs, US Senate, April 28, 2009.

115   In a recent simulation exercise, "Mr. Lynn, one of the Pentagon's top strategists for computer network operations, argues that the billions spent on defensive shields surrounding America's banks, businesses and military installations provide a similarly illusory sense of security." John Markoff, David E. Sanger and Thom Shanker, "In Digital Combat, U.S. Finds No Easy Deterrent", *The New York Times*, January 26, 2010.

116   See John A. Gentry, "Doomed to Fail: America's Blind Faith in Military Technology", *Parameters* (2002–03): 88–103.

117   For the origin of this phrase see the Free Online Dictionary of computing at http://foldoc.org/garbage+in, viewed January 30, 2010.

information quality. According to Barbara Klein: "Data stored in organizational databases have a significant number of errors. Between one and ten percent of data items in critical organizational databases are estimated to be inaccurate."[118]

Much of the work of terrorists is planned in third world countries. However, it is in just these places that the quality of data in information systems is most suspect.[119] This deficiency in data quality severely compromises efforts to monitor terrorist activities.

In a recent US government report "Cyberspace Policy Review" a review team of government cybersecurity experts concluded that "the architecture of the Nation's digital infrastructure, based largely upon the Internet, is not secure or resilient. Without major advances in the security of these systems or significant change in how they are constructed or operated, it is doubtful that the United States can protect itself from the growing threat of cybercrime and state-sponsored intrusions and operations."[120]

An example of the weakness of various securitization technologies is biometric national identity systems.[121] These systems depend for their usefulness upon the quality of (low-security) documents such as drivers licenses, birth certificates and the like. Such documents are relatively easy to (falsely) obtain. Once this has been achieved, NIDs (falsely) authenticate individuals, thus generating false negatives.

An aspect of the quality of technology that is often overlooked is its own security – that is, how well does it prevent unauthorized users from getting access to its information and decision-making process? A military example of this is the recent newspaper article by Siobhan Gorman et al., which reported that $26 worth of commercial software is able to "intercept live video feeds from U.S. Predator drones."[122] In 2009 more than 285 million data records were compromised in the business field.[123] Although military and security agencies are secretive about the safety of their systems, there is little to make one confident that their systems comprise any better technology.[124]

---

118   Barbara D. Klein, "Data Quality in the Practice of Consumer Product Management: Evidence from the Field", *Data Quality* 4, no. 1 (1998).

119   David W. Chapman and Roger A. Boothroyd, "Threats to Data Quality in Developing Country Settings", *Comparative Education Review* 32, no. 4 (1988): 416–29. Although this report is dated, the situation in developing countries has not changed in twenty years.

120   White House, *Cyberspace Policy Review: Assuring a Trusted and Resilient Information and Communications Structure* (May, 2009), available at: http://www.whitehouse.gov/assets/documents/Cyberspace_Policy_Review_final.pdf.

121   For a detailed examination of this phenomenon, see See Bijon Roy, "A Case against Biometric National Identification Systems (NIDS): 'Trading-off' Privacy Without Getting Security", *Windsor Review of Legal & Social Issues* 19 (March 2005): 45–84.

122   Siobhan Gorman, Yochi J. Dreazen, and August Cole, "Insurgents Hack U.S. Drones, $26 Software Is Used to Breach Key Weapons in Iraq; Iranian Backing Suspected", *The Wall Street Journal*, December 17, 2009, A1.

123   Wade H. Baker, Alex Hutton, C. David Hylender, Christopher Novak, Christopher Porter, Bryan Sartin, Peter Tippett, M.D., Ph.D. and J. Andrew Valentine, *2009 Data Breach Investigations Report*, Verizon Business, available at http://securityblog.verizonbusiness.com, viewed December 14, 2009.

124   There are many examples of technology failures in the military and security fields. See, for example, the U.S. Navy's Smart Ship technology of the late 1990s that failed so spectacularly, Gregory Slabodkin, "Software Glitches Leave Navy Smart Ship Dead in the Water", *Government Computer News*, 13 July 1998.

In another example, Stephen Feinberg makes the point that data mining's success "depend[s] heavily on matching and record-linkage methods that are intrinsically statistical in nature and whose accuracy deteriorates rapidly in the presence of serious measurement error. Data mining tools cannot make up for bad data and poor matches."[125] It is absolutely essential that securitization technologies have quality data.

Another difficulty with measuring the quality of information comes through quantity: if the quantity is large enough then it is not possible to measure the quality of a given set of information. According to Minnesota Internet Traffic Studies (MINTS), the total known digital content is roughly 500 billion gigabytes, or 500 exabytes (with more than 60 exabytes produced every year).[126] With current technology it is not possible to process this much information.[127] As a result new theories for information processing (especially concerning money laundering and terrorist financing) are being developed, but researchers are not yet optimistic about the possibilities.[128] This is an especially acute problem for the military use of spy drones. In a recent article, Christopher Drew of the *New York Times* reported that the military was recording video data at a greater rate than can be analyzed.[129]

The quality of technology is underpinned by the quality of the assumptions made. In the section on surveillance we pointed out that much of the technology is not of sufficient quality to be useful. This can be seen in facial recognition software (an issue visited earlier in this discussion, reviewing James Meek's experiment) that depends upon the "idea that certain anatomical characteristics, facial configurations, gestural expressions and behaviors are universal, rather than specific or framed by the context in which they appear."[130] According to Andrew Speirs, this is a flawed notion that consistently fails to deliver suspects. Here it is the quality of the design (underlying assumptions) of the technology that fails to deliver. Also underpinning the quality of technology is the quality of the personnel employed by agencies to develop the technology. In a recent

---

125   Stephen E. Feinberg, "Privacy and Confidentiality in an e-Commerce World: Data Mining, Data Warehousing, Matching and Disclosure Limitation", *Statistical Science* 21, no. 2 (2006): 143–54.
126   An exabyte is 10246 or approximately one billion gigabytes. See Minnesota Internet Traffic Studies (MINTS), at http://www.dtc.umn.edu/mints/home.php, viewed February 1, 2010.
127   David S. Alberts made just this point and called it information swamping. See David S. Alberts, *The Unintended Consequences of Information Age Technologies: Avoiding the Pitfalls, Seizing the Initiative* (Diane Publishing Co. 1996), especially pp. 16, 31, 34, 38. The legal profession refers to the term "information inflation" to describe this phenomenon/problem: see George L. Paul and Jason R. Baron, "Information Inflation: Can the Legal System Adapt?", *Richmond Journal of Law & Technology* 13, no. 3 (2007), at http://law.richmond.edu/jolt/v13i3/article10.pdf, viewed January 25, 2010.
128   Dionysios S. Demetis, "Data Growth, the New Order of Information Manipulation and Consequences for the AML/ATF Domains", *Journal of Money Laundering Control* 12, no. 4 (2009): 353–70.
129   Christopher Drew, "Military Is Awash in Data from Drones", *The New York Times*, January 11, 2010.
130   Andrew Speirs, "The Individual and the Stereotype: From Lavater to the War on Terror", Australian Council of University Art and Design Schools (ACUADS) ACUADS 2003 Conference, Hobart 1–4 Oct 2003, http://www.acuads.com.au/conf2003/papers_refereed/speirs.pdf.

job advertisement for a business consultant, the National Security Agency (NSA) specified in the job requirements that the successful candidate would "perform various types of business analyses (e.g. Business Case, Cost/Benefit, Cost Effectiveness, etc.), as well as analysis of special topics that will be used by Senior Leadership to make better-informed decisions."[131] Yet the qualifications asked for stated: "The successful candidates should possess at least 2+ years of related experience and a Bachelor's degree in engineering, mathematics, operations research, business, or economics." There was not a word about information technology qualifications, especially analysis and design. How can such agencies be confident of their employees' ability successfully to complete complex information technology tasks without any professional qualifications? This is not a new problem. In 1996, Alberts noted the US government's inability to "maintain the expertise required to adapt" commercial software for military use.[132]

In another example of flawed assumptions, Geoff Dean found the idea of profiling terrorists as persons to be "neither simple nor necessarily helpful and could in fact be dangerously misleading. It is argued that it is more fruitful to shift the focus of the profiling paradigm by engaging in profiling the 'process' of terrorism rather than the 'person'."[133] This can be seen in the results of the NSA's domestic spying program. According to the Electronic Frontier Foundation (EFF) this program is next to useless: "Reports have shown that the data from this wholesale surveillance did little more than commit FBI resources to follow up leads, virtually all of [which], current and former officials say, led to dead ends or innocent Americans."[134]

More directly addressing the quality of technology itself is the doubt cast on the quality of many technologies. For example, in the geographic profiling software referred to earlier, Derek Paulson found that his "study casts doubt . . . on the overall accuracy of profiling strategies in predicting the likely home location of an offender."[135] A final example of the worry that technology is not up to the task is steganography. Kessler points out that "there are few hard statistics about the frequency with which steganography software or media are discovered by law enforcement officials in the course of computer forensics analysis. Anecdotal evidence suggests, however, that many computer forensics examiners do not

131   This job was posted on CareerBuilder.com on January 6, 2010, viewed January 10, 2010.

132   See Alberts, *The Unintended Consequences of Information Age Technologies: Avoiding the Pitfalls, Seizing the Initiative*, 44.

133   Geoff Dean, "Criminal Profiling in a Terrorism Context", in R. N. Kocsis (ed.), *Criminal Profiling – International Theory, Research and Practice* (Humana Press, 2007).

134   Electronic Frontier Foundation FAQ, at http://www.eff.org/nsa/faq, viewed 2 January 2010.

135   Derek J. Paulsen, "Connecting the Dots: Assessing the Accuracy of Geographic Profiling Software", *Policing: An International Journal of Police Strategies & Management* 29, no. 2 (2006): 306–34.

routinely search for steganography software, and many might not recognize such tools if they found them."[136] He further points out that "it is impossible to know how widespread the use of steganography is by criminals and terrorists".

The quality of technology can also be measured by the degree to which it meets its stakeholders' expectations. A recent Standish Report found that "in 1995, U.S. government and businesses spent approximately $81 billion on cancelled software projects."[137] Most of these projects were cancelled due to difficulties in specifying and meeting user requirements.

The use of information (and its) technology

Much of the technology described in this study creates an enormous amount of information that would be useful in the right hands. Indeed, the use of technology to gather and process information has led to significant improvements in many areas, including law enforcement. However, in some cases that information has gone not into the right hands but, indeed, into the wrong hands (as seen in the drone article above).

One of the criticisms of the various government agencies in the aftermath of 9/11 was the failure to share information.[138,139] This failure points to a general lack of protocols, procedures and governance defining the importance, scope and circumstances of information sharing. Stewart Baker, in his testimony before Congress, said that "the government's failure to find the hijackers was caused in the first instance by a lack of information technology tools."[140]

Of course, much of the foregoing discussion offers an implicit evaluation from a privacy perspective of existing information technology systems. Nevertheless, we should not forget those projects that did not get even as far as being implemented. The most outstanding example of this is the FBI's Trilogy Project

---

136   See Gary C. Kessler, "An Overview of Steganography for the Computer Forensics Examiner"(edited version), *Forensic Science Communications (Technical Report)* 6, no. 3 (July 2004), available at: http://www.fbi. gov/hq/lab/fsc/backissu/july2004/research/2004_03_research01.htm; http://www.garykessler.net/library/ fsc_stego.html.

137   The Standish Group, "Chaos", 1995, at http://www.standishgroup.com/chaos.html, viewed December 30, 2009. See also Lorin J. May, "Major Causes of Software Project Failures", at http://www.stsc.hill.af.mil/ crosstalk/1998/07/causes.asp, viewed November 20, 2009.

138   In the information field, information sharing is called information transparency. See Peter P. Swire, "Privacy and Information Sharing in the War on Terrorism", *Villanova Law Review* 51 (2006): 951–80; and Matteo Turilli and Luciano Floridi, "The Ethics of Information Transparency", *Ethics and Information Technology* 11 (2009): 105–12.

139   The Christmas 2009 attempt to bomb a commercial airliner highlights the fact that information sharing has not improved. See Eric Lipton, Eric Schmitt and Mark Mazzetti, "Jet Bomb Plot Shows More Missed Clues", *The New York Times*, January 18, 2010.

140   Testimony of Stewart Baker before the National Commission on Terrorist Attacks Upon the United States December 8, 2003.

(better known as the Virtual Case File Project).[141] It is estimated to have cost at least $100 million (cost estimates vary from $100 to $400 million) with no return for the investment. This system was intended to overcome the problem of sharing of information between those who *ought* to have had access to and those who *actually* had access to critical information. Fundamentally, it failed because of the FBI's reluctance to engage professional IT project managers, preferring to use its own (unqualified, in IT terms) agents. Although this example may seem to be an outlier, in fact it is consistent with normal commercial industry practice.[142]

---

141   There is an enormous amount of literature examining this failed software project. See, for example, Harry Goldstein, "Who Killed the Virtual Case File?", *IEEE Spectrum*, at http://lrv.fri.uni-lj.si/~franc/COURSES/VP/FBI.pdf, viewed 5 July 2009, and T. Frieden, "Report: FBI Wasted Millions on 'Virtual Case File'", *CNN* (2005, February 3), at http://www.cnn.com, viewed September 7, 2009. See also,http://www.sdtimes.com/link/28788, viewed 16 November 2009.
142   Robert N. Charette, "Why Software Fails", *IEEE Spectrum*, at: http://spectrum.ieee.org/computing/why-software-fails, viewed January 3, 2010.

VII. Surveillance Technologies and Economies

Introduction

Thus far this work has been concerned extensively with the way liberal democracies attempt to balance individual privacy with the need for collective security. Government collection of data on individuals, along with its ethical and legal underpinnings, has been our main concern. In Chapters V and VI, for example, we described surveillance technologies and systems increasingly used by governments for security purposes – passenger name records, data mining to create terrorist profiles and National Identity Cards to name a few. In those sections we touched briefly upon current, widely accepted modern communication and information systems, such as social networks that now result in unprecedented collection of data on individuals by the private sector, often through what is characterized as "participatory surveillance". Here we examine those systems, their use and their impact on individual privacy in more detail. Much of what we describe in this chapter applies more directly to the United States than to the European Union. This is no accident, because we believe that in many important respects the EU offers greater privacy protection than the US.[1] In other liberal democracies we have reviewed (see Appendix) the picture is somewhat mixed; speaking generally, there is a lack of privacy protection in the private sector. India, as noted above, has an implied right to privacy and is motivated to protect privacy and confidentiality in the private sector in part because of its large international IT outsourcing industry. However, in practice, self-regulation is the norm in the private sector. Australia's Privacy Act applies to private sector organizations as well as Australian government agencies. However, the Office of the Privacy Commissioner – the agency responsible for ensuring the Act is complied with – does not have the power to conduct audits of organizations in the private sector. Moreover, the Privacy Act does not cover businesses with less than AU$3 million annual turnover (that is, the majority of businesses in Australia).

During the first decade of the twenty-first century there has been an unprecedented rise in the collection, analysis and dissemination of information on individuals. As we have noted, privacy advocates and civil libertarians have long expressed concern over government-sponsored data acquisition and

---

1   This is not to idealize the EU. Compliance with EU directives has not been wholehearted, as individual member states have developed and implemented legislation in response to EU directives.

collection activities, which have increased markedly since 2001 as part of efforts to combat terrorism. Concern regarding government use of data is prompted by the fact that government has the ultimate power to limit freedom – it can prosecute. Thus, privacy regulation in the US often focuses on restricting the government's ability to collect and use personal data. Yet, as Garfinkel[2] and others[3,4] have pointed out for some time, in the US the greatest source of data on individuals is collected by the private sector, where it enjoys few constitutional or other statutory protections, often because this personal information is part of the public record or because individuals have been deemed to have consented to the release of their personal information as part of a transaction with another party.[5] Much of the current impetus for collection and analysis comes not from security needs but from commercial needs for information on consumers and consumer behavior in order to offer novel, attractive services, gain new efficiencies or develop new revenue sources. Increasingly, US government agencies, particularly law enforcement agencies such as the FBI, rely on major commercial data brokers such as Acxiom[6] or the Accurint division of LexisNexis[7] for both data collection and analysis.

Continued advances in computer storage and processing, computer networks and information retrieval methods have made possible a range of scalable internet-based services that provide numerous benefits to consumers, but these increasingly require the collection of personal information and its dissemination to numerous parties. The widespread acceptance of and now reliance on internet-based services such as social networking sites, web-based email and search engines, along with the gradual trend to make public and other records containing personal information readily available online, has dramatically increased the types of personal information available on individuals. Most importantly, these trends have significantly lowered the cost of obtaining that information. Moreover, we now live in what was billed in the 1990s as the age of "ubiquitous computing".[8] Networked digital technologies such as cell phones, surveillance cameras and other smart devices make possible constant data collection and surveillance systems that provide location and even detailed behavioral information. In the US, a highly effective industry for aggregating,

---

2 Simson Garfinkel, *Database Nation: The Death of Privacy in the 21st Century* (O'Reilly Media, December 2000).

3 Daniel Solove and Chris J. Hoofnagle, "A Model Regime of Privacy Protection", *University of Illinois Law Review* 2006 (February, 2006): 357–404.

4 Ari Schwartz, written supplement to testimony before the Data Privacy and Integrity Committee, Department of Homeland Security, June 15, 2005. Available at: http://www.netdemocracyguide.net/testimony/20050718schwartz.pdf.

5 By contrast, consent needs to be explicit in the EU context.

6 Available at: http://www.acxiom.com/Pages/Home.aspx.

7 Available at: http://www.accurint.com/.

8 Mark Weiser coined the term "ubiquitous computing" for where computers are embedded in all types of devices and everyone interacts with them for their daily needs. See Mark Weiser, "The Computer for the Twenty-First Century", *Scientific American* (September 1991): 94–10.

analyzing and disseminating information on individuals is in place with the capability to search terabytes of both structured and unstructured data for relevant items.

Most will agree that the ability to share and discover information as well as communicate inexpensively on a worldwide scale offers tremendous opportunities to businesses, consumers and governments.[9] For example, the online availability of personal medical records improves health care by making records readily available for diagnosis, and can lower costs by eliminating unnecessary tests. Knowledge collections are now at our fingertips and not confined to obscure locations. Current internet-based systems provide a two-way communication channel between a service provider and a consumer. Thus, organizations such as retail chains, colleges and libraries can deliver highly personalized content to consumers, students and researchers that addresses their needs or interests.[10] The ability to search vast record collections and retrieve relevant information, a highly active and fruitful area of research in computer science, has allowed both individuals and organizations to utilize knowledge and research.[11] Indeed, many of the systems common today have created opportunities for productive work and socialization that would have been unimaginable fifteen years ago.

This study has been concerned with the significant risks that the release of personal information poses for individual well-being, autonomy and dignity. The systems upon which we now rely for much of our social and economic activity result in the unprecedented release of personal information and raise many questions (albeit somewhat different ones in the EU than in the US). What are the risks associated with just about anyone, including the government, being able to know just about anything about anybody for a nominal cost? As we have noted, many of the legal protections for individual liberties arose in an environment in which physical world restrictions on data limit the flow of information. Such restrictions gave rise to situations of privacy and expectations of privacy. Legal scholars are still unclear how these protections extend to the current era, where there are few practical constraints on the flow of data or what can be known and by whom. In the hope of gaining immediate benefits from internet-based systems, are we revealing too much personal information to too many different parties? Many claim that, in the new information age, information is never lost. What is the impact on individual well-being when possibly outdated information is still available and used to make decisions as to

---

9   Again, we focus here on the US context. Within the EU, personal data are to be kept and used only for the purposes for which they are originally collected, unless there is explicit consent by the data subject, subject to broad exceptions for government purposes.

10   There has, nevertheless, been concern about the way in which Google's personalizing of responses to research requests tends to confirm "detected" biases.

11   W. Fan, L. Wallace, S. Rich, and Z. Zhang, "Tapping the Power of Text Mining", *Communications of the ACM* 49, no. 9 (September 2006): 77–82.

a person's work ethic and employability? Moreover, how do individuals correct information that is incorrect if it is held in unknown data repositories and not tethered to any authoritative data source? A key feature of Web 2.0 systems is the ability for just about anyone to post information that then can be made available to anyone. How do systems in which anyone can publish information about anyone else and make it widely available impact human dignity?

Within the US, the focus has primarily been on the risks that government data collection pose for liberal democracies. However, as has been realized in the EU, aggressive collection of personal data in the private sector, along with advancing capabilities for data synthesis and analysis, now offer not only governments but unwanted others the opportunity to obtain information on individuals that was heretofore unavailable. In Chapter IV, we examined the Supreme Court decision in *United States v. White* that (in the US) severely limits Fourth Amendment protections for data provided to third parties.[12] In current, widely used internet-based systems such as social networks and search engines, third party data controllers typically obtain personal information through consent and terms-of-use agreements. The information is often no longer subject to the usual Fourth Amendment restrictions if sought by government as part of a criminal investigation. Often, law enforcement authorities can quickly obtain information on individuals from data controllers with a subpoena instead of a warrant, which requires authorities to demonstrate probable cause. In addition, restrictions on government collection of information do not apply to information that has been made publicly available – for example, information posted on a blog or personal website.

In the remainder of this chapter we examine recent technologies and organizational practices enabled by those technologies that make it very difficult – particularly in the US – for both individuals and organizations to control the exposure of sensitive personal information. Trends we examine include the following:

- Widespread acceptance and reliance on network-enabled digital devices and services to which users continually provide personal and often highly sensitive information.

- Organizational models and practices employed by service providers such as social networking sites, web-based email hosts, and other application service providers that require users to allow personal information to be made available to third parties.[13]

- Emergence in the US (but outlawed in the EU) of an efficient data aggregation and brokerage industry, with exceptional capabilities to gather, store,

---

12   The EU, as noted earlier, places much more stringent restrictions on third-party transmissions of data.

13   Broadly speaking, whereas the US has tended to favor opt-out models, the EU has mandated opt-in ones.

synthesize and make information on individuals, available for a range of specific purposes, e.g. targeted marketing, employment screening or law enforcement investigation.

- The inability of parties holding personal information to secure it properly (though increased legal liability would incentivize increased security).

We also comment on the impact that these trends are having on commonly accepted notions of privacy (focusing in this chapter largely on the US situation).

Technologies, organizational practices and information exposure

Today, an array of technologies – as well as business practices enabled by those technologies – allow aggregators to build a detailed personal profile of just about anyone. Recent advances in the knowledge-discovery technologies, data-clustering and link analyses now make it possible to group together related records in a transactional database of billions of records and establish connections among the groups. Thus it is often possible to find information on associations, relatives, past addresses and related items with little difficulty from large-scale transactional databases.[14] Furthermore, the continued development of information storage and retrieval systems, increasing levels of surveillance made possible by rapidly improving camera technologies, and the constant collection of personal information by third parties provide the information needed to establish a detailed picture of an individual that includes current interests, recent purchase history, recent whereabouts and health and financial information.

Peter Fleischer, global privacy counsel for Google, in an address to Google's employees characterized what Google considers to be the new reality concerning concepts of personal privacy.[15] Mr. Fleischer stated that historical concepts of privacy depended on forgetfulness, incompetence or laziness. Information was simply lost, or nobody bothered to find it. Mr. Fleischer claimed that those conditions have protected individual privacy for millennia. He further stated that we now live in a world in which we can remember everything and find everything. He conjectured that such an environment considerably changes expectations of privacy, especially those derived from a physical world in which information can become obscure. He further pointed out that the internet readily

---

14 The credit industry maintains a large-scale transactional database of credit applications that is mined using these techniques to detect fraudulent credit applications. See the report, "US Identity Fraud Rates by Geography", San Diego, CA: I.D. Analytics Inc. (February 2007).
15 Peter Fleischer, "Protecting Privacy on the Internet", December 19, 2007, available at http://www.youtube.com/watch?v=2IKBke1puFw.

allows data to cross national boundaries and that systems such as Google's cannot be architected to stop at an international border. He concluded, therefore, that having different privacy regimes in different countries is out of touch with the modern reality. He noted that, historically, in phone conversations there was a "sense of evanescence" to the conversation. However, with email and chat, data are stored by third parties and the data remain. He thus concluded that expectations of privacy must change.

(i) Social networking

In the past decade, social networking websites, which began as a niche phenomenon to support hobbies and other specific interests, have become for many the *de facto* mode of communication, especially among young adults and teens. Facebook, the current leading social networking site, reports that it now has 500 million active users worldwide, and that over 50% of active users log on to their Facebook account daily.[16] According to a recent Pew Internet study, internet usage among Americans is currently 93% for teens and young adults (ages 12–29), over 70% for adults (ages 30–64) and just under 40% for adults over sixty-five.[17] The study also reports that 73% of online teens and 47% of online adults now use social networking sites, a 50% increase during the last five years. Of those who have profiles, 73% have a profile on Facebook,[18] 48% have one on MySpace[19] and 14% have a LinkedIn[20] profile. Thus a significant portion of the American population uses social networking sites and most of their profiles are posted on one or more of the three top websites.

Given the growing reliance on social networks, there has been considerable research into the impact on privacy. Most information posted on the three major social network websites is associated with the user's real identity. In social networks such as Facebook, pseudonymity is discouraged through site usage norms and the need to provide a valid email address to register. Following usage norms, most users do provide a real identity, but as many have noted it is very easy to set up an account using a pseudonym.[21] When social networking first became popular, Facebook was considered a more secure environment than MySpace because a Facebook user was associated with a physical world

---

16   Facebook: pressroom statistics. Available at http://www.facebook.com/press/info.php?statistics.
17   Pew Internet and American Life Project, "Social Media & Mobile Internet Use Among Teens and Young Adults, Pew Research Center", Feb 3, 2010, available at: http://www.pewinternet.org/Reports/2010/Social-Media-and-Young-Adults.aspx. For country-by-country Facebook usage (including the EU), see: http://www.nickburcher.com/2009/07/latest-facebook-usage-statistics-by.html.
18   http://www.facebook.com.
19   http://www.myspace.com.
20   http://www.linkedin.com.
21   For this reason Japanese social network users patronize Gree or Mixi rather than Facebook. See Hiroko Tabuchi, "Facebook Wins Relatively Few Friends in Japan", *The New York Times*, January 9, 2011.

institution such as the user's high school or university. There was some expectation that information revealed would be limited to members whom the users knew from the offline world. Social networking sites allow users to define a group of friends who can view the user's profile information. Default settings will often expose the information posted to anyone associated with the user's institution, but users can opt to limit exposure to a group of friends and user-adjustable controls enable even finer-grained control of the information exposed. In many ways, Facebook and other social network sites give the impression that they offer an intimate setting in which friends can communicate and the privacy of the group is protected.

Gross and Acquisti have examined the potential for information revelation in social networks in which the use of a real account name is typically connected to an account profile.[22] They point out that the term "friends" used on a social networking website is quite different from the idea of a friend in the physical world. On a social networking site, a friend is determined by a binary setting, yes or no, while in the real world friends are associated with various degrees of trust. On a social networking site people are often included as friends even if the user does not know the person and has no established trust relationship. The number of a user's friends is much higher on a social networking site. Although physical world friendships typically number between fifteen and twenty, Gross and Acquisiti found that on a college campus in 2004 the average number of social networking friends was over sixty, all of whom enjoyed the same level of trust. Currently, the average US Facebook user has 130 friends.[23] The ease of joining and extending a friend network on most sites means that users must exert considerable effort to control the membership of the group. Research indicates that most users are apt to accept friends they do not know well as long as they do not have a previous dislike for the person.[24] Another difficulty is that the composition of the friends group changes over time. When friend groups start, they are often small groups in which the members are intimately acquainted. As the groups grow the relationships frequently become looser. Thus information intended for the smaller, original group can find its way to members of the larger group. In addition, users may find it difficult to limit the group by denying access to someone who requests membership. Social networking sites provide numerous incentives for prospective users to join the site and become a current member's friend.[25]

---

22 Ralph Gross and Alessandro Acquisti, "Information Revelation and Privacy in On-line Social Networks (The Facebook Case)", *Proceedings of the ACM Workshop on Privacy in Electronic Society (WPES)*, November 2005, available at: http://www.heinz.cmu.edu/~acquisti/papers/privacy-facebook-gross-acquisti.pdf.

23 Facebook, Press Room, Statistics. Available at http://www.facebook.com/press/info.php?statistics.

24 Danah Boyd, "Friendster and Publicly Articulated Social Networking", Conference on Human Factors and Computing Systems, April 24–29, Vienna, Austria, 2004, available at: http://www.danah.org/papers/CHI2004Friendster.pdf.

25 Facebook's homepage presents a "find friends" option. Nonmembers can look for a member's name and are then offered an opportunity to register and join the current member's group of friends.

Leading privacy organizations and the Federal Trade Commission are increasingly scrutinizing Facebook's approach to privacy protection. The Electronic Frontier Foundation (EFF) has praised Facebook's recent decision to introduce privacy controls that allow users to restrict access to content on a per-post basis.[26] Users can limit access to a post to a particular subset of friends selected from a drop down menu. At the same time the EFF and other privacy organizations were highly critical of Facebook's default settings in a new privacy tool released in December 2009. In a complaint filed with the Federal Trade Commission[27] the EEF noted that the new settings give all Facebook users and possibly anyone on the internet access to a user's friend list, profile, photos, gender, geographic region and pages they favor. Previously only a user's name and network were available. The new settings were applied to all Facebook users, unless the user took the trouble to make the settings more restrictive.

Besides friends making personal information available, there are many other ways in which information propagates in a social networking site. In the US, the basic business model of a social networking site requires that information on users be made available to third parties for targeted marketing and other commercial purposes.[28] The importance of having unfettered access to user data is evidenced in the Facebook terms of use agreement:

> By posting User Content to any part of the Site, you automatically grant, and you represent and warrant that you have the right to grant, to the Company an irrevocable, perpetual, non-exclusive, transferable, fully paid, worldwide license (with the right to sublicense) to use, copy, publicly perform, publicly display, reformat, translate, excerpt (in whole or in part) and distribute such User Content for any purpose on or in connection with the Site or the promotion thereof, to prepare derivative works of, or incorporate into other works, such User Content, and to grant and authorize sublicenses of the foregoing. You may remove your User Content from the Site at any time. If you choose to remove your User Content, the license granted above will automatically expire, however you acknowledge that the Company may retain archived copies of your User Content.[29]

---

26   Electronic Frontier Foundation, "Facebook's New Privacy Changes: The Good, the Bad and the Ugly", December 9, 2009. Available at: http://www.eff.org/deeplinks/2009/12/facebooks-new-privacy-changes-good-bad-and-ugly.

27   In the Matter of Facebook, Complaint and Request for Injunction, Request for Investigation and Other Relief, before the Federal Trade Commission (December 17, 2010). Available at: http://epic.org/privacy/inrefacebook/EPIC-FacebookComplaint.pdf. For the fallout from this, see: http://epic.org/privacy/inrefacebook/.

28   On November 9, 2009, an addition to the EU's e-privacy Directive, Directive on Privacy and Electronic Communications, 2002/58/EC, mandated an opt-in rather than opt-out requirement that included Facebook and other US-based social networking sites. Implementation has been lax, however. See: http://www.pcworld.com/businesscenter/article/235985/eu_orders_member_states_to_implement_cookie_law_or_else.html.

29   Taken from the term-of-user agreement available at: http://facebook.com/policy.php, February 7, 2007. This would almost certainly violate EU law.

Facebook also informs users that it collects information not only from what they post but also from newspapers, blogs, instant messaging services and other users of Facebook in order to provide a more personalized experience. Privacy settings on social network sites usually default to allow for as much information sharing among users and third parties in order to maximize the utility of user data. Chris Kelly, Facebook's privacy officer, noted that about 20% of Facebook's users reset privacy controls from their default values. Thus the vast majority of users do not.

Facebook allows third-party developers to write software programs that users can install on their Facebook sites to give the site various capabilities similar to those provided by java scripts used on websites. The top twenty-five Facebook applications (referred to as Apps) have about 5.5 million active users per month.[30] Most applications do not have a privacy policy and the Facebook terms-of-service agreement provides the following warning:

> ALL PLATFORM APPLICATIONS ARE PROVIDED AS IS [and that] YOU UNDERSTAND AND AGREE THAT YOU DOWNLOAD, INSTALL AND/ OR USE ANY PLATFORM APPLICATIONS AT YOUR OWN DISCRETION AND RISK.

The *Washington Post* reports that the applications have become so popular that there are now venture capital firms devoted entirely to funding Facebook App development.[31] Felt and Evans[32] report that when a user installs a Facebook App under the default privacy settings, the App has access to all of the user's information even if it does not need it. The App can collect information and copy it to a third-party server, which may then use it for a targeted marketing campaign or other purposes. Once the information has been harvested, neither Facebook nor the user has any control over its use.

Rosenbloom examined why social networking site users are apt to post such intimate details of their personal lives in an environment in which they have so little control.[33] He states that the "porous nature of the Net has radically redefined the arena in which individuals are willing to disclose personal information . . . the comfort zone is much larger and the circle of friends more broadly defined." At the time Rosenbloom was referring primarily to college students and those who grew up using the internet. However, this general

---

30   ReadWriteWeb, "Does That Facebook App Have a Privacy Policy? Probably Not", July 29, 2009. Available at: http://www.readwriteweb.com.

31   *The Washington Post*, "A Flashy Facebook Page at a Cost to Privacy", June 12, 2008.

32   A. Felt and D. Evans, "Privacy Protection for Social Networking APIs", presented at Web 2.0 Security and Privacy 2008, Oakland, Ca, May 22, 2008. Available at: http://www.eecs.berkeley.edu/~afelt/privacybyproxy. pdf. New EU laws have limited access, though not yet with full effect.

33   David Rosenblum, "What Anyone Can Know: The Privacy Risks of Social Networking Sites", *IEEE Security and Privacy* 5, no. 3 (May/June 2007): 40–49.

tendency appears in all groups who use the sites. Acquisti has noted that in using online systems users can seldom strike an adequate balance between the immediate benefit of providing information and the long-term risks of revealing it.[34] In addition, with the social network phenomenon there is the tremendous force of peer pressure to participate, as well as the confidence inspired by using a well-known website.

The impact of social networks on individual well-being is an open question. Given the inability to control who has access to information posted on a social networking website, it is important not to assume that privacy expectations in the physical world carry over to the world of social networking. James Rachels observed that privacy is valuable because it enables us to form varied and intimate relationships with other people.[35] This is precisely how social networking sites are used. However, the intimacy needed to protect communications within small groups is an illusion.

(ii) Highly dynamic systems

US businesses have long collected data on customers, but information on the activities of specific individuals was not the primary interest. When scanning devices were introduced into supermarkets and other stores in the early 1970s it became possible to collect detailed data on items being purchased, monitor inventory more effectively and reduce the costs of marking each item.[36] By 2006, the retailer Wal-mart had amassed a 586-terabyte data warehouse that included sales and inventory data.[37] Wal-mart records every item sold to every customer in every store on a daily basis. For most consumer goods purchased in retail outlets like Wal-mart, the retailer does not care exactly who bought what. Mass-market retailers are more concerned with questions such as how many tubes of a certain toothpaste were sold and what item was most often purchased with the toothpaste. Data analysis is often done to determine why certain goods may or may not be selling and how item placement can improve sales. Wal-mart claims to keep the data for only two years and also claims not to track the purchases of individual customers.

For over ten years companies like comScore Networks[38] have monitored the behavior of millions of internet users to gain insights into consumer behavior. Data are collected to try to spot trends in consumer purchases and interests.

---

34 Alessandro Acquisti, "Privacy in Electronic Commerce and the Economics of Immediate Gratification", *Proceedings of the ACM Conference on Electronic Commerce*, 2004, 21–29.

35 James Rachels, "Why is Privacy Important", *Philosophy and Public Affairs* 4 (Summer, 1975): 323–33.

36 James Sinkula, "Status of Company Usage of Scanner Based Research", *Journal of the Academy of Marketing Science* 14 (1986): 63–71.

37 C. Babcock, "Data Data Everywhere", *Information Week Global CIO*, January 9, 2006.

38 comScore, Inc., http://www.comscore.com.

The company enlists about two million internet users (who are compensated) and claims that user privacy is protected. For most of the company's activities, individuals are not the main concern; general trends are. The company monitors users in order to assess the effectiveness of ad campaigns, the use of web sites and to develop detailed profiles of users who might be purchasing certain kinds of goods or visiting particular websites. comScore clients rely on the company's research to build customer profiles and target consumers based on those profiles. In this type of targeted advertising the user's recent behavior or contextual information is used to present targeted ads. Although this type of marketing has raised privacy concerns, an identity is not required and is typically not associated with a behavioral pattern.

What is dramatically changing the picture is a collection of technologies often referred to as highly dynamic systems (HDS) that allow personalized services and products to be delivered to a particular consumer.[39] Like the client server computing paradigm upon which e-commerce is based, HDS provide a one-to-one communication channel with a customer. Such systems are built with wireless technologies, sensor networks, RFID tags, smart cards, cell phones, surveillance systems, easy pass cards, surveillance cameras and internet-connected televisions. All these technologies are used to establish a one-to-one communication channel between customer and provider which enables the provider to deliver content appealing to the customer. Of course, the provider is constantly changing; many different entities have the opportunity to provide content and many different entities need access to personalized data. Often the user simply makes a selection and obtains a desired product or service. However, the more the provider knows about the individual on the other end of the channel, the more likely something appealing can be presented, for example, an ad the customer might click on, a movie the customer might download or a restaurant the consumer might visit if a location-enabled cell phone indicates that he or she is in a particular area.

HDS provide a host of opportunities to collect data. They frequently need both personal and contextual information (e.g. a person's current location or recent purchase history) to provide personalized services. Extensive and unobservable data collection is inherent in these systems and loss of control of the data collected is inevitable. An analysis of HDS summarizes the privacy issues for the US:

- data are collected without any indication;
- data collection takes place without a predefined purpose;
- data, once collected, persist in a variety of locations; and

---

39   K. Srikumar and B. Bashker, "Personalized Recommendations in E-commerce", *International Journal of Electronic Business* 3, no. 1 (2005): 4–27.

- different devices record multiple events simultaneously, leading to various possible interpretations of logged raw data and making the assignment of a valid privacy policy impossible.[40]

These systems certainly allow much finer levels of data collection. For example, an RFID tag in clothing and a surveillance camera in a store could be used to indicate your presence in a store, how much time you spent there and even (in the US) what aisles you visited.

Research suggests that most current privacy-enhancing technologies, which are based on concealing data, are not compatible with HDS. These systems typically involve continuous collection of data from multiple sources, usually for a variety of purposes. It is difficult, if not impossible, to build systems that would limit data collection at the source. Anonymity would prevent personalized services from being delivered. Pseudonymity would allow personalized services but would require the controlled release of personal data, which might impede personalization or limit the types of services that could be offered. Finally, data are frequently collected from so many different sources that it would be difficult, if not impossible, to guarantee that a real identity could not be discovered. Nonetheless, researchers are currently exploring techniques for developing privacy-policy-aware HDS collection devices in an effort to make "upfront notices of data collection" available to consumers.[41] Consumer privacy preferences would determine data collection parameters and consumers would be able to inspect their privacy state in a connected world.

(iii) Cell phones and targeted advertising

Cell phones provide unique opportunities to present customized content to consumers, but raise many privacy questions. A popular idea is to make banner ads appear when a user is close to a particular store or restaurant. Of course, now the user location must be tracked and revealed to a third party. In the US, companies are already developing browsers for cell phones that are location aware.[42]

The business model for most websites is click-through advertising. In other words, the website gains revenue when a visitor clicks on an ad displayed on the site. Google, for example, uses your search term to decide what ads to display in

---

40   S. Sackmann, J. Struker and R. Accorsi, "Personalization in Privacy-aware Highly Dynamic Systems", *Communications of the ACM* 49, no. 9 (September 2006): 32–38. Some of these issues are covered by the EU e-Privacy Directive.

41   Marc Langheinrich, "Personal Privacy in Ubiquitous Computing – Tools and System Support", PhD dissertation, ETH Zurich, Switzerland, May 2005. Available at: http://www.vs.inf.ethz.ch/res/papers/langheinrich-phd-2005.pdf.

42   Marin Perez, "Opera Add Locations Awareness", *Information Week*, March 9, 2009.

the hope of presenting something interesting and relevant that will elicit a click on the ad and perhaps a purchase. Thus there is tremendous incentive to know as much as possible in order to present highly relevant ads.

Cell phones and communications devices are ideal for targeted advertising because the content of the conversation or text message and the user's location can be used to determine relevant content. For example, a company called Pudding Media plans to offer extremely low-cost internet phone service.[43] Users have only to agree to have the content of their calls monitored. Essentially this is the same model that Google uses to provide targeted advertising to its Gmail users. Both companies claim that their systems target ads only contextually and do not employ any demographic or identity information in the process. Both claim that the content of the communications is not saved. In tests of the Pudding Media service, the company reports that the targeted ads presented often influence the content of the conversation, causing the participants to focus on the ads.

Both services exemplify a basic business model that pervades the modern internet – free or low-cost services are provided in exchange for access to personal information. Jonathan Sackett, chief digital officer for Arnold Worldwide, a unit of the advertising company Havas, summed up the current concerns of internet marketers: "Still, it makes me caution myself and caution all of us as marketers. We really have to look at the situation, because we're getting more intrusive with each passing technology."[44]

(iv) A sample of Web 2.0 technologies

Unlike the static pages of the early web, the Web 2.0 environment provides various mechanisms for uploading content to websites and making it available to a wide audience. One of the most successful websites to emerge in the Web 2.0 era (the past five years) is YouTube.[45] Originally started to foster the communication and sharing of musical ideas and techniques among musicians, the site rapidly expanded to include all types of video and is now the world's preeminent video sharing site. According to the internet research company Alexa,[46] YouTube is the world's third most popular website behind Google and Facebook. Google purchased YouTube, a company with only sixty-five employees, for 1.65 billion in Google stock in 2006.

YouTube videos can be uploaded by anyone who has a YouTube account, which requires only a valid email address. Videos can be made available to all on the

43   Louise Story, "Company Will Monitor Phone Calls to Tailor Ads", *The New York Times*, Sept. 24, 2007.
44   *Ibid.*
45   http://www.youtube.com.
46   Alexa, Top 500 Sites on the Web, http://www.alexa.com/topsites/global.

site or restricted to friends and family. Videos are usually followed by posts of texts from users who are either anonymous or frequently use pseudonyms. The uploader of a video can control whether posts are permitted or not and only the person who uploaded the video can remove it; others must appeal to YouTube.

Numerous privacy issues arise in relation to YouTube. The company does little monitoring of uploaded video; so almost anyone can upload just about any video. Copyright infringement has resulted in a major federal lawsuit against the company by Sony Viacom.[47] YouTube now has a department that routinely removes videos of copyrighted materials upon complaints from copyright holders. For others, the process of having an objectionable or harmful video removed can require considerable time, and there are frequent complaints that the company is unresponsive. Web 2.0 technologies scale only when any work to be done is spread over the user base not relegated to the site operator. In addition, YouTube collects the following information: each occasion on which a video is watched; the unique "login ID" of the user who watched it; the time at which the user started to watch the video; the Internet Protocol (IP) address and other information needed to identify the user's computer; and the identifier for the video. As with Google, this information is used to present targeted advertising each time the user logs into the site. In the *Viacom vs. YouTube* judgment, YouTube was ordered to release the logged information to Viacom for each Viacom video viewed.[48]

Privacy issues with YouTube also center on users uploading videos intended for only a small group of individuals but made available to anyone on the internet. Business organizations can suffer when the intimacy they require in conversations with clients or employees is compromised. A recent video involving the law firm of Cohen and Grigsby offers an example.

An extremely contentious practice, especially in the information technology industry, is the hiring of foreign workers on H1 visas. The Department of Labor (DOL) issues a permanent labor certification (PERM) to an employer that allows the employer to hire a foreign worker to work permanently in the US.[49] Among other requirements, the employer must demonstrate that there are no US workers with the appropriate skills available for the job at the prevailing wage. Cohen and Grigsby is a law firm that advises corporate clients on how to meet

---

47   Viacom Intern. Inc. v. YouTube Inc., 253 F.R.D. 256 (SDNY 2008). However, the Southern District Court of New York (trial level court) granted summary judgment against Viacom and the case is currently on appeal before the Second Circuit, with the parties expecting that the fate of the appeal will turn on the Supreme Court's decision in Global-Tech Appliances v. SEB. See e.g. http://www.hollywoodreporter.com/thr-esq/how-an-obscure-supreme-court-207972.

48   However, YouTube's compliance was connected with its victory in a copyright suit by Viacom. See: http://www.zdnet.com/blog/btl/google-prevails-in-viacom-youtube-copyright-lawsuit-appeals-on-deck/36229.

49   United States Department of Labor, Permenant Labor Certification, available at http://www.foreignlaborcert.doleta.gov/perm.cfm.

the PERM requirements of DOL. In a frank presentation, firm representatives describe ways of placing want ads in newspapers in a manner that meet DOL requirements but which make the ads unlikely to attract qualified US applicants for the position. The firm obviously intended the presentation for current and prospective clients and certainly did not want the recorded sessions to be open to public viewing, where they would engender a wave of negative publicity and unwanted attention. Someone posted the recorded presentation on YouTube, where it was viewed over 155,000 times during the first week of posting. It attracted so much attention it eventually found its way onto CNN where it reached an even wider audience.

Data aggregators and processors[50]

During the past fifteen years a highly developed data brokerage industry has arisen that not only makes information on individuals available at relatively low cost but also can perform custom analyses of individuals or groups for various purposes, including law enforcement, employment background checks and targeted marketing campaigns. Companies such as ChoicePoint,[51] Acxiom and LexisNexis employ the latest algorithmic tools, along with computing power once reserved for large-scale scientific computation, to synthesize personal information from numerous sources and make a detailed profile of an individual available to either businesses or government. Due to the sensitivity of making personally identifiable information available to end consumers, these larger brokers today prefer to offer services only to larger, established businesses. Government agencies, particularly law enforcement agencies such as the FBI, are increasingly turning to these major data brokers for both data and analysis.

By 2005, largely through acquisitions of smaller data management companies, Acxiom, ChoicePoint and LexisNexis had grown to be the world's three largest aggregators and providers of data on individuals, each with annual revenues of over $1 billion. These organizations leveraged their significant analysis and processing capabilities, gleaned over many years of managing data for large corporate clients, to provide detailed information on and profiles of individuals to insurers, collection agencies, direct marketers, employment screeners and government agencies, including state and local law enforcement agencies. The website of Accurint,[52] the information subsidiary of LexisNexis, indicates the detailed information held and made available. For example, one product provided

---

50   It should be emphasized again that EU law prevents the existence of an industry as outlined in this section.
51   In 2008, Reed Elsevier, the parent company of LexisNexis, purchased ChoicePoint for $3.6 billion and merged it with LexisNexis.
52   Accurint, http://www.accurint.com/, last visited May 5, 2009.

by the company, People at Work, holds information on 132 million individuals including addresses, phone numbers and possible dates of employment. The site advertises the ability to find people, their relatives, associates and assets. In the next section we discuss some of the capabilities that data aggregators have for establishing detailed individual profiles.

Securing data repositories

To owners of large central repositories of valuable personal data, security is of paramount concern. However, given the large number of business partners and clients who require access to the data, protecting the sensitive information in these repositories is not an easy task. Large-scale breaches at both ChoicePoint and Acxiom earlier this decade generated a great deal of attention from privacy advocates and prompted calls for regulation of the activities of the data aggregation industry.[53] In May 2009, LexisNexis disclosed a breach that exposed the personal information of 40,000 individuals and compromised names, birthdates and social security numbers.[54] The breach appears to have taken place from June 2004 to October 2007. The company breach letter said the thieves, who were once legitimate LexisNexis customers, used mailboxes at commercial mail services and information taken from LexisNexis to set up about 300 fraudulent credit cards.[55] The breach letter indicated that LexisNexis learned of the breach from the United States Postal Inspection Service, which was investigating the fraudulent credit cards.

Other industries that maintain large central repositories of sensitive personal information are the retail and card payment processing industries. Each has suffered notable large-scale breaches during the past five years.[56] Unlike the data aggregation industry, breaches in these industries appear to have involved malware on servers that collected data and transmitted it outside the company. These breaches, however, also involved individuals with detailed insider knowledge of the systems that were compromised. Although the credit card industry and retail industries have not reported significant rises in the rates of credit card fraud,[57] the scope of recent payment card breaches, the rapidity with which stolen credit information has been used and the geographical

---

53 Solove and Hoofnagle, "A Model Regime of Privacy Protection".

54 Amy Westfeldt, "LexisNexis Warns 32,000 People about Data Breach", *San Francisco Chronicle*, May 1, 2009, 22.

55 LexisNexis Breach Notification Letter. Available at: http://privacy.wi.gov/databreaches/pdf/LexisNexisLetter050509.pdf, visited May 1, 2009.

56 Douglas Salane, "Are Large Scale Data Breaches Inevitable?", *Cyber Infrastructure Protection '09*, City University of New York, June 2009.

57 CyberSource Corporation, "Online Fraud Report: Online Payment Fraud Trends, Merchant Practices and Benchmarks", available at http://www.cybersource.com, visited May 1, 2009.

scope of the fraud raise concerns that data thieves are now taking advantage of the capabilities afforded by worldwide crime organizations to monetize vast collections of breached financial information. Loss by aggregators and data processors of sensitive personal data, especially financial data, poses significant risks to individual security.

Breaches in the data aggregation industry involved insiders such as contractors who extended their authorized access. Breaches in the payment processing industry made use of malware that relayed sensitive personal financial information to data thieves. However, regardless of the industry, basic privacy policies that (1) limit the amount of data collected, (2) limit where data are stored and the time for which they are stored and (3) restrict the use of data to the task for which they are collected play a critical role in preventing and mitigating breaches. Large-scale breaches are expensive, especially if the information lost involves sensitive personal financial data. Breaches in the payment industry can exact extremely high costs, particularly to organizations such as card processors, whose businesses depend on the trust of partners and customers. Breached notification laws, which keep both consumers and business partners aware of what is happening with their data, are changing the way all industries and organizations view information security.

Impact on basic notions of privacy

Modern information and communications systems are having a tremendous impact on basic, long-held notions of privacy. Although we offer an extended account of privacy in the next chapter, it is useful to relate some of the foregoing discussion to Alan Westin's differentiation of the four states of privacy: solitude, intimacy, anonymity and reserve.[58] In Chapter VI we examined the impact of recent securitization technologies on both intimacy and anonymity. Here is how modern information and communications systems can impact each of these states. Solitude is a state in which an individual is isolated and does not expect to be observed by others in any manner. Intimacy is the state in which an individual interacts with a small group and expects that his actions will be observed and limited to members of that group, for example, the interaction between spouses, among family members or among partners in a firm. Anonymity occurs when a person enters the public arena but surveillance does not result in identification. Thus the person has the freedom of action and expression that he or she might not have in other venues. The fourth state of privacy – reserve – may be the most important. Reserve is simply the ability to withhold information. We show reserve when we exercise discretion in the release of information, or in the

---

58   Alan Westin, *Privacy and Freedom* (New York Atheneum, 1967).

thoughts we convey, because these may be deemed either inappropriate for the occasion, offensive to another's sensibilities, to give an adversary an advantage or to have unknown, possibly negative, consequences. Yet Herman Tavani and James Moor think that privacy should not be defined in terms of what information individuals can control because they can control so little.[59] Instead, they stress that in order for individuals to have the freedom to function and prosper they must have the opportunity to limit access to personal information even if they do not have control of that information. Yet such privacy is an essential requirement for realizing the core values.[60]

The systems upon which we now rely for both business and social interactions can compromise each state of privacy. Analysis of a search history can reveal a person's innermost thoughts, fears, fantasies, aspirations or health concerns and thus undermine reserve. Online sites have replaced the usual meeting places for small groups, for example, the local tavern, club, mall or street corner. There is frequently a presumption that data posted or communications will be limited to a small circle of friends. Yet social networking site users cannot predict who will have access to their communications or how they will be used. For example, Pre-employ.com, an employment screening service, reports that in 2009 over 40% of employers obtained information on job candidates from social networking sites.[61] Although people have communicated online for years, prior to the social networking era they usually did so with a pseudonym, and data were held for only short periods. With current widely used systems a real identity is associated with a profile, and anything posted on major social networking sites may be archived indefinitely. As we have noted, most site owners state clearly in their terms-of-service agreements that the data may be used in any way the site deems reasonable. The situation is complicated by online privacy policies that are difficult to read, indicate little protection for personal data and are often considered to be simply legal disclaimers for protecting the site owner.[62] Furthermore, most terms-of-service agreements examined in this review indicate that information posted becomes part of the company's assets and, if the company is sold, those assets may be subject to a different privacy policy.

---

59   Herman T. Tavani and James H. Moor, "Privacy Protection, Control of Information, and Privacy-Enhancing Technologies", *Computers and Society* 31, no. 1 (March 2001): 6–11.

60   James H. Moor, "Towards a Theory of Privacy in the Information Age", *Computers and Society* (September 1997): 27–32.

61   Pre-employ.com, "Background Checks and Social Networking Sites", February 24, 2009.

62   Irene Pollach, "What's Wrong with On-line Privacy Policies?", *Communications of the ACM* 50, no. 9 (September 2007): 103–108.

Protecting consumer privacy

In Chapter IX we examine the complexity of oversight and accountability, largely with regard to government sector surveillance. That section makes the point that, "as liberal writers from as far back as John Locke realized, good social order requires more than reliance on individual good will and good judgment. Structural supports and incentives are needed." Yet in determining how information is protected by those who control data in the modern internet, particularly social networks, search engines and sites that share information with third-party advertisers, there is exceptional reliance on the individual good will and judgment of the data controllers. Most users count on the data controllers to protect their information and not use it in a way that would cause them harm. A recent letter[63] to the US Committee on Commerce, Science and Transportation by a coalition of fifteen major American privacy and consumer groups representing millions of Americans notes that internet users face the following choice – "either stay off-line and ignore the benefits of new technology, or plug in and run extraordinary risks to privacy and security." The letter states that current privacy laws are inadequate and that self regulation has failed. The letter further states there is nothing in US law similar to the National Do Not Call Registry[64] to protect consumers from unwanted advertising and profiling by internet firms.

In the US, the Federal Trade Commission (FTC) is the primary government agency responsible for protecting consumers from harm that results from the collection and sharing of their personal information.[65] This role grew out of the FTC's longstanding mission as the enforcer of the Fair Credit Reporting Act, which mainly protects consumer credit information. Since the 1990s the FTC has increasingly concerned itself with privacy issues beyond the scope of consumer credit, with authorization derived primarily from specific sector statutes enacted during the past fifteen years and Section 5 of the FTC Act, which gives the commission authority to take action against deceptive or unfair trade practices.[66] For protecting consumer privacy outside of specific sector legislation the FTC relies heavily on Section 5 of the FTC Act, which allows it to bring actions against organizations that misrepresent the way in which they collect and use consumer information.

---

63 "Congress needs to act on privacy", Coalition Letter of Consumer and Privacy Orangizations, July 1, 2011. Available at http://epic.org/privacy/consumer/Privacy_Groups_to_US_Congress_final.pdf.

64 National Do Not Call Registry, https://www.donotcall.gov/default.aspx.

65 However, it should be noted that even if the FTC could enact and enforce a more rigorous privacy program (as suggested below) it would do nothing to regulate government intrusions. This is markedly different from what is happening in the EU, in which both the Commission and the European Data Supervisor are calling for an extension of data protection laws to policing and criminal justice as well as the private sector.

66 15. U.S.C. § 1681.

The FTC is in the process of conducting a thorough examination of its enforcement practices in the area of privacy protection.[67] Up to now the FTC has employed two approaches as guides to protecting consumer information: (1) the notice and choice approach; and (2) the harm-based approach. As part of the notice and choice approach the FTC has brought actions against organizations that engage in unfair and deceptive practices by using or collecting information in ways which violate stated privacy policies and terms-of-use agreements. Under the harm-based approach the FTC has taken action when organizations handle data in ways likely to cause physical or economic harm, or result in unwanted intrusions. The harm-based approach triggers FTC action when organizations fail to protect consumer information adequately, for example, by exposing consumer information that might result in economic loss through identity theft. Aside from the approaches being used as guides for enforcement actions, the FTC uses them to promote industry self-regulatory practices. The agency encourages organizations to put in place systems that inform consumers about privacy issues and give them the choice as to whether or not to release their personal information. The FTC also promotes industry practices that protect consumer data.

In its current review, the FTC has cited limitations with both approaches. It claims that the notice and choice approach is unworkable because typical privacy policies have now become long, complex documents that consumers cannot possibly read. The agency also notes that an increasing number of privacy policies are simply legal disclaimers. According to the FTC, the harm-based approach is too narrow as it limits harm to specific areas, often indicated by sector specific legislation. The approach does not address the wide array of harms that result from making sensitive personal information available to many different parties. The agency notes that it has little authority to address situations that lead to reputational harm, a common occurrence when, for example, social networks fail to regulate what users post regarding other users.[68] The agency can also do little when consumers agree to surveillance without being aware of the consequences. Overall, the FTC has relied extensively on promoting industry best practices as part of a self-regulatory approach to privacy. The FTC chairman, Jon Leibowitz, recently remarked, "Despite some good actors, self-regulation of privacy has not worked adequately and is not working adequately for American consumers."[69]

---

67 FTC Preliminary Staff Report, "Protecting Consumers in an Era of Rapid Change: Proposed Framework for Business and Policy Makers", December 2010, available at: http://www.ftc.gov/os/2010/12/101201privacyreport.pdf.

68 Daniel J. Solove, *The Future of Reputation: Gossip, Rumor, and Privacy on the Internet* (New Haven: Yale University Press, 2007).

69 Edward Wyatt and Tanzina Vega, "FTC Honors Plan to Honor Privacy of Online Users", *The New York Times*, December 1, 2010.

In its attempt to protect consumers in the modern internet environment the FTC is largely trying to promote industry-wide practices that follow the Fair Information Practice Principles that it presented in 2000.[70] The FTC 2000 framework arose from classic work done at HEW in the early seventies to derive a general privacy framework.[71] The proposed new FTC framework emphasizes privacy by design, simplified choice and greater transparency, and embodies its Fair Information Practices Principles. In order to implement the framework in view of specific technologies and current business practices the FTC has sought input from consumer and industry groups through a series of roundtable meetings.[72] Although the FTC does not seek a legislative mandate for its new proposed framework, as part of its privacy by design initiative the agency has called for an effective and enforceable Do Not Track Tool that would give consumers the technical means to protect their online behavior from unwanted intrusion.[73]

In Chapter IV we discussed the dramatically different approaches to privacy protection in the US and EU and examined some of the cultural and historical factors that account for these differences. We noted that privacy protection in the US, unlike in the EU, is highly fragmentary and sector based. Often privacy legislation arises in response to a specific harm caused to consumers by existing data use practices. As we have noted, lack of an enforceable uniform privacy framework creates numerous gaps and results in a complex array of legislation to close the gaps. Although the public increasingly looks to the FTC to force organizations to protect consumer data, the agency does not have a broad legislative mandate for privacy protection. Given the rising consumer alarm over online privacy issues and the threat of increased legislative remedies, many organizations that provide internet-based services are now increasingly open to an overarching privacy framework. The FTC approach, however, still relies heavily on self-regulation to protect consumer data. Without a mandated framework to protect consumer privacy it appears that the FTC and Congress are in a never-ending game of plugging holes in a dyke as new harms surface that cannot be predicted in advance.

The FTC's recent reexamination of its consumer privacy protection policies provides additional impetus for a national data protection authority with a

---

70   FTC, *Privacy Online: Fair Information Practices in the Electronic Marketplace (2000)*, available at: http://www.ftc.gov/reports/privacy2000/privacy2000.pdf.
71   US Dept. of Health, Education and Welfare, *Records, Computers and the Rights of Citizens: Report of the Secretary's Advisory Committee on Automated Personal Data Systems (July 1973)*, available at: http://aspe.hhs.gov/DATACNCL/1973privacy/tocprefacemembers.htm
72   FTC Press Release, FTC to Host Public Roundtables to Address Evolving Privacy Issues (Sept. 15, 2009), available at: http://www.ftc.gov/opa/2009/09/privacyrt.shtm.
73   Testimony of David Vladeck, Director of the Bureau of Consumer Protection, Federal Trade Commission, before the Subcommittee on Commerce, Trade and Consumer Protection, US House of Representatives, Dec. 2, 2010, available at: http://www.ftc.gov/os/testimony/101202donottrack.pdf.

mandate to oversee privacy protection. Given the FTC's extensive history of privacy protection and current mandates through a range of legislation, the agency would certainly play a critical role in such an authority. We spoke earlier of a grassroots movement that could be a motivating force for a national data authority. Indeed, in response to widespread consumer outrage over the handling of sensitive personal data and the inability of organizations to secure it, a strong group of highly effective privacy advocacy organizations has arisen to represent consumer privacy interests. In addition, a number of industries now have an interest in a uniform privacy framework that would eliminate high compliance costs of a severely fragmented legislative regime of privacy protection. Without a uniform framework in place the nation faces continued proliferation of legislation and regulation, which makes oversight, enforcement and compliance extremely difficult and costly. The challenge is not only to put in place an adequate privacy protection framework but also to implement it in a way that provides adequate consumer protections and at the same time promotes innovation and development.

VIII. The Underlying Values and their Alignment

We have made repeated references to the liberal democratic values at stake in contemporary digital technologies. It is now time to attempt to articulate them in greater detail and, in particular, to offer accounts that might have some claim to broad, if not universal, acceptance within liberal polities. We focus initially on security, a value in any society, but distinctively construed within a liberal polity, before reviewing the ways in which strategies for assuring it may come into tension with other important liberal values – privacy, autonomy and dignity – and thus impinge on liberal identity.

Security

Both crime and terrorism threaten our security, and it is in the name of security that some of the controversial measures identified in earlier chapters have been deployed. But "security" is a slippery term. It may be individual or collective, and we need to be clearer about what is to be secured. Is it security against a physical threat, a threat to a way of life, a threat to a particular regime . . . ?[1]

Background

Traditional liberal democratic political theory is nicely represented by John Locke's *Second Treatise of Civil Government*, where he argues that human beings are endowed – by God, as he puts it – with certain fundamental rights that he characterizes as life, liberty and property.[2] The purpose of the *Second Treatise* is to argue that although humans should not view themselves as being under the tutelage of an absolute sovereign – a position that he had vigorously attacked in the *First Treatise* – they nevertheless still need the firm hand of central/

---

1   Our focus here will be on the threats to security that are posed by others – in particular as a result of crime and terrorism. Although the account we provide will highlight threats posed by these, it is not meant to exclude – and occasionally adverts to – non-personal threats to security, such as those posed by infectious disease. More generally on the ideas of individual and collective security, see Allen Buchanan, *Justice, Legitimacy, and Self-Determination: Moral Foundations for International Law* (New York: Oxford University Press, 2004).

2   John Locke, *Second Treatise of Civil Government*, available at: http://www.constitution.org/jl/2ndtreat. htm. The Lockean account is usually secularized by seeing in the capacity for rational thought and action an alternative foundation for fundamental rights. There has been a lively dispute over whether Locke can be so secularized. See e.g. Jeremy Waldron, *God, Locke and Equality: Christian Foundations of Locke's Political Thought* (Cambridge, UK: Cambridge University Press, 2002); Jeffrey Reiman, "Towards a Secular Lockean Liberalism", *Review of Politics*, 67 (2005): 473–93. Although, for convenience, we focus on Locke, our discussion might well have started, as it does in Waldron, with Hobbes.

civil government. Locke's attempt to reconcile this with the individual rights he has been advocating takes the form of what is known as the social contract in which, in exchange for certain benefits (the ability to exercise their rights), individuals see it to be to their advantage to cede some small portion of their rights to those who will secure those benefits for them.

How so? Although the occupants of a Lockean state of nature (pre-civil society) possess basic rights to life, liberty and property, such a state of affairs offers little security. The possession of rights is not sufficient for their enjoyment.[3] The rights must also be exercisable, and for this the state of nature does not and cannot provide. Those who inhabit a state of nature cannot be entirely trusted to acknowledge the rights of others, some preferring instead to aggrandize themselves in various ways. As Locke puts it, although a person in a state of nature has — by right — dominion over himself, "the enjoyment of [that dominion] is very uncertain, and constantly exposed to the invasion of others: for all being kings as much as he, every man his equal, and the greater part no strict observers of equity and justice, the enjoyment of the property he has in this state is very unsafe, very unsecure."[4]

Security, in other words, is a security against X so that we can be secure to Y. This can be easily forgotten, but is implicit in debates about security and liberty. If security removes or seriously compromises liberty (and/or autonomy, privacy, and dignity) then one might wonder whether it retains its foundational value.

In social contract reasoning, to effect their security rational occupants of a state of nature would choose to enter into a "civil society" — that is, one characterized by institutions that are designed to secure for its members conditions that enable the exercise of their rights.[5] Security is therefore no peripheral social condition but central to the prosecution of a life that is able to realize its potential. Some level of security will be needed not only to ensure the social conditions of our rights (various critical social institutions) but also to foster the conditions for our individual human flourishing (through enforceable criminal law).

---

3   "Enjoyment" may be a particularly apt term. The Latin term *securitas* referred, "in its classical use, to a condition of individuals, of a particular inner sort. It denoted composure, tranquillity of spirit, freedom from care, the condition that Cicero called 'the object of supreme desire', or 'the absence of anxiety upon which a happy life depends'", E. Rothschild, "What is Security?", *Daedalus* 124, no. 3 (1995): 61.

4   Locke, *Second Treatise*, §123.

5   In the *Second Treatise*, ch. 9, Locke identifies these as legislative, judicial, and executive. The critical importance that security has for the enjoyment of rights is argued at greater length in Henry Shue, *Basic Rights: Subsistence, Affluence, and U.S. Foreign Policy*, second ed. (Princeton, NJ: Princeton University Press, 1996), esp. ch. 1. The text of ch. 1 is the same as in the first edition. See also Seumas Miller, *The Moral Foundations of Social Institutions: A Philosophical Study* (New York: Cambridge University Press, 2010), chapters 1, 9 and 12, and also Seumas Miller and John Blackler, *Ethical Issues in Policing* (Aldershot: Ashgate, 2005), ch. 1.

Personal security

Henry Shue refers to personal (or physical) security as a basic right; that is, a right whose enjoyment "is essential to the enjoyment of all other rights".[6] If personal physical security is at risk, non-basic rights can be sacrificed in order to secure the basic right. Assault, rape, torture and murder disenable us (temporarily or permanently) from exercising our rights to education or free association. Even though the right to personal security may not have in itself the rich human possibilities presaged by the rights to education or free association it is nevertheless prior to them because it is the precondition of our ability to enjoy the benefits of education and free association.

The point here is that humans are ineluctably embodied, and if their physical selves are endangered then so is everything that depends on those physical selves. Given our physicality, it is not surprising that Shue also argues for a basic right to subsistence. Shue thus draws attention to something that is only implicit in Locke (though barely below the surface), whose focus on the rights to "life, liberty, and property" may tend to obscure the underlying right to security.

Although *physical security* (against bodily harm and death) is critical to any valuable personal security, mere physical security (which Jeremy Waldron usefully designates as (pure) *safety*[7]), does not comprehend the whole of what is intended by "personal security". As Waldron puts it, spending one's days huddled in a bomb shelter is not the kind of security that we wish to promote or ensure.

What is envisaged in the Lockean tradition (and Shue[8]) is *individual* security – the security of fundamental rights. Although Locke sees the state as a vehicle

---

6 Shue, *Basic Rights*, 19.

7 Useful, though stipulative. Waldron quotes from Hobbes (ever a stickler for words): "by safety one should understand not mere survival in any condition, but a happy life so far as that it possible", *De Cive*; see Jeremy Waldron, "Safety and Security", *Nebraska Law Review* 85 (2006): 458.

8 Shue does not specifically align himself with Locke, though he draws attention to a very similar passage in Mill, whose overarching position is utilitarian rather than contractarian:

> To have a right, then, is, we conceive, to have something which society ought to defend me in the possession of. If the objector goes on to ask, why it ought? We can give him no other reason than general utility. If that expression does not seem to convey a sufficient feeling of the strength of the obligation, nor to account for the peculiar energy of the feeling, it is because there goes to the composition of the sentiment, not a rational only, but also an animal element, the thirst for retaliation; and this thirst derives its intensity, as well as its moral justification, from the extraordinarily important and impressive kind of utility which is concerned. The interest involved is that of security, to every one's feelings the most vital of all interests. All other earthly benefits are needed by one person, not needed by another; and many of them can, if necessary, be cheerfully foregone, or replaced by something else; but security no human being can possibly do without; on it we depend for all our immunity from evil, and for the whole value of all and every good, beyond the passing moment; since nothing but the gratification of the instant could be of any worth to us, if we could be deprived of anything the next instant by whoever was momentarily stronger than ourselves. Now this most

for that − primarily through the promulgation of protective laws that are impartially applied and enforced − the Lockean state does not take its eye too far off the individualistic ball. To be sure, the Lockean state is probably too individualistic, since it tends to overlook the extent to which the capacity to exercise our rights is dependent on a plethora of social institutions that sustain us in various ways. Some later liberal writers − especially those with somewhat Hegelian leanings, such as T.H. Green, D.G. Ritchie and L.T. Hobhouse − were much more communitarian.[9]

An important dimension to Shue's discussion of the right to personal security is his claim that it should not be understood as a negative (in contrast to a positive) right. Although he does not object to talk of the negative as well as the positive features of rights such as to security (or liberty etc.) − a distinction that often tends to track the distinction between acting and omitting/refraining − the right to security is not merely a (negative) right that others not interfere with one by way of assault, rape or murder but also and just as importantly a (positive) right to be protected from assaults on and other threats to one's person.[10] It is the latter that the Lockean state provides through its law enforcement (executive) activities.[11]

What this means is that to ensure our security we will also need to contribute in some way − either by means of taxation or service − so that the structures needed for our protection can be sustained. Without the capacity to exercise our rights they count for little, and so the right to security that is supposed to enable us to exercise our rights to liberty etc. will need to be such that it includes the means for its enforcement.

Before turning to various kinds of collective security, let us note some additional features of personal and individual security. Although dependent on physical security, individual security includes rather more than that. We talk about the security of an historical way of life and its various social, cultural and institutional supports. Thus Waldron talks usefully of a "deepening" of the

---

indispensable of all necessaries, after physical nutriment, cannot be had, unless the machinery for providing it is kept unintermittedly in active play. Our notion, therefore, of the claim we have on our fellow-creatures to join in making safe for us the very groundwork of our existence, gathers feelings around it so much more intense than those concerned in any of the more common cases of utility, that the difference in degree (as is often the case in psychology) becomes a real difference in kind.

Utilitarianism, ch. 5: http://www.gutenberg.org/files/11224/11224-h/11224-h.htm#CHAPTER_V.

9   For a useful if flawed overview, see Gerald Gaus, *The Modern Liberal Theory of Man* (New York: St Martin's Press, 1983). See also Miller, *Moral Foundations of Social Institutions*, ch. 1.

10   Shue, *Basic Rights*, 37–39. This tracks an important and longstanding debate about negative and positive liberty. See Gerald C. MacCallum, Jr., "Negative and Positive Freedom", *Philosophical Review* 76 (July, 1967): 312–34.

11   Of course, it may also violate the former right through its executive activities (as Robert Mugabe's Zimbabwe currently illustrates).

notion of individual security to accommodate these things,[12] including freedom from fear (and provision of assurance).[13] With the metaphor of depth, Waldron associates a metaphor of breadth to which we will return.

> Because the right to security is a basic right it is a right that each human being has, insofar as human beings have any rights. It may not be a right that we value particularly for its own sake; its value may reside more in what it makes possible. Nevertheless we should not be altogether skeptical of seeing security as something that we also value for its own sake.[14]

True, Waldron is reluctant to move in this direction: "security is not so much a good in and of itself, but . . . something 'adjectival' – a mode of enjoying other goods, an underwriting of other values, a guarantor of other things we care about."[15] At the same time, he is also cautious about casting the alternatives too starkly, especially as the security in question might be seen as security in the enjoyment of our liberties.[16] We believe that Waldron may slightly shortchange security by focusing too much on its "adjectival" qualities.

Insofar as security is a right and insofar as a right provides someone with a justified claim, it provides others – the state, in Locke's case, though others may also be implicated – with a reason to address whatever is threatening their security.

National security

> *When political formulas such as "national interest" or "national security"*
> *gain popularity they need to be scrutinized with particular care. They may*

---

12   "An adequately deep conception of security should aim to protect people's individual and familial modes of living themselves, and not just the life, health, and possessions that are necessary for it." (466). This discussion continues at length from pp. 461–73, esp. 466 et seq.

13   Waldron has a nice discussion of freedom from fear (negative) and assurance (positive) that indicates some of the complexities involved in building them into our conception of security (467–71).

14   In fact, Mill warned against valuing it (only) as an end: "A man who has nothing which he cares about more than he does about his personal safety is a miserable creature who has no chance of being free, unless made and kept so by the existing of better men than himself", "The Contest in America", in J.M. Robson (ed.) *The Collected Works of John Stuart Mill* (Toronto: University of Toronto Press, 1984), vol. XXI, 141–42. This passage occurs in the context of the necessity, sometimes, of going to war (and thus jeopardizing one's safety): "war to protect other human beings against tyrannical injustice; a war to give victory to their own ideas of right and good, and which is their own war, carried on for an honest purpose by their own free choice – is often the means of their regeneration." (A copy of its early reprinting in *Harper's New Monthly Magazine* (1862) from *Fraser's Magazine* (1862) can be found at: http://cdl.library.cornell.edu/cgi-bin/moa/moa-cgi?notisid=ABK4014-0024-103.)

15   Waldron, 471; cf. 458.

16   And people will fight for their survival in and for itself. Nevertheless, on pp. 472–73 Waldron offers some valuable caveats in relation to Henry Shue's argument in ch. 1 of *Basic Rights*.

not mean the same thing to different people. They may not have any precise meaning at all. Thus, while appearing to offer guidance and a basis for broad consensus, they may be permitting everyone to label whatever policy he favors with an attractive and possibly deceptive name.[17]

What Waldron speaks of as a "depth" to security is helpfully juxtaposed with "breadth", in which the question of *whose* security is encompassed (all equally, or some more than or at the expense of others). One of the helpful aspects of Waldron's depth/breadth distinction is that it enables us to grapple with their connections as well as their differences. Insofar as a suitably deep conception of security embodies something we might want to call "the American way of life" or "liberal democratic values", a "narrowed" implementation of security measures that severely disadvantages one segment of the population to ensure the security of another segment would violate the expectations of depth.[18] The depth/breadth nexus gets additional discussion toward the end of his paper: we cannot separate our conception of the security that is worth having from the way in which it is distributed, as a matter of identity as well as achievement.[19]

The issue of breadth also provides an entrée for Waldron's discussion of the large question – the fundamental political question, perhaps – of whether the security of a population should be construed aggregatively or distributively (or even in both ways). He takes issue with Hobbesian and Benthamite accounts that tend toward a largely aggregative conception and he leans toward an account of breadth that is underlain by a notion of "equal protection".[20] He suggests that the legitimacy of a state that does not provide or seek equal protection ("or at least a minimum security for everyone") is called into question.[21]

A review of the current debate about security indicates that the focus is not primarily on personal security. The focus is generally on some form of collective security – such as public safety or, more commonly, national security – and the latter in particular is said to justify a significant number of constraints on our individual liberty interests (including privacy). In other words, the constraints

---

17   Arnold Wolfers, "'National Security' as an Ambiguous Symbol", in *Discord and Collaboration: Essays on International Politics* (Baltimore, MD: Johns Hopkins University Press, 1962), 147.

18   Waldron also warns about trying to build so much into depth that legitimate security measures are ruled out (463). Consider the absolutizing of freedom of speech, association, religion or privacy that would see any constraints on them as a compromise of its depth dimension. By the same token, each constraint needs to be argued for and not simply accepted because proposed by the incumbent regime.

19   Waldron, 494-502.

20   See the discussion on pp. 474 et seq. This does not mean that distributive considerations will always/ necessarily trump aggregative considerations – a kind of "let justice be done though the heavens fall" position – but it gives a special weighting to distributive assumptions, sufficient to require falling heavens (and not simply conjectures about terrorist attacks and weapons of mass destruction).

21   *Ibid.*, 491–94.

on our liberty interests that are said to be justified by the need for individual security are now imposed for the sake of some collective or national security to which individual security is tied.

At first blush, that may not seem all that problematic, just because, in a *liberal* society, we can anticipate that the two will be linked in some way. It is arguable that *collective* security will generally be structured to enhance the security of the *individual*. Public safety will be correlated with individual safety. Indeed, that is the message behind Lockean social contract theory: if individual security is to be assured there needs to be a secure state to ensure it. But whether or to what extent that is the case is an issue to which we will need to return.

As presaged above, although we have said that collective security commonly translates into the language of national security, it has, in fact, a number of intermediate forms that – in day-to-day matters – might be of more critical (and certainly of more immediate) importance to individual security. There will, for example, be the collective security provided by local or state police departments or by private security organizations. National security,[22] on the other hand, will tend to comprehend institutions of the larger society – the state or country. In the US, the military, National Guard and various federal agencies (e.g. FBI, CIA, DHS) will (in theory) work together to secure nationally critical institutions against outside and even some inside threats. In so doing, it is argued, such national security institutions will also secure us individually against threats.

On Waldron's account, however, collective security is not the natural complement to personal or individual security but "concerns security as among the nations of the world (or various subsets of them) determined by institutions, alliances, and the balance of power."[23] This he contrasts not only with individual security but also the security of "populations", "the people of the nation" or "whole population" (which we have included in our category of collective security). What we have referred to as national security Waldron views as the security of the state or of governmental institutions, which provide a form of security that he considers to have a somewhat problematic connection to the security of individuals and populations: "the integrity and power of the state itself as an institutional apparatus . . . is something which may or may not be related to ordinary citizens' being more secure."[24]

---

22 *State* security might seem a bit more accurate, since we are usually referring to political jurisdictions rather than nations or nationalities. Sometimes, of course, a nation-state will be involved. However, as we will suggest, it is probably no accident that we speak of national rather than simply state security, since it is not simply jurisdictional integrity that is at stake but also institutional and cultural integrity. The more recent notion of *homeland* security seems to focus mainly on domestic or geographically localized threats to national security.

23 *Ibid.*, 459.

24 *Ibid.*, 460; cf., 474.

In fact, there appear to be at least three related distinctions in play here. Firstly, there is the security of the individual person in relation to other persons and collective entities, including the state. Secondly, there is the (so to speak, internal and external) collective security of a population of such persons, for example, of the members of the Australian community in relation to some of their own number (internal) and in relation to other communities and, in particular, nation-states other than Australia (external). Thirdly, there is the (internal) collective security of a population of collective entities in relation to some of their own number, for example, the community of nation-states. Note that *qua* community, the community of nation-states does not have a need for *external* collective security; there is no external collective entity (for example, invading Martians). There are, of course, transnational entities, including crime organizations, which constitute a security threat to nation-states, but these are not, in the required sense, external to the community of nation-states; rather they are to be understood as enemies within.

The differences with respect to adjectival and more substantive conceptions of security reflected in the above discussion may indicate more about where Waldron − and we − stand on the individualist–communitarian axis and on policy preferences than some difference over deep theory. True, some of Waldron's writing is quite cosmopolitan, and we do not think he has too much time for patriotism.[25] Although states/governments may be quite toxic as far as the security of those who populate them (both individuals and groups) is concerned − so that national security in *his* sense is not the kind of security about which we should be primarily concerned − we tend to think that, for the time being at least, states/governments (not regimes) represent our best shot at securing what needs to be secured. We may be wrong about that. It may be that we should qualify our support for national security with some reference to accountability mechanisms that would check the state's power (though our references to a liberal democratic state may have been idealized by presuming some system of checks and balances).

Nevertheless, there could still be a more far-reaching difference. The distinction that Waldron makes between individuals and populations may be intended to reflect the view − or at least to show some partiality toward the view − that populations are simply aggregates of individuals and have no identity over and above the individuals who make them up. If that is so then our implicit conception of collectivities as having a distinctive identity and even, perhaps, a distinctive mode of action and responsibility may differ from his.[26] Here we

---

25   Jeremy Waldron, "Minority Cultures and the Cosmopolitan Alternative", *University of Michigan Journal of Law Reform* 25 (1992): 751–793.

26   This is a large issue, some of whose outlines are traced in Marion Smiley's *Stanford Encyclopedia of Philosophy* article, "Collective Responsibility", at: http://plato.stanford.edu/entries/collective-responsibility/. For a relational account of collective action and collective responsibility see Seumas Miller, "Collective

note the possibility of relational accounts of collective action, identity and responsibility as well as the atomistic individual accounts (typically assumed to be required by individualism) and the supra-individualist accounts (typically associated with communitarianism). We are not absolutely sure about all of this,[27] in part because there is some ambiguity in Waldron's discussion at this point. For example, one of his complaints about the pure safety conception of security is that it is "a purely individual measure" and does not provide a basis for our "talking critically about the security of the whole community."[28] And he talks about "securing the security of society as a whole."[29] True, he notes that we should not abandon the individualistic pure safety conception for "some more amiable notion of communal solidarity",[30] though of course we need not think in terms of either/or; indeed, relational accounts are framed in part precisely to avoid this dilemma. Perhaps the closest he comes to a more individualistic conception is when he argues that the legitimacy of a state security apparatus is determined by its significance for individuals: "the basic theory of political legitimacy is individualistic, not collective. Its starting point is that political regimes make demands on individuals one-by-one."[31] This probably ties in with his reluctance – near the end of the essay – to view security as a "collective good", despite his showing some sympathy for it.[32] Our sense, however, is that it is better to construe his argument as one against viewing security solely as a collective good rather than it also being considered a collective good:

> It would be wrong to exaggerate the communal element or pretend that it exhausted the concept. Much of the work in this Essay has sought to deepen and broaden what is called the pure safety conception of security. From the beginning, however, it has been said that it is important for the concept of security to remain anchored in the safety of individual men and women. That anchoring is irreducible and non-negotiable.[33]

This is not really a point with which we disagree. However, once we begin to deepen our concept of security to encompass more than physical security, then we enter the world of collective as well as individual goods. It is not (as Waldron tends to cast it) a matter of either/or.[34]

One possibility that Waldron canvasses – but which we do not – is that security may be viewed as a public good, something to which all are entitled, thus

---

Responsibility: An Individualist Account", in *Midwest Studies in Philosophy* 30 (2006): 176–93.

27   It may be the case that Waldron has elsewhere expressed himself more clearly on this matter.

28   Waldron, "Safety and Security", 462.

29   *Ibid.*, 474.

30   *Ibid.*, 463.

31   *Ibid.*, 493.

32   *Ibid.*, 500–02.

33   *Ibid.*, 501–02.

34   ". . . most of the complications here have attempted to show that security is a complex and structured function of individual safety, not an amiable communal alternative to it" (502).

setting aside the distributive question.[35] He canvasses and critiques different understandings of this option, though he concludes that even if it is a public good there remains a question about how that good is in fact distributed.

With this excursus on Waldron's valuable discussion, we return to the dominant collective idea of national security. Although often appealed to, the idea of national security has never been entirely clear cut, and a number of commentators have argued that it is "essentially contestable".[36] If that is so, as is likely to be the case, then its articulation is not going to be a neutrally characterizable enterprise such as might be involved in measuring the dimensions of a physical object.[37]

In addition, national security is rarely defined in legislation or elsewhere and, when it is, it tends to be defined extremely broadly.[38] Traditionally and most simply — at least until the collapse of the Soviet Union — it referred first and foremost to the security of borders and to the conditions for insuring a state against conquest or serious attack. Its primary agent was a standing army ready to defend those borders against an invading army (or weapons of mass destruction). As some writers (especially those working in peacemaking studies[39]) have put it, often as a prelude to its criticism, national security has traditionally had a militaristic ring to it.

But even in that traditional sense, national security referred to something more than merely uncontested or secure borders. There was the associated idea of an absence of *threat*.[40] That is, there was also an implicit subjective dimension — an absence of fear or, as we might put it, of a sense of insecurity.[41] And the threat

---

35   *Ibid.*, 482–85. Miller offers this kind of account in his *Moral Foundations of Social Institutions*, chapters 2 and 9.

36   See Steve Smith, "The Contested Concept of Security", Institute of Defence and Strategic Studies, Singapore, May 2002, at: http://www.ntu.edu.sg/idss/publications/WorkingPapers/WP23.PDF.

37   On essential contestability, see Chapter IV.

38   Thus the US Intelligence community defines "national security" as: "The territorial integrity, sovereignty, and international freedom of action of the United States. Intelligence activities relating to national security encompass all the military, economic, political, scientific, technological, and other aspects of foreign developments that pose actual or potential threats to US national interests", see: http://www.intelligence. gov/0-glossary.shtml. Clearly this allows national security to cover almost anything. For other discussions of the conceptual issues, see the editorial introduction, "A Conceptual Framework", in Daniel J. Kaufman, Jeffrey S. McKitrick, and Thomas J. Leney (eds), *U.S. National Security: A Framework for Analysis*, (Lexington, MA: Lexington Books, 1985), 3–26; Robert Mandel, *The Changing Face of National Security: A Conceptual Analysis* (Westport, CT: Greenwood, 1994).

39   Such writers see development and the reduction of invidious inequalities, not the possession of strong borders, as the key to national security. To be honest, we are not sure why authors have to think — or so often tend to think — in terms of either/or, but the debate already points to contested issues.

40   The notion of a threat might well repay attention. See Daniel Lyons, "Welcome Threats And Coercive Offers", *Philosophy* 50 (1975): 425–36; Theodore Benditt, "Threats and Offers", *Personalist* 58 (1977): 382–84; Martin Gunderson, "Threats and Coercion", *Canadian Journal of Philosophy* 9 (1979): 247–59; Andrew Hetherington, "The Real Distinction between Threats and Offers", *Social Theory and Practice* 25 (1999): 211–42; Claire Finkelstein, "Threats and Preemptive Practices", *Legal Theory* 5 (1999): 311–38.

41   "Security, in an objective sense, measures the absence of threats to acquired values, in a subjective sense, the absence of fear that such values will be attacked": Wolfers, "'National Security' as an Ambiguous

in question was not simply to borders. It usually included the threat to a *way of life* – to institutional and cultural traditions and values.[42] Borders do not mark out the boundaries of a sovereign state alone but also a sphere within which an historical narrative is unfolding – a richly textured institutional and cultural history, characterized by distinctive memories and myths. In other words, national security secures not only geographical borders but also a complex set of traditions and ways of living.[43]

Territorial border issues remain significant, though for many countries they have been transformed from a concern with armed conquest to a concern with terrorism and the influx of illegal immigrants and refugees. In response, internationally recognized but porous borders have sometimes been strengthened or even supplemented by "smart borders" that do not provide a fixed or internationally recognized geographical but rather a politically expedient demarcation of territorial boundaries.[44] At the same time – indeed, as part of that transformation – the idea and element of threat has increasingly encompassed actual and potential hazards to domestic tranquility and stability other than those posed by simple conquest.[45]

Threats to national *interests*[46] may take many forms and, *if sufficiently dire*, such threats may be considered threats to national *security*. Pandemic or contagious disease (both human and agricultural), environmental conditions (such as

---

Symbol", in *Discord and Collaboration,* 150. Zedner also draws attention to a tradition in which a sense of security is not seen as desirable but as a form of complacency ("The Concept of Security: An Agenda for Comparative Analysis", *Legal Studies* 23 (2003): 157).

42   Cf. Hans Morgenthau: "National security must be defined as integrity of the national territory and its institutions", *Politics Among the Nations: The Struggle for Power and Peace,* third ed. (NY: Alfred A. Knopf, 1960), 562; and Richard Ullman: "A threat to national security is an action or sequence of events that (1) threatens drastically and over a relatively brief span of time to degrade the quality of life for the inhabitants of the state or (2) threatens significantly to narrow the range of policy choices available to the government of a state or to private non-government entities (persons, groups, corporations) within the state", "Redefining Security", *International Security* 8 (Summer, 1983): 129. The last phrase in Ullman's account strikes us as overbroad.

43   That can be true not only of free societies but also of oppressive ones. One of the volatile issues confronting Iraqis has been the preservation of the "character" of Iraqi society – no small feat in a country that encompasses at least three major traditions. Borders may change, and with the change in borders also comes internal change – sometimes like adding another patch to a quilt, at other time seeking some form of assimilation.

44   See Leanne Weber, "The Shifting Frontiers of Migration Control", in *Borders, Mobility and Technologies of Control,* ed. Sharon Pickering and Leanne Weber (Springer, 2006), ch. 2.

45   The most influential developments seem to be associated with what is called the Copenhagen School (at the Copenhagen Peace Research Institute), primarily – though not exclusively – in the work of Barry Buzan. See B. Buzan, O. Wyer, J.D. Wilde, and O. Waever, *Security: A New Framework for Analysis* (Boulder, CO: Lynne Rienner Publishers, 1997). Its members employ the language of "securitization" to indicate ways in which various social phenomena (political, economic, societal and environmental) are marketed as relevant to national security. (Securitization requires only the successful *portrayal* of these phenomena as threats.)

46   We consider interests to be those matters in which one has a stake, particularly the ingredients of well-being. However, there is some ambiguity here between "national interests" and what is sometimes spoken of as "the national interest". See further, Hans Morgenthau, *In Defense of the National Interest* (New York: Alfred A. Knopf, 1951).

pollution and global warming) and extra-territorial economic circumstances and decisions (such as trade barriers and currency decisions) are now frequently spoken of as impinging on national security interests. Whether they also constitute threats to national security *simpliciter* will depend on how damaging they are. Moreover, threats to national security need not necessarily be external. Internal dissension and poverty may also rise to the level of threats to national security. Therefore, not only outside dangers posed to a national collectivity will be seen as threats to national security but also internal challenges – perhaps those arising from a failure to create or secure conditions for a significant segment of the local population.

Even beyond these considerations, national security has recently been broadened to include the establishment of or support for a variety of international initiatives – most critically, broadly democratic or rights-based polities.[47] It was the success of this expansion that enabled a switch from "weapons of mass destruction" threatening American freedom to "forces of undemocratic tyranny" threatening American freedom or, even more broadly, to honoring the "nonnegotiable demands of human dignity". The thought here has been that national security requires, if not anything as universal as global security, then some *commonality* or *sharing* of concern for societal integrity. Thus a number of writers have tried to focus on what is called "common security" or "cooperative security".[48] For them, national security has become, if not secondary to a broader form of interstate or international security, then equal with it.[49] These writers are concerned with what we referred to above as the internal collective security of the community of nation-states.

---

47 The assumption here is that such polities are less likely to threaten each other. For discussions of this old chestnut, see Matthew White, "Democracies Do Not Make War on One Another. . . Or Do They?", at: http://users.erols.com/mwhite28/demowar.htm; and Per Ahlmark, "How Democracy Prevents Civic Catastrophes", at: http://www.unwatch.org/speeches/demcat.html. See also the speech of President George W. Bush to the United Nations General Assembly: "In this young century, our world needs a new definition of security. Our security is not merely found in spheres of influence, or some balance of power. The security of our world is found in the advancing rights of mankind." (September 21, 2004, at: http://www.cbsnews.com/stories/2004/09/21/world/main644795.shtml.)

48 Some of these have argued that national security concerns should give way to broader cooperative security arrangements. Alternatively, other writers have pushed for the replacement of a concern for national security with one for human security.

49 One other movement and countermovement should be noted. Whereas Lockean thinking places the focus of security on individuals (i.e. needing their rights secured against predatory others, leading to the formation of a protective/securing state) a number of contemporary writers have shifted their attention almost completely from the security of the individual to that of the state. The state and its interests are not seen as the sum of those of the individuals who make it up, neither is its security reducible to the security of its citizens. It has its own identity and interests, and what secures it is not determined by what secures the interests of these or those individuals who inhabit it. In the opposite direction, there have been those who believe that the state is secondary only to the individuals who make it up and who have therefore asserted the claims of what they call *human* security, in which state relevance consists simply in the fact that, in a global human order, it is the actor "with the greatest relative power" (Francisco Rojas Aravena, "Human Security: Emerging Concept of Security in the Twenty-First Century", *Disarmament Forum* 2 (2002), at: http://www.unidir.ch/pdf/articles/pdf-art1442.pdf).

Tensions

Even though we shall return to it, it is appropriate at this point to note how different kinds of security may stand in some sort of tension. We have already referred to a possible tension between state security and individual security, depending on whether the individual or state is seen as security's primary object.

Another tension of particular relevance to the present project has been magnified by 9/11, and that is a tension between national and computer security. Security has become an important concern in computer technology – hackers may steal or destroy one's data and viruses may infect one's system and disable one's computer or otherwise ruin one's data. In response, devices of increasing sophistication have been developed to secure computer systems – for example, firewalls have been developed and data have been encrypted.

At the same time, however, computer technology has become a tool for terrorist activities, whether as a simple communication device or as a means of disabling target systems. National security concerns have thus come into conflict with those of computer security: at some level, the more effective computer security has become, the better it has been able to serve the purposes of terrorism: terrorists can communicate using encryption, steganography (digital camouflage) or otherwise deceptive communicative techniques; money can be electronically and covertly transferred;[50] and our increasing dependence on networked digital technology exposes ever larger portions of our infrastructure to sabotage.

In response, governmental technologies have been developed (in the name of national security) that have made our individual or personal security less secure.

The importance of national security

Salient to an assessment of the moral force of appeals to national security will be not only what is embodied in our understanding of it but also what, given that understanding, is then taken to constitute a (significant) threat to it. It is almost always in the interest of those in power to give national security the widest possible interpretation as well as to overestimate the actual threat posed by what they consider will endanger it. In the US, the communist witch-hunts of the 1950s were justified in terms of national security and, as noted previously, we have more recently seen the issue of "weapons of mass destruction" exploited

---

50 Online payment processing systems (OPPS) such as Paypal are making such transfers harder to trace. They allow for informal transfer of monies across the globe and, unlike the other international transfer systems (banks etc.) are subject to little or no regulation. See Holger Bürk and Andreas Pfitzmann, "Digital Payment Systems Enabling Security and Unobservability", *Computers & Security* 8, no. 5 (1989): 399–416; Kim-Kwang, Raymond Choo, and Russell G. Smith, "Criminal Exploitation of Online Systems by Organized Crime Groups", *Asian Journal of Criminology* 3, no. 1 (June 2008).

to similar effect. Not only that, it is often in the interests of those in power to clothe their more partisan concerns in the language of national security.[51] License may be an enemy of liberty but, because national security is often made to bear more moral weight than it can reasonably bear, it may also be its own enemy.[52] It is important, then, in considering arguments grounded in appeals to national security, to look at both its scope and substance.

What we consider to be a particular problem in the discussion of national security is the tendency (hinted at earlier) to slide from threats to "national security interests" to threats to "national security." Although national security is concerned with the protection of various state interests – for example, in secure borders, the preservation of cultural traditions, the perpetuation of key civil institutions – it does not follow that whenever some national interest is threatened, compromised or damaged "national security" will also be at risk. It will depend on the nature, magnitude and imminence of the threat/risk. Even *threatening* national security will not necessarily put it *at risk*. There may be those who believe that the "Great Satan" needs to be put down – at least, that is their stated ambition – but if their resources cannot match up to their desires it can hardly be argued that they place national security at risk. If national security is to be placed at risk, the risk must be *dire, imminent* and *real*.[53]

Furthermore – and this is no small matter – we must link national security to the kind of security that figures in discussions of the conditions under which our human rights (including our liberty rights) may be expressed. Although we believe that this can and must be done there are some problems to be resolved and arguments to be made. On the one hand, we need to confront arguments for forms of cosmopolitanism that seek to diminish if not erode the significance of national boundaries for human flourishing. On the other hand, we need to address arguments that move in libertarian, anarchist or anarcho-syndicalist

---

51   In the run-up to the 2004 US elections, it was frequently claimed that electing John Kerry would endanger national security. Thus, Vice-President Dick Cheney stated, "It's absolutely essential that eight weeks from today, on November 2nd, we make the right choice, because if we make the wrong choice then the danger is that we'll get hit again, that we'll be hit in a way that will be devastating from the standpoint of the United States, and that we'll fall back into the pre-9/11 mind-set, if you will, that in fact these terrorist attacks are just criminal acts and that we are not really at war." (Dana Milbank and Spencer S. Hsu, "Cheney: Kerry Victory Is Risky; Democrats Decry Talk as Scare Tactic", *The Washington Post*, September 8, 2004, A01). Senator Kerry was not beyond such tactics himself. The Kerry campaign quickly responded with an ad featuring a close-up of 9/11 widow Kristen Breitweiser in which she says, "I want to look into my daughter's eyes and know that she is safe, and that is why I am voting for John Kerry." (Walter Shapiro, "With Scare Tactics Aplenty, Election Rivals Halloween: Hype & Glory", *USA Today*, October 19, 2004, 4A). What is merely "regime security" often seeks to represent itself as "national security".

52   It was in partial recognition of this that in *US v. Robel* the Court also affirmed that "implicit in the term 'national defense' is the notion of defending those values and ideals which set this Nation apart." It would be ironic "if, in the name of national defense, we would sanction the subversion" of those liberties that make "the defense of the Nation worthwhile" (389 U.S. 258, at 264 (1967)).

53   To comment in this way courts some sort of political backlash. To ignore or downplay such threats may be to encourage their expression in increasingly effective ways. Likewise, to respond to them overactively may also strategically advantage those who make them.

directions. In other words, we need to be able to argue that for the foreseeable future human security is best achieved via national security. This is not the place to resolve such issues, but they cannot be ignored. Appeals to national security cannot be introduced as though they require no further explication or justification, including by reference to individual liberty rights.[54]

Our point here is not to claim that we should stick with a simplistic or outmoded understanding of national security. The world in which we live is not the world of one hundred years ago and our national interests are not as localized as they were one hundred years ago. Even though talk of a global village takes it too far there is nevertheless a sense in which *we* (understood as a "particular people") are now more easily impacted by events (and not just hostile armies) beyond our geographical and jurisdictional boundaries. Conflict overseas may bring pressures to accept refugees or may threaten energy supplies, and distant economies may threaten global environmental disaster. However, if national security is to be invoked as a trumping consideration, the links need to be spelled out and, if necessary, defended and quantified. Otherwise we will find ourselves on a politically slippery slope in which neither the slipperiness, the slope nor the end point will be clear. The Vietnam War was almost certainly sustained by means of a flawed argument (the domino theory) about the international spread of communism. Its mistakes are repeatable, and probably have been repeated in Iraq.

The account of security that we have so far provided views it largely as a means toward, or a precondition for, the enjoyment of our rights and other goods, not as something to be valued or sought for its own sake. This has obvious implications for the extent to which private, public and national security measures are legitimately undertaken. Should security involve significant derogations of the rights (and other goods) to which it is a justifying means then it will have been taken too far. In the article "Too Much Security?" Lucia Zedner posits and discusses six paradoxes of security. Her concern is principally with private and public security rather than with national security, though it is not too difficult to recast her discussion to apply to national security:

1. Security pursues risk reduction but presumes the persistence of crime.

2. The expansion of security has enlarged not diminished the penal state.

3. Security promises reassurance but in fact increases anxiety.

4. Security is posited as a universal good but presumes social exclusion.

5. Security promises freedom but erodes civil liberties.

---

54   John Kleinig offers some reflections on these issues in "Patriotic Loyalty", *Patriotism: Philosophical and Political Perspectives*, ed. Aleksandar Pavkovic and Igor Primoratz (Aldershot, UK: Ashgate, 2008), ch. 2. A brief account of such an argument is offered later.

6. Security is posited as a public good but its pursuit is inimical to the good society.[55]

We doubt whether all these so-called paradoxes are indeed such. Nevertheless, they point to ways in which the concern for security may overreach, or imperil other values. Her discussion of (1), for example, warns us against thinking that we should try to secure ourselves against all threat. Security is concerned with *diminishing* risk, not with *eliminating* it. Even if at time t_1 we can effectively eliminate risk it is likely that new risks will appear at time t_2. Not only is the elimination of risk a virtually unattainable goal but at a certain point it is also likely to become an unacceptably costly one. We need to make judgments about how much risk is acceptable and therefore how much security is needed. As we see from items (3) to (6), efforts to remove (or even diminish) risk may serve to undermine or compromise other values we support.

Item (3) reminds us that the *enjoyment* of our rights involves more than a bare ability to exercise them. We should be able to exercise them without undue anxiety – whether that anxiety is based on actual risk or (more problematically) on fears created by those who manage the apparatuses of security and who may have their own reasons for maintaining anxiety and creating social docility. Security measures ought not to create or exploit anxieties disproportionately to the risk involved.

Item (4) speaks to the egalitarian concerns of a liberal democratic society, and notes how the burdens of security often tend to fall more heavily – and indeed unfairly – on some groups.[56] For reasons of convenience, much profiling has the practical effect of shifting security burdens to particular ethnic groups.

---

55 Lucia Zedner, "Too Much Security?", *International Journal of the Sociology of Law* 31 (2003): 155–84. Though informative, we are not always persuaded by Zedner's discussion.

56 Most of us are probably not affected by the USA PATRIOT Act or other measures introduced following 9/11. Ostensibly, our security has been increased or restored, but most of us will not have borne any significant costs in return. However, there have been significant costs for some – and they have fallen disproportionately on a small segment of the population – those with Middle Eastern appearances, those with visa irregularities and those who, for some reason or other, have had governmental attention turned on them. Those satisfying certain profiles or who have appeared on various "watch lists" have borne the brunt of the costs of "our" greater security. Now, it might be argued that this is precisely how it should be, since it is from among those groups that our security has been jeopardized. This might look a bit more plausible – at least as a matter of policy – were it arguable that a high proportion of those made to bear the cost are also linked to terrorism in some active or conspiratorial way. But this is not arguable at all. Only a minute proportion of those on whom the burden of heightened security has been thrust has and has had any sympathy with – let alone constructive connection to – the cause of terrorism. They are no more morally tainted than those who have suffered no appreciable diminution of liberty (or, more significantly, abrogation of their liberties). Not only do we not gain in security from the investigation of those who pose no threat to it but, if the investigation is sufficiently ill conceived, it may actually diminish security by creating sympathy for the terrorist cause where there was previously none.

Those who speak about the relation of security to civil liberties often talk of an innocuous "balancing" of the two, but item (5) correctly notes the trade-off, derogation or sacrifice that is involved and the frequent erosion of those liberties in the name of security.[57]

In (6) we can observe the ways in which the focus on security can display a lack of trust, or at least diminishes it. Insofar as a good society is one in which trust is abundant, an over-concern with security will tend to undermine it.[58]

To the extent, then, that security is a means to the enjoyment of our rights it has a limited claim on our liberties and other rights.

However, security – or at least the national security that now tends to dominate our horizon – may also be valued for its own sake. If it is so-valued then it will make more sense to trade it off against those things for which it is (also) intended as the means. It is then no longer a mere means but also an end.

We are not dealing with a hypothetical possibility. National security *is* often treated as though it were something to be ensured in its own right and not merely for what it makes possible. Part of the reason for this is that many of us have come to identify with the state, nation or country of which we are a part so that securing our state/nation/country is securing something that is not only a means to our various individual (and perhaps collective) human rights but also something that has become valuable for us in its own right. The nation has become one of the associations with which we as associational beings have come to identify.

To recapitulate: the process of human growth and development is not itself an individualistic one, even if it may sometimes result in persons who are extremely individualistic. Unlike trees that have their "final form" (more or less) encoded in the DNA of their seeds, or many animals, whose nurture is more or less co-extensive with their development of survival and reproductive skills, humans come to be what we normatively represent them to be (i.e. ends in themselves, possessors of waivable rights etc.) only as the result of a fairly long process of nurture and learning, much of which is social in nature, and resulting from a

---

57   For critiques of the balancing metaphor, see Jeremy Waldron, "Security and Liberty: The Image of Balance", *Journal of Political Philosophy* 11 (2) (June 2003): 191–210; James E. Fleming, "Securing Deliberative Democracy", *Fordham Law Review* 72 (2004): 1435–76; T.M. Scanlon, "The Constitutional Essentials of Political Liberalism: Adjusting Rights and Balancing Values", *Fordham Law Review* 72 (2004): 1477–86; Lucia Zedner, "Securing Liberty in the Face of Terror: Reflections from Criminal Justice", *Journal of Law and Society* 32(4) (December 2005): 507–33; and John Kleinig, "Liberty and Security in an Age of Terrorism" in *Security and Justice in the Homeland: Criminologists on Terrorism*, ed. Brian Forst, Jack Greene and James Lynch (Cambridge University Press, 2011), ch. 15.
58   See also John Kleinig, "The Burdens of Situational Crime Prevention: An Ethical Commentary", in *Ethical and Social Perspectives on Situational Crime Prevention*, ed. Andrew von Hirsch, David Garland, and Alison Wakefield (Oxford: Hart Publishing, 2000), 37–58.

significant immersion in families, friendships, educational institutions and so forth.[59] Not only this but, for most of us, many of the activities that, as the people we have become, we subsequently value – both as means and as ends – are social in nature. They may be orchestras, social groups, religious communities, political parties, cultural traditions, national rituals, professions and so forth. Our lives, therefore, come to be partially encompassed by associative arrangements that are of both instrumental and intrinsic value to us. Included in those associations may be our state/nation/country.

This is not an uncontroversial claim. Indeed, it could be argued that friendship is the only relationship that is properly valued for its own sake,[60] whereas families and other associations are valued primarily (and justifiably) because of their instrumental value. However, we think that this is a nonviable position, in part because of what is sometimes referred to as institutional entropy – namely, the endemic tendency of institutions/associations/affiliations/relationships to decline over time. Their capacity to sustain themselves in the face of this tendency is dependent on the non-instrumental commitment of (at least some of) their members, a commitment that will sustain them during both downturns as well as prompt efforts to recuperate them.[61] That, however, is not in itself sufficient to pick out nations/states/countries as appropriate associations for intrinsic valuing. There are many associations, often quite close and often valued in themselves, that are inappropriately so valued (i.e. gangs, organized crime rings, rogue states and so forth).

So why, if at all, should we value a state, nation or country – a *patria* – in such a way that its security is important to us not simply because it enables the exercise of our rights but also because of the kind of association it is? We can construct a *contingently* affirmative response, though we need to enter some brief initial caveats before providing a somewhat roundabout argument in favor of intrinsically valuing national security.

The caveats. Historically speaking, *patriae* have not been essential to human flourishing. Many humans have flourished – not, perhaps in our fashion, though in their own way – in tribal communities that it would be anachronistic to characterize as countries, states or even polities. However we may have wanted

---

59   Human beings (i.e. members of the species *Homo sapiens*) who lack this long period of communal nurture also come to be significantly lacking in the traits that we identify with normative personhood. See the discussions of feral children in Michael Newton, *Savage Girls and Wild Boys: A History of Feral Children* (New York: Faber & Faber, 2002).

60   We probably need to distinguish here between what are sometimes referred to as end-friends and means-friends. See e.g. Neera Kapur Badhwar (ed.), *Friendship: A Philosophical Reader* (Ithaca: Cornell University Press, 1993); idem, "Friends as Ends in Themselves", *Philosophy and Phenomenological Research* 48 (1987): 1–23.

61   The classic discussion of this thesis is to be found in Albert O. Hirschman, *Exit, Voice, and Loyalty: Responses to Decline in Firms, Organizations, and States* (Cambridge, MA: Harvard University Press, 1970).

to characterize their tribal and other particularistic commitments, they were not recognizably commitments to a nation, state or country. The state, or *patria*, though not entirely modern, does not have the deepest of historical roots and, moreover, does not appear to be as central to our sense of being as we may consider friends (and family and tribe) to be.

Given these caveats, however, *our* (post-Enlightenment) sense of being probably could not have been created or sustained by a merely tribal life. What *we* count as *our* flourishing is not generally something we could have conceptualized or realized had our lives remained tribally based. What *we* require as the arena for *our* growth and satisfaction has demanded much greater social complexity, involving a fairly elaborate social infrastructure along with fairly advanced technological possibilities. The point is not simply that *patriae* provide the conditions for our flourishing but that, for many of us, *our* individual *patria* is partially constitutive of *our* flourishing. Many of what constitute aspirations and possibilities for us are given through our socio-political arrangements.

We (those reading this study) are expressions of the potentiality that particular social formations have enabled, thus our conception of what it is that constitutes a good life and the social conditions for our achieving it will be significantly influenced by the social environment within which we have been formed.

At this point, at least two questions immediately arise. Firstly, to what extent does our self-conception presume the existence and maintenance of the *patria* in which we find ourselves? Secondly, might we conceive our possibilities differently within a different socio-political environment (in which our *patria* no longer existed)? Since the two questions are connected, our response will bear on both.

Liberal selves – the kind that we are considering here – are often adaptable. They are not usually wedded to a single way of living as the only or best way for humans, or even as the only or best way *for them*. We can be born and raised in the US and move to Australia or the UK without too much trauma. For many so born and raised, the US may not be critical to their flourishing (or continued flourishing). However, we might think that *some* liberal democratic *patria* is important to our way of being – the thought of relocating to or being taken over by a fascist or Stalinist regime would be highly threatening to our sense of self.[62]

Some liberal selves might also develop cosmopolitan tendencies or even aspirations, finding themselves equally at home in Sydney, London, Paris and New York, and probably other places, without any particular (or at least strong) patriotic or national ties. That is certainly a possibility. Not all, however, will thrive in such a multicultural environment. They will retain strong patriotic

---

62   It is not uncommon for those who must relocate to problem regimes then to live in enclaves.

allegiances to their countries of origin because they have imbibed – and feel particularly at home in – distinctive aspects of their early culture (we think of Annette Baier refusing to give up her New Zealand citizenship and later retiring to New Zealand[63]). Certain of its features resonate with their deepest sense of who they are. Yet other liberal selves may come to identify so strongly with the culture and ways of the country to which they have relocated that their commitments/loyalties shift. This is often – though certainly not always – the case with those who migrate to establish better lives for themselves and their children.

However, the attraction that cosmopolitans feel for a world community is, we suspect, an attraction partly because they conceive of it in fairly liberal terms. Were cosmopolitanism to have the form of a Trotskyite international communist regime or of an extended Muslim *umma wahida* (universal community), it would not be as attractive (for most of *us*, at least). For *us* it is often *our patria*, and for some *others*, *their patria*, that constitutes the expression as well as guardian of a way of life that sustains both the requisites and "vocabulary" for flourishing. It may not constitute an exclusive venue for flourishing, but insofar as there are perceived to be "forces" abroad that might and indeed want to change it radically, we may acquire considerable attachment to it and value its security. Were circumstances to arise in which our liberal democratic way of life was radically challenged, our loyalty might well prompt us to defend our particular *patria* with our lives.

There need not be anything chauvinistic or jingoistic about such patriotism and the commitment to national security that goes with it. The popular critique of loyalty generally (and of patriotism in particular), in which it is claimed that loyalty enjoins or requires a belief in the superiority of the object of one's loyalty and/or denigrates the objects of others' loyalty (especially their country), is misguided. Chauvinism, like many exploitations of loyalty, hijacks loyalty for nefarious purposes.[64] Just as there is no need to think that the family and friends to whom we are loyal are *ipso facto* superior to those of others, there is no need to build claims of superiority into patriotic loyalty.

Nevertheless, there is little doubt that, given a very different socio-political environment, we might conceive of the possibilities for *our* flourishing differently. In a more expansive socio-political environment than we now inhabit we might be able to conceive of possibilities for ourselves that do not currently cross our radar screen. As women and historically suppressed

---

63 Annette Baier, "Some Virtues of Resident Alienage", in *Virtue*, NOMOS XXXIV, ed. John W. Chapman and William Galston (New York: NYU Press, 1992), 291–308.

64 As a side note on a theory of the virtues, almost any – if not every – virtue if taken in isolation or absolutized will lead to some form of excess. As Portia memorably observed in *The Merchant of Venice*, even justice, that pre-eminent of virtues, needs to be tempered with mercy (and probably prudence).

or marginalized minorities in liberal democracies know from their own (and historical) experience, significant socio-political changes have been required for many members of those groups to have even conceived of certain social roles and possibilities for themselves. For others, such changes have been essential to their ability to translate such broader conceptions into some sort of reality.

A *patria*, in other words, though important enough for many of us, is not deeply necessary to human flourishing. Were the conditions of our socio-political environment different from what they are, many of us might move relatively easily from one *patria* to another or into some more cosmopolitan federation of communities. Some security of our social environment would be necessary, but it might not need to be conceived of as *national* security.

We are not postulating a completely malleable conception of human flourishing. We have the biological structure we have, along with its potentialities (albeit incompletely mapped).[65] If enabled, we would anticipate that our self-conception as reasoning and responsible beings (characterizations that are, admittedly, contestable) is likely to translate itself into non-oppressive polities. Except when seen through the lens of certain ideologies (protection against which there are no guarantees), there is likely to be a desire for movement from polities that are closed to polities that are open. But that need not lead to a rejection or downgrading of patriotism and the demand for security associated with it. Patriotism is likely to be a reasonable expectation in an open society. Within such open societies, patriotism and unreasonable expressions of national security are more likely to be kept in check, and a plurality of free societies is more likely to keep each in check — but only *more* likely.

Although there are rich cultural possibilities to membership in some *patria*, especially a pluralistic one, we suspect that the deeper roots of patriotic loyalty probably lie in the desire to secure from serious encroachment or destruction the elements of a way of life with which we have come to identify, and which are components of our own flourishing. And that is risk laden.

Endangerments to our national security might be construed in largely cultural terms. We might fear and even resent the cultural changes brought about by immigration or foreign media, and even if we are not averse to cultural change — if, indeed, we welcome it — we may wish for it to occur at a pace that does not leave us feeling culturally stranded.[66] We do not want to find ourselves isolated from the social environment that has provided important elements of meaning

---

65   We prescind from the issue of future genetic manipulation, however, see Fritz Allhoff, Patrick Lin, James Moor, and John Weckert, "Ethics of Human Enhancement: 25 Questions and Answers", *Studies in Ethics, Law, and Technology* 4, no. 1 (2010), doi: 102202/1941-6008.1110.

66   Joel Feinberg usefully addresses some of these issues in *Harmless Wrongdoing* (New York: Oxford University Press, 1988), ch. 29.

for our lives.[67] There are often historical as well as current dimensions to this *status quo* – considerable pain may be involved if one's socio-political history is "swallowed up" in the history of another.

Also important, however, is the sorry and ongoing history of human predation. The lion, cosmopolitans need to recognize, is not yet ready to lie down with the lamb. In a world that will foreseeably remain deeply divided by inequality of opportunity, the *patria* is always "at risk" of conquest (or secession), and to assure ourselves in the event of challenge we need the patriotic loyalty of citizens who are prepared to defend a way of life they value not only instrumentally but for its own sake. Even – perhaps especially – liberal states need armies (or military alliances) and a population willing to make sacrifices for their preservation.[68] We may – and should – work to diminish some of those inequalities, but it is unlikely that we will eliminate them. Though patriotic loyalty may be an imperfect obligation, it is not dispensable.

The foregoing constitutes a fairly discursive argument for seeing national security not simply as an instrumental value but also as having a contingently intrinsic value for us. It does not, however, constitute an argument for seeing every appeal to national security as legitimate, though it may sometimes constitute an argument for seeing a potential in arguments for national security for some (limited) sacrifices of other values and liberties. We need to recognize that there are limits to this.

Because we tend to identify with our *patria* in a way that gives national security an intrinsic value, there is usually *implicit* in our loyalty a judgment that its objects are compatible with what we stand for. That is, embedded in those relationships to which our loyalty is owed are certain presumptions about the compatibility of values attributable to the objects of loyalty with those for which we stand.[69] To the extent that we learn otherwise we have a reason for taking some action – either to try to bring about change in the object of our loyalty or (in the event of failure) to abandon it (on the grounds that it has forfeited its claims to our loyalty). We have what Albert Hirschman refers to as *voice* and *exit* options.[70] Appropriate loyalty will generally encourage voice and delay exit until we have sufficient reason to think that necessary change is unlikely to be forthcoming, and that the associational object no longer expresses the values

---

67   This can happen on micro as well as macro levels, changing neighborhoods as well as changing societies.
68   This is a major theme in Alasdair MacIntyre's *Is Loyalty a Virtue?* Lindley Lecture (Lawrence: University of Kansas Philosophy Department, 1984).
69   This is not to be confused – as is so often the case – with grounding our loyalty in the qualities that we presume to be implicit in the object of our loyalty. In that case we might be tempted to argue that our loyalty is to the qualities. Rather, our loyalty is to the *object of our association* – the friend, organization, or whatever. It is the *association with that object* that we value – not just the object and not just the association.
70   Hirschman, *Exit, Voice, and Loyalty*. We may, of course, as people often do, compromise our values and live with a contradiction.

we deemed essential to the relationship. Nevertheless, the loyalty we have to an affiliational object or person is not a loyalty to the particular values that are instantiated by them. The loyalty is to *the objects of an association or relationship*.

Because we identify with the objects of our loyalty, critical and often painful decisions will need to be made should we discover significant dissonance between the values exemplified by the object of loyalty and our own. If, for example, we learn that our lover once murdered someone, that our country is engaging in something close to genocide or that our university is sponsoring research into biological weaponry, we will be confronted with the possibility of severing our connection with something that has become part of us. In the case of our country, its security may no longer hold great value for us.

The metaphors of balance and trade-off

Having made a case for both personal and collective security, as well as noting their interconnections as well as tensions between them, it is appropriate at this point of transition to other values with which security is often in some kind of tension (e.g. liberty and privacy) to first explore two metaphors that are commonly employed to characterize these tensions. Waldron himself refers to the pervasiveness of the balancing/trade-off metaphors in the literature on liberty (in particular) and security (though one might link the discussion as readily with privacy as with liberty). They repay further discussion, as there are some serious inadequacies to the balancing metaphor that have political and policy implications. Waldron has himself provided some discussion of them, and though we agree largely with his critique of the balancing metaphor, we believe that he conflates it inappropriately with the trade-off metaphor.[71]

Balances

In considering the relations between liberty and security – how they are to be "played off" against each other – it is very common, almost standard, to use the metaphor of a scale in which liberty/privacy and (possibly national) security are placed in opposing pans, one to be "balanced" against the other in zero-sum fashion.[72] The underlying or at least implied idea is that there is an appropriate

---

71　Waldron has a few comments on the metaphor in "Security and Safety", 502–06. His main discussion, however, is to be found in Jeremy Waldron, "Security and Liberty: The Image of Balance", *Journal of Political Philosophy* 11 (2003): 191–210.

72　Presumably the inspiration for the balancing metaphor goes back to Themis, the goddess of justice and war, holding the sword in one hand and scales in the other. However, the metaphor also pervades the language of the Supreme Court. Of course, the interests, values or rights to be "balanced" are not restricted to "liberty" and "security". Only a few writers have challenged the usefulness or appropriateness of the metaphor.

level or balance to be achieved – one, moreover, that does not threaten the integrity of the other. Appropriate liberty[73] is that which balances appropriate security.

The need for such balancing is seen as an essential and pervasive feature of our social existence. Given Lockean or, even more gloomily, Hobbesian presumptions about the subjects of liberty, some constraints will always be required in order that our security can be assured. The problem, it is said, is to get the right balance, namely, one in which constraints on liberty are *appropriate* to an *appropriate* level of security.[74]

(1) How balancing works

Securing the right balance is not something that can be determined in the abstract, or once and for all, but something that will change depending on the gravity of a threat and the level of risk (to security). Where the risks are small, appropriate constraints on liberty will be few, but where the risks are large and imminent we might expect liberty to be substantially, and appropriately or justifiably, diminished. An appropriate balance is also a function of the importance we attach to liberty and security. Some constraints on liberty might be seen as more important than others, though this will be complicated by the fact that people may disagree as to their importance. The level of security that we consider necessary will also offer opportunities for contestation. Some of us are more risk-averse than others, so even if the balancing metaphor works it will have to confront some complexity in its application to social life.[75]

The balancing metaphor has a surface plausibility, or at least it strikes us as familiar and easy to work with. Both liberty and national security can be thought of as matters of degree – of more and less – and, on the face of it, it seems reasonable to think that where security threats are great, liberty might reasonably be contracted, and that where security threats are minimal, liberty might – indeed, ought to – be expanded. The only significant issue might appear to be one of getting the balance right – of judging the gravity and probability of risk to security accurately enough to make appropriate adjustments to liberty.[76]

---

73 We will continue – as does Waldron – to talk about liberty (it can function as an umbrella term) even though much of our interest here is more narrowly concerned with privacy.

74 The picture involves an oversimplification in that it fails to accommodate other "values" – such as efficiency and economy – that might also need to be "balanced" against liberty or security.

75 Perhaps we will need to introduce some notion of what are reasonable risks to take – though that, of course, may not be easy to determine.

76 We are assuming that we can compute degrees of liberty in a relatively unproblematic way. That is not an unproblematic assumption. Even leaving to one side the challenge posed by the liberty/liberties distinction it is not clear how to compare the constraint on liberty constituted by a change of speed limit of 65 mph to 55 mph with a change of drinking age from 18 to 21. Are these equivalent constraints or different, and if so, which is the greater? Included in these questions are thorny distributional matters on the side of both who

Many have said that the balance changed dramatically, if not irrevocably, on 9/11; what we thought to be an appropriate balance of liberty and security was shown not to be so. An appropriate balance needed to be restored. Grave threats that we thought were theoretical and remote before 9/11 were shown to be real and imminent. To re-ensure the level of security that we valued (that is, that we considered appropriate) we would need to give up a measure of liberty.

We did not have to react in the way that we did. We might have argued that the balance was adequate as it was and that we simply needed to recognize that even an appropriate balance would not rule out every contingency. It was a cost that would need to be borne from time to time (like the occasional conviction of an innocent person despite the procedural safeguards we have instituted).

(2) Is rebalancing needed?

However we might have reacted, the invocation of a balancing argument makes certain important assumptions. One concerns the balancing metaphor – to which we will return, but other important presumptions may also need examination. Central among those is the presumption that what was lacking on 9/11 was a proper balance of liberty and security rather than *the functionality of existing mechanisms*. If, as it seems reasonable to argue, particularly in light of *The 9/11 Commission Report*, the existing mechanisms for security were dysfunctional in various ways, then what was lacking may not have been an appropriate balance of liberty and security but well-functioning security mechanisms and agencies that needed to be brought up to standard.[77] No shift in the balance might have been called for but a more efficient administration of what already existed. Alternatively, the evident requirement for greater security might reasonably be purchased not simply by greater efficiency but also by greater expenditure of resources on security. The latter alternative, like the former, does not necessarily involve any significant reduction in liberty.

(3) Problems of commensurability

Returning to the balancing metaphor, are liberty and security balanceable in the way that is suggested? The metaphor presumes that national security and liberty are commensurable values appropriately balanced against one another. No doubt, to the extent that our ethic is a straightforwardly consequentialist

---

bears the costs and who the benefits, questions we take up later. (Note that one constraint affects a narrower group of people than the other – this presumably will require some justification, no doubt along the lines that drinkers between the ages of 18 and 21 are disproportionately responsible for risky behavior.)

77   *The 9/11 Commission Report: Final Report of the National Commission on Terrorist Attacks Upon the United States*, 2004, at: http://www.9-11commission.gov/report/index.htm. Other reports have come to similar conclusions. This is a critical consideration because, even if it were decided that the balance had been wrongly struck, any rectificatory change would be of little value were the new mechanisms not to function properly. Why should we assume that dysfunctional intelligence agencies with new powers will function any better than the same ones with the old powers?

one – that is, to the extent that our moral values are subordinate to some end, such as the greatest happiness or good for the greatest number[78] – then this will seem to be a reasonable presumption. The right balance of security and liberty will be the ratio that maximizes happiness, good and so on. For example, in the interests of security and overall social good we may no longer enter certain venues without a picture ID or without subjecting our backpacks to X-ray scrutiny. There does not seem to be anything particularly problematic about that if there is some reason to think that failure to have a valid ID shown or a backpack X-rayed would actually heighten a security risk.

However, even on straightforwardly consequentialist premises there are problems. Remember that what we have are two values that are not equally "substantial". Constraints on liberty are likely to be more certain than risks to security. *Actual* constraints on liberty must be weighed against *risks* to security. How do you weigh an actual contraction of liberty to do X against an increase of "security" from 70% to 95% (or even from low to high)? It's not easy. It is made even more problematic by the fact that it is *notoriously* difficult to estimate levels of risk with any kind of accuracy. Moreover, the political sphere – and this is where policy is made – is highly prone to partisan taint. We need not look further than calculations of dangerousness in the criminal justice arena, in which sex and violent offenders have found themselves victims of what are barely more than ideological judgments. Risk data are very spongy, and those who make policy may be inclined to draw conclusions from the data according to their prior leanings.

However, the view that liberty and security can be balanced in some consequentialist manner is highly tendentious, both morally and constitutionally. Morally, as has already been noted, there are certain liberties – or, as we often refer to them, rights – that cannot be easily accommodated to the balancing metaphor. They function as constraints on consequentialist or maximizing doctrines. Robert Nozick spoke of such rights as *side-constraints*,[79] or considerations that should not be entered into a utilitarian calculus, and Ronald Dworkin, in his view of rights as *trumps*,[80] suggests that when utility conflicts with rights, utility must normally give way. To the extent that liberty encompasses what we may consider to be our "civil liberties" or "rights", the simple balancing metaphor is problematic or, indeed, inappropriate. It is not,

---

78   Here we will have to assume that notions of happiness and good are unitary. Otherwise we get into the Millian problem of quality v. quantity (in *Utilitarianism*) or of the commensurability of different kinds of goods.

79   Robert Nozick, *Anarchy, State, and Utopia* (New York: Basic Books, 1974), 28 et seq.

80   Ronald Dworkin, "Rights as Trumps", in *Theories of Rights*, ed. Jeremy Waldron (Oxford: OUP, 1984), 153–67.

as Nozick's and Dworkin's terminology perhaps misleadingly suggests, that values and "goods" such as national security can *never* take precedence but that, should they do so, it will not be as the result of a simple balancing process.

Civil liberties do not inhabit the realm of liberty in a purely additive way. Even though privacy, freedom of speech and freedom of association may be expanded or contracted they are not expanded or contracted as part of a continuum – for example, with the expansion or contraction of speed limits or drinking ages – as part of a more general liberty of action or movement. Privacy and the freedoms of speech and association have a special place within the sphere of liberty. Briefly, they are seen as necessary conditions – indeed, elements – of human flourishing and not merely its catalysts. Their abrogation or constriction requires a special kind of argument, not simply some consideration about greater security or efficiency or social welfare.

Americans give constitutional recognition to the special status of liberties via the Bill of Rights, in which agents of government are inhibited from engaging in maximizing reasoning. Even if it is more efficient to tap phones or enter premises at will when a murder is being investigated such invasions are not permitted unless certain stringent conditions have first been satisfied. Arguments from efficiency (utility) are not sufficient. A different kind of argument is required if we are to engage legitimately in such activities.

We might want to argue that these aspects of liberty (our liberties) are simply weightier than other parts, and that when they are constrained the security interests just have to be higher. It is certainly true – as was awkwardly recognized by their initial proponents[81] – that the side-constraining and trumping effects of certain considerations, such as rights, are not absolute. Justice need not be done if the heavens will fall.[82] But this does not leave the balancing metaphor intact. When, as in emergency situations, rights must be compromised lest disaster (and not simply some maximizing end) occur, what results is not a balance in which appropriate levels of liberty and security are secured, but a situation in which there is a *derogation* from or *infringement* of (some) liberty; it is not merely *diminished*.

The balancing metaphor – at least in the present context – will not do. It fails to capture the complexity of our moral universe.

(4) Distributive problems

The balancing metaphor, to the extent that it is seen as a weighing of commensurables, is problematic in yet another way. Appeals to the metaphor

---

81 See Dworkin, *Taking Rights Seriously*, London: Duckworth, 1977, 191; Nozick, *Anarchy, State, and Utopia*, 30n.
82 Though some have asserted otherwise.

suggest that what we lose in liberty we gain (or regain) in safety and security. *We*. It tends not to work that way. Most of us are probably not affected by the USA PATRIOT Act or other measures introduced following 9/11. Ostensibly, our security has been increased or restored, but most of us will not have borne any significant costs in return. However, as we noted earlier there have been significant costs for some, and these costs have fallen disproportionately on a small segment of the population – those with Middle Eastern appearances, those with visa irregularities and those who, for some reason or other, have had governmental attention turned on them. Those satisfying certain profiles or who have appeared on various "watch lists" have borne the brunt of the costs of "our" greater security.[83] What we may have in each pan of the scales, therefore, is increased security for the large majority on the one side and, on the other, decreased liberty for a much smaller minority.

(5) Establishing connections

In means-end reasoning of the kind that suffuses the "war on terrorism" it is important to ensure that certain conditions are satisfied if the end is to be appealed to in justifying the means. One of those conditions is that the means actually achieve the end sought (or, less stringently, make it highly probable that the end will be accomplished).[84] It is all very well to argue that, in the name of security, our liberties need to be curtailed, but we first need some assurance that such contractions *will* (likely) increase our security. More than say-so is required. If, as has been suggested, our security on 9/11 was inadequate not because more stringent controls were not available but because controls that were already in place were ineptly employed then we have no reason to think that additional controls will be correlated with greater efficiency/security. As Waldron expresses the point, it is not enough to argue that "reducing a given liberty is *necessary* for combating terrorism effectively. It may be a necessary condition, and yet – because sufficient conditions are unavailable – the terrorist threat may continue unabated." The point is important, because there *are* significant costs to the curtailment or contraction of liberties, especially for certain members of the community – aliens, members of particular religious or ethnic groups, political dissidents and so forth. If what is done to them is to have any justification, it needs to be correlated with significant security benefits that would not otherwise have been realized.[85] The worry, of course – and this

---

83   Many innocents and, it would appear, not too many guilty, were scooped up in post-9/11 sweeps. See "One Man Still Locked up from 9/11 Sweeps", *MSNBC.com* (October 14, 2006) at: http://www.msnbc.msn.com/id/15264274/from/ET.

84   On these different accounts, see John Kleinig, "Noble Cause Corruption or Process Deviance: Ruminations on Means and Ends in Policing" in *Police Corruption – Paradigms, Models and Concepts*, ed. Stanley Einstein and Menachem Amir, *Uncertainty Series, Vol. 4* (Huntsville, TX: OICJ Press, 2004), 129–46.

85   Waldron suspects that such contractions have more symbolic than real value because they show that the authorities "care about" or are "doing something about" a situation – like presidents visiting areas devastated by hurricanes. What is the moral worth/weight to be accorded such symbolic acts?

is why such consequentialist arguments need to be looked at carefully and realistically – is that even mild crackdowns of various kinds may contribute to social alienation and worsen the security situation.[86]

A further condition for valid means-end reasoning is that unintended side-effects be taken into account. Just as profiling – even if seen as an effective law enforcement tool – may have as an unwanted effect the aggravation of historically troubled relations between different ethnic groups, so too may the constriction of liberties have unintended and undesirable side-effects. As Waldron puts it:

> When liberty is understood (as it usually is) in a negative sense, it is something that cannot be reduced without increasing something else, namely the powers and means and mechanisms that obstruct or punish the ability of individuals to do what they want. Reducing liberty may prevent an action taking place which would otherwise pose a risk of harm. But it necessarily also increases the power of the state, and there is a corresponding risk that this enhanced power may also be used to cause harm.[87]

The point is an obvious one but, viewed through the lens of liberalism, is also one of some importance. Liberal thought, even in its democratic version, is predicated on a distrust of concentrated power, especially power that is less than transparent.[88] Even republican liberals[89] strongly committed to the importance of governmental mechanisms believe that those mechanisms need to be carefully circumscribed through "checks and balances". We might argue that any governmental powers exercised on "our" behalf will be exercised benevolently, but that would be overly sanguine, given the history not only of the previous US government but also of almost any other government. Government officials generally have strong incentives to err on the side of security; elected public officials in particular are rarely voted out of office for either protecting the public too vigorously or placing the safety of the majority above the liberties of a minority.

We should not forget that the boundaries of terrorism have been cast very broadly to maximize governmental flexibility: political dissent may sometimes be enough to trigger governmental attention. That is troubling enough, but in addition we have seen a number of provisions that were introduced explicitly

---

86   Thus, despite former Attorney General John Ashcroft's comments (March 20, 2002) on the "voluntary" interview program initiated by the US government on November 9, 2001, that "the process of reaching out to foreign nationals and their communities fostered new trust between law enforcement and these communities" (see: http://www.yale.edu/lawweb/avalon/sept_11/ashcroft_018.htm), a great deal of ill will was created.
87   Waldron, "Security and Liberty" 204 (footnote omitted).
88   This, of course, has been one of the major complaints about the governmental response to 9/11 – the lack of access to what is going on in Guantánamo Bay, the secret handling of aliens and certain provisions of the USA PATRIOT Act.
89   See e.g. Philip Pettit, *Republicanism: A Theory of Freedom and Government*, Oxford: Oxford University Press, 1997.

and specifically for the "war on terrorism" now transferred to the wider "war on crime".[90] Such measures would have been considered overly intrusive had they been intended for ordinary law enforcement purposes.

Trade-offs.

If we want a more promising metaphor to characterize the situation, we might do better with that of a trade-off. From time-to-time Waldron and others slide from the balancing metaphor to that of the trade-off as though they had similar implications.[91] We think not. When we trade one value off against another, we not only acknowledge an adjustment to the balance – the restoration of an equilibrium that has been upset – but have in view a *cost* or *sacrifice* to one when the other is given priority. There is an *infringement* or *derogation* of liberties or rights when liberty is traded off for security. Naturally, as noted above, the necessity for a trade-off – if, indeed, there is such a necessity – implies that more security cannot be had without a reduction in liberty, and this, as we have seen earlier, is by no means self-evident.

A trade-off is not a trade. In a trade – at least in theory (a "fair" trade) – one value is exchanged for another and no party to the trade loses. Each party sees the exchange as being advantageous: A had x and B had y; B wanted x and A wanted y; the trade, because consensual, satisfies both. A trade-off, on the other hand, involves a tension or conflict whereby A, if he is to get y, must sacrifice x. If he deems it an acceptable trade-off, it nevertheless comes at some cost. A would have preferred to secure y without sacrificing x. In a trade-off, the key issue will be to determine whether the sacrifices can be justified or sustained, and how the costs incurred should be responded to.

If many values that we might pursue are side-constrained by our liberties or rights, national security has at least the potential to be involved in a trade-off. The courts have long recognized that even constitutionally guaranteed rights may be infringed in the name of national security or some other broad social interest (such as public safety or territorial integrity). However, such interests are not to be casually invoked. Any claim must be subject to strict scrutiny in which the interests invoked in favor of constraining the liberty in question must be specified and explicitly defended.[92] Thus, vague references to "national

---

90 Most of these expansions have so far focused on financial crimes, though urban gangs are now being targeted with legislation originally designed for terrorists.

91 Waldron, "Security and Liberty", 196–198, 203. See also Philip A. Thomas, "Emergency and Anti-Terrorist Power: 9/11: USA and UK", *Fordham International Law Journal* 26 (April 2003): 1193 and 1208.

92 Strict scrutiny requires that "some compelling state interest" be shown. It stands in contrast with what is called a "rational relations" test, in which liberty is constrained (say, a dress code for employees or a lowering of the speed limit) and all that usually needs to be shown is that there is a plausible connection between the restriction on liberty and the purposes of the restricting body. In the broad gap between these two, a third level of scrutiny ("heightened") is developed to secure interests that are deemed "important" but not "fundamental" (say, the interests of gay men).

security" will not do. The national security interests that are threatened will need to be specified, the ways in which they are threatened will need to be articulated, the threat will need to be quantified in some way and some reasonable case will need to be made to sustain such claims.

Security, of course, may be seen in the same way as liberty – as a right – though what is likely to be in view will not be *national* security so much as *personal* security. (The two kinds of security may be related, since national security may facilitate or provide an environment for personal or individual security.) To the extent that securing our right to personal security comes into conflict with our liberties, the tension will not be between some good and our liberties but between two rights – or, to put it in a way that encompasses a modest view of national security, between a good (national security) that secures a right (personal security) and some other rights (our liberties). How are such tensions to be resolved? Although we may use the term "trade-off", it is a different kind of trade-off from that involved when a liberty is traded off against some communal or social good.[93]

To a degree, we are assuming that, though the interests of both national security and individual liberty will be in some tension, they will also be mutually supportive. As with courage and discretion, generosity and caution or even justice and happiness, we expect that in the ordinary transactions of life we will be presented with choices that do not violate the demands of either. Discretion will temper courage and courage will save discretion from cowardice; caution will contribute to wise expressions of generosity and generosity will overcome the inertia of caution; justice will check the aggregative tendencies of happiness and respect for happiness will save justice from rigidity. And so we anticipate that security will enhance our freedom and that freedom will guide security. Indeed, violations of personal security typically consist in part of violations of liberty rights; slavery is perhaps the most graphic illustration of this. Accordingly, insofar as national security is taken to be in large part constituted by aggregate personal security then national security is, or ought to be, ultimately in the service of liberty rights (as well as rights to life and so forth). Were this not to be the case, our lives would be wretchedly torn. However, circumstances sometimes arise in which we are faced with what seems to be a moral necessity to give one precedence over the other – not merely a

---

93   The choice of term can also reflect much deeper debates within moral theory between those who view ethics as a rational system grounded in some single principle or set of compatible principles and those who claim that we are confronted by a plurality of values – either (as Alasdair MacIntyre has suggested in *After Virtue*, second ed., University of Notre Dame Press, 1984) because we have inherited fragments from competing moral schemata or because (try as we might) our human condition is such that we are confronted by a moral plurality that calls for judgment rather than calculation. Debates over deontological and consequentialist theory, or between universalists and particularists, often reflect such deeper debates. This, however, is not the place to do more than to acknowledge them. See also the symposium on conflicts of rights in *Legal Theory* 7 (2001): 235–306.

precedence that arises because one has some inherent priority over the other but a precedence that serves to compromise or undermine the other, leaving a residue of moral loss or even taint.

Judgment.

At the end of the day, there are reasons for thinking that both terms (balance and trade-off) fail to do justice to the complexity involved in clashes between security and liberty – even though the term "trade-off" comes rather closer to the mark.[94] That is also Waldron's position.[95] What is required is judgment, and judgment is not a matter of algorithmically drawing conclusions from premises but of incrementally bringing reasons to bear on one another – point and counterpoint – until we can reach a conclusion that is defensible. This will involve the assembling of relevant considerations, prioritizing them and making determinations about whether or to what degree, in the particular case (or in respect of a particular policy, if that is the level at which we are seeking to reach a decision), one is to be sacrificed to the other. The process is one of the interplay of reasons enabling one to perhaps warrant trading off a measure of one in favor of the other. The trade-off, if any, is determined though a judgmental process. Stanley Benn puts it well:

> The metaphor of 'balancing' or 'weighing', with its image of weights held in the balance or in the hands, is not altogether perspicuous when applied to arguments or claims. For one thing, weighing and balancing suggest the achievement of a state of equilibrium – equal weights – while judgment requires the determination of an outcome because some reasons 'outweigh' others. More important than this, however, is the consideration that judging claims and reasons generally proceeds *seriatim*. There is commonly a presumption of right, which counterclaims are then designed to override. These in turn may be undercut or overridden, as may be those adduced against them in their turn. Admittedly, deciding whether a claim has indeed been undercut or whether a counterclaim overrides may itself demand judgment, and secondary disputes employing precisely similar tactics can develop at

---

94   Scanlon (following Rawls) makes use of the language of "adjustment":

> To summarize this discussion: Rawls holds that basic liberties such as freedom of expression (once defined) cannot be balanced against other interests. But they need to be 'adjusted'. The powers and prerogatives (and limits on powers and prerogatives) that define these liberties need to be specified. What is specified in this process is, among other things, the grounds on which expression may legitimately be regulated. In determining these limits we need to take various potentially conflicting interests into account. But in this process of balancing and adjustment, our interest in assuring conditions for the development and full exercise of the two moral powers has the primary role: If allowing some other interest to justify restrictions on expression in a certain way would pose a threat to the full exercise of these powers, then that justification for restriction cannot be allowed. ("The Constitutional Essentials of Political Liberalism: Adjusting Rights and Balancing Values", 1484)

95   Waldron, "Safety and Security", 502–06.

each point in the argument. It will always help in settling such disputes to understand precisely what kind of argument is going on. To describe it as one in which 'considerations are being weighed' or 'balanced' is not helpful, because the metaphor does not really illumine the process.[96]

Privacy

As we have had occasion to note, ensuring security may come into conflict with other important liberal values such as privacy, liberty, autonomy and dignity, thus threatening the identity of persons. Trade-offs may have to be made in which, to ensure the former, the latter may be compromised in certain ways. We can see what is at stake in these trade-offs by reviewing the ways in which privacy and other values are to be construed and valued within a liberal framework. We begin with privacy.

Although occasional references to privacy can be found earlier, and the expectation of it goes back much further,[97] the modern debate about privacy was not really kicked off until Samuel Warren and Louis Brandeis published their seminal law review paper in 1890.[98] Controversially, they characterized the right to privacy as "the right to be let alone". It captured something of what is involved – concerned as they were about the growing intrusiveness of the press, paparazzi etc. – but did not do so very well or accurately. Interestingly, it was there cast in terms that do not reflect or even presage its later appearance in US Constitutional law as a Constitutional right against governmental intrusion.

The right to privacy did not come to possess explicit (US) Constitutional status until the 1965 case of *Griswold v. Connecticut*, in which a law prohibiting the advocacy and use of contraceptives was said to have violated a "right to marital privacy".[99] The judges had some difficulty locating such a right in Constitutional provisions and, in fact, they varied in the ways in which they sought to account

---

96 *A Theory of Freedom*, Cambridge, UK: Cambridge University Press, 1988, 296–97. Cf. *Science Research Council v. Nassé H.L.(E.)*, (1980) A.C. 1028 at 1067, (1979) 3 W.L.R. 762 at 771 (Lord Wilberforce).

97 Eavesdropping is a very old offense (see William Blackstone, *Commentaries on the Laws of England*, (c. 1765) vol. IV: *Of Public Wrongs* (169), (Boston: Beacon Press, 1962), 189. The derogatory notion of a "Peeping Tom" goes back even earlier. See Daniel J. Solove, "A Taxonomy of Privacy", *University of Pennsylvania Law Review* 154 (2006): 491.

98 Samuel D. Warren and Louis D. Brandeis, "The Right to Privacy", *Harvard Law Review* 4 (1890): 193–220, available at: http://www-swiss.ai.mit.edu/6805/articles/privacy/Privacy_brand_warr2.html.

99 381 US 479 (1965). The relevant statutes were 53-32 and 54-196 of the General Statutes of Connecticut (1958 rev.). The former provided: "Any person who uses any drug, medicinal article or instrument for the purpose of preventing conception shall be fined not less than fifty dollars or imprisoned not less than sixty days nor more than one year or be both fined and imprisoned." The latter provided: "Any person who assists, abets, counsels, causes, hires or commands another to commit any offense may be prosecuted and punished as if he were the principal offender." Estelle Griswold was Executive Director of the Planned Parenthood League of Connecticut, and the League provided information, examinations and advice on contraceptives.

for it. It was then invoked again, though much more controversially, in *Roe v. Wade*,[100] in which a woman's right to an abortion was defended – in part – by reference to her right to privacy under the Fourteenth Amendment's due process clause. Although the right appears to have gained a reasonably secure Constitutional toehold in the US, its meaning, scope, moral status and limits remain highly controversial.

Here, however, our primary interest will not be in the legal (or Constitutional) right to privacy but in privacy as a moral notion.[101]

Privacy and publicity are complex and multi-layered concepts, part of an even more complex domain of privateness and publicness, and here we do no more than note certain aspects of that complexity.[102] As for the larger domain, consider the differences in the understanding of "private" and "public" in distinctions between private property and public property, private interests and the public interest, private officials and public officials, private goods and public goods, private meetings and public meetings, and private bathrooms and public bathrooms.[103]

---

100   410 US 113 (1973).

101   Constitutional interpretations may develop in directions that cannot be readily accommodated by moralized accounts. Thus one might want to argue for a moral right to privacy without thinking that it should encompass abortion, even though, Constitutionally, the right to privacy does encompass abortion. Compare the debate about whether capital punishment constitutes cruel and unusual punishment. Some argue that – morally – capital punishment is cruel and unusual, though as far as Constitutional argument is concerned it is not (at present, anyway).

102   There is, in addition, a further set of overlapping distinctions between privacy and secrecy. That which we keep secret (at least with respect to *A*, *B* and *C*, though not necessarily everyone) may or may not also be private. Indeed, what we keep secret (such as criminal acts that we have committed) may be a matter of public concern and should be made public. There are some critics of privacy who maintain that we would be better off if our lives were more transparent, and that we should – more or less – eschew privacy. We would not be (as) vulnerable to blackmail and fraud, there would be less hypocrisy and deceit, and greater candor. Some would maintain that we would be healthier psychologically if we had fewer hang-ups over things we tend to treat as private (e.g. matters of sexual preference and potency, penis size and religious commitment), or that the desire for privacy is connected to shame – our having something to hide. No doubt privacy can function as a cloak for secrecy, but often what seems to be complained about is not privacy but secrecy. Secrecy – deliberately concealing information from others – is a topic in its own right, even though arguments for when it may or may not be justified will sometimes intersect with arguments concerned with privacy. See Sissela Bok, *Secrets: On the Ethics of Concealment and Revelation* (New York: Vintage, 1989); Carl J. Friedrich, "Secrecy Versus Privacy: The Democratic Dilemma", in J. Roland Pennock and John W. Chapman (eds.), *Privacy*, NOMOS XIII (NY: Atherton Press, 1971), 105–20; Carol B. Warren, "Secrecy", in *The Encyclopedia of Privacy*, ed. William G. Staples, Greenwood Press: Connecticut, (2007): 482–85; C. Warren and B. Laslett, "Privacy and Secrecy: A Conceptual Comparison", *The Journal of Social Issues* (1977): 1ff; Paul B. Thompson, "Privacy, Secrecy and Security", *Ethics and Information Technology* 3, no. 1 (March, 2001): 13–19; Judith DeCew, *In Pursuit of Privacy: Ethics and the Rise of Technology* (Cornell UP, 1997), 48; Julie Inness, *Privacy, Intimacy, and Isolation* (Oxford University Press, 1992), 60ff; Michael Barkun, "Religion and Secrecy After September 11", *Journal of the American Academy of Religion* 74, no. 2 (2006): 275–301, at 277.

103   For a valuable and detailed representation of that complexity, see S.I. Benn and G.F. Gaus, "Public and Private – Concepts in Action", in *Public and Private in Social Life*, ed. S.I. Benn and G.F. Gaus (NY: St. Martin's Press, 1983), 3–27. The contrast is not always between private and public but, say, between "private (use)" and "business (use)". Moreover, what is public may also have a private dimension – the categories are not exclusive. One is entitled to privacy in a public toilet (an issue about which there have been public debates and court cases).

As a way into the discussion of privacy as we shall be mainly concerned with it here, consider the following situations, often taken to involve breaches of privacy:

(1) A person rigs up a device that enables him to listen in on his neighbors' conversations;

(2) Government agents use a thermal sensor to detect heat patterns in a person's home;[104]

(3) A passer-by stops and peers through the slightly parted shades of a lighted bedroom;

(4) A person moves up and down the escalator of a public mall, carrying a small video camera that enables him to take up-skirt photos of young girls who are using the escalator. He posts them on YouTube;[105]

(5) Someone leans over to hear what a couple is saying to each other on a park bench on which they are sitting;

(6) A company pledges not to sell personal customer information, but does so when the price is right;[106]

(7) A tabloid publishes the name of a rape victim;[107]

(8) A company markets a list of five million elderly, incontinent women; and

(9) Security devices that X-ray through people's clothing to the skin are installed at airports.[108, 109]

Insofar as it is agreed that there has been a breach of privacy in each of these cases, we think it is fair to say that it involves our gaining (or seeking to gain)

---

104   See *Kyllo v. US*, 533 U.S. 27 (2001). In this case, government agents, suspicious that Kyllo was growing marijuana indoors, used a heat sensor to determine whether parts of his house were hotter than others, consistent with the use of heat lamps to grow marijuana. After determining that some parts of the house were hotter than others, they obtained a search warrant. The Supreme Court considered the use of this device an unreasonable search, even though it could only detect variations in heat. It is interesting to compare this case with *Illinois v. Caballes*, 543 U.S. 405 (2005), in which police used a sniffer dog to check for drugs in the trunk of the defendant's car. It was argued that because the dog was trained to detect *only* that to which Caballes had no right, no violation of his Fourth Amendment rights was involved. It is also interesting to compare these cases with *Florida v. Riley*, 488 U.S. 445 (1989), in which marijuana plants growing in a greenhouse in Riley's backyard were spotted using a surveillance aircraft. Here it was argued inter alia that overflying aircraft had become commonplace, and that Riley had no reasonable expectation of privacy with respect to that location.
105   See, for example, *State v. Glas*, 54 P. 3d 147 (2002).
106   See *In re Geocities*, 127 FTC, 94 (1999).
107   See *Florida Star v. B.J.F.*, 491 U.S. 524 (1989).
108   See Austin Considine, "Will New Airport X-Rays Invade Privacy?", *The New York Times*, October 9, 2005, TR3; also the Rapiscan website: http://www.rapiscansystems.com/sec1000.html and, more graphically, http://www.electromax.com/rapiscan%20secure%201000.html. Jeffrey Rosen has spoken of the scanning device as an "electronic strip search" in "The Naked Crowd: Balancing Privacy and Security in an Age of Terror", *Arizona Law Review* 46 (Winter, 2004): 608.
109   Airports themselves have become topics of interest in the surveillance field. See Peter Adey, "Surveillance at the Airport: Surveilling Mobility/Mobilising Surveillance", *Environment and Planning A* 36, no. 8 (2004): 1365–80.

access to or information about, or disseminating (or seeking to disseminate) information or knowledge about, others that is thought to be rightfully *theirs* to control.

So, underlying (1) there is a view that certain *spaces* are private and that what goes on in them is out of bounds and not (ordinarily) the business of any others. Within certain limits, this is irrespective of what goes on in them – whether or not it is a matter that one would otherwise see as private. Of course, because that particular space – the home – is considered private, it is also a major venue for matters that would be seen as private. Whether or not what goes on inside a home is made known to others is generally for those inside it to determine. Advances in technology enable such private spaces to be invaded without physically entering them.

The case of the thermal scanner in (2) reinforces the point about a private space – the home – but part of its interest arises from the fact that the information obtained is not verbal but, at best, probabilistic. It also raises an important question about the lengths to which *government* may go in gathering information concerning us and the extent to which it may gather and use such data.[110] We can already observe here the particular US preoccupation with governmental infringements of privacy.

In (3), we have a further permutation on the "private domain". Though the shades are drawn, presumably as a measure to secure privacy (while dressing or engaged in some intimate/private activity), the voyeur takes advantage of a failure in the mechanism designed to exclude the possibility of surveillance. However, the intention of the drawn shades is clear enough,[111] even though the voyeur may mean no harm beyond the harm of invading privacy.

Case (4) occurs in a public space, though one might presume that what can be seen using such a camera would be considered an intrusion into a private domain. Posting it on a video-sharing site such as YouTube would aggravate the invasion.

Although the couple on the park bench in (5) are conversing "in public", their conversation would normally be considered a private one, overheard by others in snatches at most. Despite its being "in public", leaning over to listen to their conversation would be a breach of privacy. As with the previous case, there has been a vigorous discussion about the extent to which one might be said to

---

110 Wiretapping is also an interesting case in which the government may not physically penetrate but nevertheless "invade" the home. In *Olmstead v. US*, 277 U.S. 438 (1928), wiretapping was not seen to breach privacy. However, forty years later the Supreme Court reversed this decision in *Katz v. US*, 389 U.S. 347 (1967).
111 Compare this with the case of a toilet stall whose doors leave a narrow crack through which someone could peer.

possess privacy rights in public. This discussion is often associated with the installation of CCTV cameras. Is it *activities* or *locations* that are private, or, depending on circumstances, either or both?

Case (6) is interesting in that the information may or may not be private, but the company has pledged to treat it as private by not selling it. Selling the information may expose the person to bombardment with advertising (or other approaches) or it could be purchased by a data mining company that could then integrate that information with other information; cumulatively, it could allow for more information about individuals to be available to others than those individuals would reasonably agree to.

Case (7) operates against a background of the social opprobrium or prejudice to which even rape victims are sometimes subject, making it the case that publishing the name of a rape victim – unlike, perhaps, the name of a mugging victim – constitutes a violation of privacy. This case also indicates the extent to which privacy interests are tied up with social conventions and expectations.

Case (7) also has some similarities to (8), which deals with information that people would not wish to make available to others, except on terms of their own choosing. Consider a company that delivers adult diapers by mail order. It could be tempted to sell the list to other companies with niche products. Although there are now privacy disclosure regulations for much commercially gained marketing information,[112] this has not always been the case, and marketing information that people would be embarrassed to have others know and that in ordinary circumstances would be deemed private can be seen as a breach of privacy.

As with (2), case (9) also raises a question about the kind of information that a government may legitimately collect about its citizens and others. As we have already seen, those who travel – at least since 9/11 – must expect that, for security reasons, special care will be taken that they do not pose a security risk to others. Given that those who pose such a risk could seek to conceal dangerous objects on their persons, officials must determine how to ensure that passengers do not exploit their privacy rights for nefarious purposes. We are now familiar with X-ray (or similar) machines for carry-on (and even checked) luggage, frames that pick up metallic objects, wands and devices that are sensitive to the presence of explosives, but as the concealment of dangerous implements has become more sophisticated so has a need developed for increasingly sophisticated detectors. Pat-down searches are sometimes used but are often claimed to be violative of privacy, and there have been moves to subject people to a type of X-ray or backscatter ray scrutiny that avoids unwanted touching. However, the base

---

112   One important issue in the development of these disclosures concerns "opt-in" vs. "opt-out" provisions.

machines which penetrate to the skin reveal more than most of us would care to reveal to strangers, and there has been strong opposition to them.[113] On the other hand, it may be that technology can come to the rescue here by ensuring that the operators of scanning devices do not view "pornographic" images but only images of hidden metal objects and the like. If so, this would be an instance of what Jeroen van den Hoven refers to as "designing-in-ethics".[114] In general terms, what van den Hoven has in mind is the possibility of not having to make trade-offs between (in this case) security and privacy. We can have security with at most a very minor reduction in privacy.

There is a not-very-clear debate in the literature about whether privacy is always concerned with *information* or whether it is to be distinguished from privacy that involves *access*.[115] Although there is a distinction of some sort between A's reading of B's mail and A's peeking into B's bedroom, in each case there is some invasion of a personal space/domain over which B should be able to exercise control. In both cases A gains access to aspects of B's person (e.g. information concerning the terms of B's relationships with others and what B looks like when naked) that it is preferred that A did not have (without consent). In both cases A gets information that is B's to determine whether A has. In A's breaching of B's privacy, B loses some control over A — or over themselves and his/her self-presentation. However, we are not convinced that the distinction between information and access is ultimately of any great ethical significance.

Some of the foregoing cases, particularly (6) and (8), are concerned with confidentiality as well as privacy. Confidential information is information that is shared with specific parties on the understanding that it will not then be shared with others. The information in question may be private or personal, though it need not be. The person who confesses his crimes to a priest expects that the priest will not then share that information with others, even though it is not private in the traditional sense. A lawyer is bound by confidentiality expectations not to share with others information the client has provided without that client's permission. Confidentiality is usually justified in consequentialist terms, though where the thing confided is also private there may be other considerations that tell against its sharing with others. In the case of lawyers, physicians or priests, confidentiality is justified as a means whereby certain services can be more adequately provided — clients, patients or parishioners will be more inclined to provide relevant information if they believe that it will

---

113   As we have seen, there are technological solutions, even if they have not been fully exploited.

114   Jeroen van den Hoven, "Computer Ethics and Moral Methodology", *Metaphilosophy* 28, no. 3, (1997): 1–12.

115   Whether these exhaust the scope of privacy is debated. Helen Nissenbaum writes that "the scope of privacy is wide-ranging – potentially extending over information, activities, decision, thoughts, bodies, and communications"; "Privacy as Conceptual Integrity", *Washington Law Review*, 79 (2004): 119–57. However, we think the notion of *informational* privacy is central.

not be shared with others or, in the event that it is shared, that it will be shared on an appropriately "need to know" basis. Because justification of the duty of confidentiality is largely based on consequentialist grounds, consequentialist considerations can also be appealed to in order to justify overriding it (e.g. some significant public interest). For the most part, the duty of confidentiality lapses if and when the information enters the public domain.

What is it that makes the unconsented-to gaining of access to or dissemination of information concerning oneself a breach of privacy?

At the heart of privacy is a certain notion of agency – that is, of someone's standing as an autonomous chooser or moral agent who, by virtue of that status, warrants the respect of others.[116] The respect that is due to agents requires that we permit them to control the conditions of their self-disclosure to others. When privacy is invaded, such agency is usually violated, and it can be violated in a number of ways:

(i) It is violated when one leans over to listen to another's conversation on the park bench, since, when the other becomes aware of one's presence, it alters the conditions under which the other carries on the conversation and may affect not only what the other wishes to include but also how the other says what he or she wants to. The other becomes aware that there are some things that are being said that are meant for their companion's ears alone and that, given the presence of a further set of ears, the other no longer wishes to say them. Further, even if the other is not so worried about the content of what is being said, he/she may come to realize that what is being said to the other is being conveyed against a background of knowledge and assumptions that is unlikely to exist with respect to the eavesdropper and that it may therefore be misunderstood and misinterpreted. The other will therefore be under some pressure to put what he/she wants to say rather differently.

The control to which one is entitled as a chooser is not simply a matter of intellectual but also of emotional control. Privacy is a condition of personal wellbeing or, as Ruth Gavison puts it, of "mental health, autonomy, growth, creativity, and the capacity to form and create meaningful human relations."[117] Informational control concerns *how* as well as *what*.

---

116   That is, in the classical liberal sense of respect for persons and respect for one's status as a person (recognition respect), not necessarily respect for the particular person one is (appraisal respect). See Stephen L. Darwall, "Two Kinds of Respect", *Ethics* 88 (1) (1977): 36–49.
117   Ruth Gavison, "Privacy and the Limits of Law", *Yale Law Journal* 89 (January, 1980): 442.

(ii) Privacy is violated even if one is not aware of the other person's presence and therefore does not make adjustments for it. One may not be aware of the person who is peering through the slightly parted shades of one's bedroom, but that person has still violated one's agency, since agency consists in part in determining what others may know of those matters that are appropriately deemed to be private – for example, one's naked body or one's activities in the bed. That, after all, is why one pulled the shades in the first place, even if they failed to exclude prying eyes. Being denied that power, one's agency has been compromised.

(iii) What is violated, therefore, when privacy is violated is the person as conceived of within liberal democratic theory. Liberal democratic theory arose as a reaction against hierarchical and paternalistic polities in which some were judged or thought to be inherently superior to others and were therefore appropriately accorded powers of rulership. Liberal democratic societies – in theory at least – are populated not only by equals but also by those whose capacities (at least when "of age") fit them to be full participants in the life of the community.

It is within a social framework in which privacy is acknowledged and fostered that the kind of person well-suited to the demands and expectations of a liberal democracy is nurtured – one who is characterized by thoughtfulness, imagination, independence, courage and vitality. As Hyman Gross puts it, "respect for privacy is required to safeguard our changes of mood and mind, and to promote growth of the person through self-discovery and criticism."[118]

(iv) A somewhat different kind of violation occurs when information that is gathered is then used to harm one in some way. For example, somebody gets one's social security number, puts that together with other information that is available about one and opens a bank account that enables one's assets to be stolen.

This suggests that there are different kinds of wrongs that may be involved when privacy is violated. Traditionally, they have been divided between deontological and consequentialist wrongs – between those that are intrinsic to breaches of privacy and those that are contingent on them but often found. The former are usually said to be more fundamental than the latter.

(a) Consider some of the deontological dimensions to the breaches of privacy enumerated above. There is, first of all, an objectification of those whose privacy is breached. The neighbors (1) or people on the park bench (4) who are eavesdropped upon and the person whose bedroom is spied on (3) are treated as objects of curiosity by others and their feelings about being overheard or viewed in that way are ignored or discounted or even deliberately ruffled. In other words, their agency is left out of account or downgraded, at least as far as

---

118   Hyman Gross, "Privacy and Autonomy", in *Privacy*, NOMOS XIII, ed. J. Roland Pennock and John W. Chapman (NY: Atherton Press, 1971), 176.

the eavesdropper/voyeur is concerned. In some cases, there is also a deliberate deception involved in that those who are violated believe they are conducting their activities away from the presence of others – i.e. that their private activities are occurring "in private".

Having privacy – that is, having a sphere of activity within which one may exercise control or express one's status as an agent – is critical to being a person and not a mere thing. Centrally, though not exclusively, it involves being able to think for oneself without the monitoring of one's thoughts. Almost as importantly, it involves the ability to determine (within reason) the audience to which those thoughts are expressed. Agency requires that others respect that control. Traditionally, the home and, even more particularly, certain areas of the home have been deemed private spaces within which, within broad limits, one might express oneself without the intrusions of others.

A number of writers have argued that intimacy and friendship are in some important sense dependent on and expressed through our being able to control access and information concerning ourselves to others. Intimates and friends are those to whom we make special disclosures, disclosures that not only express a certain closeness (a drawing of them within certain boundaries) but also a trust that they will not jeopardize our interests. There is some truth in that, though it is not the case, as some (for example, Charles Fried[119]) have suggested, that the value of privacy resides in its enablement of intimacy or in its power to mark out different kinds of relationships.

To the extent that we become aware of our world as one without privacy – as one in which what we wish to think, say or do is (or is vulnerable to) being monitored by others – our status as moral agents is threatened. Rather than determining the terms of the presentation of ourselves in decisions and actions, our own sense of appropriateness or inappropriateness, our presentation is determined by factors outside us. Rather than being the primary controllers of the terms of our social interactions the terms under which our social interactions take place are determined by (the scrutiny of) others.

The private sphere is not identical to, nor is it unrelated to, the sphere of self-regarding conduct about which Mill spoke and which he distinguished from other-regarding conduct. Both connect up with the idea of a person as an "individual", a "normative agent" or a "progressive being", and the similarities are to some extent responsible for reductionist accounts of privacy that see it simply as an aspect of autonomy.[120] Here is Mill's account:

---

119 Charles Fried, "Privacy", *Yale Law Journal* 77 (1968): 475–93; see also Robert Gerstein, "Intimacy and Privacy", *Ethics* 89, no. 1 (1978): 76–81; and Innes, *Privacy, Intimacy and Isolation*.

120 Cf. Joel Feinberg: "The United States Supreme Court in recent years appears to have discovered a basic constitutional right suggestive of our 'sovereign personal right of self-determination', and has given it the highly misleading name of 'the right to privacy'" ("Autonomy, Sovereignty, and Privacy : Moral Ideals in the Constitution", *Notre Dame Law Review* 58 (1983): 445–92, at 483). However, Feinberg is taking a swipe at

> [T]here is a sphere of action in which society, as distinguished from the individual, has, if any, only an indirect interest; comprehending all that portion of a person's life and conduct which affects only himself, or if it also affects others, only with their free, voluntary, and undeceived consent and participation. When I say only himself, I mean directly, and in the first instance: for whatever affects himself, may affect others through himself; and the objection which may be grounded on this contingency, will receive consideration in the sequel. This, then, is the appropriate region of human liberty. It comprises, first, the inward domain of consciousness; demanding liberty of conscience, in the most comprehensive sense; liberty of thought and feeling; absolute freedom of opinion and sentiment on all subjects, practical or speculative, scientific, moral, or theological. The liberty of expressing and publishing opinions may seem to fall under a different principle, since it belongs to that part of the conduct of an individual which concerns other people; but, being almost of as much importance as the liberty of thought itself, and resting in great part on the same reasons, is practically inseparable from it. Secondly, the principle requires liberty of tastes and pursuits; of framing the plan of our life to suit our own character; of doing as we like, subject to such consequences as may follow: without impediment from our fellow-creatures, so long as what we do does not harm them, even though they should think our conduct foolish, perverse, or wrong. Thirdly, from this liberty of each individual, follows the liberty, within the same limits, of combination among individuals; freedom to unite, for any purpose not involving harm to others: the persons combining being supposed to be of full age, and not forced or deceived.[121]

Millian liberty is concerned with conduct rather than information, conduct in which others have no business interfering because it does not affect their interests detrimentally. Privacy, on the other hand, concerns a zone of informational control that is central to moral autonomy. Not everything that is self-regarding (in the Millian sense) is private; not everything that is private is self-regarding.

(b) The consequentialist dimensions to privacy. When people – be they individuals or institutions – obtain information that we would consider to be private to us, they may be in a position to do us considerable harm. The crime of blackmail is structured around the threat to reveal (usually) private (though sometimes just secret) information unless some "payment" is made to keep quiet about it.[122] Although the

---

judicial reasoning rather than rejecting the idea of privacy. For a different reductionist account, See Judith Jarvis Thomson, "The Right to Privacy", *Philosophy & Public Affairs* 4, no. 4 (1975): 295–314, who considers privacy rights to be reducible to, for example, property rights and right to self-ownership. For a critique, see *inter alia*, Innes, *Privacy, Intimacy, and Isolation*, 28–41.

121   John Stuart Mill, *On Liberty* (1869), see: http://www.bartleby.com/130/1.html.

122   As noted earlier, what is secret (e.g. the fact that we murdered someone) need not also be private.

person in possession of another's private information may choose to reveal it without the threat of penal consequences, using that threat to exact from another a payment is considered an improper exploitation of the other.[123]

The securing of private information by other individuals and organizations may subject individuals to various forms of invasion or threat, but so may its collection by governments. Not surprisingly, given its history, much of the US debate about privacy has concerned the gathering of data by governments. Although communitarian liberals tend to have a relatively benign attitude to governmental power – seeing it as an affirmative social structure and not simply as a lesser evil than the state of nature – such liberals are still wary of collective power and the ways in which it may be misused. This was a major concern during the years of the Cold War, with governmental worries about Communist conspiracies (Orwell's *1984* was published in 1949) and various other initiatives designed to centralize governmental data on individuals, eventually leading to the Privacy Act of 1974, which was tightened after Watergate by FISA (1978). However, since 9/11, with a somewhat weakened public resolve, there has been a re-emergence of governmental data collection initiatives as part of the "war on terrorism", along with, more recently, some half-hearted resistance to those initiatives.[124]

There has always been a tendency, even among liberal democratic governments, to "do what it takes" to retain power, and information can be an important source of power.

Privacy and cultural relativity

One reason privacy has generated a lot of debate is that it appears to be culturally variable. What one person considers to be private information (e.g. whom X is going out with; one's telephone number or address) another person may think not; what one person thinks is extremely private (e.g. that she has had breast cancer) another may think only moderately so. What one culture treats as private (e.g. certain bodily parts) another may not. Some people think of those who treat certain matters as private simply as thin-skinned.[125]

---

123   It also gives rise to the so-called "paradox of blackmail" – beloved of libertarians – whereby two acts, neither of which is illegal (making known to others the truth about someone and asking someone for money) become illegal when conjoined (cf. prostitution).

124   On August 4, 2007, Congress approved expanded surveillance powers. The Protect America Act of 2007 (see: http://thomas.loc.gov/cgi-bin/bdquery/z?d110:s.01927:). For different perspectives, see James Risen and Eric Lichtblau, "Concerns Raised on Wider Spying Under New Law", *The New York Times*, August 19, 2007; Philip Bobbitt, "The Warrantless Debate over Wiretapping", *The New York Times*, August 22, 2007; and as follow-up to the USA PATRIOT Act, see Eric Lichtblau, "F.B.I. Data Mining Reached Beyond Initial Targets", *The New York Times*, September 9, 2007: 1, 31.

125   Moreover, there are those who seem to have no sense of privacy and who gossip about the most intimate details of their lives in such a way that we may consider them lacking in self-respect. This has become part of the world of Facebook, YouTube and Twitter.

Although it can be argued with respect to almost any value, it is especially the case that privacy is often argued to be a value that is culturally relative. The claim can take one of at least two forms. Firstly, it can be claimed that, whereas privacy is a value in some cultures,[126] it is not valued greatly or at all in others. Were this to be the case (though unlikely) then either we might argue that privacy does not constitute a *human* (and is at best only a cultural) value and therefore a right to privacy does not constitute a human right, or we might argue (and would need to establish) that cultures that fail to recognize the importance of privacy are significantly lacking in normative resources (morally impoverished). Secondly, it can be argued that although privacy is universally valued, it is valued in different ways in and within different cultures, depending on other values (e.g. prevailing religious traditions) and social circumstances (privacy expectations on a beach may differ significantly from those on a crowded street).[127] To the extent that this is so, we will need to be careful to distinguish general claims about privacy from particular instantiations of information or access as private, and, further, to the extent that we choose to enforce a right to privacy, we will need to exercise considerable care in differentiating what is acceptably protected from what is unacceptably individual.[128]

Privacy in public

It has often been said that people have "no reasonable expectation of privacy in public spaces". If it is reported that *X* was seen cavorting with a woman not his wife in a shopping mall, can *X* complain that his privacy was being violated? Can *X* complain if others look in his direction while he is travelling on the subway? Are these rhetorical questions? What if a gay man, wishing to remain closeted in his hometown, nevertheless marches in a gay pride rally in a town several hundred miles away? Is his privacy violated if pictures of him marching are distributed in his hometown? What if the look on the subway becomes a stare? And what if *Y* cleans out her cupboards, getting rid of old medical records, bills and personal documents by tearing them in half and putting them in the garbage, from which someone "retrieves" them and then "uses" them against her? Has her privacy been violated?[129]

---

126 For present purposes, we leave largely to one side what constitutes a "culture".

127 See further, Alan Westin, *Privacy and Freedom* (New York: Atheneum, 1967); Anita Allen, *Uneasy Access: Privacy for Women in a Free Society* (Totowa, NJ: Rowman and Littlefield, 1988); James Rachels, "Why Privacy is Important", *Philosophy & Public Affairs*, 4 (1975): 323–33; A. Moore, "Privacy: Its Meaning and Value", *American Philosophical Quarterly*, 40 (2003): 215–27. We are unfamiliar with what is available on privacy in the anthropological literature, though see John M. Roberts and Thomas Gregor, "Privacy: A Cultural View", in *Privacy*, NOMOS XIII, ed. J. Roland Pennock and John W. Chapman (NY: Atherton Press, 1971), 199–225, where they talk about widely divergent "patterns of privacy" at the same time as they see privacy as a "promising cross-cultural variable".

128 We might want to compare such debates with those surrounding what is deemed offensive. For the latter, see Joel Feinberg's magisterial *Offense to Others* (New York: Oxford University Press, 1985).

129 No, according to *California v. Greenwood*, 486 U.S. 35 (1988). The legal argument for shredders!

The view that we have "no reasonable expectation of privacy in public spaces" is surely only part of the story. Not everything that happens in public view or in a public space is public. If *X* takes out and reads a letter on the subway, his activity, though engaged in public, is not thereby reasonably open to the close scrutiny of others. There is a moral etiquette to conduct in public that acknowledges the privacy of certain conduct that occurs in public. A public kiss should not be gawked at, and looking intently down the cleavage of a low-cut dress may be felt intrusive, even though the low-cut dress may have been worn in order to display one's "endowments". Sometimes people may not seem to care too much about the fact that their private affairs are being carried out in public, but that does not in itself show that they are no longer private, and it may be inappropriate for others to focus on or record them. A mother who must breast feed her baby in public is not *ipso facto* indicating that it is all right for others to stare. At the same time, those who conduct in public what are conventionally considered private affairs can sometimes seriously inconvenience or embarrass others who have such matters thrust upon them (the loud cell phone discussions, public arguments between spouses, expressions of sexual intimacy and so forth).

Privacy in public is not just a matter of activities "in plain view". A lot of theoretically public information about us is now available in digital format, is relatively easily accessible and is able to be combined (aggregated) in ways that we would find quite intrusive. One's address and changes of address, property transactions, purchases, dealings with the law and so forth have always been "public" in some sense, but for someone to track these and consolidate them into some sort of profile has previously involved a great deal of effort – unlikely to be made unless that person has a specific purpose and determination in doing so. The digitalization of records and their internet accessibility has changed all this. Not only that, but the development of niche marketing, credit checking, securitization and so forth have brought in their wake companies that specialize in developing dossiers on individual people which can be sold (not always to reputable people) and even demanded by security organizations.[130]

Helen Nissenbaum complains that the factors/considerations that tend to bear on ordinary cases of privacy do not operate as well in the public domain (i.e. when in public or publicly available), and that we need to develop an alternative way of accommodating our privacy concerns. That is, most privacy doctrine has developed around private spaces (such as homes), sensitive information (such as medical records) or limitations on government intrusiveness (whereas most of the information in public is harvested by commercial firms).

---

130 Check ChoicePoint, LexisNexis, and Axiom. A large portion of the business of some of these companies is with government agencies such as the FBI. We have already spelled out some of the dimensions of this in Chapter VII.

One thing that happens when the sorts of things that were referred to a couple of paragraphs ago occur is that a *presumption of anonymity* in public is eroded. That is, much of what we do in public we allow ourselves to do in part because – so far as others are concerned – it is done in a fleeting and anonymous way. It is part of the etiquette of conduct in public that it is (for the most part) fleeting and anonymous. Were we to be aware that we were being watched at length, that those watching knew us or that our actions were being recorded and reviewed, we would (probably) act differently (or more discreetly).

Anonymity is one of the ways in which we can conduct ourselves in public without others knowing our identity – or, sometimes more literally, our name.[131] We may publish a book or article anonymously, give to charity anonymously or blow the whistle anonymously for a variety of perfectly legitimate reasons. Although a free society is generally characterized by transparency rather than secrecy, there are often good reasons – as can be seen from the kinds of cases enumerated above – for acting in a way that does not reveal our identity/name.

A degree of anonymity in public enables us to retain some of the benefit of privacy in a public setting. It provides some kind of moral freedom in public settings, a space in which we can retain some control over the information about ourselves that we make available to others. Consider the effects on conduct if it were the case that once we stepped out of our doors and onto the public street everything we did was recorded and made available to others as they wished – every look, every gesture, every word and every movement.

Helen Nissenbaum makes the case for anonymity as follows:

> For situations that we judge anonymity acceptable, or even necessary, we do so because anonymity offers a safe way for people to act, transact, and participate without accountability, without others "getting at" them, tracking them down, or even punishing them. This includes a range of possibilities. Anonymity may encourage freedom of thought and expression by promising a possibility to express opinions, and develop arguments, about positions that for fear of reprisal or ridicule they would not or dare not do otherwise. Anonymity may enable people to reach out for help, especially for socially stigmatized problems like domestic violence, fear of HIV or other sexually transmitted infection, emotional problems, suicidal thoughts. It offers the possibility of a protective cloak for children, enabling them to engage in internet communication without fear of social predation or – perhaps less ominous but nevertheless unwanted – overtures from commercial marketers.

---

131 Anonymity is, literally, without our name. Our name, however, is just a dummy for something more – our person or identity. See the later notes on identity.

Anonymity may also provide respite to adults from commercial and other solicitations. It supports socially valuable institutions like peer review, whistle-blowing and voting.

In all these cases, the value of anonymity lies not in the capacity to be unnamed, but in the possibility of acting or participating while remaining out of reach, remaining unreachable. Being unreachable means that no-one will come knocking on your door demanding explanations, apologies, answerability, punishment or payment. Where society places high value on the types of expression and transaction that anonymity protects (alluded to in the previous paragraph) it must necessarily enable unreachability. In other words, this unreachability is precisely what it at stake in anonymity. If, in previous eras, namelessness, that is choosing not to reveal one's name, was the best means of achieving unreachability, it makes sense that namelessness would be protected. However, remaining unnamed should be understood for what it is: not as the end in itself of anonymity, but rather, the traditional means by which unreachability has been achieved. It has been the most effective way to keep others at bay, avoid ridicule, and prevent undeserved revenge, harm, and embarrassment, and so forth.[132]

Nissenbaum focuses fairly heavily on the consequential value of anonymity, a value that has to be weighed against the value of transparency. The calculus may vary, as we know from the issue of anonymous whistle blowing. Because of the history of retaliation against those who blow the whistle – a history that is hard to reverse, given the subtleties of organizational retaliation – we have, in many cases, provided for anonymous whistle blowing. However, the provision of anonymous whistle blowing also allows for vindictive attacks on others, and whether and under what conditions anonymous whistle blowing is permitted will often reflect some sort of cost-benefit analysis. Internet anonymity is problematic for the same reason; though the child may engage with others without unwanted solicitations, others may insinuate themselves anonymously and dangerously.[133]

But the benefits are not straightforwardly consequential. The presumption of anonymity is the condition for "being oneself" in public. For many, the possibility of anonymity is the attraction of a large urban center – and lack of anonymity is correspondingly the burden of a small community in which "everyone knows everyone and everything" and in which personal independence, particularly in

---

132 Helen Nissenbaum, "The Meaning of Anonymity in an Information Age", see: http://www.nyu.edu/projects/nissenbaum/paper_anonimity.html.

133 It is instructive to think about internet anonymity in relation to the Myth of Gyges as told by Plato in the *Republic*, II 359d–360b. See e.g. http://falcon.tamucc.edu/~sencerz/Myth_of_Gyges.htm. See also "Gyges Goes Surfing": http://www.applelust.com/one/index.php?option=com_content&task=view&id=35.

public, is very difficult to achieve. True, anonymous urban centers may also be lonely, alienating and depressing, but on the other side, though we may value the "community of care" that a small center provides, we may also be suffocated by it. The issue is one of achieving a balance.[134]

The proliferation of CCTV cameras makes public anonymity much more difficult to sustain than it used to be. What was fleeting and lost in the great surge of public activity is now, with CCTV's advent, recorded, sometimes indefinitely. It can be played back, played over and over, shared (sometimes widely) and combined with other data, all but destroying the anonymity one thought one had. For the most part, we block out the fact that much of our public behavior (in Manhattan, for example) is recorded by CCTV, for we trust that the technical possibilities will not be taken advantage of. However, if there were to be enough counterexamples, this would have a chilling effect on our behavior in public. At the moment we can generally count on recording tapes that are overplayed after several days, that are not archived or indexed in certain ways, that are consulted only in the event of some critical need, that are not coordinated and so on. But things could change along with the technology, even though there are problems in principle with the image of ubiquitous, continuous, real-time surveillance of everyone in every public space and at all times. Specifically, there are significant limits on the number of people who could be employed to do the surveillance; real-time, continuous surveillance is hugely expensive.

The presumption of anonymity in public is reflective of a larger concern that constitutes the heart of Nissenbaum's alternative approach to privacy. If what is in the public domain is treated as "fair game", there is a subversion of what she speaks of as "contextual integrity",[135] which is – in her view – what constitutes a violation of privacy. If teacher X turns up to the cash register in the supermarket, and it is recorded – as indeed it would be – that on this particular occasion he bought, *inter alia*, three cans of Spam, two bottles of rather cheap wine, suppositories and a pack of flavored ribbed condoms – a public but anonymous act – and a copy of his purchases was then distributed to his students, this latter act could be seen as a breach of privacy, even though what X did was public, done in public, recorded and even viewed (albeit casually, though maybe with eyebrows raised) by those in the line behind him. If, in addition, X has a supermarket discount purchasing card then, over time, some patterning to his supermarket acquisitions may be developed that could be sold or used (for marketing purposes) or perhaps to suggest he has a drinking problem or a very active sex life. Once again, one might claim, as Nissenbaum might, that there had been a violation of X's privacy by virtue of a violation of contextual

---

134   In this case it is a balance rather than a trade-off as we are seeking to determine for ourselves an appropriate level of individuality in community.
135   Helen Nissenbaum, "Privacy as Contextual Integrity", *Washington Law Review* 79 (2004): 119–57.

integrity. Information that X willingly and virtually anonymously provided to the checkout worker has now been re-contextualized and given a new context that X could find embarrassing, threatening or otherwise unacceptable.[136]

Informing the idea of contextual integrity is a recognition that our lives are constituted – in part, at least – by various arenas or spheres of activity, each of which is governed by certain norms of appropriateness, including, especially, norms relating to information acquisition and flow.[137] These spheres of activity may include those of family, workplace, religious community, friendships, medical care, local grocery and so on. There may be some overlap (say, between the spheres of friendship and family) and there is often internal complexity ("not in front of the children" might be a norm governing certain communications between parents). Allowing for such overlaps and complexity, what constitutes appropriate behavior and information sharing in one context may be inappropriate in another context. Norms of behavior that are appropriate in regard to one's priest, doctor, banker or workmates may be inappropriate in relation to each of the others, and what is appropriately shared or communicated in relation to one may be not appropriately shared with each of the others. Contextual integrity is constituted by acting appropriately and observing certain norms of informational flow in relation to each of the contexts.

Such norms may be challenged, refined, added to or dropped over time, though one presumes, at least within relatively stable cultures, that there will be a fair degree of longevity, continuity and specificity.

Limits to privacy

While we consider privacy important, and even *a right,* it does not follow that it is absolute. That is, it is not incapable of being legitimately constrained or overridden. The important question concerns the conditions under which it may be contracted or overridden, and that presumes that we know what is at stake in privacy. There have been times when claims of privacy have been overvalued just as there have been times at which they have been undervalued. Various forms of marital or partner assault have sometimes been "secured" behind a cloak of privacy.[138] At the same time, a bomb-making factory in a home cannot claim the protections of privacy, even if a warrant to access it

---

136   We do not wish to argue that, just because we find something embarrassing, threatening or otherwise unacceptable, it is therefore unjustified. There may be countervailing reasons that make it appropriate that information is used in ways we would prefer that it not be.

137   The account we give of Nissenbaum's position is – as we see it – "touched up": we think she casts her net too widely.

138   For some examples, see James J. Fyfe, "Structuring Police Discretion", in John Kleinig (ed.), *Handled with Discretion: Ethical Issues in Police Decision Making* (Lanham, MD: Rowman and Littlefield, 1996), 183–205.

needs to be obtained, and not even the latter may be required if police are in hot pursuit of someone who manages to run into his home. What is done "in private" need not be private, but even what is ordinarily deemed "private" (i.e. information or space) may be invaded if the stakes and probabilities are high enough. Police may apply to wiretap one's phone if there is some appropriate level of probability that one is engaged in certain kinds of criminal activities. Here, because the stakes are not as high, a greater probability has to be shown (to a court) to override one's claims to privacy. But maybe the probabilities do not have to be too high. One's suitcases may be inspected at the airport, even if there is no particular reason to believe that *one's own* bags are being used to conceal a bomb.

Privacy, in other words, may compete or come into conflict with other values. Security and public safety are major issues, but they are not the only ones. Privacy may conflict with freedom of expression, of speech and of the press, with ideas of governmental transparency, with economic efficiency and others. We draw lines – not always very satisfactorily, as we know all too well with respect to freedom of the press – and we continue to debate and sometimes revise them.

In *The Limits of Privacy*, Amitai Etzioni outlines four criteria that he believes should be invoked to determine whether privacy or some other value should be given precedence in the event of a clash. He then uses these to review the following issues: HIV testing of infants; registration and community notification of sex offenders; limits on encryption in the "war on terror"; ID cards and biometric technologies; and medical privacy. He argues that limitations on privacy can be justified only:

(i) in the event of a "well-documented and macroscopic threat to the common good";[139]

(ii) if there is no alternative to the invasion of privacy;

(iii) if the invasion is as "minimally intrusive" as possible; and

(iv) if "measures that treat undesirable side effects of needed privacy-diminishing measures are to be preferred over those that ignore these effects".[140]

To some extent these criteria track those that must be satisfied whenever we engage in means-end reasoning – that is, whenever we seek to secure some value that requires the employment of means that may be problematic. We have already discussed these at length. Etzioni casts his account in the communitarian

---

139   Amitai Etzioni, *The Limits of Privacy* (New York: Basic Books, 1999), 12.
140   *Ibid.*, 13. For a critique of Etzioni, see Miller and Blackler, *Ethical Issues in Policing*, 92–98.

terms for which he has become the major spokesperson.[141] His general position is that we tend to go a bit overboard on privacy, especially insofar as it applies to governmental access to information (he is more concerned with the intrusiveness of big business than big government). However, what he may underplay are not the abstract trade-offs that may sometimes be necessary but the abilities of those who may have access to private information to secure or control it in the way that they profess. Exposés of loss, hacking or unintentional disclosure of information may lead to a practical concern for privacy that might not be justified on abstract theoretical grounds.[142]

Quite apart from that, there are substantial challenges to applying the criteria to particular cases. The criteria do not function algorithmically but simply begin a process of deliberation that does not have any tightly determined outcomes. What, for example constitutes a sufficiently documented and macroscopic threat to the common good? What is the common good? When it is claimed that there is no alternative to the invasion of privacy, how hard must one have looked at/for other possibilities? And what if some alternatives maintain privacy but would compromise other values? Part of the value of Etzioni's discussion – whether or not one agrees with his own conclusions – is that the chapter-length discussions of the issues he reviews indicate how complex they can be.

Autonomy

In "Privacy and Autonomy", Hyman Gross warns against the "danger that privacy may be conceived as autonomy".[143] What Gross has in mind (as did Feinberg in n. 120 above) is the US Supreme Court's tendency (following Warren and Brandeis) from *Griswold* on to see the appeal to privacy as a way of stopping government from regulating personal affairs rather than as a way of stopping it from getting information on them – as seeing privacy simply as a "right to be let alone". Gross's contention, with which we are in substantial agreement, is that whereas "an offense to privacy is an offense to autonomy, not every curtailment of autonomy is a compromise of privacy."[144]

So what is the autonomy that violations of privacy are said to compromise? Any review of the literature throws up a cluster of cognate terms – freedom, liberty,

---

141   Amitai Etzioni, *The Responsive Society* (San Francisco: Jossey-Bass, 1991); *The Spirit of Community: Rights, Responsibilities and the Communitarian Agenda* (New York: Crown Publishers, 1993).

142   See Ragib Hasan and William Yurcik, "Beyond Media Hype: Empirical Analysis of Disclosed Privacy Breaches 2005–2006 and a DataSet/Database Foundation for Future Work", at: http://wesii.econinfosec.org/draft.php?paper_id=37. We have heard that data for 110,000,000 people have been hacked or lost.

143   Hyman Gross, "Privacy and Autonomy", *Privacy*, NOMOS XIII, ed. J. Roland Pennock and John W. Chapman (NY: Atherton Press, 1971), 180.

144   *Ibid.*, 181.

individuality, authenticity, independence and personal sovereignty – that are sometimes used interchangeably with autonomy and sometimes distinguished from it. Our inclination is to draw various distinctions among (at least some of) them, and what follows in the next paragraph – as a prelude to the more detailed discussion of autonomy – is a bonsai version of the central distinctions.

We see liberty as a *social* state of affairs, either an absence of external, social (human-generated[145]) constraints on action (negative liberty) or (and probably including) certain requisites for action (positive liberty).[146] It may have individual and collective dimensions (often thought to be causally connected).[147] We tend to associate freedom (though it is frequently used generically) with a level of *personal* development. We think of it more specifically as an individual (though not isolated) achievement of maturation and learning – specifically, as a state of largely personal development in which individuals have acquired the capacity to reflect on and revise their attitudes, reasons, motives and desires and to act upon them.[148] With such freedom comes a measure of responsibility for what we do, both morally and otherwise.[149] Such personal freedom is related, though not identical, to *personal autonomy* or individuality.[150] Autonomy refers not

---

145   There may be non-social constraints on action that do not constitute limits on liberty. Gravity and our physiological structure both have some bearing on how high we may be able to jump, but they are not constraints on our liberty.

146   Debate about this distinction goes back to at least the nineteenth century, where it revolved around the question of whether liberty/freedom required not merely the absence of social constraints but also access to the wherewithal that would enable a person to make use of such negative liberty. For without such wherewithal one's (negative) liberty might not be said to be worth much. See W.L Weinstein, "The Concept of Liberty in Nineteenth Century English Political Thought", *Political Studies* 13 (1965): 145–62. In the twentieth century, the debate was given a Cold War cast in Isaiah Berlin's influential essay, *Two Concepts of Liberty* (Oxford: Clarendon 1958). He saw in positive liberty, and the "self-mastery" he believed it implied, the seeds of a paternalistic perfectionism. For a better discussion, see Gerald C. MacCallum, Jr., "Negative and Positive Freedom", *Philosophical Review* 76 (July, 1967): 312–34.

147   It is often argued that liberty, as an absence of constraint or domination by others, is primarily individual. However, we believe this to be somewhat misleading. Individual liberty is most likely to exist in an environment of liberty – in which collective rules operate to secure individual liberty and, with it, the conditions for individual flourishing. It is the reference to securing the conditions for individual flourishing that helps to link liberty in its collective and individual aspects with freedom, in both its basic sense and its heightened autonomous expression. They are causally intertwined – with free persons developing more successfully and being better sustained in a society that is characterized by liberty. Were it not for our concern with personal freedom we would not have the interest we do in liberty. We have left the notion of human flourishing unanalysed. There is obviously much that could and should be said on the issue. Here we do no more than reference some of the discussions in a special issue of *Social Philosophy & Policy*, 16 no. 1 (1999).

148   This is not to deny a relational dimension to individual autonomy. See Seumas Miller, "Individual Autonomy and Sociality", in *Socializing Metaphysics: The Nature of Social Reality*, ed. F. Schmitt (Lanham: Rowman and Littlefield, 2003).

149   Here we shall prescind from a longstanding and important debate (going back to Plato and Aristotle) on whether this account should be supplemented by certain substantive beliefs that must be held if a person is truly to be said to be free. Elements of that debate reappear in the debate over whether liberty (or freedom) should be construed as positive or negative.

150   Although in this study we generally speak of personal autonomy, much of what we say relates more specifically to its narrower specification in moral autonomy. We also leave to one side a distinction that can be drawn between autonomy as a state and autonomy as a quality of particular acts or decisions. What we

only to a level of personal development compatible with responsibility but also to a heightened level of individual freedom – a dispositional commitment to and capacity for rational living. In Chapter 3 of *On Liberty*, "Individuality, as One of the Elements of Well-Being", John Stuart Mill says that a person "must use observation to see, reasoning and judgment to foresee, activity to gather materials for decision, discrimination to decide, and when he has decided, firmness and self-control to hold to his deliberate decision."[151] He is speaking here of what we characterize as autonomy. The autonomous person does more than go with the flow or conform to whatever is the prevailing fashion. In the larger passage from which the quote is taken, however, Mill makes it clear that autonomy is not simply a matter of "rational" or calculative development – it also has emotive and conative dimensions: it concerns the capacity to choose well and it involves both authenticity (whereby the reasons, feelings, attitudes and judgments one has have become one's own – one identifies with them[152]) and competence (a level of development of rational capacities and other discriminative sensibilities that secure one against systematic ignorance, self-deception and other debilitating pathologies).[153] Moreover, the development of individuality is something generally achieved in concert with others rather than in social isolation.

Some background

Like privacy, the idea of personal autonomy has clearly emerged as only a product of modernity, though traces can be found much earlier. Even today, Socrates stands in some sense as an exemplar of autonomy. But what the elders of Athens may have found threatening, contemporary liberalism tends to foster as an ideal not just for an exceptional few but for people generally. When praising the virtue of originality, Mill recognizes that that kind of creativity belongs to only a few: "The initiation of all wise or noble things, comes and must come from individuals; generally at first from some one individual. The honour and glory of the average man is that he is capable of following that initiative; that he can respond internally to wise and noble things, and be led to them with his eyes open"[154] – an ability that he distinguishes clearly from hero-worship.

It is often noted that the idea of autonomy has its background in political theory, where it refers to self-government, self-rule, self-determination or institutional

---

characterize as autonomy can be possessed as a matter of degree.

151   See *On Liberty* at: http://www.bartleby.com/130/3.html.

152   The notion of authenticity has generated a huge and problematic literature, some of which is referred to in John Christman, "Autonomy in Moral and Political Philosophy", *Stanford Encyclopedia of Philosophy*, at: http://plato.stanford.edu/entries/autonomy-moral.

153   One of the problems often associated with Kantian conceptions of autonomy concerns its overconcern with a passionless rationality.

154   Mill, *On Liberty*, ch. 3.

independence. An autonomous individual is thus to be construed on a rough analogy with a country or institution that has charge of its own affairs and is not beholden to other powers.

Feinberg usefully suggests that personal autonomy can be understood in four closely related ways: (1) as a *capacity* to govern oneself that can be possessed to a greater or lesser degree; (2) as the *actual condition* of self-government; (3) as an *ideal of character* derived from the latter; or (4) as the *sovereign authority* to govern oneself.[155] While (1) is fundamental, much of the purport of autonomy, at least in liberal thought, is the authority (4) that it is intended to convey.

The capacity that constitutes autonomy refers to a level or threshold of competence reached so far as one's natural abilities are concerned – self-control, the capacity for making wise and prudent judgments, developed sensibilities and self-reflectiveness – the kinds of factors mentioned above regarding Mill's notion of individuality. We would argue that it involves not only a capacity but a disposition to govern oneself. (1) differs from (2) insofar as a person who has the capacity for self-government may be prevented from actualizing it by bad luck or powers beyond his or her control. When we speak of someone as autonomous, we are ruling out certain kinds of descriptions as applying to them – they are free from indoctrination, compulsion, manipulation or coercion.

Individuality and individualism

As we have suggested on a number of occasions, autonomy and individuality need not be thought of individualistically. It has been a common complaint against classical liberal theory, not only by those who have had more socialistic or communitarian leanings but also by recent feminists (who have adopted the vocabulary of "relational autonomy"[156]), that liberal autonomy is framed in a way that does not have adequate regard to the social dimensions of human life. The complaint is either that autonomy is construed as a natural endowment of humans ("man is born free, and everywhere he is in chains"[157]) or that the relational and communal aspects of mature life are underestimated.

Although we have no doubt that some classical accounts of autonomy are excessively individualistic, it does not seem to us necessary that autonomy be construed individualistically. It takes a village, so to speak, to produce

---

155   Joel Feinberg, *The Moral Limits of Criminal Law*, vol. 3: *Harm to Self* (New York: Oxford University Press, 1986), 28.

156   See, particularly, *Relational Autonomy: Feminist Perspectives on Autonomy, Agency, and the Social Self*, ed. Catriona Mackenzie and Natalie Stoljar (NY: Oxford University Press, 2000); see also Miller, "Individual Autonomy and Sociality".

157   Rousseau, *The Social Contract*, at: http://www.wsu.edu:8080/~wldciv/world_civ_reader/world_civ_reader_2/rousseau.html.

an autonomous person; moreover, autonomous persons frequently find that "villages" are integral to their projects and plans. A good deal of our autonomy is realized through relational activities. The big challenge is not to choose between individualism (or atomism) and socialism (or some other relational option) but to get an appropriate balance between the individual and relational elements of our personhood.

It is easily forgotten that, in becoming the individuals we are, we acquire – and in some sense cannot shrug off – both a language, with its embedded cultural understandings, and the trappings of a broader culture and its traditions. Autonomy is not to be thought of as the absence or negation of these so much as the capacity to question or interrogate them. We may not be able to do this all at once (we are, after all, sailing on Theseus' ship), but there may not be any aspect of our lives that is permanently shielded from scrutiny.

Sovereign authority

As noted above, it is commonly claimed by many liberal writers that personal autonomy (understood as capacity and disposition) provides a basis for according individuals autonomy in another sense (sovereignty over their personal affairs, which is compatible, it is assumed or argued, with according a similar sovereignty to others). That usually provides an argument for opposing any strong form of paternalism in which individuals are prevented from making decisions that are seriously detrimental to their own interests. Mill's "harm principle" provides a classic statement:

> The object of this Essay is to assert one very simple principle, as entitled to govern absolutely the dealings of society with the individual in the way of compulsion and control, whether the means used be physical force in the form of legal penalties, or the moral coercion of public opinion. That principle is, that the sole end for which mankind are warranted, individually or collectively, in interfering with the liberty of action of any of their number, is self-protection. That the only purpose for which power can be rightfully exercised over any member of a civilized community, against his will, is to prevent harm to others. His own good, either physical or moral, is not a sufficient warrant. He cannot rightfully be compelled to do or forbear because it will be better for him to do so, because it will make him happier, because, in the opinions of others, to do so would be wise, or even right. These are good reasons for remonstrating with him, or reasoning with him, or persuading him, or entreating him, but not for compelling him, or visiting him with any evil in case he do otherwise. To justify that, the conduct from which it is desired to deter him, must be calculated to produce evil to some one

else. The only part of the conduct of any one, for which he is amenable to society, is that which concerns others. In the part which merely concerns himself, his independence is, of right, absolute. Over himself, over his own body and mind, the individual is sovereign.[158]

As a statement this is about as absolute as you can get. Nevertheless, as Mill himself recognizes, there are hard cases.[159] What he sees as the hardest case is the decision to sell oneself into slavery, though the argument that he uses to back away from it is uncharacteristically opaque:

> In this and most other civilized countries . . . an engagement by which a person should sell himself, or allow himself to be sold, as a slave, would be null and void; neither enforced by law nor by opinion. The ground for thus limiting his power of voluntarily disposing of his own lot in life, is apparent, and is very clearly seen in this extreme case. The reason for not interfering, unless for the sake of others, with a person's voluntary acts, is consideration for his liberty. His voluntary choice is evidence that what he so chooses is desirable, or at the least endurable, to him, and his good is on the whole best provided for by allowing him to take his own means of pursuing it. But by selling himself for a slave, he abdicates his liberty; he foregoes any future use of it beyond that single act. He therefore defeats, in his own case, the very purpose which is the justification of allowing him to dispose of himself. He is no longer free; but is thenceforth in a position which has no longer the presumption in its favour, that would be afforded by his voluntarily remaining in it. The principle of freedom cannot require that he should be free not to be free. It is not freedom, to be allowed to alienate his freedom.[160]

One might question Mill's coherence on this point, or at least ask for greater clarity on why it is not (an exercise of) freedom to give up one's freedom.[161]

---

158   *On Liberty*, ch. 1, at: http://www.bartleby.com/130/1.html.

159   "If either a public officer or any one else saw a person attempting to cross a bridge which had been ascertained to be unsafe, and there were no time to warn him of his danger, they might seize him and turn him back, without any real infringement of his liberty; for liberty consists in doing what one desires, and he does not desire to fall into the river. Nevertheless, when there is not a certainty, but only a danger of mischief, no one but the person himself can judge of the sufficiency of the motive which may prompt him to incur the risk: in this case, therefore, (unless he is a child, or delirious, or in some state of excitement or absorption incompatible with the full use of the reflecting faculty) he ought, I conceive, to be only warned of the danger; not forcibly prevented from exposing himself to it." Ch. 5, at: http://www.bartleby.com/130/5.html.

160   *Ibid.*, ch. 5, at: http://www.bartleby.com/130/5.html.

161   John Kleinig has tried to unravel Mill's claim in "John Stuart Mill and Voluntary Slavery Contracts", *Politics* 18, no. 2 (November, 1983): 76-83. But see also: David Archard, "Freedom Not to be Free: The Case of the Slavery Contract in J. S. Mill's *On Liberty*", *Philosophical Quarterly* (October, 1990): 453-465; Alan E. Fuchs, "Autonomy, Slavery, and Mill's Critique of Paternalism", *Ethical Theory and Moral Practice* 4, no. 3 (September, 2001): 231-51; John D. Hodson, "Mill, Paternalism, and Slavery", *Analysis* 41 (January, 1981): 60-62; Andrew Sneddon, "What's Wrong with Selling Yourself into Slavery? Paternalism and Deep Autonomy", *Critica: Revista Hispanoamericana de Filosofia* 33, no. 98 (August, 2001): 97-121 (see also: http://critica.filosoficas.unam.mx/pdf/C98/C98_sneddon.pdf); Mark Strasser, "Mill on Voluntary Self-enslavement",

More recently, a German case of consented-to cannibalism has once again pushed the limits of an absolutist anti-paternalistic stance.[162] Suicide (unassisted and assisted) has elicited a great deal of discussion, though part of that discussion has concerned not intervention so much as criminalization.

What is not absolutely clear about the move from the capacity account to the sovereignty account is how it is to be understood. Is there a (non-arbitrary) threshold autonomy such that, once one has met the threshold, others may not intervene? That seems to be Mill's position and why he has to meet the self-enslavement challenge in the way he does (it is not freedom to be allowed give up one's freedom). However, given that autonomy may be a matter of degree, is it the case that the greater a person's autonomy, the heavier the burden that must be faced by those who would paternalistically intervene? Paternalism would not be ruled out but simply made increasingly difficult to justify.[163] Opposition to it may be viewed as presumptive without being absolute.

Perhaps the sovereign authority that goes with personal autonomy is not absolute but, like the political sovereignty from which the metaphor originates, simply provides a strong but not overriding reason for not intervening in the affairs of others.

Dignity

As has become clear in the foregoing discussion, lurking behind most of the concepts we have been discussing and fundamental to much of the liberal tradition has been the idea of human dignity – an idea with a long history in Western thought but with renewed prominence in post-World War Two political rhetoric. Violations of privacy and autonomy tend, at their deepest level, to be also violations of dignity.

Although Immanuel Kant has been the most influential architect of modern ideas of human dignity, he built on and extended a Renaissance tradition that included, among others, Giannozzo Manetti (1396-1459) and Giovanni Pico

---

Philosophical Papers 17 (November, 1988): 171-83; Ten Chin Liew, *Mill on Liberty* (Oxford: Oxford University press, 1980), ch. 7; Samuel V. La Selva, "Selling Oneself into Slavery: Mill and Paternalism", *Political Studies* 35, no, 2 (1987): 211-23.

162 See Armin Meiwes at: http://en.wikipedia.org/wiki/Armin_Meiwes. For *New York Times* articles on the case, see: http://topics.nytimes.com/top/reference/timestopics/subjects/c/cannibalism/index. html?query=BRANDES,%20BERND-JURGEN&field=per&match=exact. There is a useful discussion of this and other cases in Vera Bergelson, "The Right to Be Hurt. Testing the Boundaries of Consent", *George Washington Law Review* 75 (2007): 165 (see also: http://works.bepress.com/vera_bergelson/4).

163 In such cases other factors, such as the kind of intervention (e.g. criminal, civil), the identity of the intervener (e.g. friend, state) and the intrusiveness of the intervention (e.g. seat belt laws, enforced dieting) might also be taken into account.

della Mirandola (1463-1494).[164] That tradition helped to transplant[165] an older tradition in which *dignitas* was most closely associated with social rank. This was done by universalizing a standing and bearing associated with rank. There was a raising up, not a leveling down.[166] The big question prompted by this universalization of dignity was, naturally: In what does such *human* dignity consist? Pico located this generalized dignity in the human power of self-transformation; that is, in our capacity as humans to be whatever we wish to be. This was innovative in more ways than one. It accorded powers to humans that many Christian theologians considered to have been radically lost when Adam and Eve rebelled against their Maker.[167] But its most distinctive feature was to universalize the idea of dignity.

There is much to be said for the Kantian tradition of understanding human dignity. We take as our starting point a position that is articulated in numerous recent international documents. This is the view that human dignity is not simply another value – to be traded off against autonomy and such like – but one that possesses foundational significance. Thus, in the Preamble to the UN Convention Against Torture (1987), it is affirmed that "the equal and inalienable rights of

---

164 See, Giannozzo Manetti, *De dignitate et excellentia hominis libri IV*; Book 4 translated by Bernard Murchland in *Two Views of Man: Pope Innocent III On the Misery of Man; Giannozzo Manetti On the Dignity of Man* (New York: Frederick Ungar, 1966); Giovanni Pico della Mirandola, *De dominis dignitate oratio*, translated as *Oration on the Dignity of Man*, by A. Robert Caponigri (Chicago: Gateway, 1956). Some see the seeds of a general idea of human dignity in Cicero or even earlier in Judeo-Christian thought. For overviews, see Izhak England, "Human Dignity from Antiquity to Modern Israel's Constitutional Framework", *Cardozo Law Review* 21 (May 2000): 1903-27; Charles Trinkhaus, "Renaissance Idea of the Dignity of Man", *Dictionary of the History of Ideas*, vol. 4, 136-46 (see also: http://etext.virginia.edu/cgi-local/DHI/dhiana.cgi?id=dv4-20); Richard C. Dales, "A Medieval View of Human Dignity", *Journal of the History of Ideas* 38, no. 4 (October-December 1979): 557-72.

165 We say "transplant" because, in many cases, including that of Kant, there was not so much a rejection of older traditions of rank-based dignity as the addition of a distinct kind of dignity, one attaching to all humans. This universal dignity also needs to be distinguished from another contemporary account of transplanted dignity – the dignity of each *citizen*.

166 Admittedly, there were those (e.g. Thomas Paine) who sought to *replace* the dignity of rank with the equal dignity of all, and several influential writers have spoken of this development as a "leveling up" (e.g. James Q Whitman) or an "upwards equalization of rank" (Jeremy Waldron). For the most part, though, Kant and others who wished to advocate a universal human dignity did not wish to abandon traditional forms of rank. Instead, contrary to tradition, they thought that by virtue of their humanity all possessed a dignity comparable to that associated with traditional rank. See Thomas Paine, *The Rights of Man* (New York: Anchor, 1973), 320; James Q. Whitman, "The Two Western Cultures of Privacy: Dignity versus Liberty", *Yale Law Journal* 113 (2004): 1151-221; Jeremy Waldron "Dignity and Rank", *Archives Européennes de Sociologie* 48 (2007), 201-37; also idem, "Cruel, Inhuman and Degrading Treatment: The Words Themselves", New York University School of Law, Public and Legal Theory Research Paper Series, Working Paper # 08-36 (November 2008), 36 (see also: http://papers.ssrn.com/sol3/papers.cfm?abstract_id=1278604).

167 Some later Christian theologians spoke of the partial restoration of this dignity, located in the *imago Dei*, "in Christ". Nevertheless, the awkwardness of connecting dignity with some universally possessed inherent characteristic led other theologians, especially in the Lutheran tradition, to construe human dignity as an "alien dignity" – an "infinite worth" that is not constituted by qualities such as rationality but by the distinctive relationship we have with God – created in love, called in love and redeemed in love. For a useful exposition of this idea, see Karen Lebacqz, "Alien Dignity: The Legacy of Helmut Thielicke for Bioethics", in *Religion and Medical Ethics: Looking Back, Looking Forward* ed. Allen Verhey (Grand Rapids: Eerdmans, 1996), 44-60.

all members of the human family . . . derive from the inherent dignity of the human person."[168] A similar point is implicit in German Basic Law (1949), which opens with the claim that "human dignity shall be inviolable" (Art. 1) and follows with the assertion that "the German people *therefore* acknowledge inviolable and inalienable human rights as the basis of every community" (Art . 2).[169]

In the *Groundwork of the Metaphysic of Morals*, Kant is quite explicit about what he thinks is intended by the idea of human dignity: "the dignity of man consists precisely in his capacity to make universal law, although only on condition of being himself also subject to the laws he makes."[170] This is an enormously illuminating understanding of human dignity, especially if abstracted from some of the more complex elements of Kantian doctrine. If we understand correctly what Kant is saying here, there are two dimensions to human dignity that are now deeply embedded in our cultural understanding of human dignity.

On the one hand, there is, as Kant puts it, the human capacity to make universal law — what he elsewhere explicates in terms of the categorical imperative. For present purposes we can leave the problems associated with Kant's understanding of the categorical imperative aside. The important underlying point is that human dignity does not consist primarily in some idea of rationality or freedom, however important those may ultimately be to his account. It is the capacity to make universal law — that is, the capacity to bind or obligate oneself — that is central. Or, to put it a bit more generally, it is to be found in our status as normative beings whose decisions are not to be resolved in terms of simple means-end determinations but as judgments of appropriateness and inappropriateness. It is our standing as moral agents (especially), given to evaluating courses of action as a condition of determining them, that is a critical element in our dignity.

On the other hand, Kant says that the capacity to make human universal law is constitutive of human dignity only if those who exercise such capacity also subject themselves to the law that they make. Again, we do not want to get bogged down in Kantian scholarship. However, what Kant is adverting to is that there is more to human dignity than the capacity for certain kinds of decisional

---

168   See: http://www.unhchr.ch/html/menu3/b/h_cat39.htm. A similar ordering is found in the preamble to the UN International Covenant on Civil and Political Rights (1966):

Considering that, in accordance with the principles proclaimed in the Charter of the United Nations, recognition of the inherent dignity and of the equal and inalienable rights of all members of the human family is the foundation of freedom, justice and peace in the world, recognizing that these rights derive from the inherent dignity of the human person . . ."

169   Grundgesetz, GG, at: http://www.iuscomp.org/gla/statutes/GG.htm. Additional references to – and discussion of – the internationalization of human dignity can be found in Man Yee Karen Lee, "Universal Human Dignity: Some Reflections in the Asian Context", *Asian Journal of Comparative Law* 3, no. 1 (2008) (see: http://www.bepress.com/asjcl/vol3/iss1/art10).

170   *Groundwork of the Metaphysic of Morals,* translated by H. J. Paton (New York: Harper & Row, 1956), sect. II, Akad. 440.

determinations. Such determinations must also be reflected in one's own person. We must carry ourselves in a certain way if we are to be creatures with dignity. There is an expressive aspect to human dignity.

These two elements of dignity have often been sundered in discussions of dignity – to the point that dictionaries will often distinguish, as two distinct meanings of "dignity", one that focuses on certain capacities and the other that focuses on a certain bearing or way of being. The *Oxford English Dictionary*, for example, offers as its second usage of dignity: "honourable or high estate, position, or estimation; honour; degree of estimation, rank"; and as its fourth usage: "nobility or befitting elevation of aspect, manner, or style; becoming or fit stateliness, gravity". Although treated as distinct and separate, these two accounts really belong together as two dimensions of a single account.[171] If we recall the roots of the current conception of human dignity as a kind of social rank, we are confronted with a person who not only had a certain status but was expected to manifest it in certain forms of social behavior. There were not two kinds of dignity – dignity of status and dignity of bearing – but a single dignity that had two dimensions.

Before moving on, let us briefly comment on what we see as the connection between the understanding of human dignity as normativity and the common identification of human dignity with autonomy or rationality – connections that are also strong in Kant. The human capacity for moral discernment and determinations – our normativity – is to an important extent premised on our capacity for rationality and autonomy. Compromise that and you threaten our normative capacity; you challenge our dignity.

If this account of human dignity is somewhere near the mark, the question that then arises is: how does it help us to understand the claim that the inherent dignity of the human person is foundational to our rights? We could worry – as Jeremy Waldron does – that such international statements might simply be expressions of pious rhetoric,[172] but once we grasp the central connection between dignity and the capacity for determining the course of our lives by means of moral considerations, dignity's foundational character becomes much clearer.

We are rights-possessing creatures – that is, we are in a position to make enforceable claims on others – by virtue of our normative capacity. It is our normative capacity, our capacity to guide our lives by means of considerations

---

171 We do not mean to imply that they cannot be sundered – indeed, they have been. But we want to suggest that there goes with the first usage an expectation of the second.
172 Jeremy Waldron, "Dignity and Rank", 235.

of appropriateness (and not mere efficacy), that undergirds our status as rights bearers, and those who act in ways that would compromise, subvert or destroy that capacity violate us.

We are not suggesting that we can directly infer from our possession of dignity what rights we should have. To be sure, Waldron attempts such an exercise by considering the accoutrements of rank as the substance of our human rights. He considers whether what those with rank were entitled to by virtue of their rank we might all be entitled to – the entitlement to vote and a voice in public affairs, a right not to be struck, a right to have one's wishes respected in the conduct of personal life and so on.[173] Our own claim is the much more modest one that whatever others may do that jeopardizes our capacity to act as normatively determined beings *ipso facto* jeopardizes our rights.

Nevertheless, there is something else implicit in the idea of dignity that is important. Whereas Waldron focuses on the positive trappings of dignity as rank, it might be more appropriate to focus on the situation of those who lack dignity. In *The Metaphysical Elements of Justice*, Kant observes that the head of state – the chief dignitary – possesses the right to distribute "positions of dignity that are distinctions of rank not involving pay and that are based on honor alone; these distinctions of rank establish a superior class (entitled to command) and an inferior class (which although free and bound only by public law), is predestined to obey the former".[174] What we may infer from this is that those lacking in dignity are beholden to others – they are not authors of their obligations but are obligated as those under authority. What our human dignity does is morally entitle us to treatment by others that acknowledges our status as normatively determining beings.

Identity

We have already looked at some of the values associated with anonymity, particularly as a means of retaining a certain measure of privacy in public and, along with that, a constituent of personal autonomy. Anonymity enables one to retain some control over one's identity.[175] However, control over one's identity is something of a two-edged sword. Although it may express and protect autonomy,

---

173   *Ibid.*, 226 et seq.

174   Kant, *The Metaphysical Elements of Justice*, translated by John Ladd (Indianapolis: Bobbs-Merrill, 1965), Akad., 328.

175   A useful listing of reasons for anonymity, more detailed than those of Nissenbaum, can be found in Gary Marx, "Identity and Anonymity: Some Conceptual Distinctions and Issues for Research", in *Documenting Individual Identity: The Development of State Practices in the Modern World*, ed. J. Caplan and J. Torpey (Princeton, NJ: Princeton University Press, 2001): 326, available at: http://web.mit.edu/gtmarx/www/identity.html.

as with Gyges' ring it also constitutes an opportunity for harm to others. The control we have may enable us to present ourselves to others deceptively, as someone other than who we are, and this possibility is made easier with the increasing use that is being made of automated transactions. This is exacerbated in large and complex societies that have made themselves responsible for the disbursal of a large number of benefits and burdens (social security benefits, banking systems, tax collections, neighborhood protection, penalties, welfare, education and so forth). The most dramatic recent expression of this has been identity theft, now numbering in the millions each year. Protection against the stealing of identities requires increasing use of increasingly sophisticated identifiers, and the increasing use of such identifiers also increases the potential for privacy violations as well as harm done to one through them. The social challenge is to secure privacy at the same time as one secures appropriate identification.

Control over one's identity is made increasingly problematic by the development of digital technologies that seek to identify one by means of certain identifiers. Among other things, many digital technologies store, move and integrate data about people. If someone was to Google John Kleinig's name, that person would find online data about him (and perhaps others of that name) at various sites that might then be integrated to create a composite that could then be used to qualify or disqualify a co-author of this study for some kind of social response. It might provide enough information to enable someone to engage in identity theft; it could provide pertinent information to a prospective employer who might, because of some posting (say, on MySpace), decide not to offer him a job; it might enable him to be targeted for certain kinds of merchandise; or it might trigger an FBI (or other governmental) investigation into his politics or sexual proclivities. There are lots of possibilities – and that is just Google. However, in addition to Google there are lots of other repositories of digitalized information about John Kleinig to which someone is able to get access by paying a fee. Alternatively, those who do not wish to pay fees to get private or personal data about John Kleinig may seek to trick him into revealing it by means of phishing.

LexisNexis[176] and ChoicePoint[177] use sophisticated search software to gain access to and combine a great deal of data about John Kleinig, much of which might be considered personal and private. Even if the discrete bits of data are not private, the composite that can be produced as a result of its integration (like a jigsaw puzzle) might be seen by him as too revealing or even as distorting.[178]

---

176   See: http://global.lexisnexis.com/us>; but see also <http://www.lexisnexis.com/gov/.

177   See: http://www.choicepoint.com/index.html and also: http://www.epic.org/privacy/choicepoint/.

178   For example, it so happens that there are (at least) two John Kleinigs of almost the same age and same national origins who, because of certain similarities, have often been confused.

The composite in question can be sold to financial institutions, marketers, the FBI or other interested parties. In the case of the FBI, it is used in the process of compiling travel watch lists.

Sometimes, of course, it is perfectly legitimate for others to ask for some private data from one. If one wants to make an online purchase, the seller has every reason to ask for one's credit card number.[179] Or, as a sign of good faith with respect to some online contribution one has made, one's name and address might need to be entered. Or one's social security number might need to be provided to determine one's eligibility for some service or benefit. Some way or other, certain more or less uniquely identifying information may need to be provided.

There are two important terms/concepts that crop up in this connection – those of identity and identification:

1.   The notion of *identity* is already the topic of multiple and somewhat divergent philosophical inquiries, whether it is the "identity of indiscernibles", "personal identity" or "identity politics".[180] The kind of identity that we are concerned with here is different again, though not entirely unrelated. It is closer in meaning to "identity" as we use it in talking about "identity theft",[181] though even that constitutes a particular take on something that has become increasingly multi-layered and elusive.

Let us start with a simple and simplified account of identity. As a particular person, John Kleinig, a co-author of this study, might be said to have a specific identity or individuality. It is constituted by certain uniquely identifying characteristics that make him the particular person that he is.[182] This core identity (what makes him "him") is likely to have some invariant features (date and place of birth, names of parents etc.) but it need not be fixed; indeed, it will almost certainly change over time as he develops, matures and declines. Sometimes we want to say of ourselves that we are no longer the persons we were: we have a different identity now from that which we once had. We sometimes find it galling that people remember us as we were and do not see us as we are. And sometimes, perhaps, we would prefer people to remember us as we were rather than know us as we have become.

---

179   If we are antsy about even supposedly secure sites, companies will sometimes provide a phone option (though that, too, may be less secure than we think).

180   The *OED* distinguishes at least ten major meanings.

181   See: http://www.ftc.gov/bcp/edu/microsites/idtheft/.

182   Later we indicate how this apparently unique identity can also – because of the categories upon which it draws, such as ethnicity, religion and so forth – function to dis-identify one and to merge one with a group that is either privileged or discriminated against.

But even this notion of a core identity is fraught with complications.[183] At one level it seems to be constituted by a series of "objective" facts about one, allowing that some of those facts may change over time (or, perhaps better, need to be seen as historically mutable – e.g. was a pain in the neck when growing up and is now the salt of the earth, began as a girl but is now transgendered). But we also want to connect the idea of core identity with some notion of self-identity that links with the idea of one as an individual autonomous agent. Insofar as we connect these things there will be an irreducibly "subjective" aspect to one's core identity. Our current sense is that there is an ongoing tension between these two elements within the idea of a core identity.

However, one's current core identity may not be one's only identity, for one may seek to create alternative identities for oneself.[184] For example, one may seek to pass oneself off as a wealthy *bon vivant* so that one can insinuate oneself into certain social circles. One may create an online identity for oneself so that one may enter certain chat rooms from which one would otherwise be excluded.[185] Less problematically, one may create an online identity for oneself simply for the purpose of experiencing an alternative identity, much as an actor may temporarily enter into the persona of a script character. Or one may go to live in a distant city so that one can create a new identity for oneself, either having tired of or wishing to escape an old one.

Even if one makes no conscious effort to do so, one may project a different identity to different people, and each may be – so far as it goes – "real". To one's students one may be an aging, white male philosopher; to one's children one may be an easy touch and supportive presence; to one's friends one may be funny and laidback; and to one's bank manager one may be the guy who has trouble managing his finances. Some will have a better or fuller grasp than others of the "I" one really is; that is, they will have a better sense of the range of characteristics that constitute one's identity. Although we are sometimes glad if people see us "in the round" (and not simply as the person who . . .), at

---

183   Even the very notion of a core identity is being called into question, and not just because Judith Butler says so. Has the notion of identity itself become a victim of self-creative postmodernism? Do we display our prejudices and/or unwillingness to let go of Linus's rug? Is the elusive "I" non-existent? It may be, at least insofar as many time-worn – and seemingly fixed – categories (such as gender, religion, and nationality) become less permanent (or exclusive).

184   Sometimes, as we know from well-researched biographies, even what are seen as the core identities of individuals are radically reconstructed. Birth names, dates and places are reconfigured so that what their subjects present as their true selves are at variance with important facts about them. In some cases, it would appear that even the persons themselves have come to identify with the identity that they have now claimed for themselves.

185   Some of these identities may be reflective of or consonant with our wider identity. Others may not. The pedophile who pretends to be a teenager looking for sex is expressing, albeit deceptively, his identity as a pedophile, whereas the FBI agent who enters the same chat room as a 14-year-old girl is acting deceptively but (we presume) not expressing his identity as a sexually hungry person. Of course, to identify someone as a pedophile may be to impose on that person an identity with more associations than ought to be the case (e.g. predator, rather than desperately lonely).

other times we may wish to conceal aspects of our identity from others. Our identities may contain a variety of contradictory characteristics, the result of our (or others') attempts to create alternative identities for alternative purposes.

Thus we may be ambivalent about our identities, should it happen to be the case that some aspect of our identity will benefit or burden us in ways that we do not want. One's identity as an "Astor" may (to one's embarrassment) privilege one in the job market as one will be seen to be "connected" to certain social circles; whereas one's identity as "Robert Zimmerman" may be thought to prejudice one's chances in certain WASPy circles, leading one to change one's name to "Bob Dylan". On the other hand, there may be contexts in which we wish to assert our identity (e.g. as Australian or American) rather than conceal it. Our identities do not exist in a vacuum, whether we "own" them or are simply ascribed them. Some of our identifying characteristics tend to pick us out uniquely, others link us to groups (ethnic, national, religious, political and so on). Problematically, some of the factors that we think of as contributing to our uniqueness (because they narrow the field), may also serve to link us to others, thus including us – for some purposes – in socially significant groups (e.g. Jewish, gay).

We can crudely link identity in the sense(s) we have been outlining with identity in other senses as follows. In the philosophical literature, personal identity is usually taken to refer to the persistence of a particular individual over time[186]; that is, the John Kleinig who is co-authoring this study is the same person who went to Nedlands Primary School in the 1940s. However, the personal identity issue focuses on continuity and persistence, not on what might be called one's identity at age five and one's identity at age sixty-five. In the latter sense, one is a different person now from the person one was then. The latter (change in identity over time) is sometimes used to deny that there is personal identity in the former sense.[187] The debate may have normative importance. Suppose John Kleinig at age ten broke into a neighbor's house and stole money that he used to

---

186   In the sociological and psychological literature, "personal identity" tends to be understood differently. For example, Erving Goffman understands by personal identity what we initially characterized as a person's identity: "Personal identity, then, has to do with the assumption that the individual can be differentiated from all others and that around this means of differentiation a single continuous record of social facts can be attached, entangled, like fairy floss, becoming then the sticky substance to which all other biographical facts can be attached", *Stigma: Notes on the Management of Spoiled Identity* (1963; Englewood Cliffs, NJ: Prentice Hall, 1968), 74–75. Susan Hekman states: "Each of us possesses a personal identity that is constituted by an array of influences and experiences that form us as a unique person. These forces are both public, the hegemonic discourses that define our social life, and individual, the character and situation of those who care for us as infants, and through whom the public concepts are transmitted to us. The result of these influences is . . . our core self. But in addition to possessing a personal identity, each of us is subsumed under an array of public identities: woman/man; white/nonwhite; middle class/working class, and so forth", *Private Selves, Public Identities, Reconsidering Identity Politics* (University Park, PA: Penn State University Press, 2004), 7.
187   See, in particular, Derek Parfit, *Reasons and Persons* (New York: Oxford University Press, 1984), esp. 326; and also L. Fields, "Parfit on Personal Identity and Desert", *Philosophical Quarterly* 37 (1987): 432–41.

purchase chemicals and equipment for his chemistry experiments. In his later teens he underwent a major change of outlook and subsequently became an exemplary citizen. Forty years later, he meets the neighbor again, and somehow the matter of the theft arises. Can fifty-year-old John be held responsible for what ten-year-old John did? Certainly the fifty-year-old John does not have the same identity as the ten-year-old John; he's now the kind of person who would never steal from others. But can he hide behind that change of identity to conceal his continuity with the ten-year-old who burgled the neighbor? Can he deny responsibility for what was done when he was ten? *Pace Parfit*, we think not. There does not seem to be anything inappropriate about his apologizing for what he did when he was ten.

In the case of identity politics, what we are talking about is political decision making designed to foster the interests of a particular group on the basis of some shared feature — often one feature, such as gender or race — that is also often included as part of a person's identity. In such cases, the feature in question, now being advanced as a reason for special recognition, was perhaps once exploited as a reason for invidious discrimination.

So far we have been talking about (more or less) self-ascribed identities — how we characterize ourselves as the particular persons we are (presumably on the basis of features that also hold true of us). Identities are also ascribed to us by others. Indeed, identities are first ascribed to us by others and it is only later that we are likely to claim an identity as our own. That later, self-ascribed identity may include (mostly) elements of what has been ascribed to us by others, or it may involve a repudiation of some or much of that other, other-ascribed identity. The co-author of this study was an Australian by birth, baptized as John Kleinig in a Methodist church and raised in a right-wing family. Each and all of these elements of his identity he may later wish to repudiate — not that they were never part of his identity but that they may come to have no significance for the person who forty years later is an American citizen called Roscoe Mann who worships in a working-class Catholic church. As far as personal identity is concerned, Roscoe Mann is continuous with John Kleinig, and if it turns out that John Kleinig went to the US to reconstitute himself as Roscoe Mann after he murdered someone in a robbery gone bad, he will not be able to wriggle out of it if he is found out fifty years later by claiming that he is not John Kleinig etc. but Roscoe Mann etc.[188]

The identities that are ascribed to us are much more varied and complex than the ones that we have just alluded to. Governments and other organizations have multitudinous purposes in ascribing particular identities to us and they

---

188 The co-author of this study hastens to add that a number of the identifying factors that are being referred to here are fictional.

may do so in ways that we may wish to disavow.[189] Consider something that tends to be (relatively) anonymous – a census. By filling in a census form we will check a variety of boxes (number of people in household, zip code, ethnic identity (possibly a limited number of choices), income, etc.), information that will be aggregated and become the basis for distributions of federal funds – to age groups, communities etc. However, the identities that we may thereby acquire, albeit only for aggregative purposes, may not be identities that we want to "own". If one of John Kleinig's parents was German and the other Sorbian, he may be proud of his ethnic heritage, but the census will not allow him the option of identifying with that, even though it gives others the option of identifying with their heritage.[190] If one and one's family are (normally) resident in Harlem, but at the time of the census one is incarcerated in an upstate New York prison, one will be counted (for census purposes and the distribution of certain federal funds) as a resident of the county in which the prison is located.[191] In the 1930s many German Jews thought of themselves as more German than Jewish, but governmental policy prioritized (and denigrated) their Jewishness even if, as had occurred in a fair number of cases, they had converted.

For purposes of taxation, welfare, health benefits and salary, one's identity (in the US) is largely structured around one's social security number, supposedly a uniquely referring identifying number. It may serve to verify one's identity but will not in other ways say very much about one's identity (and because of that it may enable one's identity to be stolen more easily). Other factors about one – such as one's belonging to an underrepresented (for certain purposes) group (as determined by others) may make one eligible for certain opportunities that one may or may not otherwise have had and whether or not one wishes to have them.[192] One's passport does not include a social security number, even though an increasingly nonreplicable (but also not private) photograph is central. For other purposes, a fingerprint or other biometric data may be used. What we should note is the potential for divergence between our identity as it is construed by governmental agencies and our identity as we construe it for ourselves. It is unlikely to figure in a government account of one's identity that one has a morbid fear of spiders or elevators, even if those fears may tend to dominate one's everyday behavior.

---

189   We focus here on identities that may be ascribed to us for various governmental purposes. However, they may be ascribed to us for various marketing purposes as well – as people fitting various lifestyle or age classifications.

190   Intermarriage of various kinds creates havoc with the options provided by censuses and other registers. See Marx, "Identity and Anonymity: Some Conceptual Distinctions and Issues for Research".

191   There are some – as yet unsuccessful – moves afoot to rectify this. The poor communities from which prisoners ordinarily come are further deprived of benefits and the communities in which the prisons are built are glad of the extra income. They also tend to have greater political clout.

192   Consider the offense felt in the 1990s by some African-American sergeants in the NYPD as those they supervised speculated about whether they were "affirmative action sergeants".

We shall return to issues of identity, but first we go to the other term of our distinction.

2. *Identification* is what we do to establish an identity, and we do this by means of identifiers. Thus one may be identified as a particular person by one's name (though not uniquely so), one's parentage (though not uniquely so), one's height, weight and skin color (though not uniquely so), one's ethnicity (though not uniquely so), one's profession (though not uniquely so), one's address (though not uniquely so) the websites one visits (though not uniquely so) and so on, though it may well be the case that there is no other person who answers to all these identifying characteristics. Different identifiers may be used for different purposes. One's address, for example, may be used to locate one (for purposes of interrogation), to classify one (as middle class) or to render one as eligible for certain benefits/burdens.[193] One's name may be used to classify one (e.g. German lineage, gender, to sort one in a process) and so on. A biometric identifier (such as fingerprint, voiceprint or DNA) may identify one for purposes of immigration eligibility, criminal guilt or access to a restricted site.

In digital contexts, identities are fixed through a process of identification in which various identifiers are employed or brought together. A critical question will concern the match between a digitally created identity and the (core or self) identity of the person it is intended to "capture". Does the identity of the John Kleinig who is digitally identified match the John Kleinig who is co-authoring this study? Although there has always been an issue about the match between some public or official identity and the identity of the person it refers to, it was not until the development of digital tools that this became a significant issue.

One's digitally stored or available identity may be accurate so far as it goes (though it may not go far enough), or it may contain inaccuracies. Insofar as that identity may then be used to make various decisions that bear on one's interests (e.g. one's ability to take out a loan or fly on an aircraft, or one's capacity to be electronically surveilled), it is important that it should be adequate to the purposes to which it is put.

Not only is the accuracy of an ascribed identity for particular purposes important, it is also important to be able to correct misidentifications. One of the huge problems encountered in the so-called "war on terrorism" has been the misidentification of those who are deemed to pose a terrorist threat and the enormous difficulty such people have had in correcting such misidentifications.

---

193 Some identifiers will usually contribute to one's being uniquely identified (such as name, address, and SS#), whereas others may be of a comparative nature, enabling one to be classified (e.g. using income range, IQ or SAT scores for marketing purposes, welfare eligibility, college admission and so forth).

Creating a set of identifiers that accurately and sufficiently capture or secure a person's identity is not an easy task.[194] Most names are not unique and even a name that is unique may be spelled in different ways, sometimes arising from simple typos and sometimes because of digital constraints.[195] Even a combination of name and address is not likely to remain stable. A more reliable identifier may be some code, such as a social security or employee number, though, like a name, it may not carry a lot of information with it, and if it does link to other information it may not always be accurate. It may be mined, stolen or misused, as may also be the case with passwords and PINs, which are used to protect a person from some invasion of his or her identity.[196] Such devices are protective rather than descriptive – and, of course, there may be some inaccuracies in what is protected. Various tokens (such as smart cards, drivers licenses, birth certificates and passports) may also serve to identify a person to others and secure that person against another's misuse of his or her identity. Currently, no widely used set of identifiers is foolproof, though some emerging biometric techniques such as retinal identification[197] may be very difficult to steal or forge.

Arguments for privacy and anonymity center on the idea of autonomous agency, both constitutively and instrumentally. Privacy and anonymity can assure our identity as something that we can control, but, insofar as we wish to secure the viability of various social activities and participate in them (activities that themselves may be expressive of our identities), we must enable our identity to be verified. That will be achieved via various forms of identification. Gary Marx suggests ten normative uses for identification. It may be used to:

1. assist accountability;

2. determine reputation;

3. pay dues or receive just deserts;

4. assist efficiency and improve service;

5. determine bureaucratic eligibility;

6. guarantee transactions distanced or mediated by time/space;

7. assist research;

8. protect health and consumers;

---

194   We may control some identifiers (even if socially adopted) ourselves. For example, we may choose to get a tattoo that identifies us as a member of a particular gang.

195   Roger Clarke notes some of the ways in which a name can go wrong in "Human Identification in Information Systems: Management Challenges and Public Policy Issues", *Information Technology & People*, 7 (1994): 6–37 (See: http://www.anu.edu.au/people/Roger.Clarke/DV/HumanID.html).

196   Vulnerability is exploited through practices such as phishing (see: http://www.antiphishing.org) or the attachment of trojans (see: http://en.wikipedia.org/wiki/Trojan_horse_(computing)) to emails or internet files.

197   See: http://www.cse.msu.edu/~cse891/Sect601/textbook/6.pdf.

9. assist relationship building; and

10. assist social orientation.

(Marx's paper was written before 9/11. No doubt he would have expanded one of the above categories or emphasized a security use of identifiers had he written it later.)

Though these social purposes may justify the development and implementation of increasingly sophisticated — because of failures or subversions — forms of identification, they bring in their train a series of normatively charged questions, lest these forms of identification jeopardize the identities of those whom they are intended to identify:

1. *Questions concerning necessity.* Are the identifying materials asked for really necessary? Why does *Y* need one's phone number when he/she has one's email address? Does Y really need one's social security number for this?

2. *Questions of reliability.* How good are the various forms of identification at doing the tasks for which they were intended? What are the problems of false positives and false negatives?[198] Are particular identifiers (religion, ethnicity, gender etc.) as relevant as they might once have been?

3. *Questions concerning rectification.* If the identifiers fail, will procedures be in place for setting records straight? Will they be easily accessible and responsive? Will there be some form of recompense for those falsely excluded from benefits or subjected to burdens?

4. *Questions concerning enforcement.* If matters go awry, what procedures are in place to *ensure* that rectificatory or punitive strategies will actually work?

5. *Questions concerning updating.* Will mutable identifiers have a mandated life? Will information be eliminated or reconfirmed after a certain period? How long?

6. *Questions concerning use.* Will use of the identifiers be restricted to the purposes for which they were originally developed or, if used for other purposes, will these be known (how?) and consented to (how?)? Will information that is given be sold or made available to others? If made available to others, will there be constraints on use? Will this information be aggregated with information given for other purposes? If so, to what further uses might this consolidated information be put? Does one have any control over such uses — or the imputations involved in such uses?[199]

---

198 Gary Marx notes the number of communications he receives that are addressed to Georg Simmel, Emile Durkheim and Karl Marx, efforts he has made to deflect the intentions of marketers.

199 Consider how one's zip code could include or exclude one with respect to a range of benefits or burdens — higher real estate values, marketing targeting etc.

Aligning the values

We have endeavored to provide a broad articulation of the values at stake in the development of new technologies. We have sought to provide an account that will have traction for a wide spectrum of liberal democratic viewpoints, even though the policy traditions of different liberal polities have diverged considerably. Is it possible that out of this analysis some rapprochement may be achieved? We have some hope that this can be so. Although the current divergences track different strands and roots within the liberal tradition, they are more reflective of political responses to historical circumstances than of deep and intractable normative divisions.

At an earlier point in this study (Chapter III), we drew attention to James Q. Whitman's paper, "The Two Western Cultures of Privacy: Dignity versus Liberty".[200] As we saw, his history of the development of privacy in Europe and in the US nicely illustrates their divergence from a common history (prior to US Independence) as well as the possibilities for rapprochement.

Whitman contended that European conceptions of privacy view it as an aspect of dignity, whereas the US conception of privacy tends to see it as an aspect of liberty. But dignity is closely connected to liberty, both in the latter's sense as autonomy as well as in its social sense of political liberty. There is a well-trodden path from political liberty to personal autonomy (and back) and from the acknowledgment of human dignity to the recognition of autonomy and support for political liberty. It should not be impossible to develop an account of privacy (especially) that will reunite or at least bring into fruitful dialogue the seemingly divergent conceptions that have developed in the EU and the US. What will then be needed is the political will to bring them into more practical alignment. Of course, this would by no means constitute the completion of the larger task of bringing all or most liberal democracies into such practical alignment. In the case of some liberal democracies, such as Australia, if alignment between the US and the EU were to be achieved, then alignment with Australia would be all but complete. However, in the case of others such as India, there would likely be some considerable way to go.

We believe that some motivation for a more fruitful dialogue and the possibility for some rapprochement might be fostered by recognizing the ways in which specifically US values have been exploited. Deeply embedded in US culture is a concern about governmental overreaching that goes back to the situation that prompted the Declaration of Independence – the British exploitation of the colonies and the eventual refusal of those colonies to accept this. A great

---

200   James Q. Whitman, "The Two Western Cultures of Privacy: Dignity verses Liberty", *Yale Law Journal* 113 (2004).

deal of US culture since then – including the Constitutional Bill of Rights – can be explained as a project to curb federal (and later state) excess. "Liberty" is construed primarily in terms of freedom from certain governmental constraints. A "free market" – commercial liberty – has been seen as one of the guarantors of this. One consequence of this stance – which reached its apogee/nadir in *Lochner*[201] – has been the failure to see the extent to which prized individual liberty (and the autonomy which it fostered) could be subverted by institutional structures other than governmental ones. Because they have seen commercial freedom as a bulwark against governmental oppression, American citizens have been remarkably sanguine about the collection of their personal information by commercial companies – such as ChoicePoint and LexisNexis – believing this to be an expression of legitimate social freedom (liberty). What has not been appreciated is the extent to which – especially since 9/11 – governmental agencies have sought to avail themselves of these commercially collected personal data. What Americans have been loath to permit their government to collect, their government has purchased or otherwise obtained from private/commercial sources. Indeed, government agencies (especially the FBI) have been the largest customers of some personal data-gathering agencies.[202]

We believe that, were this commercial/governmental nexus better appreciated, there would be a serious concern about existing privacy arrangements and a much greater sympathy for the privacy arrangements that exist in EU countries. In the latter, no distinction is made between governmentally and commercially gathered personal data. Personal data are viewed as private, no matter who collects them.

It is true that because the events of 9/11 occurred on US soil there have been greater concerns about terrorism in the US than in European countries (though we should not forget Madrid, London and Glasgow). But this should impact only secondary issues, such as the length of time that legitimately gathered personal data can be retained or with whom such data can be shared. It should not have manifested itself in a different conception of what constitutes appropriately private data.

In general, it appears to us that the countries of the EU have a more rigorous and defensible conception of privacy than the prevailing one in the US (even if, as we also believe, they do not always manage to live up to their own expectations). At the same time it appears to us that the dominant conception of privacy in the US trades on a misunderstanding of the independence of government and commerce, and that were American citizens to be more aware of the ways in which their federal government obtains backdoor access to personal data there would be a significant rethinking of the status quo.

---

201   *Lochner v. New York*, 198 US 45 (1905).
202   This is developed at some length in Chapter VII.

We do not want to suggest that this will resolve all differences between the US and EU regarding the privacy of personal data. However, if the foregoing enhanced awareness were to be realized we believe that it would move us in the direction of some form of liberal rapprochement. To reaffirm Whitman's judgment: "There is no logical inconsistency in pursuing both forms of privacy protection: It is perfectly possible to advocate both privacy against the state and privacy against non-state information gatherers to argue that protecting privacy means both safeguarding the presentation of self, and inhibiting the investigative and regulatory excesses of the state."

IX. The Complexities of Oversight and Accountability

Assuming that there are ways of aligning the values that infuse various liberal democratic societies, there is still the important question of how to implement them within the diverse institutional arrangements in which they are or will be embedded.[1] What regulatory or oversight arrangements would be most suited to their realization?

Ideally, oversight arrangements within liberal societies will reflect their undergirding values. Oversight mechanisms should gravitate in the direction of structures that exemplify those values. In particular – and apposite to the concerns of this study – there will be a determination to ensure social arrangements in which personal accountability is both fostered and maximized.

However, as liberal writers from as far back as John Locke have realized, good social order requires more than reliance on individual good will and good judgment. Structural supports and incentives are needed. As civil society itself exemplifies – with its legislative, judicial and enforcement structures – the human condition requires more formalized approaches to social ordering than a *laissez faire* expectation will be able to deliver. Even so, more formalized approaches can differ significantly in the level of compulsion they involve. Although we noted in Chapter IV of this study the need and our desire to eventually move the US in the direction of creating an independent National Office of Data Protection, we understand that traveling this path is likely to be slow going. Recognizing this reality, our inclination here is therefore first of all to advocate for better development of what we term a "soft-law" approach to accountability. We recommend this tactic in conjunction with the development of appropriate legislation and enforcement mechanisms. Ultimately, in this area as elsewhere, there is a need for an integrated mix of soft law and coercive hard law.[2]

---

1 The Appendix provides some insight into the complexity of implementing common global standards for security and privacy, even within liberal democracies. Reviewing the variety of institutional structures and oversight mechanisms established by Australia and India gives perspective to the wider challenge beyond that posed by the EU–US focused discussion that has primarily occupied us.

2 We are mindful of T. H. Green's warning – albeit in a somewhat different context – that the precise measures to be adopted as social policy need to have regard to what people will tolerate: "to attempt a restraining law in advance of the social sentiment necessary to give real effect to it, is always a mistake." See T.H. Green, "Liberal Legislation and Freedom of Contract", (1881), published in *Works*, ed. R.L. Nettleship (London: Longmans, 1888), vol. 3, 265–86. The Appendix to this study adds grist to this mill. The countries reviewed clearly operate at different points of what could reasonably be construed as a security/privacy continuum. Recognizing that such variation exists requires sensitivity in establishing mechanisms for achieving the common end of desired protection for multiple stakeholders. Providing a flexible framework for choosing and implementing a menu of means, which we are attempting to articulate here, is essential to enabling success in what are often dissimilar settings.

A soft-law approach to enhancing oversight can serve as an intermediate mechanism for managing already legislated or regulated surveillance activities where guidance for achieving accountability is vague and where the political will to clarify confusion is not exercised. It can also be useful in cases in which emerging surveillance issues require clarification before hard law is explored and introduced. The recommendations that we make in this chapter focus specifically on increasing accountability in electronic surveillance, profiling and data mining efforts through the utilization of an accountability assessment tool that allows an organization to take stock of its surveillance operations, and through the creation of multi-disciplinary Techno-ethics Boards that could be worked into the process of building and applying surveillance programs.

Soft law and oversight

To date, hard law has served as a less-than-ideal means of achieving accountability in surveillance operations across levels of government in the US and elsewhere. Although such legal tools hold a necessary place among the approaches to monitoring and controlling surveillance operations, even after long and detailed public discussion (resulting in actual laws and codified rules of implementation for techniques such as wiretapping), they have nevertheless sometimes proven ineffective in certain areas of practice. Such failures of foresight have required the employment of effective practical oversight methods so that problems that have emerged can be identified and rectified. As a recent example, we need look no further than the dilemmas that the FBI has encountered with its surveillance activities. Although the USA PATRIOT Act authorized the use of National Security Letters (in effect, administrative subpoenas) by the FBI in investigations of international terrorism and foreign spying,[3] a Department of Justice Office of Inspector General (OIG) report indicated that in the earlier part of this decade there had been insufficient monitoring of the implementation of this strategy by its field officers. These findings raised questions of impropriety and illegality in the FBI surveillance activities that had been implemented.[4] It was fortunate that this step was taken by the OIG before problems found their way into the court system for settlement through judicial review of administrative operations. It is just this type of occurrence that points out the weaknesses and openings for abuse that can arise between the development of hard law and its resulting implementation. As we have previously noted, another problem that has

---

3 See Charles Doyle, "National Security Letters in Foreign Intelligence Investigations: A Glimpse of the Legal Background and Recent Amendments", *CRS Report for Congress Received through the CRS Web*, March 31, 2006, Order Code RS22406.
4 See Julie Hirschfeld Davis, "Lawmakers Warn FBI Over Spy Powers Abuse", Associated Press, March 21, 2007.

come to light involving the FBI regards the illegal soliciting of phone records between the years 2002 and 2006.[5] A Justice Department OIG report examines these issues in depth.

In other situations, developers of hard law can find themselves struggling to offer the insight required to do the job of managing surveillance activities effectively where newer forms of technology are involved. This too can result in problems developing during implementation that will not be rooted out early, and are left to be caught only after they have impacted upon the public. For example, unique expertise that exists among private sector professionals developing technology and innovations within certain fields, such as facial recognition imaging, enables them to operate at such high levels that without commensurate knowledge at their disposal government regulators and elected officials may find themselves challenged to create well-targeted and effective control mechanisms within legislation. Understanding these shortcomings, a more flexible means of ongoing oversight needs to be sought out that can provide stability as the development and eventual implementation of hard law requirements are pursued.

One approach to shrinking this gap in effectiveness and accountability is to heighten flexible governmental regulation and oversight activities through the exploration of "soft law". Discussions of soft law can be considered part of an emerging discourse on the overall value of regulation and governance that in academic circles has recently come to the foreground in a multi-disciplinary fashion.[6]

"Soft law" is an inexact term that covers a multitude of quasi-legislative, often non-binding instruments used to enhance government efforts to regulate service delivery areas. These instruments are intended to enable policy changes to emerge and harden through voluntary application and adherence in both confrontational and politicized atmospheres in which a wide array of players from public, private and non-governmental sectors are involved.[7] Such tools have been referred to broadly as "unofficial guidelines" that deliver information to those being regulated.[8]

---

5 See John Solomon and Carrie Johnson, "FBI Broke Law for Years in Phone Records Searches", *The Washington Post*, January 19, 2010, A01. Additional information about the role of the ill-fated White House Privacy and Civil Liberties Oversight Board in this case can be found in Allen Charles Raul's Letter to the Editor, "The Missing Privacy and Civil Liberties Oversight Board", *The Washington Post*, January 24, 2010.

6 See John Braithwaite, Cary Coglianese, and David Levi-Faur, "Editors' Introduction: Can Regulation and Governance Make a Difference?", *Regulation & Governance* 1 (2007): 1–7.

7 See Taco Brandsen, Marcel Boogers, and Pieter Tops, "Soft Governance, Hard Consequences: The Ambiguous Status of Unofficial Guidelines", *Public AdministrationReview* 66, no. 4 (July/August 2006): 546–53; and Peter Mameli, "Managing the HIV/AIDS Pandemic: Paving a Path into the Future of International Law and Organization", *Law & Policy* 22, no. 2 (April 2000): 203–24.

8 Brandsen, Boogers and Tops, 546.

Some of the instruments that communicate these ideas include codes of governance, quality standards, letters of advice, handbooks, manuals, reports, declarations, recommendations, guidelines and resolutions, to name a few.[9] They can be used to fill gaps between existing legal norms and implementation shortcomings, or to exercise initiative where no legal guidance currently exists. The result is intended to be a collaborative effort at ensuring quality service delivery by all parties involved in the process. Sometimes they can even result in the drafting of enhanced or new binding legal agreements, after a slow process in which policy diffusion is accepted and validated by the players affected.

In the case of government surveillance programs that rely on electronic surveillance, profiling or data mining activities, construction and delivery of mutually acceptable soft-law guidelines for their ongoing management and oversight would likely enhance reliability in the eyes of the public. Among the guidelines provided could be agreement to the need for time-driven audits and program evaluations, ongoing development of relevant performance measurement indicators, public reporting expectations on the results of the measurement systems created and the use of Techno-ethics Boards to resolve issues of ethical concern at the same time as developing advice for carrying out surveillance activities from the beginning of operations through to their conclusion. These ideas will be expanded on in later sections of this chapter.

Soft governance, trust and success

Although a soft law approach to oversight promises to relieve problems and pressures that have surfaced with surveillance programs, there are also quandaries to address well before such programs are productively employed. Quasi-legislative instrumentation of the nature discussed here is voluntarily adhered to and presents an uncertain edict to those on the receiving end. The intent is obvious; the authors of soft law believe that others should follow these "suggestions" and upgrade their operations accordingly. Yet there is no "authority" determining that action be taken. These are not new laws or regulatory rules that must be followed. They are something else: important enough to be taken note of, but ignored at one's own professional and personal peril.[10] Complicating matters further, soft law often suggests that new implementation norms be followed and attested to through self-reporting by the entities that are charged with providing a particular service. Yet, given

---

9   Brandsen, Boogers and Tops, 546; and Mameli, 203.
10   Brandsen, Boogers and Tops, 550–51.

that a gap exists between hard law and regulation and implementation in this sensitive policy area, a soft-law approach does offer opportunities to begin the process of deepening oversight.

The conundrum noted above frames a central discussion point that needs to be entertained here: how does soft law consistently result in something more than soft, or even abdicated, governance? Even if governance was found lacking before, does this yield a better answer? How can you be sure you have not let the fox guard the henhouse when you are counting on the fox to give you a daily testament to his/her actions? Given this problem, it is important to begin by noting that there are two sides to the coin of soft law.

The first side of the coin views the use of such unofficial guidelines as necessary tools for distributing new information to agents perceived as needing to update and improve their services, while still creating room for innovative practices to flourish. This view assumes good faith on the part of those being regulated to honestly address the suggested course of action, or to offer a better path to follow. The other side of the coin is one in which the suggested changes are not implemented due to a lack of comprehension or ability on the part of the receiver, a lack of leverage on the part of the sender or, worst of all, a desire by one or both to engage in fraud, waste or abuse by keeping loopholes open and outside eyes closed.[11] Both sides of the coin are relevant parts of the discussion about the implications that these instruments have for practitioners of soft law in complex environments.

When constructed well, the use of soft law to close gaps between hard law and implementation efforts opens doors to programmatic innovation and improvement. In practice it can also serve to increase accountability by mitigating administrative confusion and folly due to imprecise understandings of how to accomplish desired ends. However, it is also true that political stressors and unclear messages from central authorities regarding unofficial guidelines can drag down the potential gains of the process by causing those being regulated to stifle innovation and simply toe the line in order to avoid being cited during inspections and oversight – even though these are not clear infractions that they will be called on.[12] In such a scenario, the process that should lead to an active interchange of ideas between the center and the periphery that results in continuous improvement leads only to a game of follow-the-leader or, worse, resistance. Further still, poorly developed unofficial guidelines that do not provide effective problem resolution can also allow for abuse in application by practitioners.

---

11 See *Ibid*, 547–48, for a nice breakdown of possible paths that regulated parties can take in reaction to unofficial guidelines.
12 *Ibid.*, 550–51.

We should be striving to shut off the mains that allow illegal activity to flow forward by crafting useful soft law that also improves results. In the world of surveillance operations such a goal is of great value in and of itself, given the threats to liberty, privacy, and civil rights that hang in the balance. The question that emerges becomes: How can the relationship between those sending the soft forms of guidance and those receiving it be made to work better? Can we ensure transparency, attain accountability, improve effectiveness, prevent misconduct and enable innovation all at once? Can individuals charged with overseeing government surveillance programs help this development along in a front-to-back process? The answer seems to boil down to partnership and how to achieve it.

If creative interchange between all parties is what is desired then trust must be created to allow the interchange to flourish. That trust needs to run through the entire process. Trust must exist in the formulation of the quasi-legislative instruments and advice up front, as well as in the oversight process that is created afterward. However, it is hard to create that level of trust when there is resistance to oversight in sensitive areas of national security (e.g. involving surveillance operations, or any other activity).

Certainly, recent problems between the US CIA and its own OIG, where the former challenged the investigative methods of the latter in politically sensitive reviews, attest to this dilemma.[13] Indeed, at this time the agency has successfully managed to create two new positions to oversee the actions of its own internal watchdog![14] Yet oversight and accountability of national security activities must exist, and so the conundrum surrounding trust is laid bare. One undeniable finding from the CIA's situation so far is that at the very least a lack of trust in oversight operations distracts an organization from accomplishing its mission. Therefore, if government is to function effectively it seems clear that trust needs to be established early on rather than as an afterthought or as the result of a crisis.

In unpacking these concerns we first examine weaknesses that complicate the processes of soft law implementation and then note how particular forms of collaborative (rather than adversarial) interaction between oversight entities and those being inspected can improve accountability through enlightened, triangulated oversight. In conjunction with this analytical effort, addressing elements of performance measurement and management that can be used in constructing transparent and accountable partnerships between oversight agents and those being inspected must be further developed. Taken in total,

---

13   Mark Mazzetti and Scott Hane, "CIA Watchdog Becomes Subject of CIA Inquiry", *The New York Times*, October 12. 2007, A1, A25.
14   Greg Miller, "CIA Places Controls on Inspector General", *Los Angeles Times*, February 2, 2008, retrieved February 9, 2008 at: www.latimes.com/news/printedition/a/la-na-cia2feb02,1,6583760.story.

our recommendations represent an attempt to stretch the current discourse on regulating new and existing surveillance operations into less-well-traveled areas of thought. Here we are considering a role for oversight personnel in government surveillance that is essentially counter to the logic of reaction and punishment that often permeate such dialogues, and then offering tools to build trust between these parties and enhance capacity to achieve success. It may be hoped that the framework we lay out here can create room for free thinking and discussion about soft law in regard to better managing the surveillance society of the future.

Surveillance technology accountability assessment tool

What we initially offer below is a soft accountability assessment tool, designed to encourage those who engage in surveillance, data mining and profiling, to reflect on the nature and consequences of what they are doing. In many respects it particularizes the various means-end questions that we raised at an earlier stage of this discussion, linking those questions specifically to what we can characterize broadly as surveillance technologies.

The rationale behind such a tool is that within a liberal society we ought to encourage surveillance strategies that acknowledge, draw upon and foster the dignity of those who use them as well as those who are subject to them. This we do when we implement strategies that encourage individual accountability rather than presume a lack thereof. If these fail, harder strategies should be available to ensure that important liberal values are not left vulnerable and unprotected.

In addition, this tool brings focus to the channels by which oversight can be exercised on surveillance programs in order to grow accountability and ensure that reasonable levels of control and scrutiny are met.[15] Activities such as improved contracting requirements, audits, inspections, program evaluations and the establishing of ongoing performance measurement and management systems can all aid in this effort. Ingrained within the logic of the "new public management" is a heavy reliance on these practices to aid in the effective steering of government programs as they navigate the real world flows and barriers that cross the ship of state's path.[16] Bringing these concepts to bear on surveillance programs is both proper and necessary. However, though

---

15   See Donald F. Kettl and James. W. Fesler, *The Politics of the Administrative Process,* fourth ed. (Washington, D.C.: CQ Press, 2009), 9–12 for a useful description of the layers of government accountability.
16   Donald F. Kettl, *The Global Public Management Revolution,* second ed. (Washington D.C.: The Brookings Institution, 2005), 17–18.

it is essential to understand the methods for achieving and maintaining accountability, the way in which they are executed is also crucial to their success or failure.

Some of the modes of oversight noted above can be used upfront in the development of surveillance programs (strict requests for proposal and contracting requirements as well as formative program evaluations), while others can be carried out during the life of surveillance operations (performance and financial audits, interim and summative program evaluations and performance measurement reporting). The problems arise with the willingness and ability to build these activities into the entire lifespan of surveillance programs across levels of government. For instance, it is not at all clear that such oversight activities are legislatively mandated into government surveillance programs, or are expected to happen in regular patterns in all law enforcement and intelligence agencies. In addition, even if such oversight of surveillance operations is taking place, the degree to which there is regular reporting to elected officials and the public no doubt varies. Is such reporting simply desired and left to occur at the will of the agencies and oversight bodies involved, or mandated and handled in a more regimented fashion? It appears that, due to the need for operational secrecy, the former is the case more often than not, and this needs to change. The question is how to create change and enhance accountability without endangering the effectiveness of the surveillance program in question? To this end we offer a tool that will allow for self-assessment in order to begin the process of improvement in oversight and accountability activities. The tool can be used by practitioners of surveillance interested in growing accountability within their organizations, as well as those interested in carrying out oversight of these groups.

SURVEILLANCE TECHNOLOGY ACCOUNTABILITY ASSESSMENT TOOL*

1. What external agencies are charged with carrying out oversight of the creation and use of the surveillance technologies you work with? Please name the oversight agencies and explain their roles.

2. What internal units within your agency are charged with carrying out oversight of the creation and use of the surveillance technologies you work with? Please name the oversight units and explain their roles.

---

3. How is oversight carried out for the surveillance technologies you create and/or work with? Please explain for each condition noted below and differentiate by type of technology or method if necessary. Also, please provide documentation if possible.

    (A) Consultation with experts beyond the organization?

    (B) Closed/open meetings within the organization?

    (C) Closed/open hearings with the public or an oversight body?

    (C) Closed/open hearings with the public or an oversight body?

    (D) Program evaluations of success in implementation?

    (E) Performance audits for accountability?

    (F) Financial audits for accountability?

    (G) Investigations of fraud, waste, abuse and mismanagement?

    (H) Performance measurement and management system development and monitoring?

    (I) Other.

4. Are experts external to the organization utilized to ensure that the surveillance technology being constructed and/or utilized satisfies appropriate ethical concerns for development and implementation? Please explain. What about regulatory concerns? Please explain. What about statutory legal concerns? Please explain.

5. if your agency issues a Request for Proposal (RFP) for development of a surveillance technology, or employs a subcontractor for such a purpose, what accountability mechanisms (if any) do you require to be built into the resulting submissions to provide service? Please explain.

6. Does your agency establish performance measures in its contracts when dealing with the creation of surveillance technologies by outside parties?

    If yes, please explain the steps, benchmarks and measures that are to be built into the contract for provision of such services to determine if a vendor is effectively achieving desired outcomes.

    If you do currently establish performance measures in contracts in which surveillance technologies are created, how do you think this process could be improved?

    Finally, please explain what happens if a vendor or subcontractor fails to perform adequately.

7. Has your agency established performance measures for methods of using surveillance technologies?

   If yes, please explain the steps, benchmarks and measures that are used to monitor such services and determine if the process is effectively achieving desired outcomes. If necessary, differentiate by type of surveillance technology.

   If you do currently establish performance measures for methods of using surveillance technologies, how do you think this process could be improved?

   Finally, please explain what happens if performance is inadequate.

8. Does your agency have an articulated rule defining inappropriate and/or personal use as it relates to surveillance technologies? If yes, please explain and/or provide a copy of the rule(s).

9. Suppose that someone is suspected of misusing surveillance technology; is there a formal process for investigating and adjudicating the breach? If yes, please describe the process and/or provide a written copy of it.

10. What systems do you have in place for actively detecting potentially inappropriate or personal uses of your surveillance technologies? Please explain how this is done and whether you utilize an automatic alerting of suspected misuse systemically.

11. What systems do you have in place for passively detecting potentially inappropriate or personal uses of your surveillance technologies? Please explain how this is done and whether you have established a system of "whistle blowing" protections for people so that they feel they can alert managers and other relevant parties when misuse is detected.

12. If you work with third-party vendors to build and implement new or enhanced surveillance technologies, how does your agency ensure that the vendors and their employees do not re-use or re-sell the code for creating the resulting systems that are developed?

13. How does your organization secure proprietary algorithms for its surveillance technology activities? Please explain and/or provide written copy of the process.

14. If your organization procures third-party algorithms for surveillance technology do you have a process for checking the validity and reliability of the algorithms? If yes, please explain and/or provide written documentation of how this process would work.

15. If your organization procures data from third parties how are they securely stored when the original purpose for its use is completed? Please explain and/or provide written documentation of this process.

16. Considering how information and databases can be re-purposed and mined for an indefinite number of applications, how do you ensure that the systems you create do not exceed their legal or ethical boundaries after implementation? Please explain and/or provide written documentation of this process.

* This tool was developed by Peter Mameli and Vincenzo Sainato.

If the foregoing soft law questions are diligently asked and responded to by either internal or external parties, we might expect that liberal values will be sustained at an acceptable level. Nevertheless, it is acknowledged that a culture supportive of such an approach is not easily achieved or sustained, especially in times of apparent crisis. Therefore, various "harder" approaches may be required.

Harder approaches may take various forms. Some may take the form of (a) building ("hard-wiring") appropriate values into the surveillance technologies themselves; (b) imposing various administrative or civil penalties on those who disregard or contravene such values; and, as a last resort, (c) implementing criminal mechanisms in cases in which such values are egregiously flouted.

For a culture supportive of oversight and accountability to take root, trust must be ingrained among the parties involved. Trust can be developed in a number of ways at the beginning of operations when advice is crafted and distributed to surveillance practitioners in soft or hard forms. The first way is to utilize the accountability assessment tool provided to ease concerns that issues of oversight are being glossed over or ignored. An additional layer of protection offers the opportunity to bring a variety of parties together early in order to craft mutually agreeable guidance on surveillance operations. Such an approach could accomplish this goal in a number of ways. One is where the public sector defers to nongovernmental parties from the start in the development of said guidelines.[17] This is similar to a model of rulemaking that Weimer refers to as

---

17   Brandsen, Boogers and Tops, 552. For additional examples, see Steven Bernstein and Benjamin Cashore, "Can Non-State Global Governance Be Legitimate? An Analytical Framework", *Regulation & Governance* 1 (2007); 347–71.

"private rulemaking".[18] It is important to note that the private rulemaking model is different from the "negotiated rulemaking" approach, in which external parties engage in the process but do not control it, or the "agency rulemaking" approach, in which experts and advisory boards are invited in only to offer their insight and support.[19] Each of these approaches can create buy-in early on that will help to support positive relationships as problems arise in the future. However, neither fully addresses the negative reactions to oversight discussed earlier that follow once guidance is provided. Another level of trust needs to be developed in order to get over this hurdle, and it is incumbent on the personnel charged with such oversight to help facilitate that trust. But how can this goal be achieved when thinking in the world of inspection is colored by expectations of adversarial relationships rather than collaborative ones?

Techno-ethics Boards: guiding and growing accountability

One way to build trust between practitioners and oversight entities involved in responsibly carrying out surveillance operations is to explore the creation of a means of constructive engagement between the parties. However, the form of interaction must include those who would be involved in such a process from front to back. To achieve this purpose we suggest developing Techno-ethics Boards. Akin to Institutional Review Boards (IRBs) in universities, and Bioethics Boards in health settings, Techno-ethics Boards in law enforcement and intelligence settings would be charged with advising surveillance practitioners on how to go about implementing hard law and regulation on these matters. They would also be responsible for addressing ongoing questions of acceptable practice that would evolve as technology (and criminality) changes. However, as opposed to IRBs, they would not have the ability to prevent the implementation of official policies existing in surveillance programs. Due to the need for security and the sensitive nature of information that may need to remain protected even from the board itself, final calls on implementation would still remain with law enforcement and intelligence personnel directly involved with the activity. Hence, the board's oversight of said surveillance operations would still have limits. Yet this additional layer of scrutiny would no doubt aid in clarifying problems and halting preventable errors through the application of mutually accepted soft governance, built on soft law and soft instrumentation.

---

18   David L. Weimer, "The Puzzle of Private Rulemaking: Expertise, Flexibility, and Blame Avoidance in U.S. Regulation", *Public Administration Review* 66, no. 4 (July/August 2006): 569–82.

19   *Ibid.*, 569.

IRBs have been used within universities for decades to protect human and animal subjects from research abuses.[20] Although the protections of subjects and procedures for construction of a Techno-ethics Board to provide guidance to government surveillance programs might indeed differ from an IRB, it is a worthwhile enterprise to begin exploring. Could such a body stop abuses from happening in cases in which law enforcement and intelligence efforts are trying to protect national security but go beyond acceptable norms of practice? If so, it is at least worth the effort to take a close look at the possibilities for such boards. Why risk making the error of creating a new type of Stanley Milgram scenario, where both surveillance practitioners and their subjects become victims of overzealous observation efforts, if it can be short-circuited?[21]

As with federally mandated IRBs a Techno-ethics Board would require a spray of appropriate expertise and talent, with a recommended membership of at least five parties.[22] The members would include, at a minimum, one lawyer, one ethicist, one technology expert, one oversight expert and one field practitioner. As with IRB appointments, sensitive demographic information would also need to be taken into account in the development of a Techno-ethics Board in order to ensure that a balance of backgrounds is represented.[23] All may come from government circles, or none. However, there are complications that come with including non-governmental entities in security driven operations that make for a quandary in this regard. It is more likely that, given the information and the context under which surveillance reviews would take place, personnel would need to be drawn from across differing law enforcement agencies (and perhaps levels of government) more so than from outside parties. However, regardless of who is chosen to serve, the goal would not be to create a confrontational atmosphere but rather a mutually supportive one in which professionals concerned with surveillance and its implications could gather to address real-world implementation issues.

Evaluating the difficult choices that must be made by governmental entities, in which adherence to protections of civil rights and liberties are traded against the need for protection, is no easy task. Given that matters of security are at stake, parties granted entrance to a given Techno-ethics Board at any level of

---

20   Lawrence W. Neuman, *Social Research Methods: Quantitative and Qualitative Approaches*, fifth ed. (Boston, MA: Allyn and Bacon, 2003). Recently Christine Grady surfaced concerns about the effectiveness of IRBs in her article entitled, "Do IRBs Protect Human Research Participants?", *Journal of the American Medical Association* 304, no. 10 (2010): 1122–23. A key point made was that a lack of evidence exists allowing such a question to be resolved, and that new approaches to measure the work of IRBs must be developed. Clearly, the best way to build a Techno-ethics Board would be to benefit from the improvements in IRBs that will likely be generated from the ensuing discussion of Grady's comments.

21   Royce A. Singleton, Jr. and Bruce C. Straits, *Approaches to Social Research*, fourth ed. (NY and Oxford: Oxford University Press, 2005), 519.

22   Singleton and Straits, p. 530.

23   Elizabethann O'Sullivan, Gary R. Rassel, and Maureen Berner, *Research Methods for Public Administrators*, fifth ed. (US: Pearson Longman, 2008), 261.

government should not be chosen without careful consideration. As such, it is important to turn to those who have the levels of clearance necessary to be involved with these matters. One such participant could be found within OIGs. OIGs have already been awarded oversight responsibility at the federal level of surveillance operations in the US through the Foreign Intelligence Surveillance Act Amendments Act of 2008. Considering personnel from these organizations for inclusion within a Techno-ethics Board is therefore no great leap of logic. Now that the OIG concept is found in many countries around the world and operates at many levels of government, OIG members would constitute a good population to explore for the purposes of this discussion.

By taking some time to look at the theory that underpins OIGs in the US we can begin to see how one type of inspection and oversight body's personnel can be deployed constructively and justifiably in a Techno-ethics Board. If welded together carefully with other relevant members, surveillance practitioners can be provided with a feeling of comfort that they remain free to innovate solutions to crime and intelligence problems despite the existence of the board. Further still, they will feel that they have somewhere to go for support and guidance as the inevitable tough decisions arise.

Offices of Inspector General and Techno-ethics Boards

Over the last twenty years in the US, OIGs have become common entities on the government oversight landscape. With a growing realization that the costs of corruption and abuse devastate all sectors of society, there has been an increasing reliance on oversight bodies such as OIGs to step up and ensure accountability and transparency. Yet OIGs do not need to be only reactive in their work, seeking out wrongdoers for punishment after infractions have occurred. OIGs can also be proactive and can become engaged in constructive efforts to ensure that processes of change occur smoothly and, in select circumstances, that innovation is encouraged without fear. As such, there is an increasing role for OIGs in facilitating soft governance by engaging in a type of consultative capacity building that can enhance oversight.

OIGs have a straightforward purpose that is reflected in the US Association of Inspectors General's (AIG) explanation of its role:

> Accountability is key to maintaining public trust in our democracy. Inspectors general at all levels of government are entrusted with fostering and promoting accountability and integrity in government. While the scope of this oversight varies among Offices of Inspectors

General (OIGs), the level of public trust, and hence public expectation, embodied in these offices remains exceptionally high. The public expects OIGs to hold government officials accountable for efficient, cost effective government operations and to prevent, detect, identify, expose and eliminate fraud, waste, corruption, illegal acts and abuse.[24]

The AIG further notes that the qualifications and skills that should exist in these offices include:

> Skills needed to evaluate the efficiency, economy, and effectiveness of program performance within the OIG's area of responsibility . . . and state-of-the-art technical skills as needed such as computer auditing, detection of computer fraud, review of information technology design requirements, statistical sampling and analysis, factor analysis, trend analysis, systems and management analysis, undercover techniques, and covert surveillance.[25]

The language above casts OIGs in a reactive oversight role to those they are overseeing. This role has most recently been seen in the efforts of five federal OIGs to examine the President's Surveillance Program as required by the FISA Amendments Act of 2008.[26] However, the work of OIG staff does not have to be restricted to post-implementation analysis once they become part of a Techno-ethics Board. Where compliance efforts are voluntary to start with, rather than mandated, members of OIGs working on Techno-ethics Boards can take on more of a capacity-building face than they might normally do when they maintain their regular oversight watches. In fact, the skills identified above can be put to use in a multitude of ways so as to build operational understanding as part of a Techno-ethics Board's abilities. Expertise brought to the table by OIG personnel can enhance adherence to unofficial guidelines upfront, or can at least increase understanding of why such guidelines are being ignored or improved upon by the parties being asked to implement them. Under such a rationale, members of OIGs on Techno-ethics Boards could view themselves as being in position to get ahead of problems, rather than be trapped behind them. The parties being asked to conform to such soft-law advice would feel that they are being worked with, rather than being worked over. This would be especially true if surveillance practitioners were given time to comment on board advice prior to it being finalized and recommended. In addition, OIG personnel would not find themselves totally out of the loop as implementation (or the lack of it) moves forward. Finally, when OIG personnel on Techno-ethics Boards receive the self-

---

24 Association of Inspectors General, *Principles and Standards for Offices of Inspector General, 2004* (Philadelphia: Association of Inspectors General, 2004).
25 *Ibid*.
26 Offices of Inspectors General, *Unclassified Report of the President's Surveillance Program — Report No. 2009-0013-AS* (Washington, D.C., 2009).

reported attestations of those being overseen, they will have a much better understanding of what is being presented in the final documents. The ways in which they would then address issues of non-compliance and enforcement could proceed with greater understanding.[27] Similar benefits would likely be gained by all participating members of a Techno-ethics Board.

In this chapter of the study we are suggesting that creative soft-law approaches to government surveillance programs can supplement – and in some cases, obviate the need for – hard law by successfully addressing and containing abuses of power that occur through negligence, overzealous application or outright abuse. They can also aid in simply containing random error. The utilization of the Surveillance Technology Accountability Assessment Tool to assess current surveillance oversight practices, and the creation of intermediary bodies such as Techno-ethics Boards that can be used to provide advice and guidance at points between those who create hard law and regulation regarding surveillance operations and those who practice its implementation, are the touchstones of this offering. Future research in this area should, at the very least, explore: (1) The possibilities for such enterprises to be developed; (2) The procedural hurdles that would need to be overcome to make Techno-ethics Boards a reality in law enforcement settings across levels of government; (3) the selection of proper participants in such endeavors; and (4) the piloting of the Surveillance Technology Accountability and Assessment Tool in a variety of settings to determine its overall usefulness.[28]

---

27 See Christopher S. Decker, "Flexible Enforcement and Fine Adjustment", *Regulation & Governance* 1 (2007): 312–28, for some private sector examples.

28 Vincenzo Antonio Sainato's criminal justice dissertation, "Situational Surveillance Control" (City University of New York, John Jay College of Criminal Justice, 2009), explored the value of this tool as part of an ethnographic examination of the Branford, Connecticut, Police Department.

X. Recommendations

Here we articulate a series of recommendations with respect to the use of technologies identified in Chapters VI and VII that will bear on both accountability mechanisms and legal constraints/requirements. Although these recommendations focus particularly on the current US situation, they have clear implications for democratic polities writ large. To some degree, our recommendations arise out of a review of the EU experience which, even if flawed in the implementation, strikes us as formally well-developed.

(1) That steps be taken to make the American public more aware of the extent to which its expectations of privacy have been compromised.

The point here is that compromises of individual privacy — via the collection of data by government agencies — are not limited to newspaper exposés such as those undertaken by the *New York Times* but are a much more pervasive feature of contemporary life, engaged in not only by government agents but also by private information-gathering firms. Further, these gathered materials are in many respects vulnerable to unauthorized access by others via hacking, non-encryption of databases and so on. Despite the willingness of individuals to make private personal data known to others via social networking sites, we believe that if awareness of the extent to which personal data is available, accessible and collected is raised there will be an increased concern about privacy and the extent to which it has been compromised. One opportune time to initiate a more visible national discussion would be the next International Data Privacy Day, currently celebrated on January 28 of each year. If a coalition of data protection advocates, private sector organization representatives charged with protecting privacy, and public officials engages in the concerted promotion of such a dialogue, it will constitute a good first step in this direction. Using this opportunity to begin debate on the recommendations of this study would allow for a more focused conversation to surface on security and privacy than we have seen to date.

(2) That this process draw attention to the collapse of the traditional distinction between the commercial and governmental collection, use and retention of personal data.

We are particularly concerned – especially in the case of the US – that it be made known to what extent a traditional division between the government's access to private data and commercial access to that data – for legitimate commercial purposes – has broken down, in order that there will be increased concern about issues of privacy and the legitimate expectations that we may have concerning its protection. The relationship between these growing infringements on information privacy and the resulting uses of data by law enforcement, intelligence and national security organizations should be highlighted as a part of the ensuing activities.

(3) That this process also include a clear articulation of the values that inform personal privacy, and that this extend to expectations of privacy in public.

Along with an increased awareness of the extent to which private data are now widely available – and of course the various uses to which they are and may be put – we believe that there should also be more public articulation of the importance of privacy to individual and social wellbeing, to the preservation of dignity and to the securing of our identities as citizens in a liberal democracy. Recent revelations of how the New York Police Department's Intelligence Division has worked with the US CIA to engage in questionable domestic surveillance operations indicates how urgent it is to engage in this clarification.[1] Given the current terrorist threat environment, brighter lines of demarcation must be drawn to separate acceptable and unacceptable impacts on these values.

---

1 Adam Goldman and Matt Apuzzo, "With CIA Help, NYPD Moves Covertly in Muslim Areas", Associated Press New York, August 24, 2011, available at: http://abcnews.go.com/Politics/wireStory?id=14368992.

(4) That there be greater transparency regarding the kinds of data digitally collected, stored and used.

Transparency is a significant liberal value, and a liberal democratic society that lacks transparency is seriously compromised. Although we do not doubt the importance of the challenge posed by transnational crime and terrorism, we believe that responses to it should be conducted in ways that do not unnecessarily compromise the privacy, autonomy and ultimately the dignity of citizens. That will happen only if there is transparency about how those who represent us in government are transparent about what personal data are collected and how they are being used. To this end, we recommend that government agencies construct and publicly report on performance measurement indicators within their organizations' performance management systems that clearly display activities in these areas.

(5) That a national public discussion be initiated concerning the legitimate extent and limits of privacy, and of ways of protecting it.

We believe that social changes have significantly affected the nature and extent to which the privacy of citizens is construed and secured, especially (though not exclusively) as a result of technological advances and their deployment to counter crime and terrorism. We believe that these changes need to be publicly acknowledged and discussed as part of the deliberative life of a liberal democratic community.[2]

---

2   Recent discussions in the UK and the US about limiting the use of social media sites during times of political and social unrest display the need for early reflection on such concerns. Decisions relating to restricting free speech in these contexts could lead to a future erosion of privacy rights in others. Although they are not dominoes, many issues intersect with the way in which we construct our image of privacy. Waiting for riots and protests to break out in order to address such complexities is akin to closing the barn door after the horses have already fled. See James Robinson, "Twitter and Facebook Riot Restrictions Would Be a Mistake, Says Google Chief", Guardian.co.uk, August 27, 2011, available at: http://www.guardian.co.uk/media/2011/aug/27/twitter-facebook-riot-restrictions-eric-schmidt. See also Daniel B. Wood, "BART Puts Social Media Crackdown in Uncharted Legal Territory", *The Christian Science Monitor*, August 16, 2011, available at: http://www.csmonitor.com/USA/Justice/2011/0816/BART-puts-social-media-crackdown-in-uncharted-legal-territory.

(6) That the US federal government create a National Office of Data Protection (NODP) charged with responsibility for developing national policy guidelines and recommendations for associated legislation for the protection of personal data, and with responsibility for oversight of compliance with such guidelines and legislation.

In part because transnational crime and international terrorism are of national concern, and also in order to avoid a piecemeal approach to an issue of national concern, we believe that a federally funded and nationally focused office should be set up to gather data concerning privacy-related issues as well as to develop national guidelines and associated legislative provisions for the protection of privacy. This office should also oversee compliance with privacy legislation and guidelines, including implementation of program evaluations, audits, receipt of complaints and investigation of infringements of privacy rights.

(7) That these guidelines and recommendations for associated legislation take into account both commercial and governmental collection, use and retention of personal data.

The NODP should see its role as encompassing all significant compromises or threats to private data, whether they are initiated by government or commercial agencies. Especially given the nexus that has developed between commercial data gatherers and governmental interests, we do not believe that the existing conventions concerning governmental and commercial or private data gathering retain any significant validity. Only an NODP charged with recommending the regulation of both public and private sector entities involved with privacy matters can adequately satisfy this need.

(8) That the NODP recommend a graduated series of guidelines and legislative provisions for the oversight of personal data collection, use and retention by private and public agencies, including but not limited to soft-law self-regulatory measures, privacy enhancement of software, administrative measures designed to protect privacy and the identification of situations in which criminal penalties ought to be levied.

Recognizing that the social history of the US is distinct from that of the EU, we believe that a graduated system, commencing with voluntary compliance with general guidelines, is best suited to the former's distinctive culture. However, we also recognize that self-regulation has had only a modest success and that it needs to go hand in glove with more coercive options given the inevitability of noncompliance.

(9) That the NODP also have a communicative responsibility to ensure that the American public is aware of current concerns about the privacy of personal data, as well as recommendations concerning protection enhancements.

It is critical to liberal democratic communities that information concerning data protection issues and contemplated responses to them be made available in fora that enable public discussion to play an effective role in reviewing problem areas and responding to them. Although some watchdog and advocacy organizations already exist for that purpose, we believe that the NODP should have a responsibility of its own for ensuring that a public debate occurs.

(10) That the NODP explore the possibility of the formation of Techno-ethics Boards to provide practical oversight of institutional data collection and surveillance operations.

It is not enough to have a general office of data protection such as the NODP; a more focused body is required to provide immediate oversight of operations that threaten privacy boundaries, whether they are engaged in by government or commercial agencies. Internal to organizations, Techno-ethics Boards have the ability to engage in proactive troubleshooting and problem solving. Where programs of data collection, retention and use, as well as surveillance and profiling, are formed and implemented, the varied expertise of board members can help to achieve and maintain a successful equilibrium between security and privacy interests.

(11) That the NODP liaise with the European Data Protection Supervisor and those similarly situated in other liberal democratic countries to develop a set of standards that can be generally implemented within such societies.

As we have indicated, there is a rich international resource of experience in data protection and oversight to be drawn upon, and though we do not question the distinctive circumstances of social and political life in the US, we believe that there is a great deal to be learned – not only by the US – through developing firm links with similar kinds of agencies in other liberal democratic societies. However, we see the purpose of such liaisons not only to be one of mutual enrichment but also as a means whereby – in an increasingly connected world – universal standards for data collection, processing, dissemination and retention can be developed.

Appendix: Security and Privacy Institutional Arrangements: Australia and India

Australia

Introduction

The Commonwealth of Australia is a federation of states. The purposes for which the Commonwealth was established are known and (to an extent) codified within the Australian Constitution. There are a number of sections in the *Constitution of the Commonwealth of Australia* that explicitly establish a framework for law enforcement activities. These are:

Section 51:

(xxiv) The service and execution throughout the Commonwealth of civil and criminal process and the judgments of the courts of the States:

And:

Section 119: The Commonwealth shall protect every State against invasion and, on the application of the Executive Government of the State, against domestic violence.

Having said this, the Constitution is silent concerning which rights (if any) of citizens are meant to be served by the government. To that extent, there is a problem in discerning the limiting factors that ought to serve as the boundaries within which the Commonwealth pursues its law enforcement activities. In fact, the absence of a Bill of Rights (or some equivalent document) leaves this important question unresolved except in the following circumstances:

1. Where the Commonwealth legislates to create a right.

2. Where a treaty to which the Commonwealth is a party creates a right (as in the United Nations Declaration of Human Rights).

3. Where the courts discern that a right exists under the common law.

4. Where the courts find that a stated or implied right exists under the Constitution.

Although the Commonwealth has law enforcement powers and agencies, law enforcement is and remains primarily a state responsibility, and each of the states has its own police service (e.g. New South Wales Police, Victoria Police).

Moreover, although there is no Commonwealth Bill of Rights, one of the states (Victoria) and one of the territories (Australian Capital Territory (ACT)) have recently introduced human rights legislation (Victoria's Charter of Human Rights and Responsibilities Act 2006 and the ACT Human Rights Act 2004), and each requires that any statutory provisions that are found to be incompatible with the human rights thus established are identified and a justification provided. However, the relevant parliaments are not required to rescind legislation that is found to be incompatible with the relevant human rights legislation. Both the Victorian and ACT human rights legislation explicitly establish a human right to privacy. There are also moves afoot to establish a Commonwealth Bill of Rights (Brennan Commission of Inquiry).

Some of the key federal agencies relevant to security and privacy are those with law enforcement or defense functions and their respective oversight bodies.

Regarding law enforcement, key agencies include the Australian Federal Police (AFP), the Australian Crime Commission (ACC) and Australian Transaction Reports and Analysis Centre (AUSTRAC). The AFP has an analogous role to that of the FBI. For example, it is concerned with serious trans-jurisdictional crimes, such as organized crime and terrorism. The focus of the ACC is on organized crime; its functions include collecting and analyzing criminal intelligence and maintaining criminal intelligence systems. AUSTRAC gathers and analyzes information about financial transactions. The various Australian police databases of information, including those containing names and details of offenders (photographs, fingerprints, criminal history, outstanding warrants and, in many cases, DNA records), names of gun owners and missing persons, listed telephone numbers and addresses, stolen cars and names and aliases of "persons of interest" are linked through the National Police Reference System. An important oversight body is the Australian Commission for Law Enforcement Integrity (ACLEI). The main focus of ACLEI is the prevention, detection and investigation of serious corruption in federal law enforcement agencies. The Parliamentary Joint Committee on the Australian Crime Commission is the main oversight body for that organization.

Regarding intelligence and defense intelligence, key agencies include (in regard to intelligence) the Australia Security Intelligence Organization (ASIO), the Australian Secret Intelligence Service (ASIS) and (in regard to defense intelligence) the Defence Intelligence Organisation (DIO). ASIO is principally concerned with the domestic security of Australia; it has both an intelligence collection role and an assessment role. Security in this context means the protection of Australia from espionage, sabotage, attacks on the Australian defense system, terrorism and the like. ASIS collects intelligence outside Australia and engages in counter-intelligence. DIO assesses foreign intelligence and exists principally to support the Department of Defence. An important oversight body is the Inspector-General of Intelligence and Security (IGIS). The latter is an independent statutory officer responsible for ensuring that the activities of the intelligence and defense agencies are lawful and have appropriate regard to human rights, including privacy.

The Office of the Privacy Commissioner is the federal agency with responsibility for overseeing the operation of the key piece of Australian legislation pertaining to privacy, namely, the Privacy Act 1988. Most law enforcement agencies in Australia are covered by the Privacy Act, including the AFP and AUSTRAC, though the ACC is exempt. The intelligence and defense intelligence agencies are partially or completely exempt from the Privacy Act.

Some of the key pieces of federal legislation pertaining to security and privacy are: the Privacy Act 1988 (in partial fulfillment of Australia's international obligations under the International Covenant on Civil and Political Rights, which recognizes a basic right to privacy); the Anti-Money Laundering and Counter-terrorism Financing Act 2006; the Telecommunications (Interception and Access) Act 1979; the Telecommunications Act 1997; the Surveillance Devices Act 2004 (which outlines the circumstances under which surveillance devices can be used by federal law enforcement agencies in particular); the Freedom of Information Act 1982 (which outlines the rights of access of individuals to government-held documents); and the Data-matching Program (Assistance and Tax) Act 1990 (which regulates data-matching that makes use of tax file numbers). In addition, the states have legislation in relation to privacy and various associated agencies, such as privacy commissioners.

In Australia, no jurisdiction has legislated into existence a cause of action for invasion of privacy; rather, any such cause of action is part of the common law.

In Australia, identity theft is not currently a federal offense. However, it is a federal offense to dishonestly obtain or deal in personal financial information without the consent of the relevant person. Although the legislation clearly captures credit card fraud and a range of other kinds of identity fraud/theft, it is not clear that it is wholly adequate.

The Privacy Act 1988 and privacy principles

The Privacy Act gives effect to Article 17 of the International Covenant on Civil and Political Rights and the OECD's Guidelines on the Protection of Privacy and Transborder Flows of Personal Data. The Privacy Act regulates the collection, use, storage, disclosure and correction of personal information. The requirements of the Act include the National Privacy Principles (NPP) (applying to private sector organizations) and the Information Privacy Principles (IPP) (applying to Australian government agencies).

The NPP include principles that relate to: (1) collection of information by an organization from an individual (e.g. that information collection is lawful, not unreasonably intrusive or necessary for one of the organizations purposes); (2) use and disclosure (e.g. that information is lawful, is consented to by an individual, is necessary to prevent serious or imminent threat to life or is not sensitive); (3) data quality (e.g. that information is accurate and up-to-date); (4) data security (e.g. that information is protected from unauthorized access by members of an organization); (5) openness (e.g. that an organization make available how it manages personal information); (6) access and correction (e.g. that an individual has access to information about him/herself, unless providing access would be unlawful); (7) identifiers (e.g. that an organization not adopt as its own identifier of an individual an identifier of the individual that has been assigned by a government agency – to reduce the possibility of data-matching); (8) anonymity (e.g. that individuals have the option of not identifying themselves in transactions with organizations); (9) transborder data flows (e.g. a presumption against transfer of personal information to someone in a foreign country); and (10) sensitive information (e.g. a presumption against the collection of sensitive information).

The IPP consists of most of the principles constitutive of the NPP. However, it does so in the context of some requirements specific to Commonwealth agencies, for example, with respect to legal requirement for archival record-keeping. Moreover, there are some important differences. For example, unlike the IPP, under the NPP there is no obligation to destroy or de-identify personal information data when they are no longer required for the purpose for which they were originally collected.

Agencies

Office of the Privacy Commissioner (OPC)

The OPC's responsibilities include overseeing and monitoring compliance with the Privacy Act (see below), investigating breaches of the Data-matching Program (Assistance and Tax) Act 1990 and monitoring compliance with record-keeping requirements of the Telecommunications Act 1997. As a consequence, the OPC conducts audits and examines records, receives and investigates privacy complaints and enforces the acts through determinations and court proceedings.[1]

---

1 See *The Operation of the Privacy Act: Annual Report 2008–2009* (Canberra: Office of the Privacy Commissioner, 2009).

The Australian government has announced the establishment of a new statutory Office of the Information Commissioner, to be headed by an Information Commissioner, but which will also include the Privacy Commissioner and a Freedom of Information Commissioner (another new statutory office).

The Privacy Commissioner is a member of various government committees and groups, such as the National Identity Security Group, convened by the Attorney-General's Department, and in these fora the Privacy Commissioner provides advice on privacy issues.

The OPC is an active participant in various international organizations (e.g. the Organization for Economic Cooperation and Development (OECD)), fora (e.g. Asia Pacific Privacy Authorities Forum) and developments (such as the Asia Pacific Economic Cooperation (APEC) Data Privacy Pathfinder, endorsed by the APEC economies under the APEC Privacy Framework). Under the Pathfinder work plan are projects such as cooperation arrangements for cross-border cooperation on privacy enforcement and cross-border complaint handling.

The OPC makes numerous submissions to government and elsewhere. For example, in 2009 the OPC made a submission to the Australian Law Reform Commission's Review of Secrecy Laws on secrecy laws and, specifically, the interaction between secrecy laws and the Privacy Act.[2] Among other things, the OPC recommended "that where an agency identifies a need to require or authorize the handling of personal information where that handling would otherwise breach the Privacy Act, the agency should have a clear and appropriate policy basis for doing so."[3]

Although the Privacy Act applies to private sector organizations as well as Australian government agencies, the OPC does not have the power to conduct audits of organizations in the private sector. Moreover, there are various public sector agencies that are exempt from the Privacy Act and, therefore, from oversight and monitoring by the OPC (see below). Further, the Privacy Act does not cover businesses with less than AU$3 million annual turnover (i.e. the majority of businesses in Australia).

The federal Privacy Act does not cover state public sector agencies and the OPC does not have jurisdiction with respect to state public sector agencies. These come under the jurisdiction of the various state privacy commissioners (e.g. the Office of the Victorian Privacy Commissioner) and are covered by state legislation. However, not all the states have privacy legislation or privacy commissioners – Western Australia, for example, does not. Moreover, some state law enforcement agencies have partial exemptions from the relevant state

---

2   Australian Law Reform Commission, *Review of Secrecy Laws* – Issues Paper 34 (2009).
3   *Annual Report 2008–09*, 1.4.1.

privacy legislation. Victoria Police, for example, does not have to comply if it has a reasonable belief that, in relation to a particular matter, compliance would prevent it from conducting its law enforcement function.

In Australia, other than the Victorian Commissioner for Law Enforcement Data Security, there is no statutory body concerned exclusively with data security. At the federal level and in other states data security and, specifically, law enforcement data security are simply functions of oversight agencies with a wider remit. Thus the Crime and Conduct Commission in Queensland oversees the Queensland Police (and other Queensland public sector agencies) and has a concern with data security.

Australian Security Intelligence Organisation (ASIO)

As stated above, ASIO is responsible for protecting Australia and Australians from espionage, sabotage, attacks on the Australian defense system, terrorism and the like; moreover, ASIO has both an intelligence collection and an assessment role.

ASIO collects security information under warrant and only the Director-General of Security or an ASIO officer authorized by the Director-General can communicate such information. Under the Attorney-General's guidelines articulated in the Performance by the Australian Security Intelligence Organization of its Function of Obtaining, Correlating, Evaluating and Communicating Intelligence relevant to Security (including Politically Motivated Violence),[4] ASIO must: obtain intelligence in a lawful and timely manner; ensure the means it uses to obtain information are proportionate to the threat; and ensure such means are the least intrusive possible. The Director-General must ensure that any personal information held or disclosed is accurate and protected against unauthorized disclosure.

As noted earlier, ASIO's compliance with the Attorney-General's guidelines is overseen by the Inspector-General of Intelligence and Security (IGIS). The IGIS has access to ASIO's records and the power to require persons to answer questions and produce documents, including documents with a national security classification.

However, ASIO is exempt from the Privacy Act and the Freedom of Information Act. In addition, according to the Australian Law Reform Commission's Privacy Inquiry, the privacy rules that are applicable to ASIO do not cover persons who are not Australian citizens.[5] Nevertheless, these rules need to be updated with respect to classified (as opposed to security-classified) information in respect of the incorrect disclosure, accuracy of records and storage of personal information.

---

4   Available at: www.asio.gov.au/About/Content/AttorneyAcountability.aspx.
5   Australian Law Reform Commission, *Australian Privacy Law and Practice* – Report 108 (2008), 17–18,
available at: http://www.austlii.edu.au/au/other/alrc/publications/reports/108/.

Australian Crime Commission (ACC)

As stated earlier, the focus of the ACC is on organized crime. The ACC's projects have included drug trafficking, targeting suspected pedophile rings and determining the nature and extent of organized crime within particular ethnic communities. The ACC has the full array of intrusive law enforcement powers, such as the use of surveillance devices, the capacity to intercept telephone and internet communications, the use of undercover operatives and participation in controlled operations ("traps"). In addition, the ACC has special powers that are not possessed by normal law enforcement agencies, such as the power to issue a summons requiring a person to give evidence under oath and for which failure to attend may attract imprisonment. The ACC also provides strategic and tactical intelligence to other law enforcement agencies in relation to serious crimes, including murder and violent crime, drug trafficking, fraud, organized motor vehicle theft, organized gambling and extortion.

As mentioned above, the functions of the ACC include collecting and analyzing criminal intelligence and maintaining criminal intelligence systems. The ACC uses and adds to a variety of criminal intelligence data bases. It deploys techniques such as data-matching and profiling. As noted elsewhere in this study, profiling consists of developing a profile or set of characteristics of an offender or class of offenders, based in part on the characteristics of the types of person who commit that sort of crime. Once a profile has been developed, people with that profile can become the subjects of targeted investigations.

Besides data provided by law enforcement agencies, including surveillance sheets, the ACC relies on data from public records, company records, the National Missing Persons Unit, Telstra and government departments, including taxation, social security, health and immigration. Although provision of confidential information by these government departments is at the discretion of these departments, it is usually provided after a request from the ACC. Such requests are made for the general reason that the information will assist investigation into a serious crime.

As noted above, the Privacy Act does not apply to the ACC; nor does the Freedom of Information Act. The ACC does not destroy but archives information that it possesses, including transcripts and files on individuals. Although there are audit trails on ACC activities, it is not known whether there are procedures in place that actually monitor these audit trails.

In the area of organized crime, there is some tension between privacy and law enforcement. This tension is especially evident with respect to third parties — that is, persons who are not themselves suspects but who communicate with suspects whose communications are being intercepted.

Whether the ACC should be exempted from the Privacy Act is an issue that remains unresolved. One option here would be to bring the ACC under the Privacy Act, albeit *qua* law enforcement body (as is the case with, for example, the AFP). This would ensure it was subject to privacy principles, except to the extent that its law enforcement activities exempted it. The view of the Australian Law Reform Commission is that the ACC should remain exempt from the Privacy Act, but that: "The Australian Crime Commission (ACC) in consultation with the Privacy Commissioner, should develop and publish information-handling guidelines for the ACC and the Board of the ACC."[6] In that case, the Parliamentary Joint Committee on the Australian Crime Commission should then monitor the ACC's compliance with these guidelines.

Australian Transaction Reports and Analysis Centre (AUSTRAC)

Under the Anti-Money Laundering and Counter-terrorism Financing Act 2006 and related legislation, AUSTRAC concerns itself with money laundering activities. Illegal activities, such as drug dealing and major fraud, generate large amounts of money that need to be laundered. In addition, terrorist organizations seek to acquire and transfer funds illegally. One of the most effective ways of combating these kinds of crime is to follow the so-called money trail. AUSTRAC gathers and analyzes data about financial transactions, and the data – at least in the first instance – is of two kinds: (1) data automatically provided in accordance with the law, including domestic bank and other transactions over $10,000, and international telegraphic transfers over $5,000; and (2) data furnished in suspect transaction reports (STRs) on the basis of the discretionary judgment of bank tellers and the like. These discretionary judgments are based on "suspicious" behavior or situations – for example, someone apparently structuring deposits in such a manner as to avoid the $10,000 reporting requirement. (STRs go directly to law enforcement agencies as well as AUSTRAC.)

These two kinds of data are entered on AUSTRAC's database and might provide the starting point for an investigative analysis by AUSTRAC. This investigative analysis might make use of computerized techniques such as data-matching and may have recourse to additional data, the precise nature of which is not publicly available. Should the investigative analysis fail to allay the suspicions that triggered the initial interest of AUSTRAC, the material is handed over to law enforcement agencies for further investigation. For example, frequent deposits in a number of banks by person X of sums of $9,900 might trigger an investigative analysis that, because X is unemployed, yields no apparently legitimate explanation. Alternatively, X might turn out to be a legitimate businessman whose product retails for $9,900.

---

6   Australian Law Reform Commission, *Australian Privacy Law and Practice*, Recommendation 37–1 (a).

AUSTRAC has some accountability mechanisms covering its activities. For example, its staff will have had their security checked and they have limited access to data. Moreover, their activities leave audit trails, and the Director of AUSTRAC has the right to follow these trails. Nevertheless, although there are audit trails, there is evidently no set of procedures in place that will routinely follow those trails. According to the OPC website's list of agencies audited, the OPC has to date not audited AUSTRAC. Moreover, state agencies that have access to AUSTRAC data may not have the same accountability under the Privacy Act as federal agencies. Specifically, it is unclear whether some state agencies are using AUSTRAC-provided data for purposes other than those provided for in the anti-money laundering and counter-terrorism financing legislation.

In some instances AUSTRAC's capacity to provide data and intelligence in relation to money laundering might be undermined by recent technological developments. For example, money launderers who use smartcard technology, high-level encryption and the internet might be able to make international transfers that bypass the financial system and that are not able to be intercepted.

India

India is a sovereign democratic republic and a British Commonwealth nation; in fact, this former British colony is the world's largest democracy. India has the parliamentary form of a union government and a unitary construction of twenty-eight states – each with its own elected legislative assembly – and seven union territories administed by India's union government.

The Constitution of India provides for various Fundamental Rights (e.g. the protection of life and personal liberty (Article 21)) that cannot be removed by the state and that are legally enforceable against the state. The Constitution is interpreted by the Supreme Court, and states that "the law declared by the Supreme Court shall be binding within the terrority of India" (Article 141).

India's legislative authority is divided between the legislative assemblies of the states that form the Union of India and Parliament (the central government). In some matters both have concurrent legislative powers. Section 246 of India's 1950 Constitution makes policing the responsibility of its states (entries 1 and 2 in List II of the Seventh Schedule of India's 1950 Constitution).

Although each of India's states has legislative authority, the structure and practices of the states' police forces either are governed by India's Police Act 1861 or use that Act to provide the model for their own police procedure manuals. That Act, together with the operation of other legislation, such as the Indian Penal Code 1860, the Indian Evidence Act 1873 and the Criminal Procedure Code 1973 (which replaced the Criminal Procedure Code 1861), apply throughout India, imposing uniformity on Indian policing.

From time to time special laws to combat terrorism have been enacted in India. The Terrorist and Disruptive Activities Prevention Act (TADA) was in use for quite a few years. However, strong and vociferous criticism about its draconian provisions and misuse in some cases led to it being repealed. The Prevention of Terrorists Activities Act (POTA) was introduced in its place, but that Act is also no longer in force, and there is now no special law to deal with terrorist activities in India.

Policing and security organizations

India's state police organizations are headed by Director-Generals/Inspector-Generals of police, accountable to the relevant state government for the administration and good order of the state's police.

Unfortunately, even after Independence (1947), the original hierarchical police structure in India has remained substantially intact, and no serious attempt has been made to redefine the relationship between the police and the government so as to better reflect the needs of a democracy. In particular, it needs to be made clear that the police are not simply an instrument of the executive arm of government – and, as such, highly susceptible to corruption – but are rather servants of the law and protectors of the rights of the ordinary citizenry.

Numerous commentators and commissions of inquiry have made this point, including the Kerala Police Commission (1959), the National Police Commission (1981) and the National Commission to Review the Working of the Constitution of India (2002). The National Police Commission, for example, recommended that the investigative wing of the police needed to be insulated from external pressures and that the head of the police be given statutory tenure.

Each state has a Criminal Investigation Department (CID). The CIDs are divided into two cohorts, the Crime and the Intelligence branches. Each of these CID branches is headed by an Inspector-General or an Additional-Inspector-General.

In the "Company" era, some of India's great cities (Calcutta, Madras, Bombay) modelled the police of London rather than the paramilitary forces of the British colonies. Such police forces were commanded by a Commissioner of Police who was accountable not to the state government via an Inspector-General but directly to the local city government. Police Commissioners enjoyed judicial-executive authority and licensing and regulatory powers that elsewhere lay within the purview of District Magistrates. In modern India, larger cities or developmental areas with special needs have established Commissionerates.

Thus Cyberabad Commissionerate is located in India's "Silicon Valley", the home of its burgeoning IT industry. This go-ahead Commissionerate is conducting a community-interactive Culture Change Management Programme, a staple of which is "constabulary empowerment", intended to overcome the limitations of an "officer-centered" orientation imposed by the 1861 Police Act. Constables have been retitled constable officers, and up-skilled as problem-solving "police executives", with ownership of and responsibility for the execution of solutions to policing problems, including the use of IT.

The central government's responsibility under the Constitution includes protecting states against internal disturbances, guarding India's 14,090 km land border, providing security for infrastructure and the like.

As well as "communalism" (inter-communal violence) and foreign invasion (China in 1962 and Pakistan in 1965), India faces cross-border terrorist incursions and its own internal terrorism, including: (a) leftist extremism (Naxalism) in the states of Andhra Pradesh, Maharashtra, Chattisgarh, Jharkhand, Bihar, Madhya Pradesh, Orissa and West Bengal; (b) ethnic extremism in Nagaland, Tripura, Assam and Arunachal Pradesh in furtherance of demands for seccession from India; and (c) religious extremism in Kashmir, where the Muslim majority variously seek the freedom (Azadi) of an independent Kashmir state, or unification with Pakistan. In recent years Kashmir-based terrorist groups, notably Lashkar-e-Toiba, have undertaken terrorist attacks in Indian cities outside Kashmir, such as Mumbai and Delhi. Moreover, although the majority of the population of India still do not possess computers, mobile phones and the like, there has nevertheless been an exponential growth in the use of communication and information technology and, as a consequence, a steady increase in cybercrime. Among other things, the Indian government is concerned about cyber-terrorism, cyber-warfare and transnational crime involving the use of communication and information technology.

The central government's Minister for Home Affairs has a coordinating function, and may deploy central government police assets to assist states. Such central government police asset forces as have been deployed lifted Indian police numbers to 1.8 million and include: the Central Reserve Police Force (CRPF); the Border Security Force (BSF); the Indo-Tibetan Border Police (ITBP); the Central Industrial Security Force (CISF); and the Railway Protection Force (RPF).

Central government organizations concerned with intelligence and investigation include: the Central Intelligence Bureau (CIB) (which focuses on domestic intelligence); the Research and Analysis Wing (RAW) (which focuses on external intelligence, e.g. regarding India's conflict with Pakistan); the Central Bureau of Investigation (CBI); the National Investigation Agency (NIA); and the National Crime Records Bureau (NCRB). Other central government agencies include the Bureau of Police Research and Development and the Institute of Criminology and Forensic Science.

Privacy and information technology

In India, the right to privacy derives from the Constitution as well as the common law of torts. The Constitution does not explicitly recognize the right to privacy but, as mentioned earlier, Article 21 provides for personal liberty, and in various cases this has been taken by the Supreme Court to include the right to privacy against the state.[7] For example, in *Kharak Singh v State of Uttar Pradesh* (1964) the Supreme Court held that police intrusions into a person's house were a violation of privacy. In *People's Union for Civil Liberties v. Union of India* 1997, the Supreme Court held that telephone tapping by the government under the Telegraph Act 1885 constituted an infringement of privacy. On the other hand, in the course of these judgments it emerged that the right to privacy is not absolute and can be lawfully infringed for the prevention of crime and disorder. So telephone tapping on the part of law enforcement agencies is permissible under certain conditions.

In India, there is no right against infringements of privacy by individuals or other private entities. Nevertheless, individual or other private entities who infringe one's privacy are subject to the common law of torts and are liable for damages. That said, there is no privacy protection authority in India.

Data protection is not explicitly provided for in the Constitution and, under its right in the Constitution to legislate in relation to matters not enumerated in the relevant lists, the central government has taken it to be an appropriate matter for its involvement. Accordingly, it has enacted the Information Technology Act 2000. The Act declared computers and computer networks to be protected systems and provided for various civil and criminal offenses in respect of unauthorized computer access, theft of computer data, destruction of data, corruption of data, fraud and so forth. The Act also set up various regulatory authorities, such as the Cyber Regulations Appellate Tribunal. However, there is no data protection authority in India. On the other hand, computerization has a long way to go in India, including among law enforcement agencies, and there are few comprehensive electronic data bases of a kind that would enable efficient and effective data mining or profiling.

---

7   This also enables India to partially fulfil its international obligations under the International Covenant on Civil and Political Rights, in which a basic right to privacy is recognized.

In 2009 the Information Technology (Amendment) Act 2008 was enacted in part to address not only domestic and regional security issues, including cyber-crimes and cyber-terrorism, but also, and very importantly, the security concerns of foreign companies in respect of India's huge outsourcing industry. The Act provides penalties for various new cyber-crimes (e.g. cyber-terrorism and identity theft), the recognition of new electronic documents (e.g. electronic documents with e-signatures) and enhanced data security (e.g. for intermediaries (any person who receives, stores or transmits data for another person such as internet service providers)).

In 2007, the Indian IT software and services industry generated export revenues of US$31.3 billion (especially from the US and EU) and it is projected to increase this to US$60 billion in 2010.[8] Approximately 80% of the world's 500 largest companies outsource some of their sales calls, technical help desks, payroll management and/or legal services etc. to India.[9]

As already noted, data security is not simply a general concern, it constitutes a specific threat to India's billion-dollar IT outsourcing industry and, as a consequence, the Indian government and the Indian IT industry have joined forces with respect to legislation and on several other fronts to deal with the data security issue. The Information Technology (Amendment) Act 2008 is part of the legislative response. The establishment by NASSCOM of the Data Security Council of India (DSCI) is part of the broader institutional response – in this instance, a self-regulatory part, for the DSCI represents software companies and the business process outsourcing (BPO) and related IT industries. The function of DSCI is to establish, disseminate, monitor and enforce privacy and data protection standards for India's IT and outsourcing industry. Obviously, enforcement is the key challenge for DSCI; however, it is difficult to see how what is essentially a voluntary organization can effectively enforce the standards it establishes other than by the threat of expulsion.

The Information Technology Act 2000 and the Information Technology (Amendment) Act 2008 do not set out a comprehensive set of specific privacy and data protection principles in the manner of, say, the EU Directive or the OECD Guidelines. Rather, they require the use of "reasonable security practices and procedures", defined in terms of practices and procedures designed to protect sensitive personal information from unauthorized access, damage, use, modification, disclosure etc. However, the DSCI has recommended that companies implement one of the available industry-recognized standards such as the OECD

---

8   N. Saravade (former Director of Cyber Security and Compliance, National Association of Software and Service Companies (NASSCOM)), available at: http://nationalskillsregistry.com/winwin.html.)
9   See: http:www.reuters.com/article/idUSSP4999820060207.

Privacy Principles for Information Management Systems. Nevertheless, there is no requirement that companies undergo an audit to verify the existence and efficacy of the controls they have in place to meet any such industry standards.

The Indian government and, specifically, the Department of Information Technology (DIT) within the Ministry of Communication and Information Technology, has embarked on an ambitious program of e-governance known as the National eGovernance Program (NeGP) in relation to the delivery of citizen services at both central and state government levels. This program faces prodigious challenges in terms of resources, skill levels of personnel and IT infrastructure and equipment, although more so in some states than in others. The implementation of such an e-governance program in the Indian social and institutional context brings with it multiple security threats. Recognizing the vulnerability of the information infrastructure to e-crime and e-corruption, the government has formulated an information security policy, established various bodies (notably the Computer Emergency Response Team (CERT-In) within the DIT) and required that the government's information infrastructure be subjected to an annual audit. However, the focus of this audit is principally on the technical IT systems and networks.

Agencies

Central Bureau of Investigation (CBI)

The CBI is a central government agency and India's leading investigative agency. The CBI's remit is very wide and includes criminal offenses, corruption and national security matters. It can investigate offenses anywhere in India. The authority of investigation of the CBI can be exercised only on a specific case-by-case authorization by the concerned state government or High Court.

Its power to investigate derives from the Delhi Special Police Establishment Act 1946, according to which it can investigate offenses only in the union territories. However, its jurisdiction can be extended by the central government to the states, provided that the state government in question consents.

Cases investigated by the CBI include: those involving employees of the central government or in which a central government organization is involved; breaches of the Official Secrets Act involving the central government; serious breaches of import/export laws; trans-jurisdictional crime; serious fraud; and organized crime.

The Director of the CBI is a Director General of Police within the Delhi Special Police Establishment. Although the CBI is an administrative unit of the Ministry of Home Affairs, in operational and policy terms the CBI is controlled by the

Department of Personnel and Training under a Minister of State who reports to the Prime Minister. However, the investigation by the CBI of offenses under the Prevention of Corruption Act 1988 (involving offenses by public officials of the central government) are controlled by the Central Vigilance Commission (CVC). The CVC also oversees the CBI.

Central Vigilance Commission (CVC)

The CVC is a statutory body established under the Central Vigilance Commission Act 2003. It consists of a Central Vigilance Commissioner and two Vigilance Commissioners. Its principal focus is corruption within central government agencies. It identifies high-risk areas, conducts surprise inspections to detect system deficiencies and malpractices and advises in relation to, and monitors the workings of, anti-corruption systems. It also receives written complaints on any allegation of corruption or misuse of office and recommends appropriate action. It does not act on anonymous complaints. However, the identity of the complainant is not revealed and the CVC can direct the relevant authorities to provide protection to complainants.

The CVC is not an investigative agency. Rather, as noted above, it initiates and supervises corruption investigations carried out by the CBI or by departmentally based vigilance (anti-corruption) officers. An exception is the investigation by the CVC of civil works/contracts (e.g. scrutiny of financial controls, reasonableness of prices, tender documents, purchase manuals, filing systems etc.), conducted by the Chief Technical Examiners Organization, which is the Technical Wing of the CVC.

The CVC has undertaken a number of new initiatives including naming corrupt officials on its website ("naming and shaming"), and enhancing transparency in high-risk areas such as procurement by the use of new information technology processes, for example, e-bidding and e-payment.

Intelligence Bureau (IB)

The IB has an intelligence-gathering and an assessment function. It also has a preventive function, for example, in developing security checks, vetting procedures and the like. The IB is focused on internal security, including public order, terrorism, sabotage of vital installations, VIP security and counter-intelligence, and it is an administrative unit of the Ministry of Home Affairs. However, the Director of IB is a member of the Joint Intelligence Committee (which is in turn responsible to the Cabinet Secretariat in the Prime Minister's Office) and has the authority to brief the Prime Minister should the need arise. The IB operates at both central and state levels (through state IBs). However, as noted above, the internal security situation in many states is precarious.

In the interest of national security, the IB's intelligence-gathering operations include human intelligence (e.g. from informants, mail and telephone interception). Moreover, in the interest of national security, the central government – and, therefore, the IB – has the authority to intercept, monitor and block access to electronic information and to monitor and collect data identifying a person, computer system or location to or from which the communication was transmitted.

Infringements of human rights on the part of law enforcement and intelligence agencies, including the IB, can be investigated by the National Commission on Human Rights. However, it is unclear what specific oversight mechanisms there are in relation to the IB.

Research and Analysis Wing (RAW)

RAW is India's foreign intelligence agency. RAW has intelligence-gathering, counter-intelligence and assessment functions. It also engages in covert operations, for example, covert assistance to the ANC, training members of Liberation Tigers of Tamil Eelam and attempts to limit the supply of military hardware to Pakistan. Although its personnel and their numbers are shrouded in secrecy, it is estimated to employ around 10,000 agents.[10]

The head of RAW is the Secretary (Research) in the Cabinet Secretariat, which is part of the Prime Minister's Office. In relation to operational matters the Secretary (Research) reports to the National Security Advisor. In addition to its headquarters in Delhi, RAW has a number of regional offices and various overseas stations.

Infringements of human rights on the part of law enforcement and intelligence agencies, including RAW, can be investigated by the National Commission on Human Rights. However, the activities of RAW are highly secretive and it is unclear what specific oversight mechanisms exist in relation to RAW.

---

10 "RAW: India's External Intelligence Agency", Council on Foreign Relations, available at: http:www.dfr. org/publications/17707/.

References

Alessandro Acquisti, "Privacy in Electronic Commerce and the Economics of Immediate Gratification", *Proceedings of the ACM Conference on Electronic Commerce*, 2004, 21–29.

Peter Adey, "Surveillance at the Airport: Surveilling Mobility/Mobilising Surveillance", *Environment and Planning A* 36, no. 8 (2004): 1365–80.

Per Ahlmark, "How Democracy Prevents Civic Catastrophes", at: http://www.unwatch.org/speeches/demcat.html.

David S. Alberts, *The Unintended Consequences of Information Age Technologies: Avoiding the Pitfalls, Seizing the Initiative* (Diane Publishing Co. 1996).

Anders Albrechtslund, "Online Social Networking as Participatory Surveillance", *First Monday* 13, no. 3 (March 2008).

Anita Allen, *Uneasy Access: Privacy for Women in a Free Society* (Totowa, NJ: Rowman and Littlefield, 1988).

Fritz Allhoff, Patrick Lin, James Moor and John Weckert, "Ethics of Human Enhancement: 25 Questions and Answers", *Studies in Ethics, Law, and Technology* 4, no. 1 (2010), doi: 102202/1941-6008.1110.

Monique Altheim, "The Review of the EU Data Protection Framework v. The State of Online Consumer Privacy in the US", EDiscoveryMap, March 17, 2011, at: http://ediscoverymap.com/2011/03/the-review-of-the-eu-data-protection-framework-v-the-state-of-online-consumer-privacy-in-the-us.

Anthony G. Amsterdam, "Perspectives on the Fourth Amendment", *Minnesota Law Review* 58 (1974): 349, 428–34.

Anon., "Data Protection in the European Union", at: http://ec.europa.eu/justice/policies/privacy/docs/guide/guide-ukingdom_en.pdf.

Anon., "US Identity Fraud Rates by Geography", I.D. Analytics Inc., San Diego, CA, February 2007.

Anon., "Phishing", at: http://www.antiphishing.org/.

Anon., "A History of Surveillance in New York City", available at: http://www.notbored.org/nyc-history.html.

Anon., "Armin Meiwes", at: http://en.wikipedia.org/wiki/Armin_Meiwes.

Anon., "NSA Warrantless Surveillance Controversy", at: http://en.wikipedia.org/wiki/NSA_warrantless_surveillance_controversy.

Anon., "Trojan Horse", (Computing) at: http://en.wikipedia.org/wiki/Trojan_horse_(computing).

Anon., "Gyges Goes Surfing", at: http://www.applelust.com/one/index.php?option=com_content&task=view&id=35.

Leonora LaPeter Anton, "Airport Body Scanners Reveal All, But What About When It's Your Kid?", *St Petersburg Times*, July, 17, 2010.

Francisco Rojas Aravena, "Human Security: Emerging Concept of Security in the Twenty-First Century", *Disarmament Forum* 2 (2002), at: http://www.unidir.ch/pdf/articles/pdf-art1442.pdf.

David Archard, "Freedom not to be Free: The Case of the Slavery Contract in J. S. Mill's *On Liberty*", *Philosophical Quarterly* (October, 1990): 453–465.

Nicholas S. Argyres, "The Impact of Information Technology on Coordination: Evidence from the B-2 'Stealth' Bomber", *Organization Science* 10, no. 2 (1999): 162–80.

Association of Inspectors General, *Principles and Standards for Offices of Inspector General, 2004* (Philadelphia: Association of Inspectors General, 2004).

Association of the Bar of the City of New York and Center for Human Rights and Global Justice, *Torture by Proxy: International and Domestic Law Applicable to "Extraordinary Renditions"*, New York: ABCNY & NYU School of Law, 2004; available at *The Record* (of the Bar Association of the City of New York), 60 (2005): 13–193.

Australian Law Reform Commission, *Australian Privacy Law and Practice – Report 108* (2008), available at: http://www.austlii.edu.au/au/other/alrc/publications/reports/108/.

_____, *Review of Secrecy Laws* – Issues Paper 34 (2009).

C. Babcock, "Data Data Everywhere", *Information Week Global CIO*, January 9, 2006.

Neera Kapur Badhwar (ed.), *Friendship: A Philosophical Reader* (Ithaca: Cornell University Press, 1993).

_____, "Friends as Ends in Themselves", *Philosophy and Phenomenological Research*, 48 (1987):1–23.

Annette Baier, "Some Virtues of Resident Alienage", in *Virtue*, NOMOS XXXIV, ed. John W. Chapman and William Galston (New York: NYU Press, 1992), 291–308.

Al Baker, "Police Seek a Second Zone of High Security in the City", *The New York Times*, March 31, 2009, available at: http://www.nytimes.com/2009/04/01/nyregion/01kelly.html.

Wade H. Baker, Alex Hutton, C. David Hylender, Christopher Novak, Christopher Porter, Bryan Sartin, Peter Tippett, M.D., PhD and J. Andrew Valentine, *2009 Data Breach Investigations Report*, Verizon Business, available at: http://securityblog.verizonbusiness.com, viewed 14 December 2009.

Michael Barkun, "Religion and Secrecy After September 11", *Journal of the American Academy of Religion* 74, no. 2 (2006): 275–301.

S.I. Benn, *A Theory of Freedom*, Cambridge, UK: Cambridge University Press, 1988, 296–97.

S.I. Benn and G.F. Gaus, "Public and Private – Concepts in Action", *Public and Private in Social Life*, ed. S.I. Benn and G.F. Gaus (NY: St. Martin's Press, 1983), 3–27.

Craig Bennell and Shevaun Corey, "Geographic Profiling of Terrorist Attacks",*Criminal Profiling: International Theory, Research, and Practice*, ed. R. N. Kocsis (Totowa, NJ: Humana Press, 2007), 201.

Colin J. Bennett, "Cookies, Web Bugs, Webcams and Cue Cats: Patterns of Surveillance on the World Wide Web", *Ethics and Information Technology* 3 (2001): 197–210.

Jeremy Bentham, *The Works of Jeremy Bentham,* ed. John Bowring (London: W. Tait, 1838–43), vol. 4.

_____, *The Panopticon Writings*, ed. Miran Bozovic (London: Verso, 1995).

Vera Bergelson,. "The Right to Be Hurt. Testing the Boundaries of Consent", George Washington Law Review 75 (2007): 165 at: http://works.bepress.com/vera_bergelson/4.

Steven Bernstein and Benjamin Cashore, "Can Non-State Global Governance Be Legitimate? An Analytical Framework", *Regulation & Governance* 1 (2007); 347–71.

Calvin Biesecker, "TSA to Test Additional Personal Imaging Systems at Airports", *Defense Daily*, 8/21/2007.

Francesca Bignami, "European versus American Liberty: A Comparative Privacy Analysis of Anti-Terrorism Data-Mining", *Boston College Law Review*, 48 (May 2007): 609.

_____, "Privacy and Law Enforcement in the European Union: The Data Retention Directive", *Chicago Journal of International Law* 8 (2007): 233.

Dan Bilefsky, "Data Transfer Broke Rules, Report Says", *The New York Times*, September 28, 2006.

Charles Black, *Decision According to Law* (New York: Norton, 1981).

Edwin Black, *IBM and the Holocaust*, Time Warner Paperbacks (2001).

William Blackstone, *Commentaries on the Laws of England*, (c. 1765) vol. IV: *Of Public Wrongs* (169), Boston: Beacon Press, 1962, 189.

Philip Bobbitt, "The Warrantless Debate over Wiretapping", *The New York Times*, August 22, 2007.

Sissela Bok, *Secrets: On the Ethics of Concealment and Revelation* (New York: Vintage, 1989).

Danah Boyd, "Friendster and Publicly Articulated Social Networking", Conference on Human Factors and Computing Systems, April 24–29, Vienna, Austria, 2004, available at: http://www.danah.org/papers/CHI2004Friendster.pdf.

Taco Brandsen, Marcel Boogers and Pieter Tops, "Soft Governance, Hard Consequences: The Ambiguous Status of Unofficial Guidelines", *Public Administration Review* 66, no. 4 (July/August 2006): 546–53.

William F. Brennan, Jr., "The Bill of Rights and the States", *NYU Law Review* 61 (1986): 535.

Ian Brown, Terrorism and the Proportionality of Internet Surveillance, *European Journal of Criminology* 6, no. 2 (2009): 119–134.

Allen Buchanan, *Justice, Legitimacy, and Self-Determination: Moral Foundations for International Law* (New York: Oxford University Press, 2004).

Bureau of Justice Statistics, *State and Local Public Defender Offices*, at: http://bjs.ojp.usdoj.gov/index.cfm?ty=tp&tid=215.

Holger Bürk and Andreas Pfitzmann, "Digital Payment Systems Enabling Security and Unobservability", *Computers & Security* 8, no. 5 (1989): 399–416.

B. Buzan, O. Wyer, J.D. Wilde, and O. Waever, *Security: A New Framework for Analysis* (Boulder, CO: Lynne Rienner Publishers, 1997).

Norman S. Care, "On Fixing Social Concepts", *Ethics*, 84 (October, 1973), 10–21.

Leslie Cauley, "NSA Has Massive Database of Americans' Phone Calls", *USA Today*, May 11, 2006, A1.

Samidh Chakrabarti and Aaron Strauss, "Carnival Booth: An Algorithm for Defeating the Computer-Assisted Passenger Screening System", *Electrical-Engineering-and-Computer-Science* (2002), at: http://www.mit.strathmore.edu/NR/rdonlyres/Electrical-Engineering-and-Computer-Science/6-805Fall-2005/4E484655-6947-4D60-B789-32F2FFE6199A/0/caps.pdf.

David W. Chapman and Roger A. Boothroyd, "Threats to Data Quality in Developing Country Settings", *Comparative Education Review* 32, no. 4 (1988): 416–29.

Robert N. Charette, "Why Software Fails", IEEE Spectrum, at http://spectrum.ieee.org/computing/why-software-fails, viewed January 3, 2010.

Kim-Kwang Raymond Choo and Russell G. Smith, "Criminal Exploitation of Online Systems by Organized Crime Groups", *Asian Journal of Criminology* 3, no. 1 (June 2008).

John Christman, "Autonomy in Moral and Political Philosophy", *Stanford Encyclopedia of Philosophy*, at: http://plato.stanford.edu/entries/autonomy-moral/.

Roger Clarke, "Human Identification in Information Systems: Management Challenges and Public Policy Issues", *Information Technology & People*, 7 (1994): 6–37, at: http://www.anu.edu.au/people/Roger.Clarke/DV/HumanID.html.

_____, "Person-Location and Person-Tracking: Technologies, Risks and Policy Implications", *Information Technology & People* 14, no. 2 (Summer 2001): 206–31.

William J. Clinton & Albert Gore, Jr., A Framework for Global Electronic Commerce, July 1, 1997, available at http://www.technology.gov/digeconomy/framewrk.htm.

Simon A. Cole and Michael Lynch, "The Social and Legal Construction of Suspects", *Annual Review of Law and Social Science*, December 2006, vol. 2, 39–60 (doi: 10.1146/annurev.lawsocsci.2.081805.110001).

Committee on Assessment of Security Technologies for Transportation, National Research Council, *Assessment of Millimeter-Wave and Terahertz Technology for Detection and Identification of Concealed Explosives and Weapons* (Washington, DC: National Academies Press, 2007), at: http://books.nap.edu/openbook.php?record_id=11826&page=R1.

William E. Connolly, *The Terms of Political Discourse* (Princeton, NJ: Princeton University Press, 1993).

Austin Considine, "Will New Airport X-Rays Invade Privacy?", *The New York Times*, October 9, 2005, TR3.

Maureen Cooney, *Report to Congress on the Impact of Data Mining Technologies on Privacy and Civil Liberties* (Washington, DC: DHS, July 6, 2006), at: http://www.dhs.gov/xlibrary/assets/privacy/privacy_data_%20mining_%20report.pdf.

Daniel Cooper, Henriette Tielemans, and David Fink, "The Lisbon Treaty and Data Protection: What's Next for Europe's Privacy Rules?", *The Privacy Advisor*, at http://www.cov.com/files/Publication/44dd09f7-3015-4b37-b02e-7fe07d1403f4/Presentation/PublicationAttachment/8a89a612-f202-410b-b0c8-8c9b34980318/The%20Lisbon%20Treaty%20and%20Data%20Protection%20What%E2%80%99s%20Next%20for%20Europe%E2%80%99s%20Privacy%20Rules.pdf.

CyberSource Corporation, "Online Fraud Report: Online Payment Fraud Trends, Merchant Practices and Benchmarks", available at: http://www.cybersource.com.

Omar Dahbour, "Advocating Sovereignty in an Age of Globalization", *Journal of Social Philosophy*, 37, no. 1 (2006): 108–26.

Richard C. Dales, "A Medieval View of Human Dignity", *Journal of the History of Ideas* 38, no. 4 (October–December 1979): 557–72.

Stephen L. Darwall, "Two Kinds of Respect", *Ethics*, 88 (1) (1977): 36–49.

Eric Dash, "City Data Theft Points Up a Nagging Problem", NY Times, June 10, 2011, B1 and 7.

Julie Hirschfeld Davis, "Lawmakers Warn FBI Over Spy Powers Abuse", *The Washington Post*, March 21, 2007, available at: http://www.washingtonpost.com/wp-dyn/content/article/2007/03/21/AR2007032100225.html

Dionysios S. Demetis, "Data Growth, the New Order of Information Manipulation and Consequences for the AML/ATF Domains", *Journal of Money Laundering Control* 12, no. 4 (2009): 353–70.

Department of Commerce Internet Policy Task Force, "Commercial Data Privacy and Innovation in the Internet Economy: A Dynamic Policy Framework", 2010, available at http://www.commerce.gov/sites/default/files/documents/2010/december/iptf-privacy-green-paper.pdf.

Department of Homeland Security, *Privacy Office – Privacy Impact Assessments (PIA)*, at: http://www.dhs.gov/files/publications/editorial_0511.shtm.

_____, *Agreement Between the United States of America and the European Union on the Processing and Transfer of Passenger Name Record (PNR) Data by Air Carriers to the United States Department of Homeland Security (DHS) (2007 PNR Agreement)*, at: http://www.dhs.gov/xlibrary/assets/pnr-2007agreement-usversion.pdf.

_____, *A Report Concerning Passenger Name Record Information Derived from Flights between the U.S. and the European Union*, at: http://www.dhs.gov/xlibrary/assets/privacy/privacy_pnr_report_20081218.pdf.

_____, Office of Inspector General, *Survey of DHS Data Mining Activities*, OIG-06-56 (Washington, DC: Office of Information Technology, August 2006), at: http://www.dhs.gov/xoig/assets/mgmtrpts/OIG_06-56_Aug06.pdf.

Gijs de Vries, "Terrorism, Islam and Democracy", EurActiv.com, March 4, 2005, at: http://www.euractiv.com/en/security/gijs-vries-terrorism-islam-democracy/article-136245.

Geoff Dean, "Criminal Profiling in a Terrorism Context", in R. N. Kocsis (ed.), *Criminal Profiling – International Theory, Research, and Practice*, Humana Press, 2007.

Judith DeCew, *In Pursuit of Privacy: Ethics and the Rise of Technology* (Cornell UP, 1997), 48.

Christopher S. Decker, "Flexible Enforcement and Fine Adjustment", *Regulation & Governance* 1 (2007): 312–28.

Tamara Dinev, Paul Hart, and Michael R. Mullen, "Internet Privacy Concerns and Beliefs about Government Surveillance – An Empirical Investigation", *Journal of Strategic Information Systems* 17 (2008): 214–33.

Charles Doyle, "Administrative Subpoenas and National Security Letters in Criminal and Foreign Intelligence Investigations" (Congressional Research Service, 2005), at: http://www.fas.org/sgp/crs/natsec/RL32880.pdf.

_____, "National Security Letters in Foreign Intelligence Investigations: A Glimpse of the Legal Background and Recent Amendments", March 31, 2006, *CRS Report for Congress Received through the CRS Web*. Order Code RS22406.

George F. du Pont, "The Time Has Come For Limited Liability For Operators of True Anonymity Remailers in Cyberspace: An Examination of the Possibilities and Perils", *Journal of Technology Law & Policy* 6, no. 2 (2001): 175–218, available at: http://grove.ufl.edu/~techlaw/vol6/issue2/duPont.pdf.

Christopher Drew, "Military Is Awash in Data From Drones", *The New York Times*, January 11, 2010.

Michael Dusche, "Human Rights, Autonomy and National Sovereignty", *Ethical Perspectives*, 7, no. 1 (2000): 24–36.

Ronald Dworkin, *Taking Rights Seriously*, London: Duckworth, 1977.

_____, "Rights as Trumps", in *Theories of Rights*, ed. Jeremy Waldron, Oxford: OUP, 1984, 153–67.

Editorial, "The Cloud Darkens: As Online Security Threats Grow, Companies and Government Are Scarily Unprepared", NY Times, June 30, 2011, A26.

EDRI-gram, January 14, 2009, at: http://www.edri.org/edri-gram/number7.1.

Electronic Frontier Foundation, "Facebook's New Privacy Changes: The Good, the Bad and the Ugly", December 9, 2009. Available at: http://www.eff.org/deeplinks/2009/12/facebooks-new-privacy-changes-good-bad-and-ugly.

Yuval Elovici, Bracha Shapira, Mark Last, Omer Azzfrany, Menahem Friedman, Moti Schneider and Abraham Kandel, "Content Based Detection of Terrorists Browsing the Web Using an Advanced Terror Detection System", in *Terrorism Informatics: Knowledge Management and Data Mining for Homeland Security*, Hsinchun Chen, Edna Reid, Joshua Sinai, Andrew Silke, and Boaz Ganor (eds), 2008, Springer, 365–384.

Izhak England, "Human Dignity from Antiquity to Modern Israel's Constitutional Framework", *Cardozo Law Review* 21 (May 2000): 1903–27.

Amitai Etzioni, *The Responsive Society* (San Francisco: Jossey-Bass, 1991).

_____, *The Spirit of Community: Rights, Responsibilities and the Communitarian Agenda* (New York: Crown Publishers, 1993).

_____, *The Limits of Privacy* (New York: Basic Books, 1999).

EUROPA Press Releases Rapid, "European Commission Sets Out Strategy to Strengthen EU Data Protection Rules", IP/10/1462, Brussels, November 4, 2010, at: http://europa.eu/rapid/pressReleasesAction.do?reference=IP/10/1462.

European Data Protection Supervisor (EDPS), "Opinion of the European Data Protection Supervisor on the Evaluation report from the Commission to the Council and the European Parliament on the Data Retention Directive (Directive 2006/24/EC)", May 31, 2011, available at: http://www.edps.europa.eu/EDPSWEB/webdav/site/mySite/shared/Documents/Consultation/Opinions/2011/11-05-30_Evaluation_Report_DRD_EN.pdf.

EU Privacy Commission, "Summary of the Opinion on the Transfer of Personal Data by SCRL SWIFT Following the UST (OFAC) Subpoenas", at: http://www.privacycommission.be/communiqu%E9s/summary_opinion_Swift_%20 28_09_2006.pdf.

European Union Fundamental Rights Agency, "Data Protection in the EU: the role of National Data Protection Authorities – Strengthening the fundamental rights architecture in the EU II", 2010, available at: http://fra.europa.eu/ fraWebsite/research/publications/publications_en.htm.

Mark Evans (ed.), Special Issue: New Directions in the Study of Policy Transfer, *Policy Studies*, 30, no. 3 (June 2009): 237–402.

Kareem Faheem, "Surveillance Will Expand To Midtown, Mayor Says", *The New York Times*, October 4, 2009, available at: http://www.nytimes. com/2009/10/05/nyregion/05security.html.

W. Fan, L. Wallace, S. Rich and Z. Zhang, "Tapping the Power of Text Mining", *Communications of the ACM* 49, no. 9 (September 2006): 77–82.

Lyle Fearnley, "Signals Come and Go: Syndromic Surveillance and Styles of Biosecurity", *Environment and Planning A*, 40 (2008): 1615–1632.

FTC, *Privacy Online: Fair Information Practices in the Electronic Marketplace (2000)*, available at: http://www.ftc.gov/reports/privacy2000/privacy2000. pdf.

FTC Preliminary Staff Report, "Protecting Consumers in an Era of Rapid Change: Proposed Framework for Business and Policy Makers", December 2010, available at: http://www.ftc.gov/os/2010/12/101201privacyreport.pdf.

Federal Trade Commission, "Protecting Consumer Privacy in an Era of Rapid Change", December 2010, available at: http://www.ftc.gov/ os/2010/12/101201privacyreport.pdf.

Lukas Feiler, "The Legality of the Data Retention Directive in Light of the Fundamental Right to Privacy and Data Protection", *European Journal of Law & Technology* 1, no. 3 (2010), available at: http://ejlt.org//article/view/29/75.

Joel Feinberg, *The Moral Limits of Criminal Law,* vol. 3: *Harm to Self* (New York: Oxford University Press, 1986).

_____, *The Moral Limits of Criminal Law,* vol. 4: *Harmless Wrongdoing* (New York: Oxford University Press, 1988).

_____, "Autonomy, Sovereignty, and Privacy: Moral Ideals in the Constitution", *Notre Dame Law Review* 58 (1983): 445–92.

Stephen E. Feinberg, "Privacy and Confidentiality in an e-Commerce World: Data Mining, Data Warehousing, Matching and Disclosure Limitation", *Statistical Science* 21, no. 2 (2006): 143–54.

A. Felt and D. Evans, "Privacy Protection for Social Networking APIs", presented at Web 2.0 Security and Privacy 2008, Oakland, Ca, May 22, 2008. Available at: http://www.eecs.berkeley.edu/~afelt/privacybyproxy.pdf.

Glen W. Fewkes, "New Public Surveillance Technologies May Alter Fourth Amendment Standards", *Government Security News*, available at: http://www.gsnmagazine.com/

L. Fields, "Parfit on Personal Identity and Desert", *Philosophical Quarterly* 37 (1987): 432–41.

Peter Fleischer, "Protecting Privacy on the Internet", December 19, 2007, available at: http://www.youtube.com/watch?v=2IKBke1puFw.

James E. Fleming, "Securing Deliberative Democracy", *Fordham Law Review*, 72 (2004): 1435–76.

Michael Foucault, *Discipline & Punish: The Birth of the Prison*, translated by Alan Sheridan (NY: Vintage Books 1977) pp. 195–228.

FoxNews, "FBI Ditches Carnivore Surveillance System", at: http://www.foxnews.com/story/0,2933,144809,00.html.

Leslie P. Francis, Margaret P. Battin, Jay Jacobson, and Charles Smith, "Syndromic Surveillance and Patients as Victims and Vectors", *Bioethical Inquiry* 6 (2009):187–195.

Charles Fried, "Privacy", *Yale Law Journal* 77 (1968): 475–93.

T. Frieden, "Report: FBI Wasted Millions on 'Virtual Case File'", *CNN* (2005, February 3), viewed September 7, 2009, at: http://www.cnn.com.

Carl J. Friedrich, "Secrecy Versus Privacy: The Democratic Dilemma", in J. Roland Pennock and John W. Chapman (eds.), *Privacy*, NOMOS XIII (NY: Atherton Press, 1971), 105–20.

Alan E. Fuchs, "Autonomy, Slavery, and Mill's Critique of Paternalism", *Ethical Theory and Moral Practice*, 4, no. 3 (September, 2001): 231–251.

Christian Fuchs, *Social Networking Sites and the Surveillance Society* (Salzburg Förderung der Integration der Informationswissenschaften, 2009).

James J. Fyfe, "Structuring Police Discretion", in John Kleinig (ed.), *Handled with Discretion: Ethical Issues in Police Decision Making* (Lanham, MD: Rowman and Littlefield, 1996), 183–205.

W.B. Gallie, "Essentially Contested Concepts", *Proceedings of the Aristotelian Society*, 56 (1955–56), 167–98 (also in *Essentially Contested Concepts and the Historical Understanding*, London: Chatto and Windus, 1964, ch. 8).

EOS Gallup Europe – FLASH EB No 147, *Data Protection in the European Union: Report*, p. 5, available at: http://ec.europa.eu/public_opinion/flash/fl147_data_protect.pdf.

Simson Garfinkel, *Database Nation: The Death of Privacy in the 21st Century* (O'Reilly Media, December 2000).

Gerald Gaus, *The Modern Liberal Theory of Man* (New York: St Martin's Press, 1983).

Ruth Gavison, "Privacy and the Limits of Law", *Yale Law Journal*, 89 (January, 1980): 442.

John A. Gentry, "Doomed to Fail: America's Blind Faith in Military Technology", *Parameters* (2002–03): 88–103.

Robert Gerstein, "Intimacy and Privacy", *Ethics* 89, no. 1 (1978): 76–81.

Rebecca Givner-Forbes, *Steganography: Information Technology in the Service of Jihad* (Singapore: The International Centre for Political Violence and Terrorism Research, A Centre of the S. Rajaratnam School of International Studies, Nanyang Technical University, 2007).

Erving Goffman, *Stigma: Notes on the Management of Spoiled Identity* (1963; Englwood Cliffs, NJ: Prentice Hall, 1968).

Adam Goldman and Matt Apuzzo, "With CIA Help, NYPD Moves Covertly in Muslim Areas", Associated Press New York, August 24, 2011, available at: http://abcnews.go.com/Politics/wireStory?id=14368992.

Harry Goldstein, "Who Killed the Virtual Case File?", *IEEE Spectrum*, available at: http://lrv.fri.uni-lj.si/~franc/COURSES/VP/FBI.pdf viewed 5 July 2009.

Benjamin Goold, "Privacy Rights and Public Spaces: CCTV and the Problem of the 'Unobservable Observer'", *Criminal Justice Ethics* 21, no. 1 (2002): 24.

_____, "Open to All? Regulating Open Street CCTV", *Criminal Justice Ethics* 25, no. 1 (2006): 11–12.

Siobhan Gorman, Yochi J. Dreazen, and August Cole, "Insurgents Hack U.S. Drones, $26 Software Is Used to Breach Key Weapons in Iraq; Iranian Backing Suspected", *The Wall Street Journal*, December 17, 2009, A1.

Christine Grady, "Do IRBs Protect Human Research Participants", *Journal of the American Medical Association* 304, no. 10 (2010): 1122–23.

Stephen Graham and David Wood, "Digitizing Surveillance: Categorization, Space, Inequality", *Critical Social Policy* 23, no. 2 (2003): 227–48.

John N. Gray, "The Contestability of Concepts", *Political Theory*, 5 (1977), 330–48.

_____, "On Liberty, Liberalism, and Essential Contestability", *British Journal of Political Science*, 8 (1978), 385–402.

Mary W. Green, *The Appropriate and Effective Use of Security Technologies in U.S. Schools, A Guide for Schools and Law Enforcement Agencies*, Sandia National Laboratories, September 1999, NCJ 178265.

Hyman Gross, "Privacy and Autonomy", in *Privacy*, NOMOS XIII, ed. J. Roland Pennock and John W.Chapman (NY: Atherton Press, 1971).

Ralph Gross and Alessandro Acquisti, "Information Revelation and Privacy in On-line Social Networks (The Facebook Case)", *Proceedings of the ACM Workshop on Privacy in Electronic Society (WPES)*, November 2005, available at: http://www.heinz.cmu.edu/~acquisti/papers/privacy-facebook-gross-acquisti.pdf.

Jeremy Gruber, RFID and Workplace Privacy, on the NATIONAL WORKRIGHTS INSTITUTE website, http://www.workrights.org/issue_electronic/RFIDWorkplacePrivacy.html, 23 December 2009.

Niels Haering, Péter L. Venetianer, and Alan Lipton, "The Evolution Of Video Surveillance: An Overview", *Machine Vision and Applications* 19 (2008):279–90.

Arun Hampapur, Lisa Brown, Jonathan Connell, Sharat Pankanti, Andrew Senior and Yingli Tian, "Smart Surveillance: Applications, Technologies and Implications", available at: http://domino.research.ibm.com/comm./research_projects.nsf/pages/s3.pubs.html/$FILE$/PCM03.pdf.

David Harris, "Profiling: Theory and Practice", *Criminal Justice Ethics* 23, no. 2 (2004): 51–57.

Edward Hasbrouck, "What's in a Passenger Name Record (PNR)?", at: http://hasbrouck.org/articles/PNR.html.

Ragib Hasan and William Yurcik, "Beyond Media Hype: Empirical Analysis of Disclosed Privacy Breaches 2005-2006 and a DataSet/Database Foundation for Future Work", at: http://wesii.econinfosec.org/draft.php?paper_id=37.

Susan Hekman, *Private Selves, Public Identities, Reconsidering Identity Politics* (University Park, PA: Penn State University Press, 2004).

Richard Hillestad, James H. Bigelow, Basit Chaudhry, Paul Dreyer, Michael D. Greenberg, Robin C. Meili, M. Susan Ridgely, Jeff Rothenberg and Roger Taylor, *Identity Crisis: An Examination of the Costs and Benefits of a Unique Patient Identifier for the U.S. Health Care System* (Santa Monica, CA: Rand, 2008), available at: http://www.rand.org/content/dam/rand/pubs/monographs/2008/RAND_MG753.pdf.

Albert O. Hirschman, *Exit, Voice, and Loyalty: Responses to Decline in Firms, Organizations, and States* (Cambridge, MA: Harvard University Press, 1970).

John D. Hodson, John D. "Mill, Paternalism and Slavery", *Analysis* 41 (January, 1981): 60–62.

Bruce Hoffman, "Defining Terrorism", in *Terrorism and Counterterrorism: Understanding the New Security Environment*, ed. Russell D. Howard, Reid L. Sawyer, Natasha E. Bajema (third ed., NY: McGraw-Hill, 2009), 4–33.

Jennifer Daw Holloway, "The Perils of Profiling for the Media: Forensic Psychologists Speak Out on the Lessons Learned from the Washington-Area Sniper Case", APA Online at: http://www.apa.org/monitor/jan03/perils.html.

Chris Jay Hoofnagle, Jennifer King, Su Li, and Joseph Turow, "How Different Are Young Adults from Older Adults When it Comes to Information Privacy Attitudes and Policies?", available at: http://papers.ssrn.com/sol3/papers.cfm?abstract_id=1589864.

Patrick Howard, Chief Information Security Officer, Nuclear Regulatory Commission, "Creating a Culture of Security — Top 10 Elements of an Information Security Program", available at: www.govinfosecurity.com/webinarsDetails.php.

IAPP (International assoc. of Privacy Professionals), "House Subcommittee Hears Call for ECPA Updates", June 25, 2010, at: https://www.privacyassociation.org/.../2010_06_25_house_subcommittee_hears_call_for_ecpa_updates.

Information Policy Division, UK Ministry of Justice, Circular 2011/01, "Council Framework Decision on the protection of personal data processed in the framework of police and judicial cooperation in criminal matters 2008/977/ JHA", Jan. 25, 2011, available at: http://www.justice.gov.uk/publications/ docs/data-protection-framework-decision-circular.pdf.

Julie C. Innes, *Privacy, Intimacy and Isolation* (NY: Oxford University Press, 1992).

R. Jones, "Digital Rule: Punishment, Control and Technology", *Punishment and Society* 2, no. 1 (2001): 5–22.

Paul W. Kahn, "Interpretation and Authority in State Constitutionalism", *Harvard Law Review* 106 (1993): 1147.

Yale Kamisar, "Remembering the Old World of Criminal Procedure: A Reply to Professor Grano", *University of Michigan Journal of Law Reform* 23 (1990): 537, 562–65.

Immanuel Kant, *Groundwork of the Metaphysic of Morals,* translated by H. J. Paton (New York: Harper and Row, 1956).

_____, *The Metaphysical Elements of Justice,* trans John Ladd (Indianapolis: Bobbs-Merrill, 1965).

Gary C. Kessler, "An Overview of Steganography for the Computer Forensics Examiner" (edited version), *Forensic Science Communications (Technical Report)* 6, no. 3 (July 2004), available at: http://www.fbi.gov/hq/lab/fsc/ backissu/july2004/research/2004_03_research01.htm and http://www. garykessler.net/library/fsc_stego.html.

Donald F. Kettl, *The Global Public Management Revolution,* second ed. (Washington D.C.: The Brookings Institution, 2005).

Donald F. Kettl and James. W. Fesler, *The Politics of the Administrative Process,* fourth ed. (Washington, D.C.: CQ Press, 2009).

Mun-Cho Kim, "Surveillance Technology, Privacy and Social Control: With Reference to the Case of the Electronic National Identification Card in South Korea", *International Sociology*, 2004, 19(2), 193–213.

Neil King, Jr., "FBI's Wiretaps to Scan E-Mail Spark Concern", *Wall Street Journal*, 7/11/2000, A3.

Barbara D. Klein, "Data Quality in the Practice of Consumer Product Management: Evidence from the Field", *Data Quality* 4, no. 1 (1998).

John Kleinig, "John Stuart Mill and Voluntary Slavery Contracts", *Politics*, XVIII, 2 (November, 1983), 76-83.

_____, "Patriotic Loyalty", *Patriotism: Philosophical and Political Perspectives,* ed. Aleksandar Pavkovic and Igor Primoratz (Aldershot, UK: Ashgate, 2008), ch. 2.

_____, "Liberty and Security in an Age of Terrorism", Security and Justice in the Homeland: Criminologists on Terrorism, ed. Brian Forst, Jack Greene and James Lynch (forthcoming).

_____, "The Burdens of Situational Crime Prevention: An Ethical Commentary", in *Ethical and Social Perspectives on Situational Crime Prevention*, ed. Andrew von Hirsch, David Garland and Alison Wakefield (Oxford: Hart Publishing, 2000), 37–58.

_____, "Noble Cause Corruption or Process Deviance: Ruminations on Means and Ends in Policing", in *Police Corruption – Paradigms, Models and Concepts*, ed. Stanley Einstein and Menachem Amir, *Uncertainty Series, vol. 4,* Huntsville, TX: OICJ Press, 2004, 129–46.

Peter Kovesi, *Video Surveillance is Useless*, Presentation at the 18th International Symposium of the Australia and New Zealand Forensic Society, April 2–7, 2006, Fremantle, Western Australia.

_____, *Video Surveillance: Legally Blind*, presentation at DICTA 2009, Digital Image Computing: Techniques and Applications, December 1–3, 2009, Melbourne, Australia, at: http://dicta2009.vu.edu.au/, viewed December 31, 2009.

Samuel V. La Selva, "Selling Oneself into Slavery: Mill and Paternalism", *Political Studies*, 35, no. 2 (1987): 211–23.

Konrad Lachmayer, "European Police Cooperation and its Limits: From Intelligence-led to Coercive Measures", *The Outer Limits of European Union Law*, ed. Catherine Barnard and Okeoghene Odudu (Oxford: Hart Publishing 2009).

Marc Langheinrich, Personal Privacy in Ubiquitous Computing – Tools and System Support, PhD dissertation, ETH Zurich, Switzerland, May 2005. Available at: http://www.vs.inf.ethz.ch/res/papers/langheinrich-phd-2005.pdf.

Karen Lebacqz, "Alien Dignity: The Legacy of Helmut Thielicke for Bioethics", *Religion and Medical Ethics: Looking Back, Looking Forward* ed. Allen Verhey (Grand Rapids: Eerdmans, 1996), 44–60.

Man Yee Karen Lee, "Universal Human Dignity: Some Reflections in the Asian Context", *Asian Journal of Comparative Law* 3, no. 1 (2008), at: http://www.bepress.com/asjcl/vol3/iss1/art10.

LexisNexis Breach Notification Letter. Available at: http://privacy.wi.gov/databreaches/pdf/LexisNexisLetter050509.pdf (Last visited May 1, 2009).

Eric Lichtblau, "F.B.I. Data Mining Reached Beyond Initial Targets", *The New York Times*, September 9, 2007, 1, 31.

Eric Lichtblau and James Risen, "Bank Data is Sifted by U.S. in Secret to Block Terror", *The New York Times*, June 23, 2006, A1.

Eric Lipton, Eric Schmitt and Mark Mazzetti, "Jet Bomb Plot Shows More Missed Clues", *The New York Times,* January 18, 2010.

Eric Lipton and Scott Shane, "Questions on Why Terror Suspect Wasn't Stopped", *The New York Times*, December 2, 2009, at: http://www.nytimes.com/2009/12/28/us/28terror.html?_r=1&scp=2&sq=Umar%20Farouk%20Abdulmutallab%20&st=cse.

John Locke, *Second Treatise Of Civil Government*, 1689, ch. 9.

Steven Lukes, "Relativism: Cognitive and Moral", *Proceedings of the Aristotelian Society*, Supp. vol. 48 (1974), 165–89.

David Lyon, *Surveillance Studies: An Overview* (Cambridge, UK: Polity Press, 2007).

Gerald C. MacCallum, Jr., "Negative and Positive Freedom", *Philosophical Review*, 76 (July, 1967): 312–34.

Andrew McClurg, "A Thousand Words Are Worth A Picture: A Privacy Tort Response To Consumer Data Profiling", *Northwestern University Law Review* 98, no. 1 (2006): 63–143.

Alasdair MacIntyre, "The Essential Contestability of Some Social Concepts", *Ethics*, 84 (October, 1973), 1–9.

———, *After Virtue*, second ed. University of Notre Dame Press, 1984.

———, *Is Loyalty a Virtue?* Lindley Lecture (Lawrence: University of Kansas Philosophy Department, 1984).

Catriona Mackenzie and Natalie Stoljar (eds), *Relational Autonomy: Feminist Perspectives on Autonomy, Agency, and the Social Self* (NY: Oxford University Press, 2000).

Wayne Madsen, "FBI's Communications Surveillance Capabilities Widen", *Computer Fraud & Security*, no. 10 (October 2000): 16–17.

Peter Mameli, "Managing the HIV/AIDS Pandemic: Paving a Path into the Future of International Law and Organization", *Law & Policy* 22, no. 2 (April 2000): 203–24.

_____, "Tracking the Beast: Techno-Ethics Boards and Government Surveillance Programs", *Critical Issues in Justice and Politics* 1, no. 1 (2008): 31–56.

Giannozzo Manetti, *De dignitate et excellentia hominis libri IV;* Book 4 translated by Bernard Murchland in *Two Views of Man: Pope Innocent III On the Misery of Man; Giannozzo Manetti On the Dignity of Man* (New York: Frederick Ungar, 1966).

John Markoff, David E. Sanger and Thom Shanker, "In Digital Combat, U.S. Finds No Easy Deterrent", *The New York Times*, January 26, 2010.

Aaron K. Martin, Rosamunde Van Brakel and Daniel Bernhard, "Understanding Resistance to Digital Surveillance: Towards a Multi-Disciplinary, Multi-Actor Framework", *Surveillance & Society* 6 no. 3 (2009): 213–32.

Gary Marx, "Identity and Anonymity: Some Conceptual Distinctions and Issues for Research", *Documenting Individual Identity: The Development of State Practices in the Modern World*, ed. J. Caplan and J. Torpey (Princeton, NJ: Princeton University Press, 2001): 326, available at: http://web.mit.edu/gtmarx/www/identity.html.

_____, "A Tack in the Shoe: Neutralizing and Resisting the New Surveillance", *Journal of Social Issues* 59, no. 2 (2003): 369–90.

Mike Masnick, "Privacy: Senator Leahy Wants to Update Digital Privacy Law: Some Good, Some Bad", *TechDirt*, May 17, 2011, at http://www.techdirt.com/blog/?tag=ecpa.

Andrew Mason, "On Explaining Political Disagreement: The Notion of an Essentially Contested Concept", *Inquiry* 33 (1990), 81–98.

Lorin J. May, "Major Causes of Software Project Failures", at: http://www.stsc.hill.af.mil/crosstalk/1998/07/causes.asp, viewed 20 November 20, 2009.

Mark Mazzetti and Scott Hane, "CIA Watchdog Becomes Subject of CIA Inquiry", *The New York Times*, October 12 2007, A1, A25.

James Meek, "Robo Cop", *The Guardian*, 13/06/2002.

N. Memon, H.L. Larsen, "Investigative Data Mining Toolkit: A Software Prototype for Visualizing, Analyzing and Destabilizing Terrorist Networks", *Visualising Network Information* (2006), 14-1–14-24.

Nasrullah Memon, "Detecting Terrorist Activity Patterns Using Investigative Data Mining Tool", IFSR 2005: Proceedings of the First World Congress of the International Federation for Systems Research: *The New Roles of Systems Sciences For a Knowledge-based Society*, Nov. 14–17, 2123, Kobe, Japan.

Jeanne Merserve and Mike M. Ahlers, "Body Scanners Can Store, Send Images, Group Says", CNN News, January 11, 2010, available at: http://edition.cnn.com/2010/TRAVEL/01/11/body.scanners/index.html.

M.G. Michael, Sarah Jean Fusco, and Katina Michael, "A Research Note on Ethics in the Emerging Age of Überveillance", *Computer Communications* 31 (2008): 1192–99.

Dana Milbank and Spencer S. Hsu, "Cheney: Kerry Victory Is Risky; Democrats Decry Talk as Scare Tactic", *The Washington Post*, September 8, 2004, A01.

John Stuart Mill, "The Contest in America", in J.M. Robson (ed.) *The Collected Works of John Stuart Mill*, Toronto: University of Toronto Press, 1984, vol. XXI, 141–42.

-------, *On Liberty* (1869) at: http://www.bartleby.com/130/1.html.

-------, *Utilitarianism*, ch. 5, at: http://www.gutenberg.org/files/11224/11224-h/11224-h.htm#CHAPTER_V.

Greg Miller, "CIA Places Controls on Inspector General", *Los Angeles Times*, February 2, 2008; www.latimes.com/news/printedition/a/la-na-cia2feb02,1,6583760.story.

Seumas Miller, *Terrorism and Counter-terrorism: Ethics and Liberal Democracy* (Oxford: Blackwell, 2010).

_____, *The Moral Foundations of Social Institutions: A Philosophical Study* (New York: Cambridge University Press, 2010).

_____, "Collective Responsibility: An Individualist Account", *Midwest Studies in Philosophy* 30 (2006): 176–93.

_____, "Individual Autonomy and Sociality", *Socializing Metaphysics: The Nature of Social Reality*, ed. F. Schmitt (Lanham: Rowman and Littlefield, 2003).

Seumas Miller and John Blackler, *Ethical Issues in Policing* (Aldershot: Ashgate, 2005).

Seumas Miller and John Weckert, "Privacy, the Workplace and the Internet", *Journal of Business Ethics* 28, no. 3 (2000): 255–65.

Christopher S. Milligan, "Facial Recognition Technology, Video Surveillance, and Privacy", *Southern California Interdisciplinary Law Journal* 9 (2000): 295–334.

Minnesota Internet Traffic Studies (MINTS), at: http://www.dtc.umn.edu/mints/home.php, viewed February 1, 2010.

Tobias W. Mock, "Comment: The Tsa's New X-Ray Vision: The Fourth Amendment Implications of 'Body-Scan' Searches at Domestic Airport Security Checkpoints", *Santa Clara Law Review* 49 (2009): 213–51.

A.P. Montefiore (ed.), *Neutrality and Impartiality: The University and Political Commitment* (Cambridge, UK: Cambridge University Press, 1975), Part I.

James H. Moor, "Towards a Theory of Privacy in the Information Age", *Computers and Society*, 27–32, September 1997.

A. Moore, "Privacy: Its Meaning and Value", *American Philosophical Quarterly*, 40 (2003): 215–27.

Hans Morgenthau, *In Defense of the National Interest* (New York: Alfred A. Knopf, 1951).

_____, "National security must be defined as integrity of the national territory and its institutions", *Politics Among the Nations: The Struggle for Power and Peace*, third ed. (NY: Alfred A. Knopf, 1960), 562.

MSNBC News, "One Man Still Locked up from 9/11 Sweeps", *MSNBC.com* (October 14, 2006), at: http://www.msnbc.msn.com/id/15264274/from/ET.

Angela Murphy, Morgan Streetman and Mark Sweet, "Carnivore: Will it Devour Your Privacy?", *Duke Law & Technology Review* (2001): 0028, at: http://www.law.duke.edu/journals/dltr/articles/2001dltr0028.

National Technology Alliance, *Geographic Profiling and the Hunt for Insurgents* (2007), available at: http://www.nta.org/docs/Geoprofiling.pdf, accessed on Feb 15, 2007.

Lawrence W. Neuman, *Social Research Methods: Quantitative and Qualitative Approaches,* fifth ed. (Boston, MA: Allyn and Bacon, 2003).

Abraham L. Newman, *Protectors of Privacy: Regulating Personal Data in the Global Economy*. (United States: Cornell University Press, 2008).

Michael Newton, *Savage Girls and Wild Boys: A History of Feral Children* (New York: Faber & Faber, 2002).

Kenneth Nguyen, "Australia Hands over Man to US Courts", *The Age* (Melbourne), May 7, 2007; Alex P. Schmid, A.J. Jongman, and Irving Horowitz, *Political Terrorism: A New Guide to Actors, Authors, Concepts, Data Bases, Theories, and Literature* (Amsterdam: Transaction Books, 1998).

The 9/11 Commission, *The 9/11 Commission Report: Final Report of the National Commission on Terrorist Attacks upon the United States*, 2004, at: http://www.9-11commission.gov/report/index.htm.

Helen Nissenbaum, "The Meaning of Anonymity in an Information Age", at: http://www.nyu.edu/projects/nissenbaum/paper_anonimity.html.

_____, "Privacy as Conceptual Integrity", *Washington Law Review*, 79 (2004): 119–57.

Érika Nogueira de Andrade Stupiello, "Ethical Implications of Translation Technologies", *Translation Journal*, 2007, available at: http://translationjournal.net/journal/43ethics.htm, accessed, 3 January 2010.

Note, "Legal Authorities Supporting the Activities of the National Security Agency Described by the President", *Indiana Law Journal*, 81 (2006): 1374.

Robert Nozick, *Anarchy, State, and Utopia*, New York: Basic Books, 1974.

Office of the Privacy Commissioner, *The Operation of the Privacy Act: Annual Report 2008–2009* (Office of the Privacy Commissioner, Canberra, 2009).

Offices of Inspectors General, *Unclassified Report of the President's Surveillance Program – Report No. 2009-0013-AS* (Washington, D.C.: USA 2009).

S. Oka, H. Togo, N. Kukutsu, and T. Nagatsuma, "Latest Trends in Millimeter-Wave Imaging Technology", *Progress In Electromagnetics Research Letters* 1 (2008): 197–204.

Jo Ann Oravec, "Secret Sharers: Consensual and Participatory Surveillance Concerns in the Context of Network-Based Computer Systems", *ACM SIGOIS Bulletin* 14, no. 1 (July 1993): 32–40.

Elizabethann O'Sullivan, Gary R. Rassel, and Maureen Berner, *Research Methods for Public Administrators*, fifth ed. (US: Pearson Longman, 2008).

Susan Page, "Lawmakers: NSA Database Incomplete", *USA Today*, June 30, 2006, A1.

Thomas Paine, *The Rights of Man* (New York: Anchor, 1973).

Derek Parfit, *Reasons and Persons* (New York: Oxford University Press, 1984).

George L. Paul and Jason R. Baron, "Information Inflation: Can the Legal System Adapt?", *Richmond Journal of Law & Technology* 13, no. 3 (2007), at: http://law.richmond.edu/jolt/v13i3/article10.pdf, viewed 25 January 2010.

Derek J. Paulsen, "Connecting the Dots: Assessing the Accuracy of Geographic Profiling Software", *Policing: An International Journal of Police Strategies & Management* 29, no. 2 (2006): 306–34.

Marin Perez, "Opera Add Locations Awareness", *Information Week*, March 9, 2009.

Philip Pettit, *Republicanism: A Theory of Freedom and Government*, Oxford: Oxford University Press, 1997.

Pew Internet and American Life Project, "Social Media & Mobil Internet Use Among Teens and Young Adults, Pew Research Center", Feb 3, 2010, available at: http://www.pewinternet.org/Reports/2010/Social-Media-and-Young-Adults.aspx.

Eric Pfanner, "Data Leak in Britain Affects 25 Million", *The New York Times*, November 22, 2007.

Giovanni Pico della Mirandola, *De dominis dignitate oratio*, translated as *Oration on the Dignity of Man* by A. Robert Caponigri (Chicago: Gateway, 1956).

Plato, *Republic*, II 359d–360b.

Thomas Pogge, *Realizing Rawls* (Ithaca, NY: Cornell University Press, 1989), Part III.

Irene Pollach, "What's Wrong with On-line Privacy Policies?", *Communications of the ACM* 50, no. 9 (September 2007): 103–108.

David A. Powner, Director, United States Government Accountability Office, Information Technology Management Issues, *Management and Oversight of Projects Totaling Billions of Dollars Need Attention*, Testimony Before the Subcommittee on Federal Financial Management, Government Information, Federal Services, and International Security, Committee on Homeland Security and Governmental Affairs, US Senate, April 28, 2009.

Pre-employ.com, "Background Checks and Social Networking Sites", February 24, 2009.

James Rachels, "Why Privacy is Important", *Philosophy & Public Affairs*, 4 (1975): 323–33.

Allen Charles Raul, "The Missing Privacy and Civil Liberties Oversight Board", *The Washington Post*, January 24, 2010, available at: http://www.washingtonpost.com/wp-dyn/content/article/2010/01/23/AR2010012302190.html.

John Rawls, "The Idea of an Overlapping Consensus", *Oxford Journal of Legal Studies*, 7, no. 1 (1987): 1–25.

ReadWriteWeb, "Does That Facebook App Have a Privacy Policy? Probably Not", July 29, 2009. Available at: http://www.readwriteweb.com.

Jeffrey Reiman, "Towards a Secular Lockean Liberalism", *Review of Politics,* 67 (2005): 473–93.

James Risen and Eric Lichtblau, "Concerns Raised on Wider Spying Under New Law", *The New York Times*, August 19, 2007.

John M. Roberts and Thomas Gregor, "Privacy: A Cultural View", *Privacy*, NOMOS XIII, ed. J. Roland Pennock and John W. Chapman (NY: Atherton Press, 1971), 199–225.

James Robinson, "Twitter and Facebook Riot Restrictions Would Be a Mistake, Says Google Chief", Guardian.co.uk, August 27, 2011, available at: http://www.guardian.co.uk/media/2011/aug/27/twitter-facebook-riot-restrictions-eric-schmidt.

Jeffrey Rosen, "The Naked Crowd: Balancing Privacy and Security in an Age of Terror", *Arizona Law Review* 46 (Winter, 2004): 608.

Richard Rose, *Learning from Comparative Public Policy: A Practical Guide* (London: Routledge, 2005).

David Rosenblum, "What Anyone Can Know: The Privacy Risks of Social Networking Sites", *IEEE Security and Privacy* 5, no. 3 (May/June 2007): 40–49.

Paul Roth, "Workplace Privacy Issues Raised by RFID Technology", Privacy Issues Forum, March 30, 2006 University of Otago.

E. Rothschild, "What is Security?", *Daedalus* 124, no. 3 (1995): 61.

Jean-Jacques Rousseau, *The Social Contract*, at: http://www.wsu.edu:8080/~wldciv/world_civ_reader/world_civ_reader_2/rousseau.html.

Bijon Roy, "A Case Against Biometric National Identification Systems (NIDS): 'Trading-off' Privacy Without Getting Security", *Windsor Review of Legal & Social Issues* 19 (March 2005): 45–84.

Ira S. Rubinstein, Ronald D. Lee, and Paul M. Schwartz, "Data Mining and Internet Profiling: Emerging Regulatory and Technological Approaches", *University of Chicago Law Review* 75, no. 1 (2008): 261–85, esp. 274–80.

S. Sackmann, J. Struker and R. Accorsi, "Personalization in Privacy-aware Highly Dynamic Systems", *Communications of the ACM* 49, no. 9 (September 2006): 32–38.

Michael V. Sage, "The Exploitation of Legal loopholes in the Name of National Security", *California W. International Law Journal* 37 (Fall, 2006): 121–42.

Vincenzo Antonio Sainato, "Situational Surveillance Control", Criminal Justice PhD dissertation, City University of New York, John Jay College of Criminal Justice, 2009.

Douglas Salane, "Are Large Scale Data Breaches Inevitable?", Cyber Infrastructure Protection '09, The City University of New York, June 2009.

Sudhir Saxena, K. Santhanam and Aparna Basu, "Application of Social Network Analysis (SNA) to Terrorist Networks", *Strategic Analysis* 28, no.1 (January–March 2004): 84–101.

T.M. Scanlon, "The Constitutional Essentials of Political Liberalism: Adjusting Rights and Balancing Values", *Fordham Law Review*, 72 (2004): 1477–86.

Frederick Schauer, *Profiles, Probabilities and Stereotypes* (Cambridge, MA: Harvard University Press, 2003).

Leslie Regan Shade, "The Culture of Surveillance: G-Men Redux and Total Information Awareness", *Topia* 9 (2003): 35–45.

H. Schneider, H. C. Liu, S. Winnerl, O. Drachenko, M. Helm, and J. Faist, "Room-temperature Midinfrared Two-photon Photodetector", *Applied Physics Letters* 93, no. 101114 (2008): 1–3.

School of African and Oriental Studies, University of London, "Transfer Outside the EU", at: http://www.soas.ac.uk/infocomp/dpa/policy/outside.

Adina Schwartz, "Homes as Folding Umbrellas: Two Recent Supreme Court Decisions on 'Knock and Announce'", *American Journal of Criminal Law* 25 (1998): 545–94.

Ari Schwartz, written supplement to testimony before the Data Privacy and Integrity Committee, Department of Homeland Security, June 15, 2005. Available at: http://www.netdemocracyguide.net/testimony/20050718schwartz.pdf.

Walter Shapiro, "With Scare Tactics Aplenty, Election Rivals Halloween: Hype & Glory", *USA Today*, October 19, 2004, 4A.

Henry Shue, *Basic Rights: Subsistence, Affluence, and U.S. Foreign Policy,* second ed. (Princeton, NJ: Princeton University Press, 1996).

Royce A. Singleton, Jr. and Bruce C. Straits, *Approaches to Social Research,* fourth ed. (New York and Oxford: Oxford University Press, 2005).

James Sinkula, "Status of Company Usage of Scanner Based Research", Journal of the Academy of Marketing Science 14 (1986): 63–71.

Gregory Slabodkin, "Software Glitches Leave Navy Smart Ship Dead in the Water", *Government Computer News*, 13 July 1998.

Marion Smiley, "Collective Responsibility", *Stanford Encyclopedia of Philosophy*, at: http://plato.stanford.edu/entries/collective-responsibility/.

Andrew Sneddon, "What's Wrong with Selling Yourself into Slavery? Paternalism and Deep Autonomy", *Critica: Revista Hispanoamericana de Filosofia* 33, no. 98 (August, 2001): 97–121, at: http://critica.filosoficas.unam.mx/pdf/C98/C98_sneddon.pdf.

John Solomon and Carrie Johnson, "FBI Broke Law for Years in Phone Records Searches", *The Washington Post*, January 19, 2010, A01.

Julie Solomon, "Does the TSA Have Stage Fright? Then Why are they Picturing you Naked?", *Journal of Air Law and Commerce* 73, no 3 (2008): 643–71.

Daniel J. Solove, "Restructuring Electronic Surveillance Law", *George Washington Law Review* 72 (2004): 1706.

_____, "A Taxonomy of Privacy", *University of Pennsylvania Law Review*, 154 (2006): 491.

Daniel J. Solove and Chris J. Hoofnagle, "A Model Regime of Privacy Protection", *University of Illinois Law Review*, (February, 2006): 357–404.

Daniel J. Solove, *The Future of Reputation: Gossip, Rumor, and Privacy on the Internet* (New Haven: Yale University Press, 2007).

John T. Soma, et al., "Corporate Privacy Trend: The 'Value' of Personally Identifiable Information (PII) Equals the 'Value' of Financial Assets", *Richmond Journal of Law & Technology* 15, no. 4 (2009), available at: http://law.richmond.edu/jolt /v15i4/article11.pdf.

Andrew Speirs, "The Individual and the Stereotype: From Lavater to the War on Terror" Australian Council of University Art and Design Schools (ACUADS) ACUADS 2003 Conference Hobart, 1–4 Oct 2003, http://www.acuads.com.au/conf2003/papers_refereed/speirs.pdf.

K. Srikumar and B. Bashker, "Personalized Recommendations in E-commerce", *International Journal of Electronic Business 3*, no. 1 (2005): 4–27.

L. Story, "Company Will Monitor Phone Calls to Tailor Ads", *The New York Times*, Sept. 24, 2007.

Katherine J. Strandburg, "Freedom of Association in a Networked World: First Amendment Regulation of Relational Surveillance", *Boston College Law Review* 49, no. 1 (2008): 1–81.

Mark Strasser, Mark, "Mill on Voluntary Self-enslavement", *Philosophical Papers* 17 (November, 1988): 171–183.

P.F. Strawson, "Social Morality and Individual Ideal", *Philosophy* 36 (January, 1961): 1–17.

William J. Stuntz, "Privacy's Problem and the Law of Criminal Procedure", *Michigan Law Review* 93 (1995): 1016.

Christine Swanton, "On the 'Essential Contestedness' of Political Concepts", *Ethics*, 95 (July, 1985), 811–27.

Peter P. Swire, "Privacy and Information Sharing in the War on Terrorism", *Villanova Law Review* 51 (2006): 951–980.

Hiroko Tabuchi, "Facebook Wins Relatively Few Friends in Japan", *The New York Times*, January 9, 2011.

Kim Taipale, "Data Mining and Domestic Security: Connecting the Dots to Make Sense of Data", *Columbia Science and Technology Law Review,* 5 (2003): 24–25.

Joelle Tanguy, "Redefining Sovereignty and Intervention", *Ethics and International Affairs*, 17, no. 1 (2003): 141–48.

Herman T. Tavani and James H. Moor, "Privacy Protection, Control of Information, and Privacy-Enhancing Technologies", *Computers and Society* 31, no. 1 (March 2001): 6–11.

Chin Liew Ten, *Mill on Liberty* (Oxford: Oxford University Press, 1980), ch. 7.

Hugo Teufel III, *2007 Report to Congress on the Impact of Data Mining Technologies on Privacy and Civil Liberties* (Washington, DC: DHS, July 6, 2007), at: http://www.dhs.gov/xlibrary/assets/privacy/privacy_rpt_datamining_2007.pdf.

Philip A. Thomas, "Emergency and Anti-Terrorist Power: 9/11: USA and UK", *Fordham International Law Journal* 26 (April 2003): 1193.

Paul B. Thompson, "Privacy, Secrecy and Security", *Ethics and Information Technology* 3, no. 1 (March, 2001): 13–19.

Judith Jarvis Thomson, "The Right to Privacy", *Philosophy & Public Affairs*, 4, no. 4 (1975): 295–314.

Ying-li Tian, Lisa Brown, Arun Hampapur, Max Lu, Andrew Senior and Chiao-fe Shu, "IBM Smart Surveillance System (S3): Event Based Video Surveillance System with an Open and Extensible Framework", *Machine Vision and Applications* 19 (2008):315-27, DOI 10.1007/s00138-008-0153-z.

TSA website, at: http://www.tsa.dhs.gov/approach/tech/castscope.shtm.

Alan Travis, "Lords: CCTV is Threat to Freedom", *The Guardian*, February 9, 2009, available at: http://www.guardian.co.uk/uk/2009/feb/06/surveillance-freedom-peers.

———, "New Scanners Break Child Porn Laws", *The Guardian*, Monday, January 4, 2010 22.14 GMT.

Charles Trinkhaus, "Renaissance Idea of the Dignity of Man", *Dictionary of the History of Ideas*, vol. IV, 136–46, at: http://etext.virginia.edu/cgi-local/DHI/dhiana.cgi?id=dv4-20.

Matteo Turilli and Luciano Floridi, "The Ethics of Information Transparency", *Ethics and Information Technology* 11 (2009): 105–112.

Richard Ullman, "Redefining Security", *International Security*, 8 (Summer, 1983): 129.

US Department of Health, Education and Welfare, *Records, Computers and the Rights of Citizens: Report of the Secretary's Advisory Committee on Automated Personal Data Systems (July 1973)*, available at: http://aspe.hhs.gov/DATACNCL/1973privacy/tocprefacemembers.htm.

US Department of Labor, *Permenant Labor Certification*, available at: http://www.foreignlaborcert.doleta.gov/perm.cfm.

Jeroen van den Hoven, "Computer Ethics and Moral Methodology", *Metaphilosophy* 28, no. 3, (1997): 1–12.

Andrew von Hirsch, "The Ethics of Public Television Surveillance", in Andrew von Hirsch, David Garland and Alison Wakefield (eds.), *Ethical and Social Perspectives on Situational Crime Prevention* (Oxford: Hart Publishing, 2000), 68.

A.K. Vorrat, "Police Statistics Prove Data Retention Superfluous", EDRI-Gram, Number 9.12, June 15, 2011, http://www.edri.org/edrigram/number9.12.

Jeremy Waldron, God, Locke and Equality: Christian Foundations of Locke's Political Thought (Cambridge, UK: Cambridge University Press, 2002).

_____, "Minority Cultures and the Cosmopolitan Alternative", *University of Michigan Journal of Law Reform* 25 (1992): 751–793.

_____. "Security and Liberty: The Image of Balance", *Journal of Political Philosophy*, 11 (2) (June 2003): 191–210.

_____, "Safety and Security", *Nebraska Law Review*, 85 (2006): 454–507.

_____, "Dignity and Rank", Archives *Européennes de Sociologie*, 48 (2007), 201–37.

_____, "Cruel, Inhuman and Degrading Treatment: The Words Themselves", New York University School of Law, Public and Legal Theory Research Paper Series, Working Paper #08-36 (November 2008), 36, at: http://papers.ssrn.com/sol3/papers.cfm?abstract_id=1278604.

Carol B. Warren, "Secrecy", *The Encyclopedia of Privacy*, ed. William G. Staples, Greenwood Press: Connecticut, (2007): 482–85.

C. Warren and B. Laslett, "Privacy and Secrecy: A Conceptual Comparison", *The Journal of Social Issues*, (1977): 1ff.

Arnold Wolfers, "'National Security' as an Ambiguous Symbol", in *Discord and Collaboration: Essays on International Politics* (Baltimore, MD: Johns Hopkins University Press, 1962), 147.

Michael Walzer, *Just and Unjust Wars* (1977).

Samuel D. Warren and Louis D. Brandeis, "The Right to Privacy", *Harvard Law Review*, 4 (1890): 193–220, at: http://www-swiss.ai.mit.edu/6805/articles/privacy/Privacy_brand_warr2.html.

The Washington Post, "A Flashy Facebook Page at a Cost to Privacy", June 12, 2008

Dale Watson, "Foreign Terrorists in America: Five Years After the World Trade Center", (Senate Judiciary Committee), February 24, 1998, available at: http://fas.org/irp/congress/1998_hr/s980224w.htm.

Leanne Weber, "The Shifting Frontiers of Migration Control", in *Borders, Mobility and Technologies of Control*, ed. Sharon Pickering and Leanne Weber (Springer, 2006), ch. 2.

John Weckert (ed.), *Electronic Monitoring in the Workplace: Controversies and Solutions* (Hershey, PA: Idea Group Publishing, 2005).

David L. Weimer, "The Puzzle of Private Rulemaking: Expertise, Flexibility, and Blame Avoidance in U.S. Regulation", *Public AdministrationReview* 66, no. 4 (July/August 2006): 569–82.

Mark Weiser, "The Computer for the Twenty-First Century", *Scientific American*, September 1991, 94–10.

David Weissbrodt and Amy Bergquist, "Extraordinary Rendition: A Human Rights Analysis", *Harvard Human Rights Journal*, 19 (Spring, 2006): 123–60.

———, "Extraordinary Rendition and the Torture Convention", *Virginia Journal of International Law*, 46 (Summer, 2006): 585–650.

———, "Extraordinary Rendition and the Humanitarian Law of War and Occupation", *Virginia Journal of International Law*, 47 (Winter, 2007): 295–356.

Amy Westfeldt, "LexisNexis Warns 32,000 People about Data Breach", *San Francisco Chronicle*, May 1, 2009, 22.

Alan F. Westin, *Privacy and Freedom* (New York: Atheneum, 1967).

Matthew White, "Democracies Do Not Make War on One Another. . . Or Do They?", at: http://users.erols.com/mwhite28/demowar.htm.

White House, *Cyberspace Policy Review: Assuring a Trusted and Resilient Information and Communications Structure* (May, 2009), available at: www.whitehouse.gov/assets/.../Cyberspace_Policy_Review_final.pdf.

Zach Whittaker, "Microsoft Admits Patriot Act Can Access EU-Based Cloud Data", ZDNet, June 28, 2011, available at: http://www.zdnet.com/blog/igeneration/microsoft-admits-patriot-act-can-access-eu-based-cloud-data/11225

wik-Consult/RAND Europe/CLIP/CRID/GLOM, "Comparison of Privacy and Trust Policies in the Areas of Electronic Communications – Final Report", European Commission (2007).

James Q. Whitman, "The Two Western Cultures of Privacy: Dignity versus Liberty", *Yale Law Journal* 113 (2004): 1151–1221.

Daniel B. Wood, "BART Puts Social Media Crackdown in Uncharted Legal Territory", *The Christian Science Monitor*, August 16, 2011, available at: http://www.csmonitor.com/USA/Justice/2011/0816/BART-puts-social-media-crackdown-in-uncharted-legal-territory.

Edward Wyatt and Tanzina Vega, "FTC Honors Plan to Honor Privacy of Online Users", *The New York Times*, December 1, 2010.

P.W. Young, "Extradition to the US", *Australian Law Journal* 81 (April, 2007): 225.

Xiaoyi Yu, K. Chinomi, T. Koshimizu, N. Nitta, Y. Ito and N. Babaguchi, "Image Processing, 2008", ICIP 2008, 15th IEEE International Conference, October 12–15, 2008, 1672–75.

Lucia Zedner, "The Concept of Security: An Agenda for Comparative Analysis", *Legal Studies* 23 (2003): 157.

_____, "Too Much Security?", *International Journal of the Sociology of Law*, 31 (2003): 155–84.

_____, "Securing Liberty in the Face of Terror: Reflections from Criminal Justice", *Journal of Law and Society*, 32 (4) (December 2005): 507–33.